STRATEGIC NETWORKING

From LAN and WAN to Information Superhighways

Paul David Henry

Gene De Libero

INTERNATIONAL THOMSON COMPUTER PRESS

I(T)P™   An International Thomson Publishing Company

London • Bonn • Boston • Johannesburg • Madrid • Melbourne • Mexico City • New York • Paris
Singapore • Tokyo • Toronto • Albany, NY • Belmont, CA • Cincinnati, OH • Detroit, MI

Copyright ©1996 International Thomson Computer Press

I⊤P™ A division of International Thomson Publishing Inc.
The ITP Logo is a trademark under license.

Printed in the United States of America.

For more information, contact:

International Thomson Computer Press
20 Park Plaza, Suite 1001
Boston, MA 02116
USA

International Thomson Publishing GmbH
Königswinterer Strasse 418
53227 Bonn
Germany

International Thomson Publishing Europe
Berkshire House 168-173
High Holborn
London WCIV 7AA
England

International Thomson Publishing Asia
221 Henderson Road #05-10
Henderson Building
Singapore 0315

Thomas Nelson Australia
102 Dodds Street
South Melbourne, 3205
Victoria, Australia

International Thomson Publishing Japan
Hirakawacho Kyowa Building, 3F
2-2-1 Hirakawacho
Chiyoda-ku, 102 Tokyo
Japan

Nelson Canada
1120 Birchmount Road
Scarborough, Ontario
Canada M1K 5G4

International Thomson Editores
Campos Eliseos 385, Piso 7
Col. Polanco
11560 Mexico D.F. Mexico

International Thomson Publishing Southern Africa
Bldg. 19, Constantia Park
239 Old Pretoria Road, P.O. Box 2459
Halfway House, 1685 South Africa

International Thomson Publishing France
1, rue st. Georges
75 009 Paris France

1 2 3 4 5 6 7 8 9 10 QEBFF 01 00 99 98 97 96 95
Library of Congress Cataloging-in-Publication Data
(available upon request)

ISBN: 1-850-32203-1

Publisher/Vice President: Jim DeWolf, ITCP/Boston
Project Director: Chris Grisonich, ITCP/Boston
Marketing Manager: Kathleen Raftery, ITCP/Boston
Production: Jo-Ann Campbell • mle design • 562 Milford Point Rd. • Milford, CT 06460 • 203-878-3793

Contents

Chapter 3   **Network Components**   **65**

Chapter 7   Protocols   193

Chapter 12   Disaster Recovery and Contingency   399

Introduction

ABOUT STRATEGIC NETWORKING

Charles Dickens, the author and astute observer of human nature, had timeless advice about the ubiquity of information and the importance of knowledge. What might his observations be if he were present in this era of unprecedented technological and social change? With respect to the manner in which technology is blindly pursued without a clear sense of its purpose, he might remark: "A smattering of everything, and a knowledge of nothing" (Dickens, 1836).

As we conducted research for this book, we were quickly deluged with information. It piled up on multi-gigabyte hard drives and in storage boxes until we had to start building knowledge out of this mountain of information. Running out of room and piling up too many pages forced us to re-think what we needed to say about networking and how we needed to say it.

We pondered how the words in this book's title could suggest a practical approach to learning and working with network technology. The word *networking* is used throughout this book to denote the process of providing computing and communications on a distributed basis to many users. We also emphasize the need to plan and implement this technology with a clear understanding of the organization and the people it must serve.

Of course, we also use the term *network*. Simply put, networks are what people make. Networking is what people do with them.

Riding the Crest of Change

Networking is a highly dynamic innovation that moves quickly and broadly like the crest of a high-rising wave. Riding that crest means balancing your existing networking assets, knowledge, and skills against the steep and often risky investment in new technology. Moving ahead too far incurs risks inherent with unproven technology. Yet remaining behind courts obsolescence and the related loss of competitiveness. Riding the crest is also not without cost. It requires a constant commitment of resources for strategic planning and management.

Changes occur so quickly that standards and product compatibility constantly play a game of "catch-up." However steep the learning curve and cost, moving with each wave of technological innovation is essential to the growth and even survival of the organization which relies on it. However, moving blindly with each change based on technological and marketing pressures alone is a fool's paradise. Strategic networking means reordering this "cart before the horse" mode of thinking. We believe the best way to achieve that is to develop a useful model of networking and apply it to organizational planning.

In an era where information drives and often defines the nature of an organization, networks are its infrastructure. Although existing network technology can provide reliable service, changes in the form of repair and improvement to that infrastructure ensures that vital information can be used in a timely and effective manner. This keeps an organization competitive.

It is in that context that we use the word *strategic*. It denotes careful consideration of convergent factors (technology, people, procedures, goals, budget, etc.) when planning and implementing networks.

In a very tangible manner, networks help determine the interactions between people within an organization. Implementing new network technology not only brings technological change, but also changes to those patterns of interaction. Sometimes these changes can be anticipated and beneficial, but that is not a given.

That's where strategic planning and management of networks comes in, especially strategies that address organizational and social issues along with technological and business objectives. Sociologists have explored these issues in studies relating to planned organizational change and adoption of new technology. Despite the common sense of considering networking technology in terms of its use and setting, it is surprising how many organizations fail in this regard.

Acknowledging these issues within a strategic framework is something that has evolved from our experience in consulting, implementing, and documenting network innovations for a variety of organizations. Thus, we felt it was important to introduce networking within the context of organizational and social change.

Key Strategic Concepts

Networks and their supporting technologies and services are expanding at an unprecedented rate; yet the supply and capabilities of qualified personnel who can plan, implement, and manage them are barely keeping pace. This situation calls for products and services that acknowledge the involvement of people whose primary training and role is not necessarily in systems or networking.

We offer eight keys for unlocking the complexity of network technology. The following terms and related concepts represent many useful models for computing. These concepts are used in various ways by vendors, professional associations, standards committees, and researchers in the computer networking field. Wherever appropriate, we invoke these terms and suggest strategies built around the underlying concept, but always within the context of the topic under discussion.

> **Organizational Fit** means defining and matching the features, benefits, and risks inherent in network technology to the needs and capacities of the organization and the people it serves. This is critical during the planning and implementation stages of network innovations, but also throughout its life cycle.

Appropriate Technology means choosing and using the type of network technology that meets a given application in the most efficient and effective manner. For example, this might mean deploying satellite or other wireless technologies in any of the following situations: where the return on investment in cable is questionable, when an installation is only temporary, there is no wired infrastructure, or where distance or remoteness to hosts make it impractical.

Usable Design means selecting, modifying, and using software (and hardware) that fits the needs of the users and the organization and not vice versa. According to Terry Winograd (1995), software usability "... takes the system, the users, and the situation of its use all together as a starting point."

Whether it's software or hardware, user-centered design and implementation largely determines the usefulness of technology (Norman, 1981). Thus, bigger is not necessarily better, nor is the most powerful system or application necessarily the best choice in all situations. This strategy guided our choice of products as examples of underlying technology and strategic solutions.

Manageable and Supportable Technology refers to networks or systems that can be managed and supported by the people using the technology. This can be augmented by software management tools, vendor support, and the advantages that accrue to technology that embraces open and published standards.

Interoperable means cross-platform and multi-platform support and the ability for one type of network or system to communicate or work with another regardless of vendor.

Interoperability is most evident on the Internet, which was designed to support and maintain open standards. Using products and techniques that conform to these standards allows people from around the world to share information and use common applications despite the diverse hardware and software platforms they may be using.

Scalable means minimal change is necessary in current configurations to accommodate growth. For networks or systems, it means they can be made larger or smaller relatively easily and cost-effectively. For software products, scalability means they will run on different families of processors and from single to multi-processor systems. The Internet provides scalability in that local applications and networks can grow to global extent.

Flexible Management means monitoring and managing network resources using strategies that leverage software-based remote management tools with other resources, such as personnel, fax, and pager technology. These resources provide a way for administrators to be notified if network problems need to be addressed.

Portable means products that support several hardware platforms with different versions or built-in capabilities for switching between them. For example, network hardware such as hubs and routers can be portable. It also refers to software which can be easily converted from one hardware platform to another and often has built-in support of multiple platforms.

ABOUT THIS BOOK

Consider the following descriptions of this book's design and purpose. You can use it as a guide for learning about strategic networking.

Goals of This Book

This book has three basic goals:

1. To introduce networking technology and its related skills, products, and services.

2. To examine the relationship between networks as a technological infrastructure and an innovation that brings change to the way people interact.

3. To map the domain of networking topics and issues using Internet addresses as a resource for continuous learning.

Who Should Read This Book

This book is designed for the following readers and uses:

- Executives and managers for strategic enterprise planning and CIOs and MIS management for strategic information technology planning.

- System administrators, integrators, and network engineers for reference, training, planning and implementation.

- Educators and students in computer science, information science, and business courses, and corporate trainers for class, platform, and individual training.

- Software developers, Original Equipment Manufacturers (OEM), Value-added Resellers (VAR), and network vendors for reference, training, planning and implementation strategies.

- Other computer users who are considering the use of networks in their organizations.

How to Use This Book

This book can be used in several ways:

- Use it as an introduction, from the basic building blocks of networks to larger strategic issues of connectivity, interoperability, and security.

- Use it as a reference tool, especially for emerging network technology, protocols, and standards.

- Use it as a planning guide for network upgrades, security, disaster recovery, or change management for network innovations.

- Use it as an applications guide for systems and client/server software for LAN, WAN, and Internet.

Reading Strategies

To cover networks from the ground up, we started this book by describing transmission media and then followed with each aspect of networking that would logically build on the previous concepts. Thus, reading from Chapter 1 to the end of the book represents a progressive treatment of topics. For some readers, this may be a suitable path. However, we didn't intend for this book to be read only that way.

We believe your approach should be based on your prior knowledge and current learning needs. Consider the following reading strategies as a guide for developing your own plan for reading.

Chapter 1: Transmission Media discusses the various types of network cabling, including twisted pair, coaxial, fiber-optic, and a range of wireless media. However, you should read Chapter 6 first if you need a high-level administrative or executive view of how networks are designed and implemented in an organization, especially before delving into the details of transmission media. As Chapter 1 describes the media used to connect network users and Chapter 2 focuses on its operation, they should be read sequentially.

Chapter 2: Topologies, Techniques, and Technologies identifies and explains how transmission media are deployed and interconnected to form the foundation of a network. The techniques section provides information about how data travels over a media, and the technologies section explains the characteristics and operation of the media. All of this comes together to help you visualize which combination of topologies, techniques, and technologies are best suited for your network innovation. Thus, Chapter 2 logically follows concepts introduced in Chapter 1.

Chapter 3: Network Components describes hardware devices that connect nodes, regenerate signals, or route network traffic, including repeaters, hubs, bridges, routers, and gateways. It also covers communications, terminal, and print servers, workstations, and personal computers. Following Chapters 1 and 2, it rounds out the hardware-based description of a network infrastructure. This chapter can be read at any time for an overview of networking hardware.

Chapter 4: Operating Systems and Environments can be read at any time because it provides a overview of popular operating systems, network operating systems, and operating environments on multiple platforms including UNIX, Windows, and Macintosh. Properties such as scalability and interoperability are examined with respect to heterogeneous internetworks.

Chapter 5: Networking Services builds upon the concepts introduced in previous chapters. It provides coverage of the abundance and variety of network services that use the transmission media of cable, fiber, wireless, and satellite technologies. However, it may be a good follow-up to Chapter 6 if you first want an overview of how networks are designed and implemented.

Chapter 6: Designing and Implementing Networks is a good choice to read at any time. However, you should start your reading of this book here if you need a high-level administrative or executive view of how networking is designed and implemented in an organization. It addresses important issues and presents strategies for planning, designing, and implementing networks of all sizes. We recommend you read Chapter 10 after this one because it describes the servers that are commonly used to build networks. Other paths to take after this chapter include a ground-up approach from Chapter 1 or reading Chapters 8, 10, 11, 12, and/or 13 next for a high-level view.

Chapter 7: Protocols describes the rules and standards that govern network communications. It can be read along with Chapter 6, 8, 10, or 11 to add depth to a high-level understanding of interoperability and scalability. However, for a detailed view of network technology, Chapter 7 should follow Chapters 1 through 3 or 1 through 5.

Chapter 8: Network Applications can be read any time for a discussion of network-based software applications and their underlying concepts, including remote connectivity, e-mail, publishing and graphics, multimedia and hypermedia, database, and groupware. Chapter 11 is a good follow-up to this chapter because of its in-depth coverage of Internet applications.

Chapter 9: System Administration covers important issues relating to the administration, management, and support of networks. This chapter also covers management and security issues related to supporting an internetworking presence such as the integrated Web site discussed in Chapter 10. For these reasons, we feel this is a good chapter to read after Chapter 10.

Chapter 10: Internetwork Servers and Gateways can be read at any time. It describes the wide variety of servers and gateways commonly deployed in modern networks. It is also a high-level follow-up to Chapter 6 and/or 9 that describes the driving software behind client-server networks. This chapter is important for anyone who wants to understand how different types of servers are set up, configured, and implemented, whether to establish an Internet presence through an integrated World Wide Web site or to deliver mission objectives in enterprise networks.

Chapter 11: Internet Services and Applications is a chapter that can be read at any time by anyone interested in the Internet. Along with Chapters 8 and 10, it comprises an "Internet book within a book." It provides a comprehensive look at services and related software applications such as World Wide Web, WAIS and other search engines, e-mail, Whois, mailing lists, newsgroups, file transfer, gopher, and more. Enhanced services and applications are covered as well: Internet Relay Chat, MBONE, audio and video streaming, multimedia, virtual reality, and electronic commerce with secure transactions, and doing business on the Net. Also look here for information about the Internet, its roots, growth, and how to access it.

Chapter 12: Disaster Recovery and Contingency provides an overview of different types of disasters and the steps that organizations and people can take in preventing and responding to them. It focuses on the creation, testing, and maintenance of a documented disaster recovery plan. It can be read at any time, but is a good companion to Chapter 6 and 9 for a complete, yet high-level view of implementing and managing networks.

Chapter 13: Organizational and Social Issues explores the human issues associated with network technology to underscore the need for strategic planning and implementation. Drawing from recent research, it examines network technology as an innovation that accompanies change for individuals, organizations, and society. Rather than viewing people as passive recipients, it acknowledges our active roles in determining its effects. Thus, the Introduction and Chapter 13 elaborate the conceptual framework for strategic networking that is presented throughout the book.

Chapter 14: Resources provides contact information and brief network product and service descriptions for vendors, publications, associations, conferences, and expositions.

Learning Strategies

Conceptual Models

Throughout this book we use analogies, examples, and visual representation of networking concepts as aids to learning. Wherever possible, we use existing models that conform to common practice and build on prior knowledge.

The Open System Interconnection (OSI) Reference model provides a standard to which manufacturers can comply to make their network hardware and software components interoperable in multi-vendor and multi-platform network environments. It is a seven-layer description of network functionality that is typically diagrammed as seven building blocks. Starting from the Physical layer up to the Applications layer, it describes the functional roles that must be assumed by network hardware and software from transmission media up to software applications.

Accordingly, we have designed the order and content of the topics in this book to support this functional model. From transmission media to software applications, the progression of topics in chapters ascends through the seven layers of the OSI Reference model in a progressive treatment.

As Chapter 6 represents a high-level view of network planning and implementation and is also a point of entry to the book for some readers, it is the appropriate place to reveal the entire structure. Subsequent chapters also make links between their topics and the corresponding OSI layers.

Besides its common use in planning, implementation, and trouble-shooting of networks, we believe this use of the OSI Reference model can guide you in building an appropriate mental model as a tool for understanding this complex subject (Norman, 1988).

Continuous Learning

In the course of our research for this book, the most timely source of information on most aspects of networking was the Internet and the people who use it.

This strategy allowed us to cover the broad topic of networking in one volume. To complement a high-level discussion of key networking concepts, we cite relevant online sources for more information. You can access the cited source on the Net while the topic is still fresh in your mind, and add it as a bookmark in a Web browser or other application. In this way, you can begin a process of self-directed, online learning. This process builds a personal web of knowledge. It will contain meaningful, associative links that exist online and in your mind.

This learning strategy grew naturally out of our writing. Once we realized that we could map the complex and changing domain of networking against the resources of the Net, we knew that we were building the beginnings of personal webs. We also realized that we should carefully choose Net references that would work as the initial point of contact for our readers.

With mastery and care, the Internet and the people with whom you interact on it can be used to create your own personal web. It can be the starting point for the continuous learning that you need to ride the crest of change.

Using References

References in this book fall into two basic categories. Internal references (i.e., cross-references) refer to information found elsewhere in this book. External references refer to information found outside this book, including other books, journals, magazines, Internet sources, and organizational contacts. Internal references take the following form:

NOTE For more information, see Chapter 14.

External references for print publications cite author and date of publication within parentheses. All print citations within any chapter can be traced to an alphabetical listing by author last name at the end of the chapter under the References heading.

Net References

Net Reference, or netref for short, is the name we have given to Internet sources of information represented in this book. These are indicated in the form of citations (within a chapter) and references (at the end of a chapter).

For citations to Internet references, we indicate the citation within the body of the text as (see netref #) where # is the number of that netref as it is listed under the Net References heading at the end of the chapter. These references are numbered in the order that they appear in the chapter.

The format we have adopted for a netref is based on addressing as "service to site." For example, a reference to information on the World Wide Web about the NetManage company site would be www to http://netmanage.com/. The netrefs for other Internet services using this site as an example would be shown as:

- e-mail to info@netmanage.com
- ftp to netmanage.com
- gopher to netmanage.com
- telnet to netmanage.com

Additional information about a source is provided in the netrefs to help you in the case of changed address or content. The extended format for this type of reference is "service to site then actions/locations." For example, a reference that describes how to use the telnet service to access the White Pages listing (of e-mail addresses) at the psi.com site, then login and find a particular address would be:

> telnet to wp.psi.com then login as Fred and type the name of a person or organization whose e-mail address you want.

When using the ftp, or file transfer protocol service on the Internet, the Net reference will usually begin with the instructions in the format: ftp to name of site then log in as anonymous. This refers to a login procedure that is common to many remote ftp servers. It requires that you type the word anonymous when you are presented with a prompt for username at login. After the next prompt for a password appears, you should type in your full e-mail address in the format: username@host.domain.

Due to the dynamic nature of Internet content and addresses, we cannot provide any assurance that these references will be accurate or current. However, we have tried wherever possible to provide general information about the site, such as department or company e-mail addresses, Web home pages, and high-level directories.

Also, all of the information in this book is provided solely on an editorial basis and is only intended for informational purposes. Neither the Authors or the Publisher provide implied or explicit advice, warranty, or other assurances concerning its accuracy or usefulness to you. How you use this information and its consequences to you are responsibilities that you as the reader must solely bear and should carefully consider.

The products, services, and companies that are described in this book are the trademarks of their respective companies and are used in this book only for editorial purposes. Descriptions of these products and services can be found in Chapter 14, Resources chapter.

ACKNOWLEDGMENTS

A book is the result of more people than the authors alone and this book is no exception. Although our acknowledgment is brief, our gratitude is sincere and considerable. We thank everyone who provided advice, support, and encouragement at each step during the long period of research and writing. First and foremost is our grateful thanks for the support and encouragement of family and friends, especially Sara and Alison who waited so patiently and Joann and Frank for their advice on early drafts.

Many thanks to Carlo Cernivani at the New York University Academic Computing Facility, Brett Lynch at Global Telecom, and Robert Warren at Network-USA for providing Internet access. Special appreciation goes to the many public relations, press, and support people at the organizations we contacted, and to the many helpful "netizens" who, through their selfless generosity and enthusiasm, create the rich community we call the Internet. Words alone cannot voice our appreciation to our Publisher Jim DeWolf, Project Director Chris Grisonich, Editor Liz Israel Oppedijk, Marketing Manager Kathleen Raftery, Jay Habegger, the webmaster@thomson.com, and the rest of the ITCP staff, along with production by Jo-Ann Campbell and the staff of *mle design* of Milford, CT.

Last, but not least, we thank you, the reader, for making this book part of your learning experience. We welcome your comments and suggestions. This forum doesn't stop or fit within these pages. Look for us online at ITCP (see netref 1) and other sites where we continue the forum and welcome the feedback (see netref 2).

REFERENCES

Dickens, C. 1836-1837. *Sketches by Boz* from chapter 3 of *Tales.*

Norman, Donald A. 1981. "The Trouble with UNIX." *Datamation* 27:139-150.

Norman, Donald A. 1988. *The Psychology of Everyday Things.* New York: Basic Books.

Winograd, Terry. 1995. "From Programming Environments to Environments for Designing." *Communications of the ACM.* 38 (6):65-73.

Net References

1. For more information about the Strategic Networking book and related events, www to http://www.itcp.thomson.com/ then browse the International Thomson Computer Press home page for Strategic Networking links or search for Strategic Networking in the ITCP catalog.

2. To find more information about online and live Strategic Networking Forums, www to http://www.snf.org/ and browse the home page. You can also get current forum and event information by sending e-mail to info@snf.org with no message body. We welcome your feedback through e-mail to gene@snf.org or paul@snf.org.

1

Transmission Media

ABOUT THIS CHAPTER

Transmission media carry data over a network. Selecting the right medium to transmit data is often easier said than done. The information in this chapter will help you select the transmission medium that best suits your network needs.

Popular cable media such as twisted-pair, coaxial cable, and optical fiber are described along with the standards and gradings that determine their selection and use. Wireless transmission media based on radio and infrared technologies are similarly covered. You will also learn about preparing functional specifications, media testing and certification, and selecting a cabling contractor.

INTRODUCTION

Driving across town or traveling by train, utility poles are often a familiar sight beside the road or railroad tracks. The telephone and cable television wires stretched across their tops are examples of transmission media. They provide a vital link to a vast network of public utilities and private services. Transmission media in computer networks serve a similar function.

In this section, some basic concepts about transmission media and computer data are covered. Read it if you need background information for topics covered later in this chapter.

Physical Characteristics

Networks are designed to distribute resources. Transmission media provide the physical links between network nodes that connect users and resources whether within local networks or global internetworks. Often hidden from view or passing invisibly through the air, transmission media are an unobtrusive, yet vital component of networking.

Available in a wide array of cabling and wireless technologies, networks are often characterized by the predominant type of media employed. Despite the tendency to think first and foremost of media when planning networks, the choice of media should follow organizational objectives like form follows function.

The electrical and physical characteristics of a transmission medium determine the speed, quantity, and quality of a transmitted signal. These characteristics also determine which transmission medium is best suited to the organizational needs of a network. For example, access to network databases may not require the same speed and quantity of transmitted data as a videoconferencing link. Also, some types of data such as video, need to be transmitted without delay. Thus, it's not only the amount of data but also the speed of delivery that helps determine the transmission medium.

Signal

Computer data is encoded as a series of on-off pulses (in binary code) which represent the symbols that we understand, regardless of whether they are text, images, sound, or video. Networks transmit computer data in bundles called packets which contain both data and routing information.

As in other communications media, some computer data is transmitted by a carrier signal. The frequency of this signal is measured in cycles-per-second and named after its discoverer, Hertz. Computer data is typically transmitted by carrier frequencies in the range of millions (mega-Hertz or MHz) to billions of cycles per second (giga-Hertz or GHz). These frequencies can extend up the electromagnetic spectrum to radio and light waves.

Conductor

A conductor is any material capable of carrying an electrical signal. There are many types of conductors used in computer and communications networks; the most common are cable (wire or wired systems) and air (wireless systems). Cable is used to transmit electronic signals through wire or as photonic (light) signals through glass fiber. Both types are surrounded by sheathing material.

Wire cabling is also protected from the interference of other signals by twisting pairs of wires or wrapping the wires with a braided sheath. Wire can vary in thickness and can be solid or stranded. Twisted-pair wire is the most common type of transmission media and conductor and is frequently used in home and office telephone systems. Another type of cable is coaxial. Coaxial cable conductors can also be solid or stranded. There are several types of coaxial cable. It is typically used for high-speed data and cable television applications.

In optical fiber cabling, a glass fiber which acts as an optical data pipe is surrounded by plastic sheathing. Instead of using an electrical signal as the carrier, it transmits computer data using light waves. Thus, shielding from electronic interference is not necessary.

Wireless transmission systems are becoming increasingly popular for remote network access and other applications where wired systems are not present or practical. Using air as the conductor, computer data can be transmitted at the higher frequencies of radio and infrared light.

Transmission Speed and Capacity

Bandwidth is a term that describes the difference between the highest and lowest frequencies in a specific range of frequencies. In published standards (see netref 1) bandwidth is defined as a medium's information-carrying capacity or the size of a transmission channel expressed in megahertz (MHz).

Transmission media also have specific bit rates, or rates of throughput, as defined by various transmission media standards. Several of the more popular standards will be discussed in detail later in this chapter. Throughput is an overall measure of the data-carrying capability of both the transmission medium and the components to which it connects.

It is important to understand that the rated bandwidth or throughput of a medium does not guarantee performance. For example, unshielded twisted-pair cable has a rated throughput of 100 megabits per second (Mbps). This means it can support transmission rates of up to one hundred million data bits per second. Typical Ethernet networks offer transmission speeds up to 10Mbps. Thus, although the cable is rated for 100Mbps, the technology in use (e.g., Ethernet) as well as other variables such as overall network traffic, the number of users on a segment, and cable lengths, etc., determine the actual throughput. Throughput is also affected by the speed at which network components like routers and hubs can transmit the packets of data.

Physical Layer of the OSI Model

The Open Systems Interconnection (OSI) Reference model was developed by the International Standards Organization (ISO) and published in 1977. It is an industry standard model that helps define how devices on a network communicate. There are seven layers that make up this model and they are discussed in Chapter 6. We will refer to this model throughout this book as a conceptual tool for understanding the way networks operate.

Transmission media operate at the Physical layer of the OSI model. The Physical layer specifies the physical components used in the network, such cables and connectors. It also addresses the functions necessary to send and receive data over a particular medium. The Physical layer is the lowest layer in the OSI model and it is the layer where components such as repeaters can operate on the signal to amplify and retransmit it.

> **NOTE** For more information about repeaters and other network components, see Chapter 3.

If you are responsible for designing, implementing, or managing networks of any size, it is important to familiarize yourself with the OSI model. Understanding the layers of the model at which specific network components function can provide you with a tactical tool for solving most network problems.

If you work with network planning issues at higher levels, the OSI model can provide a common framework for discussion with network professionals. The following section provides detailed information about the many types of network transmission media in use today.

TWISTED-PAIR WIRE

The two major types of twisted-pair wire are unshielded twisted-pair (UTP) and shielded twisted-pair (STP) (see Figure 1-1). Several sets of twisted-pair wires can be enclosed in a single cable. In cables with more than 25 pairs, the twisted-pairs are grouped and bound together in a common cable sheath. Screened twisted-pair (ScTP) wire, a 100-ohm cable that uses a thinner, more flexible shielding than STP and offers many of the performance characteristics of optical-fiber cable, has also become very popular since it's introduction in 1991.

Unshielded Twisted-pair

Unshielded twisted-pair (UTP) wiring is one of the most popular network cabling methods in use today. This is due in part to its flexibility and the fact that, depending on the contruction of the cable, it doesn't take up as much room in cable ducts as STP and other media can.

Telephone companies often pre-wire buildings with UTP. This particular grade of wire is acceptable for PBX (Private Branch eXchange) telephone use, but might not be certified for network services.

Figure 1-1. Twisted-pair (UTP) Cable (AMP Incorporated).

Interference and Noise

Certain grades of UTP are more susceptible to interference and noise than other cable. In cases like these unshielded wires can act as an antenna, picking up external electrical interference. How the wire pairs are twisted can have a great impact on the ability of a cable to resist crosstalk, electromagnetic interference, and radio frequency interference (EMI/RFI).

Although most twisted-pair cable is manufactured with a certain level of quality assurance, you can expect 2 to 3 percent of wire pairs in an installation to be defective (Derfler and Freed, 1993). If your environment is prone to a high degree of electrical interference, carefully consider the features and benefits of each category of twisted-pair wire. In this type of environment, you might be better off using shielded twisted-pair (STP) or even optical-fiber cabling because of their increased resistance to noise and interference.

Installing UTP

When installing UTP, the Institute of Electrical and Electronics Engineers (IEEE) 10BASET standard recommends that the cable run for each node shouldn't exceed 328 feet from the network port on the workstation to the terminating point in the hub.

Observing this rule as closely as possible when planning your cable runs makes it easier to troubleshoot performance problems later on. At least you will know that the length of the cable is not likely to be the cause of a problem. UTP is found in Ethernet, token-ring, and ARCNET installations. While the UTP cable used with each of these technologies can be the same, pin configurations can be different in certain applications.

> **NOTE** For more information about Ethernet, token-ring, and ARCNET technologies, see Chapter 2.

Shielded Twisted-pair

The most common type of shielded twisted-pair (STP) was introduced by IBM and is called 150-ohm STP, because of its 150-ohm impedance. Widely used in earlier token-ring networks, in this type of STP cable the pairs of twisted wires are separately shielded from one another. This greatly reduces crosstalk and other interference.

The entire cable is also completely shielded, which further reduces the possible effects of EMI/RFI. However, because of the added shielding, STP can be considerably more expensive to purchase and install than UTP.

A simpler STP cable, called 100 ohm shielded cable or aluminum screened cable, has a shield surrounding the wire pairs. It provides more protection from interference than UTP and is also compatible with popular 10BASET wiring hubs.

Grounding

No matter which type of STP cable you select, make absolutely sure the cable is properly grounded. 150-ohm cable calls for grounding at both ends while 100-ohm cable should be grounded at one end, typically at the hub.

If proper grounding procedures are not followed, not only can the shielding in the cable act as an antenna, but electrostatic buildup can cause shocks and other damage. Unless you're hoping to pick up your favorite sports broadcast, this can cause real headaches!

COAXIAL CABLE

Coaxial cable is made up of an insulated center copper conductor, an outer braid or secondary conductor that functions as a ground, and a plastic outside covering. The outer braid makes up half of the electrical circuit and also functions as a shield for the center conductor. Because of this, the braid must make a solid electrical connection at both ends of the cable.

There are two types of coaxial cable used in LAN configurations, 10BASE5 thick Ethernet and 10BASE2 thin Ethernet.

10BASE5 Thick Ethernet

Thick Ethernet cabling systems use cable with 50-ohm terminators at each end. The IEEE 802.3 10BASE5 standard for baseband Ethernet allows 100 nodes on a 10BASE5 thick Ethernet segment, with a minimum distance between transceivers of eight feet. It also specifies that the maximum length of a transceiver, or drop cable (the cable running from the backbone or trunk to your workstation), should be no longer than 165 feet and that the maximum length of a single 10BASE5 segment is approximately 1,640 feet, with a limit on overall cable length of 8,200 feet.

Connecting nodes to a 10BASE5 segment is accomplished most often with device known as a vampire tap. The vampire tap has metal spikes that pierce the plastic outer sheath of the cable to make contact with the copper wire or center conductor. When installing taps on thick Ethernet cable, look for markers printed on the jacket of the cable. These markers indicate quarter wavelength points.

When you tap into a cable that is properly terminated, inserting your vampire tap at the quarter wavelength intervals, the transceiver is able to detect the correct impedance. If you should happen to miss a quarter wavelength point by more than a few inches, the impedance mismatch might cause reflections over the cable leading to lost or corrupted data. This is one reason why terminators must be installed exactly on the markers at each end of the segment.

10BASE2 Thin Ethernet

The thin Ethernet cabling system doesn't use transceiver or drop cables. Instead, the 10BASE2 thin Ethernet cable travels from node to node using a T-connector to physically connect to the workstation's network interface card (NIC) or other network component like a bridge or router. Each end of the segment has a 50-ohm terminating resistor installed, as with thick Ethernet cabling systems described above.

The thin Ethernet cable system was originally specified in the IEEE 802.3 10BASE2 standard as using RG-58 coaxial cable, with nodes arranged in a daisy-chained fashion. In this configuration, a break in the cable or a bad connector could bring your entire network down. Newer hardware lets us wire our Ethernet networks in a star-shaped or spoked-wheel pattern, with a single cable between the workstation and wiring hub.

The maximum length of a single 10BASE2, or thin Ethernet segment, is approximately 607 feet. The maximum overall cable length connected by repeaters is 3,035 feet, for a total of five cable segments linked by repeaters. If you're not planning on using repeaters, commonly used to increase transmission distances and reduce signal distortion, then a maximum 10BASE2 segment of 984 feet is permitted. Each cable run can have a maximum of 30 nodes with the minimum distance between nodes being 1.5 feet. Practical experience dictates a maximum of approximately 15 to 20 nodes per segment for thin Ethernet segments on busy networks.

> **NOTE** For more information about repeaters and other network components, see Chapter 3.

OPTICAL FIBER CABLE

Optical fiber (see netref 2) is a strand of glass thinner than a human hair, yet inch for inch is stronger than steel. It can carry information so fast that you could transmit three episodes of your favorite television show in just one second.

Fiber carries information in the form of light. Communicating with light gives some types of fiber an information-carrying capacity thousands of times greater than copper, which uses electricity to transmit signals. In fact, two strands of fiber about the thickness of a human hair can carry more data than a bundle of copper wire four inches in diameter.

A fiber is made up of two different types of glass, known as the core and cladding, covered by a protective coating. Smaller core sizes are easier to couple and interconnect and generally offer lower bandwidth capabilities. The core is the light-guiding region of the fiber, while the cladding ensures the light pulses remain within the core. Light is contained within the core because the core and cladding glasses have different indices of refraction. This refractive-index difference causes the light signal to be contained in the core as it is carried along the length of the fiber (see Figure 1-2). A protective coating is applied to the glass as the final step in the manufacturing process. This coating protects the glass from dust and scratches, which can affect its strength.

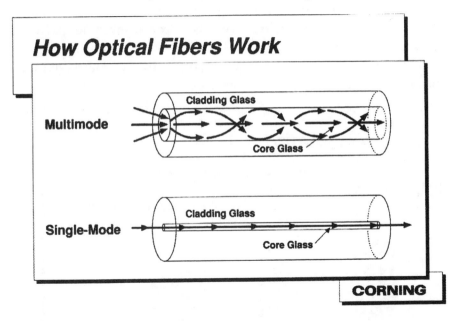

Figure 1-2. How optical fibers work (Corning Incorporated).

Due to its high immunity to electronic or radio-frequency interference (EMI/RFI), fiber cable is the perfect choice for military applications, industrial environments, or commercial installations that are susceptible to a high degree of interference. Fiber cabling is fast becoming a standard in organizations interested in providing secure, high-speed backbones in large installations. It is also highly resistant to security breaches caused by the possibility of intruders tapping into a cable. While copper cable can be tapped by directly connecting to the copper wire itself or other methods, tapping a fiber cable could release light from the cable, resulting in a power loss in the optical fiber system. Additionally, since optical-fiber cable isn't conductive, it won't radiate electromagnetic noise and other signals that can be picked up by experienced hackers seeking to break into your system.

Fiber is extremely tolerant of heat and corrosion, unlike copper cables. The smaller diameter of some types of fiber cable can save valuable space in wiring closets and raceways. Using advanced engineering techniques in testing situations, transmission speeds of more than 25Gbps have been achieved. In addition, fiber runs can span many miles, with no degradation in signal quality.

There are two types of optical fiber cable in use commercially today, multimode and single-mode (see Figure 1-3).

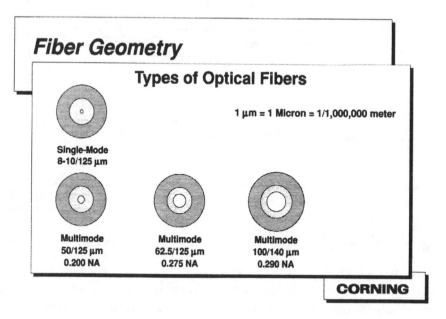

Figure 1-3. Types of optical fiber (Corning Incorporated).

Multimode Fiber

Multimode fiber was the first type of fiber to be commercialized. It has a much larger core than single-mode fiber, allowing hundreds of rays, or modes, of light to be generated through the fiber simultaneously. While you might think that multimode fibers have a high capacity to carry information, just the opposite is true.

Multimode fiber has less bandwidth capabilities than monomode, but is easier to splice than single-mode and uses inexpensive light-emitting diodes (LEDs) as an optical transmitter instead of the expensive lasers used in single-mode installations. Multimode is most often used for data communications and in private networks where transmission distances are less than approximately 6,550 feet.

Core sizes of 50 and 62.5 micron multimode are the types most commonly used in today's network installations, because they offer the best combination of available attenuation, bandwidth, and light coupling power.

Single-mode Fiber

Single-mode fiber is manufactured with the smallest core sizes, approximately 8–10 microns in diameter. This smaller core size makes single-mode fiber more difficult to splice and install than multimode. In addition, single-mode fiber allows only one mode of light at a time to be generated through the core.

Single-mode fibers retain the separation of each light pulse over longer distances, allowing more information to be transmitted. With its greater information-carrying capacity, single-mode fiber is generally used for long distance and high bandwidth applications.

Fiber Connectors

Fiber connectors (see Figure 1-4) are designed to transmit light in the most efficient manner possible. For this to happen, the ends of the cables must be perfectly polished to ensure all scratches and flaws are removed.

Let's take a look at the four most practical commercial connectors in use today.

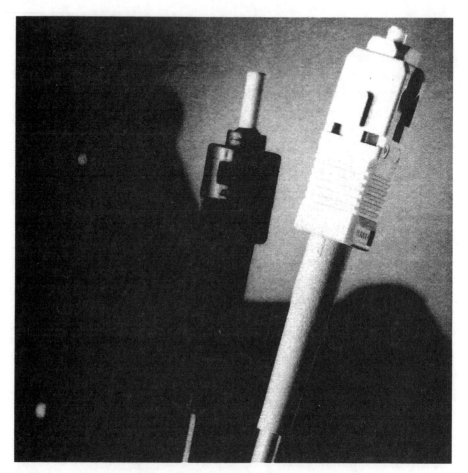

Figure 1-4. Optical fiber connectors (AMP Incorporated).

Straight-Tip Connector

The ST (straight-tip) connector is probably the most frequently used connector and is usually installed in commercial and office environments. The center of the connector is a ceramic jacket that is glued to the fiber core. The fiber comes out at the end of the jacket and must be polished to be sure it is free of scratches and imperfections. The outer shell of the ST connector looks something like the coaxial BNC connector, and locks onto the jack with a quarter-twist.

Sub-Miniature Assembly

The SMA (sub-miniature assembly) connector is used primarily by European equipment manufacturers and is similar to the ST type, but utilizes a threaded outer shell. The threaded design helps make the SMA connector more reliable than the ST connector, particularly when installed in environments prone to vibration. The SMA connector was developed by AMP, Inc. (see netref 3), and was the first connector for optical fibers to be standardized.

There are two types of SMA connectors. One has a rounded tip like the ST connector and the other a stepped-down tip, which provides better alignment when connecting your cable. The ST and SMA connectors use a single connector for each optical fiber strand. Because of this, sometimes it is easy to confuse the strands and plug the wrong fiber into a jack, even though one of the fibers is usually marked with a strip or other identifier.

Medium Interface Connector

The MIC (medium interface connector) is typically associated with the Fiber Distributed Data Interface (FDDI). A single MIC connector holds two fibers and is keyed. This ensures that the plug and socket will couple only specific way. MIC connectors are used in many popular LAN adapters and wiring hubs.

NOTE For more information about FDDI, see Chapter 2.

Style Connector

The SC (style connector) connector provides a very strong connection that is used occasionally only in rare occurrences where cable splicing is necessary. The SC connector holds two fibers, ensuring you will always plug the right fiber into the right jack. It is used in FDDI, Fibre Channel, and Broadband/ISDN (B/ISDN) applications.

NOTE For more information about FDDI and Fibre Channel, see Chapter 2. For more information about B/ISDN, see Chapter 5.

Now that we've talked about different physical transmission media used in networks, let's review a few standards and gradings that will help you differentiate one media type from another.

CABLE STANDARDS

AT&T, Digital Equipment Corporation (DEC), Hewlett-Packard (HP), IBM, and Northern Telecom (NorTel) have individually produced specifications and standards that address topics like connectors, wiring distribution centers, and cabling and its installation (see netref 4). Several of these companies have also developed architectures for structured cabling systems. Structured wiring systems are based on the entire system instead of just the wiring between LAN hubs and workstations.

In addition, several organizations and government agencies issue standards for the cabling used in your network. They include the Institute of Electrical and Electronic Engineers (IEEE), the Electronics Industries Association, Telecommunications Industry Association (EIA/TIA), and Underwriters Laboratories (UL).

EIA/TIA-568 Standard

The EIA/TIA-568 standard covers 100 ohm UTP, 150 ohm UTP, STP, and optical-fiber cabling. Here are the EIA/TIA-568 category ratings:

- **Category 1**–Typically made up of 22 or 24 American Wire Gauge (AWG) untwisted wire, Category 1 cabling is not recommended for data

- **Category 2**–This cable is derived from the IBM Type 3 cable specification and uses 22 or 24 AWG solid wire in twisted-pairs. Category 2 cable is tested to a bandwidth of 1MHz and is often used for IBM 3270, AS/400, and LocalTalk connections.

- **Category 3**–Comprised of 24 AWG solid wire in twisted-pairs, it is useful for installations requiring transmission speeds (throughput) up to 16Mbps. Category 3 is the lowest acceptable standard for a 10BASET installation and is also adequate for 4Mbps Token-ring installations. It is possible to use Category 3 UTP in 16Mbps token-ring installations, although not recommended.

- **Category 4**–Category 4 uses 22 or 24 AWG solid wire in twisted-pairs. This is a good choice when running 16Mbps token-ring over unshielded twisted-pair wire and will also work well in 10BASET installations. Category 4 cable is tested to a bandwidth of 20Mhz.

- **Category 5**–The highest capacity choice for network installations, this 22 or 24 AWG unshielded twisted-pair cable can handle data rates of 100Mbps under certain conditions. Category 5 is a high-quality cable and offers the possibility of transmitting video, images, and high-speed data over enterprise-wide networks. It is tested to a bandwidth of 100Mhz.

Annex E

While the categories listed above refer to the cable itself, Annex E of the EIA/TIA-568 draft addresses the need for a standard for link performance. Annex E includes the connectors, punch blocks, wall plates, and patch cords that, together with the cable, make up a segment or link. Descriptions of the Annex E link portion of the EIA/TIA-568 draft are as follows (Categories 1 and 2 were omitted since they are not recommended for data use):

- **Category 3**–For UTP cables and associated connecting hardware with transmission characteristics (bandwidth) up to 16MHz. Applications for this cable type could include 10BASET, 4Mbps token-ring, ARCNET, or 100VG-AnyLAN systems.

- **Category 4**–Applies to UTP cables and associated connecting hardware with transmission characteristics up to 20MHz. Applications for this category include 16Mbps token-ring and 10BASET.

- **Category 5**–For UTP, ScTP (ITT's exclusive screened twisted-pair cable technology), or STP cables and associated connecting hardware with transmission characteristics up to 100MHz. Possible

CAT5 implementations include ATM (Asynchronous Transfer Mode) over copper, 100BASE-X, and TP-PMD (Twisted-Pair Physical Medium Dependent), which is an American National Standards Institute (ANSI) (see netref 5) standard for an FDDI network that uses UTP instead of optical fiber. TP-PMD is also known as CDDI or TPDDI.

NOTE For more information about FDDI and CDDI, see Chapter 2. For more information about ATM, see Chapter 5.

UL Specifications

Underwriters Laboratories, Inc. is a privately owned, for-profit company that charges manufacturers a fee to guarantee that their cables or hardware meet the safety standards that UL has developed. The UL program addresses UTP and STP cabling and has safety standards for cables similar to those of the National Electrical Code (NEC). The NEC is established by the National Fire Protection Association (NFPA).

UL 444 is the Standard for Safety for Communications Cable. UL 13 is the Standard for Safety for Power-Limited Circuit Cable (network cable can fall into either category). UL tests and evaluates samples of cable and then continues to test and inspect the cable even after it issues a UL listing.

In January 1994, the UL system was more closely matched to the EIA/TIA category system. UL now classifies cabling as Category 1–5 instead of Level I–V. UL Categories 3–5 correspond exactly to EIA/TIA-568 Categories and have been omitted here.

- **Category 1**–This cable is intended for basic communications and power-limited circuit cable. There are no performance criteria for this cable at this level.

- **Category 2**–Performance requirements for this cable are similar to IBM's Type 3 cable. Category 2 covers cable with 2-pair to 25-pair construction.

IBM Cabling System

The first popular LAN cabling system was from IBM. The IBM Cabling System uses STP, as well as optical fiber and UTP cabling. STP is the wire type IBM recommends for 4 and 16Mbps token-ring installations. Here's a description of the 9 IBM wire types:

- **Type 1**–Made up of two twisted-pairs of 22 AWG solid wire, each pair of wires has its own shielding. The entire cable is shielded by an external braid and supports data rates up to 100Mbps. Type 1 cable can be compared with the EIA/TIA-568 Category 5 UTP cable and is primarily used in token-ring networks. Type 1 cable is tested to a bandwidth of 100MHz. IBM also offers a more rigorously tested high-speed cable classified as Type 1A. Type 1A cabling is tested to 300 MHz and is designed for use in networks requiring very high transmission rates, such as ATM.

- **Type 2**–This cable consists of four unshielded 22 AWG solid wire pairs for telephone, and two shielded pairs meeting the Type 1 data specification, all housed in the same sheath. It is designed for applications in which voice and data services will be over the same cable. IBM also offers type 2A cable, which is tested to a bandwidth of 600MHz.

- **Type 3**–Type 3 is IBM's version of twisted-pair telephone wire. The four unshielded 24 AWG solid twisted wire pairs are designed for telephone and low-speed data transmission of up to 4 Mbps, but does not meet the requirements for higher-speed data transmission.

- **Type 4**–There is no published IBM specification for this cable type.

- **Type 5**–Type 5 cabling is made up of two optical fiber strands, and measures 140 microns (with cladding) with a 100-micron core. Type 5 cable is recognized as part of the Fiber Distributed Data Interface (FDDI) specification, but is not as commonly used in network installations as is 62.5/125 micron cable.

- **Type 6**–Made up of two twisted pairs of 26 AWG stranded wire, this shielded cable is more flexible than Type 1 cable and is frequently used to connect a node to a data jack or for patch cables. It is designed specifically for data transmission. Type 6A is also available. It is tested to a bandwidth of 600MHz.

- **Type 7**–There is no published IBM specification for this cable type.

- **Type 8**–This is a flat, shielded twisted pair cable meant for installation under carpeting and other floor coverings. This cable has two parallel, untwisted pair of 23 AWG solid wire. Because of the parallel, untwisted characteristics of the cable, it isn't well suited for use in modern network installations.

- **Type 9**–Type 9 is a plenum cable consisting of two individually shielded, twisted, solid or stranded 26 AWG wire pairs. Plenum cabling is generally required by fire codes in most commercial installations because it is flame retardant. Type 9 cable is designed for low-speed data transmission. IBM Type 9A, tested to a bandwidth of 600MHz, is also available.

ISO Generic Cabling Standard

In addition to the EIA/TIA-568 standards on building wiring, there is also an important international standard being developed by the International Standards Organization (ISO) (see netref 6), founded in 1946 and headquartered in Geneva. The ISO deals with all fields except electrical and electronics, which is handled by the older International Electrotechnical Commission (IEC), also in Geneva. The ISO carries out its work through more than 160 technical committees and over 2,000 subcommittees and working groups and is made up of standards organizations from more than 75 countries.

The IEC is an organization that sets international electrical and electronics standards. It was founded in 1906 and is headquartered in Geneva. The IEC is made up of national committees from over 40 countries. Contact is via ANSI in New York. These two organizations have established a joint technical committee, JTC1, the Joint Technical

Committee for information technology. This committee has developed the Draft International Standard (DIS) 11801: Generic Cabling for Information Technology.

The 11801 standard was based loosely on the EIA/TIA standard, and became a draft standard in late 1993. It is intended to support voice and data, text, image, and video cable applications and includes configuration, implementation, performance, and conformance requirements.

IEEE

The IEEE (the Institute of Electrical and Electronics Engineers) is a transnational publishing and standards-making organization with over 300,000 members in 137 countries. It is the world's largest engineering society. The IEEE's technical objectives center on advancing the theory and practice of electrical, electronics, and computer engineering and computer science. To meet these objectives, the IEEE sponsors various conferences, publishes a wide range of professional papers, and provides educational programs.

More information about the IEEE can be found at their World Wide Web (Web or W3) home page on the Internet. Using one of the widely available Web browsers, open the following location or Uniform Resource Locator (URL): http://www.ieee.org/ and then link to further information such as the IEEE electronic bookshelves, magazines, and information about standards. Clicking on a highlighted link will load the selected URL into memory, with the results displayed by your browser. See Figure 1-5 for an example of the IEEE home page.

Figure 1-5. IEEE World Wide Web home page (©1995 IEEE).

WIRELESS NETWORKS

In certain instances, your organization may want to consider a wireless network implementation. For example, it might be difficult or impossible to cable a particular building or workgroup area. Wireless networks can be used to extend wired networks such as LANs, WANs, or the Internet

Most wireless LAN equipment falls into two categories: low-speed devices with data rates from 115Kbps to 250Kbps, and high-speed devices supporting data rates up to about 10Mbps, the speed of Ethernet. Today's wireless WANs support data rates from 19.2Kbps up to 1Mbps. However, data rates for both wireless LANs and WANs are considerably less than the 100Mbps rates being achieved today by technologies such as ATM and 100VG-AnyLan.

> **NOTE** For more information about 100VG-AnyLan, see Chapter 2.

Radio Frequency

Radio Frequency (RF) networks can be an attractive alternative to conventional LANs when there is a need to integrate wireless and standard Ethernet technologies.

RF LANs provide bandwidth capabilities up to 10 Mbps. There are two types of RF signals: local-area RF and wide-area RF. Local-area RF signals range from 2,400 to 2,483MHz while wide-area RF signals are transmitted on a fairly narrow band at about 940MHz.

Local-Area RF

The average range for local-area RF equipment is approximately 30 feet to 300 feet, though some equipment can reach as far as 1,200 feet. Local-area RF equipment is operated primarily in the Industrial, Scientific, and Medical (ISM) bands. ISM is a term the FCC uses to name several of the frequency bands in the electromagnetic spectrum. These radio frequencies don't require a broadcasting license, but the equipment still must observe the power and bandwidth restrictions enforced by the FCC and be certified by the agency as well.

Wide-Area RF

Wide-area RF equipment can consist of one-way as well as two-way data flow. One-way data flow is the technology used by some digital electronic pagers. With one-way data flow a carrier service, such as the company that provides your pager, transmits a message and an address. In this example, the transmitted address would be your pager's ID. The pager will recognize its ID and display the incoming digital message. One-way wide-area RF signals can transmit over a distance of about 10 miles.

Two-way service is almost the same, except the receiving unit also transmits data back to the carrier. This data might be forwarded to yet another organization, like an e-mail service or a node on your LAN. Some companies now provide services such as sending wireless copies of *The Wall Street Journal* or *USA Today* right to your workstation. Two-way wide-area signals can transmit over a distance of about six miles.

Access to wide-area RF services is facilitated using an RF modem. The RF modem transmits and receives data in 128-byte packets, much like the Cellular Digital Packet Data (CDPD) technology. Each packet is numbered, which means they can be re-transmitted very quickly and correctly reassembled by the receiving modem even if they are out of order, with no obvious decrease in throughput.

A typical session between two RF modems might look something like this: the sender transmits a sequence of packets, with no pause for confirmation. If one of the packets becomes corrupted by noise or interference, the receiver requests the sending modem to retransmit only the damaged packet. The sender continues transmitting new packets until it detects this retransmit request from the receiver. The sending modem resends the offending packet and then continues with normal transmission.

Profile: RAM Mobile Data

RAM Mobile Data, a business venture between RAM Broadcasting and BellSouth, offers packet-switching RF data communications and assists companies in eliminating the barriers of physical distance and time between a business and its customers or employees. This is one example of a growing number of businesses providing ways to utilize the potential of wireless communications systems.

According to statistics published by RAM, the mobile workforce in the U.S. is estimated at approximately 45 million, or nearly 40 percent of the total employed workforce of 118 million. In addition, RAM states that the emerging market for portable wireless data services is projected to climb to 15 million units by the year 2000.

RAM Mobile Data provides its service via a multiuser, two-way, wireless data communications network covering over 7,500 cities, plus airports and major transportation corridors. Their networks include 870 base stations, along with local switches and network control centers, that send and receive data messages between portable and fixed devices in the field and host computers, servers, and information services.

Some of RAM's more strategic implementations of wireless communications services include:

- Providing wireless connections to credit card processing systems for point-of-sale credit card authorization in places where it is neither desirable or possible to install dedicated phone lines.

- Transmitting job assignments and customer service history to service personnel on the road. Field personnel can respond with order status and parts/pricing requests while they are at a customer site.

- Enterprise-wide e-mail services are delivered via RAM's systems. Many LAN e-mail packages are now compatible with RAM's services. Real-time financial market information, news, commentary, and analytics are delivered via commercial information providers offering wireless data distribution of their services via RAM's network, as well.

VSAT

VSAT (Very Small Aperture Terminal) networks use small satellite dishes, approximately 2.5 to 8 feet, to provide efficient and cost-effective communications for a variety of applications. These include credit card verification, inventory control, business television for training and corporate communications, in-store music, and data distribution. VSATs are a practical option for locations where a land-based communications infrastructure does not exist. Because of this, businesses in a variety of industries use VSAT satellite networks to communicate with remote locations no matter where they are located; across town or around the world.

Hub Stations

VSAT networks rely on a central hub station to serve as the transfer point between remote locations, the satellite, and a company's headquarters or data center. The hub contains the necessary uplink and downlink equipment to transfer signals to and from the satellite.

Satellite transmissions use multiple frequency bands; the C-band (4-6gHz), Ku-band (12-14gHz), and Ka-band (20-30gHz). Outbound and inbound channels handle data transfers from hub stations and remote VSATs at speeds between 256Kbps and 512Kbps. VSAT networks use standard data interfaces to connect to the hub or remote equipment. These include serial synchronous/asynchronous and direct LAN connections.

For a company that decides not to own and operate its own dedicated hub, shared hub services are used. Using shared hub services means your organization can avoid the expense of building its own hub and maintaining a technical staff to run it.

Performance

Performance over a VSAT network depends on the protocols and applications used. Some protocols perform poorly unless they are used in a conventional LAN environment with high-speed connections between all nodes.

Generally, applications developed for WAN use perform well in a VSAT LAN/WAN environment. TCP/IP performs well over satellite networks because it requires the least amount of tuning and offers maximum use of available resources. Other protocols used in VSAT networks include AppleTalk, Banyan VINES, DECnet, SNA, and Novell IPX.

> **NOTE** For more information about VSAT, see Chapter 5. For information about protocols, see Chapter 7.

Mobile Satellite Products

A new breed of mobile satellite products have been introduced in response to the emergence of a mobile workforce.

Mobile Satellite Products Corporation (a California Microwave Company) manufactures the Mobilesat LYNXX Earth Station (see Figure 1-6). It handles high-speed data and ISDN connectivity, which makes it useful for live two-way videoconferencing via ISDN and H.320-compatible video. The unit can be used as a portable ISDN gateway to the Internet and other networks.

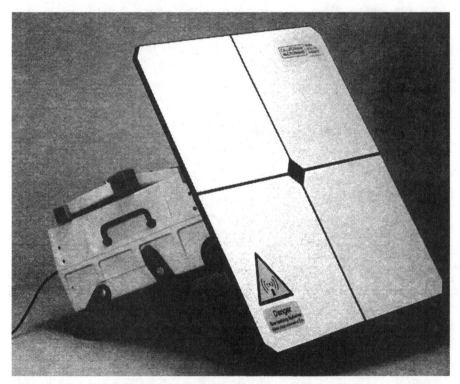

Figure 1-6. MobileSat™ LYNXX® Transportable Earth station (Mobile Satellite Products Corporation).

Cellular

Circuit-switched cellular systems, also known as voice-band cellular systems, use existing cellular telephone networks, microwave technology, and land lines to make remote communications possible. Even though information transmitted via cellular links travels over land-based copper or fiber lines at one point or another, cellular services are still considered a wireless technology.

Land-based telephone lines usually provide good quality links with little noise. Cellular channels, however, are highly susceptible to noise and interference. Because of this, throughput over cellular links can drop unexpectedly. To address this issue, many vendors are attempting to improve the reliability and throughput of data over cellular connections by introducing new, proprietary protocols. Although some vendors have reported data rates up to 14.4Kbps, you can realistically expect cellular throughput to average between 4,800 and 7,200bps. Many factors, such as the time required to set up a cellular call, are a likely source of reduced throughput.

Proprietary protocols are being incorporated into many new cellular devices. Some boost performance by shrinking and expanding the size of a data block from 8 to 256 bytes and decreasing or increasing modem speeds as line conditions decay or improve. These proprietary implementations are only effective when both the sending and receiving modems use the same protocol.

Cellular phones transmit data by using the audio signals produced by a modem. So, to transmit data over a cellular link, you will need a special cellular-ready modem that connects to your cellular phone or a cellular adapter that connects to both the modem and your cellular phone. In order to function together, a cellular modem or adapter has to be able to control the bus of the cellular phone.

While some companies publish open specifications that are broadly supported by many cellular modem and adapter vendors, others are not quite as open. Because of this, not all cellular phones, modems, and adapters are compatible. This makes interoperability an important issue to consider when buying cellular equipment.

Cellular Digital Packet Data

If Cellular Digital Packet Data (CDPD) technology isn't available in your neighborhood today, cellular carriers are working hard to have nationwide CDPD networks in place before long. Led by McCaw Cellular Communications, Inc., of Kirkland, WA (see netref 7), CDPD was developed by a consortium of the nation's largest cellular carriers.

The CDPD specification, providing a standard for using cellular networks for wireless data transmission, was released in July of 1993. The CDPD Forum (see netref 8) is a group dedicated to creating CDPD technical specifications that provide vendors with guidelines for creating CDPD hardware and software products.

Noteworthy features of CDPD include a reduced sensitivity to noise, relief from the interruptions caused by roaming between cellular transmitting regions, automatic error-detection and retransmission to ensure data integrity, and data encryption technology to protect transmitted data.

The CDPD architecture supports multiple connectionless network protocols like IP (Internet Protocol) and the OSI CLNP (Connectionless Network Protocol). Connectionless protocols do not require a circuit to be established before data is transmitted.

> **NOTE** For more information about the IP and CLNP protocols, see Chapter 7.

CDPD transmits data in 128-byte blocks, searching for available time in the digital cellular network which can be idle up to 30 percent of the time. These data packets are sent along with cellular signals already being used for voice communications, inserted into the signal path during the silences that commonly accompany normal speech. As newer methods of data compression and error correction are developed, CDPD is expected to attain transfer rates comparable to those of land-based phone lines.

Some organizations find the technology to be a useful and strategic business tool but discover performance to be slower than anticipated after contractual commitments are made. Evaluate the technology carefully to see how it fits your organization's needs and be sure to test your proposed cellular system with applications you use regularly before making any long-term commitments.

Infrared

Infrared LANs transmit data via infrared signals. Because it is not a radio frequency, infrared equipment does not require federal licensing. Infrared signals typically travel longer distances at greater speeds than radio signals. Some manufacturers offer products supporting transmission speeds of up to 16 Mbps. Since infrared cannot penetrate walls as radio waves do, it can provide better security by preventing information from passing beyond specified areas. Infrared transceivers are also immune to interference from incidental radio-frequency sources. The technology is suited to LAN installations in warehouses, retail floor areas, or other open office environments.

There are two types of infrared LANs. One uses diffused infrared light, a technique that bounces low-powered light waves off walls, ceilings, and floors to create a wireless network within a single room. This technology provides a transmission range of about 50 feet, but adapters can be prone to interference from bright visible-light sources. Base stations or access points are available that provide diffuse infrared clients with access to wired LANs. Some manufacturers claim a capacity of up to 1,000 users serviced by a single, dedicated base station.

The other type of infrared LAN is a direct, or line-of-sight configuration. Unlike diffused infrared LANs, direct infrared configurations require that a line of sight exist between both ends of a connection. Line-of-sight configurations use lenses to focus the beam tightly along a narrow path, providing relatively long transmission distances of up to 1,250 feet.

Laser

Laser communications hardware provides your business with the ability to connect LANs between buildings without wires. Lasers offer the benefits of high-speed networking, but there are some tradeoffs to consider when using these systems. One issue is that the link must be a line of sight. This is not always possible, especially if your offices are located in a large, multi-building facility where other real estate blocks the line of sight between two buildings. Another drawback to lasers is their poor performance in heavy weather. Very thick fog or heavy snow conditions may diffuse the laser beam and interrupt network communications.

Laser units are usually mounted on the top of two buildings and carefully aimed at each other. Certain products available today provide services for bridging buildings up to 3,000 feet apart at speeds up to 16Mbps. At these speeds, laser technology is compatible with existing Ethernet and token-ring installations.

Microwave

Microwave transmission technology carries data signals via high frequency, short-wavelength radio waves. Like lasers, microwave configurations are frequently used when bridging LANs between buildings. A microwave dish must be installed at each location in order to transmit and receive signals.

Available microwave products vary greatly in regard to power and performance. A typical microwave installation operating in the 23 GHz range provides data rates of 10Mbps over a distance of roughly 4.5 miles, provided that a clear line of sight is attainable between the microwave dishes. All microwave systems operating in the 23GHz bandwidth range require licensing from federal communications authorities.

Multiple microwave systems can be implemented in a daisy-chained fashion, extending the range of a network or to interconnect multiple sites. This type of system would incorporate a spanning tree algorithm, a technique that detects and eliminates logical loops in bridged networks. This approach provides performance enhancements as well as redundancy.

A strategic implementation of microwave technology might be to integrate a T1 voice module (1.544Mbps) into a microwave LAN system to connect corporate PBXs together, eliminating toll charges for off-site extensions. In this scenario, if the facilities were separated by a highway or it was not possible to install optical fiber or copper cable, this configuration would be a good solution, providing data and voice transmission at a full 10Mbps. If it were possible to install optical fiber cabling in this scenario, another approach could be to use fiber as a primary link and microwave communications for a redundant backup path.

> **NOTE** For more information about network services, see Chapter 5.

PREPARING SPECIFICATIONS

One of the first steps to ensure the success of your network cabling project is to create a functional specification (spec) detailing the exact cable, connector, termination, and testing requirements for the project. Doing this provides vendors with the information they need to properly bid on your project. Functional specs are sometimes accepted by vendors as requests for quotes (RFQ), but preparing a formal RFQ is best.

The RFQ is a document used to define your specific needs for service and equipment. The purpose of the RFQ is to determine what equipment and services are available as well as what they will cost. Frequently, RFQs are used when allocating a budget or setting aside money for an anticipated purchase.

A request for proposal (RFP) is more detailed than a RFQ and is ordinarily drafted after responses from the RFQ are reviewed. Your RFP should contain an exact list of the equipment and services you require and other important facts, such as how equipment should be delivered, installed, and paid for. Once prospective vendors have received your RFP, they can respond with the exact terms and conditions of sale. This is called a response to an RFP and should be viewed as a definite bid or quote for your business.

CHOOSING A VENDOR

Once you've received responses to your RFP, it is time to choose the vendor(s) for your project. Some organizations are content in hiring a single vendor or contractor for a project. In certain situations, you could hire several vendors. For example, one could have assisted in producing a functional spec, another to actually pull the network cable, a third to terminate wiring in your wiring closets, and yet another vendor to install connectors, test, and certify the cabling.

However, the multi-vendor approach raises an important question. If the network wiring doesn't function properly, or perhaps not at all, which vendor in the chain is responsible?

If you've taken the time to provide all of the vendors involved with the project a detailed functional spec, as well as a formal RFQ and RFP, it should be fairly easy to discover which vendor dropped the ball. One way to avoid situations like this is to assign one vendor, perhaps the one writing the functional specification, the responsibility of overall project manager. It will be the project manager's obligation to make sure that cable installation, terminations, connectors, and testing are properly carried out according to your spec.

Assigning a project manager responsible for all phases of your cable installation also provides a single point of contact for technical direction and culpability. In addition, try to hire an unbiased third party for testing and certification. If the cabling is not properly installed, the unbiased vendor should be ready and able to document any questionable test results.

CABLE CONTRACTORS

Who do you call when you need network cabling? Most likely, you've probably used your electrical contractor to run network cable for you at one time or another. Electricians are quite adept at running additional power for new users to their work areas, or perhaps adding new dedicated circuits to your existing electrical service. In fact, many electrical contractors may be able to provide qualified network cabling specialists in addition to electricians. Unfortunately, while electricians can be highly qualified when it comes to the electrical code, giving an electrician your network cabling project might not be in your best interest.

Network cabling contractors are the experts you should turn to when implementing or upgrading network cabling systems. The level of expertise available in your area will dictate the price you will pay for qualified cable installers. More experience generally nets a higher price per hour. Typically, labor accounts for about 70 percent of the total cost of a cabling project. In larger cities, you can expect to pay approximately $200 per cable run (including terminations) for Category 5 UTP.

Technical Qualifications

How can you determine if a cable contractor is technically qualified to handle your project? One way is to check for BICSI certification. The Building Industry Consulting Service International (BICSI) is a non-profit association of telecommunications professionals founded in 1974. It offers a comprehensive program intended to certify cable design professionals.

BICSI's mission, according to the organization's literature, is to provide for economical, efficient, flexible, and safe telecommunications, data, and low-voltage distribution facilities and services in commercial, campus, and multi-family buildings through their Registered Communications Distribution Designer (RCDD) program, educational conferences, programs, and publications.

What does all of this mean to you and your business? BICSI, by way of its training, testing, and certification programs, helps ensure you will get qualified technicians pulling your cable. RCDDs must pass a rigid written exam, have at least three years of experience in premises-wiring design and installation, and have the recommendation of five employers in order to take the RCDD test. In fact, many government RFPs stipulate that contractors working on government cabling projects must hold an RCDD certification.

To ensure that your network cabling performs according to spec, make use of qualified professionals, whether your cable systems link buildings or workgroups. The foundation of your network, like the foundation of a well constructed building, must be rock-solid.

CABLE TESTING AND CERTIFICATION

The last cable run has been completed. Now it is time to put your functional specification and your cable contractor to the test. Certification testing of your network cabling system is the most important step you can take to identify and remedy possible cable defects. The key is to do it before full-scale network implementation begins.

When certification tests are conducted, the entire cabling system should be checked, including cable runs, patch panels, patch cables, and outlets. Performance criteria such as electrical noise, attenuation, continuity and polarity, length verification, and near-end crosstalk are also tested.

A new standard from the EIA/TIA that directly specifies the performance criteria of a LAN cable run, or link, is expected. There are presently two link models being discussed. The first, called the channel model, includes all the elements that exist in cable runs between a workstation and a hub, including patch cables. The basic link model includes the horizontal cabling from the wall outlet or transition point to the first punch down in the wiring closet. It also includes the access cables that are part of the field test unit.

The equipment we describe in this section all adhere to a set of transmission media standards developed to ensure the measurements they provide are consistent and accurate. Under the heading "Cable Standards" (covered earlier in this chapter), we discuss these standards and the organizations and companies responsible for their creation.

Network Analyzers

The network analyzer contains a very accurate radio frequency source and a narrowband tracking receiver. By varying the analyzer's frequency over a wide range onto the transmitting wire pair and then using the tracking receiver to measure the signal on the receiving wire pair, attenuation and NEXT measurements can be made.

Attenuation is defined as the decreasing power of a signal as it travels along a cable. The longer the cable, the more signal loss there will be. Beyond a certain loss boundary, the cable may not be able to reliably transmit data. *NEXT* is also known as near-end crosstalk. This is interference that is measured on a wire adjacent to the wire over which a signal is being transmitted over. Another way of describing NEXT is to say that it is the amount of signal leakage measured close to the point of actual signal generation.

Network analyzers are expensive, with some models costing more than $20,000. They also can be fairly cumbersome, making them awkward to carry around, set up, and operate while in the field. Most network analyzers simply display data. They do not offer pass/fail results or other diagnostic output.

One example of a network analyzer that does offer diagnostic output is the Network General Expert Sniffer (see netref 9). The Expert Sniffer helps maintain, troubleshoot, and fine-tune multi-protocol networks. It automatically uncovers a wide variety of problems and offers solutions to help correct them. The core of the Sniffer package is the Network General Expert Sniffer software and PCMCIA network interface cards that can be installed on notebook computers approved by Network General.

The Expert Sniffer family of analyzers supports all major network types including Ethernet, token-ring (4/16Mbps), and FDDI. Protocol interpreters for over 140 protocols are also provided including TCP/IP, Novell NetWare, DECnet, Sun NFS, IBM SNA, AppleTalk, Banyan VINES, OSI, NetBIOS, OS/2 LAN Manager, 3Com 3+Open, and IBM LAN Server.

> **NOTE** For information about protocols, see Chapter 7. For information about network operating systems, see Chapter 4.

Field Test Units

These tools are great for network firefighters without the time, budgets, or luxury of network analyzers or the training required to operate them properly. Field test units are easy to use and physically connect to the network, usually lightweight, and very reliable when troubleshooting physical layer problems on your network. Some handheld models can operate up to eight hours on a single charge and can automate all testing and analysis into a single keystroke. Certain units even have built-in intelligence to interpret most test results.

Testers can perform many functions (but not with the same dynamic range) of a network analyzer. Features to check cable length, impedance, capacitance, NEXT, attenuation, and resistance are all part of the feature set found in most units. The wire map function, unique to twisted-pair installations, can show you how wire pairs are connected to plugs and sockets. The cost of cable testers can range from approximately $500 to more than $3,000, depending on available features.

Continuity Testers

Continuity testers are thought to be the simplest of cable troubleshooting tools. Purchased for generally less than $200, they can verify end-to-end connectivity and continuity. They can also be used to check twisted-pair wiring for crossed pairs or split pairs. These conditions exist when twisted-pair jacks are not properly connected to the cable itself.

Useful as they may be, continuity testers are not really adequate to diagnose most problems you will encounter on a LAN because they don't reveal anything about the cable's ability to reliably transfer data at network speeds.

REFERENCES

Derfler, Jr., F. and Freed, L. 1993. *Get A Grip On Network Cabling*. Emeryville, CA: Ziff-Davis Press.

Net References

1. www to http://www.cmpcmm.com/cc/standards.html then browse the Computer and Communication Standards Documentation home page.

2. For information about the latest optical-fiber developments at Corning, www to http://www.usa.net/corningfiber/whatsup/default.html

3. www to http://www.amp.com/ then browse the AMP, Inc. home page for product overviews.

4. www to http://www.att.com/ then browse the AT&T home page.

The Digital Equipment Corporation home page can be found at http://www.digital.com/

The Northern Telecom home page can be found at http://www.nt.com/

www to http://www.hp.com/ for the Hewlett-Packard home page.

www to http://www.ibm.com/ for the IBM home page.

5. www to http://www.ansi.org/ then browse the American National Standards Institute (ANSI) home page.

6. www to http://www.iso.ch/ then browse The International Standards Organization (ISO) home page.

7. www to http://www.mccaw-wdd.com/ then browse the McCaw Wireless Data, Inc. home page for more information about CDPD.

8. www to http://www.cdpd.net/ then browse the CDPD Forum home page.

9. www to http://www.ngc.com/ for the home page for Network General Corporation. Specific information about the Sniffer Analyzer can be found at http://www.ngc.com/product_info/

Suggested Reading

Brosch, E. 1993. *Cabling Guide: Planning the Computer Connection for the Office of Tomorrow, First Edition*. Shorewood, MN: E.F. Brosch.

Jones, J. 1995. Cable Ready. *LAN Magazine* 10(9):87-94.

Sheldon, T. 1994. *LAN TIMES Encyclopedia of Networking*. Berkeley, CA: Osborne McGraw-Hill.

2

Topologies, Techniques, and Technologies

ABOUT THIS CHAPTER

Network topologies, transmission techniques, and technologies determine the interconnection of a transmission medium, how it moves data, and the characteristics and operation of the medium.

Using analogies and examples, this chapter will help you to understand each of these concepts and their contribution to network design and implementation.

INTRODUCTION

Transmission media are the physical conduits used to carry data packets over a network. But what about the methods and technologies that regulate the movement of these packets? What ensures the integrity and delivery of the data? In this section, you will be introduced to network topologies, transmission techniques, and technologies. Each one has its own important place in the network infrastructure.

Topologies

Network topologies are like the varied highway systems that interconnect local roads and sites. They are physical interconnections for transmitting data through network transmission media. The most common topologies are the star, bus, and ring.

These topologies have distinct shapes, as suggested by their names. In a star configuration, all network wires or cables branch out from a single location. Bus-configured networks consist of a cable that is daisy-chained from one workstation or other network component to the next, terminating at either end. In a ring-configured network, the transmission medium makes a circle and connects back to itself.

In the section entitled "Network Topologies," you will learn the basics of the star, bus, and ring configuration for local area networks (LANs). The "Internetwork Topologies" section covers other types of configurations such as hierarchical, backbone, and mesh, that are used to interconnect LANs.

Techniques and Access Methods

Traffic lights and signs help regulate the flow of traffic on many roads and highways. If there were no traffic lights, vehicle congestion and collisions would be inevitable. Transmission techniques and media access methods serve a similar purpose on a network.

On most LANs, a single cable carries all of the messages transmitted over the network. On a busy system, more than one node could be trying to send a message over a medium at any given time. If the LAN is to provide acceptable performance without a loss of data, access to the cable must be regulated. LAN access methods address this issue by controlling the setup and maintenance of sessions and monitoring data traffic for errors. Defining the order in which nodes are authorized to gain access to the network helps avoid data congestion and collisions that would render the network inoperable.

Access methods function at the Physical and Data Link layers of the OSI model. The Physical layer addresses the functions necessary to send and receive data over a particular medium, while the Data Link layer handles logical connections.

> **NOTE** For more information about the OSI model, see Chapter 6.

In the "Transmission Techniques" section you will be introduced to two types of transmission techniques (broadband and baseband) and two types of media access methods (CSMA/CD and token-passing).

Technologies

The way roads are built define how vehicles can travel, including such factors as the direction and speed of traffic. Network technologies define the nature of the transmission medium, how it operates, and its physical characteristics. In turn, this determines how data is transmitted over a network.

The "Network Technologies" section of the chapter covers several popular LAN technologies, including Ethernet, token-ring, and Fiber Distributed Data Interface.

NETWORK TOPOLOGIES

The interconnection of network components through transmission media are associated with several unique topologies. The names of these topologies are descriptive of the shape they impose on these interconnections. The most common topologies are the star, bus, and ring.

Star

In a star topology, cables radiate from a central wiring hub or concentrator, much like spokes in a wheel (see Figure 2-1). Each node has its own cable run. In star-configured networks, the hub is the weak link. Thus, the reliability of a network depends on the reliability of the central hub. If the hub malfunctions, network nodes and components connected to the hub will be made unavailable for use. If a peripheral node fails, however, only that node is affected.

Although the physical arrangement of the nodes resembles a star configuration, the star-wired network is logically a bus. Data transmissions from network nodes enter hubs or concentrators and are re-transmitted, or broadcast, to all outgoing ports on the hub or concentrator.

Many modern network implementations are based on the star topology. Star networks provide features such as centralized device management and added flexibility when installing or removing nodes, network components, or servers. Popular configurations include star-wired 10BASET, star-wired 10BASE5 ring networks, and multiple interconnected stars called star/tree wired networks.

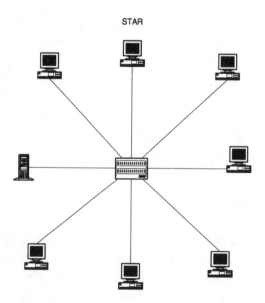

STAR

Figure 2-1. Star Topology.

Bus

The bus topology connects all nodes or devices to a common cable. This is also known as node-to-node wiring (see Figure 2-2). Many Ethernet LANs installed before 10BASET became popular use this node-to-node method. In this configuration, data is transmitted in a linear fashion over the entire length of a cable. Bus networks typically use less cable than other technologies because of this simple linear layout.

Bus-configured networks are commonly wired using thick and thin coaxial cabling. Thin coax is widely used for connectivity at the desktop level while thick coax is frequently specified for the backbone, or main cable. As in the star topology, the failure of a single bus-configured node may not bring the network to a grinding halt. The performance and reliability of coax-cabled LANs can be affected by crimped cables and bad connectors.

Similar to the star configuration, data transmitted by a node is available for reception by any other node. Baseband and broadband technologies, covered later in this chapter, make use of the bus topology, which requires a full-duplex medium. A full-duplex medium is one where data or signals can flow in either direction over a medium.

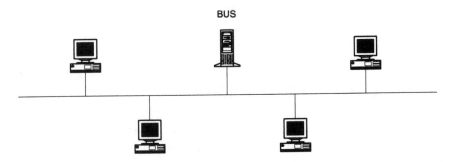

Figure 2-2. Bus Topology.

Ring

In ring-configured networks, instead of each node being connected to a central hub, link segments connect neighboring nodes to each other (see Figure 2-3). Each node passes the data it receives on to its neighbor. In this type of LAN, the loss of a single node detaches the connected node and can bring down the entire network.

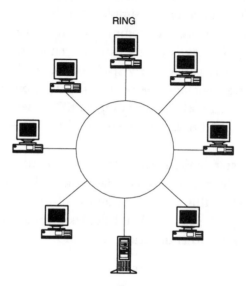

Figure 2-3. Ring Topology.

INTERNETWORK TOPOLOGIES

Internetworks are made up of several LANs connected together. The interconnected LANs could be networks operating within the same building or in separate buildings. They might even be from several geographically different areas.

When LANs separated by a geographic area are internetworked, they are collectively referred to as a wide area network (WAN). Popular internetwork configurations are backbone, hierarchical, and mesh networks (see Figure 2-4).

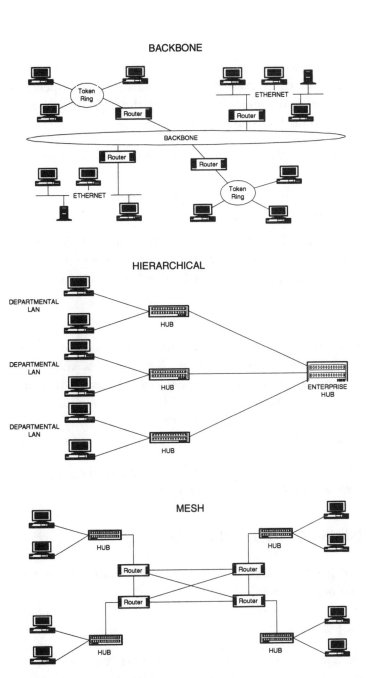

Figure 2-4. Internetwork Topologies.

Backbone

Backbone configurations are popular in office environments where departments or buildings are connected over high-speed backbone cables. Bridges and routers help manage the data passing between the interconnected networks and the backbone.

> **NOTE** For further information about bridges and routers, see Chapter 3.

Hierarchical

In the hierarchical configuration, star-configured hubs are wired to a central hub that handles inter-hub traffic. Modern office and campus installations are frequently designed around the hierarchical topology.

Mesh

In mesh configurations there are at least two pathways to each node. This is a common configuration found in WANs and MANs (Metropolitan Area Networks). Internetworking devices such as bridges and routers choose the most efficient paths for data to travel from one point to another in this configuration. Mesh networks are often used because of their reliability; when one path goes down, another can take over.

> **NOTE** For further information about bridges, routers, and other network components, see Chapter 3.

TRANSMISSION TECHNIQUES

LANs are generally characterized by their transmission techniques: broadband or baseband.

Baseband

Baseband is a single-channel environment where only one node transmits while the others listen. It uses the complete bandwidth of a medium without any multiplexing of the digital signal. Multiplexing allows multiple users to share a single transmission medium or communications link.

On a baseband LAN, a workstation or other network component transmits into the channel and waits for a reply. If it doesn't receive a reply, it retransmits. The two main baseband access control schemes are token-ring passing and carrier sense multiple access with collision detection (CSMA/CD).

Broadband

Broadband is a generic term for a wide bandwidth communications network that uses the same FDM (frequency division multiplexing) technique as cable TV. Broadband systems are used primarily for data and video communications, but are also used to provide independent communications for voice and other applications.

These systems can carry numerous voice, video, and data channels simultaneously. Each channel takes up a different frequency on the cable. There are guardbands, or empty spaces, between the channels to ensure each channel doesn't interfere with its neighbor.

Access Methods

All LANs employ shared media, but the way they share a medium plays a key role in determining the reliability and availability of the network. Access methods address this important issue by imposing rules that determine how network components can use a shared transmission medium.

CSMA/CD

The original 802.3 Ethernet specification describes two types of media-access control methods: carrier sense multiple access with collision detection (CSMA/CD) and carrier sense multiple access with collision avoidance (CSMA/CA).

CSMA/CD, the most commonly used method, allows two or more nodes to share a common bus. The idea behind CSMA/CD is simple. A transmitting node postpones the transmitting of packets until the network is quiet. When the network is quiet, the packet is sent. One advantage of this type of network is that it provides virtually instant access to network resources under the right conditions.

CSMA/CD also provides a way for the nodes to correct a collision if they've sent packets over the network at the same time. Each node transmits a few extra bytes to ensure the other nodes are aware that a collision has taken place. After a collision occurs, the original transmitting node remains quiet for a specified period of time before retransmitting. This is known as a backoff period and it prevents nodes from creating multiple collisions.

CSMA/CA

CSMA/CA is a variation of Ethernet's CSMA/CD and was designed for wireless communications. It is currently used by all Ethernet-compatible wireless networks. Since wireless networks can't detect packet collisions, certain procedures must be followed to ensure reliable data transmissions.

When a node wants to broadcast a packet, it sends a message called a request to send (RTS) to the destination device. If that workstation receives a clear to send (CTS) message from the device, it continues with its data transmission. When the data packet has been received, the receiving device sends an acknowledgment packet.

NOTE For more information about wireless networks, see Chapter 1.

Token Passing

Token passing is an alternative to CSMA/CD Ethernet networks. Tokens are special data packets that circulate from node to node when there's no data traffic. Possession of the token gives the owner exclusive access to the network for transmission of a message. When a node wants to send a message, it waits for an empty token. When it finds one, it fills it with the address of the destination station and some or all of its message. Each node on the network constantly monitors the passing tokens to determine if it is a recipient of a message. If it is, it takes the message and resets the token status to empty.

Token passing uses bus and ring topologies. Nodes in a token-passing network are physically connected to a wiring concentrator, most often in a star-wired ring topology. Popular examples of token passing are IBM's token-ring network and FDDI/CDDI networks.

NETWORK TECHNOLOGIES

Network technologies are the standards, specifications, and physical characteristics associated with the implementation of transmission media in a network environment. Several popular technologies are presented in this section.

Ethernet

Ethernet was originally developed by Xerox Corporation in the 1970s as a research project. Specifications were published in 1980 by Xerox, Intel, and Digital Equipment Corp. (DEC–see netref 1). Ethernet is a data-link protocol and functions at the Data Link and Physical levels of the OSI model.

The IEEE 802.3 Ethernet standard, which was a modified version of the original spec, has become one of the most widely deployed and supported systems in use today. Prior to the adoption of 802.3, there were actually two Ethernet specifications, Ethernet I and II. Ethernet I was the original, while Ethernet II became known as 802.3. Ethernet I devices did not work with 802.3 standard hardware and systems. In time, many hardware manufacturers produced equipment designed to work with both specifications.

Fast Ethernet

Fast Ethernet systems are also known as IEEE 802.3 100BASET. There are three media varieties that have been specified for transmitting 100Mbps Ethernet signals. 100BASETX uses two pairs of wires and is based on the data-grade twisted-pair physical medium standard developed by ANSI. 100BASEFX is based on the optical-fiber physical medium standard developed by ANSI and uses two strands of fiber cable. 100BASET4 uses Category 3, 4, or 5 twisted-pair cabling.

IEEE 802.12 100BASEVG is another Fast Ethernet technology adapted from Hewlett-Packard's 100VG-AnyLAN. 100BASEVG uses a demand-priority access method instead of CSMA/CD, which allows priorities to be given to the data being transmitted. For example, real-time voice and video could be given a higher priority than other types of data.

Applications and networking software presently running on your 10Mbps Ethernet will run unchanged on 100BASET networks. In addition, you can continue using familiar protocol analysis and management tools, which provide a way to manage Fast Ethernet systems with minimal retraining. The Fast Ethernet specifications include mechanisms for auto-negotiation of media speed. This makes it possible to use dual-speed Ethernet interfaces that can run at either 10Mbps or 100Mbps automatically.

Token-Ring

The token-ring network was developed by IBM during the period between 1982 and 1985. With IBM leading the standardization process, it was first described in the IEEE 802.5 standard. Token-ring networks can support a maximum of 256 nodes.

Token

Access to the ring is controlled by a token, circulating around the ring at a speed of 4 or 16Mbps. Only a single token can exist on a ring segment at any given time. In order to accomplish this, a delay equivalent to the time it takes for a token to circulate the ring is required to ensure that no overrun occurs. Data overrun results in a node receiving a token that it is already transmitting, confusing the node by making it think a second token exists on the ring.

A node with data to transmit has to wait for a free token to arrive and can transfer data to the ring only while it's holding a token. When this token arrives, the node changes the token into a frame, appends the data to it, and sends the frame over the ring. If the destination node is active, it copies the frame. At this point, the frame-copied and address-recognized bits of the frame are set. The sending node then strips the frame from the ring and releases a new token.

This process provides Media Access Control (MAC) layer acknowledgment to the transmitting node. The MAC layer is a sublayer of the Data Link layer, which is part of the OSI model. It controls access to the physical transmission medium on a LAN and is implemented in the network interface card (NIC).

> **NOTE** For more information about the OSI Reference Model, see Chapter 6.

Active Monitors

At any given time, one node per segment must perform an active monitor function. Any node can serve as the active monitor but only one will have this function enabled. Any node that is not performing the active monitor function acts as a standby monitor. Its purpose is to detect a failing active monitor as well as disruptions on the ring and to take over if the active monitor fails.

Token-Ring Errors

Initialization and error-recovery are the most complicated aspects of token-ring operation. The token-ring technology is susceptible to faults in the OSI Physical and Data Link layers; in fact, 60 percent of all network failures occur at these lower levels (Lumpkin, 1991). There are two categories of token-ring errors that can affect a network's performance.

A hard error is a permanent fault that stops normal traffic on the ring. It's usually first detected on the receive side of the node downstream from the fault. A change in the ring configuration is required to bypass a fault like this and restore normal operation. Reconfiguration can be done automatically or, if the automatic recovery process fails to bypass the error, it may require manual intervention.

If a node detects a hard error, it begins continually transmitting frames called beacon frames at designated time intervals. A beacon frame indicates that the node has detected a serious ring problem, such as a broken cable or medium attachment unit (MAU). A MAU is a device that allows terminals, PCs, printers, and other network components to be connected in a star-based configuration to the LAN. The beacon frame identifies the address of the nearest active upstream neighbor (NAUN) of the beaconing node and provides error information as well. When the beaconing node's NAUN has copied a number of these beacon frames, the NAUN goes off-line and performs microcode and lobe tests (each run of cable from a hub to a node is called a lobe). If the tests are successful, the node reattaches to the ring immediately. If the tests fail, the node stays off-line.

When the node begins transmitting beacon frames, it also starts what's called a beacon timer. If the node did not receive its beacon frame back, the beacon timer expires. At this point, if normal traffic hasn't been restored the node assumes that its NAUN went off-line, found no errors, and came back online. It now goes through the same testing process as its NAUN. If the tests fail, the beaconing node remains detached. If the node receives its own beacon frames, it will assume that the ring has been restored and return to the claim-token process. As indicated in the last example, normal traffic may not have been restored during automatic recovery. In this case, network management applications will be informed and will require manual intervention.

> **NOTE** For more information about network management, see Chapter 9.

Periodic faults that temporarily interrupt normal operation of the token-ring are called soft errors. Generally well-tolerated by error recovery procedures, these soft-errors can degrade normal ring operation if they're extreme or non-random in nature.

The most critical soft-errors are monitored in each node by a set of counters. Every two seconds the values of the soft error counters are sent as a soft-error report MAC frame to the ring error monitor functional address. The ring error monitor typically resides in a bridge or system management console, where the values for each counter are collected.

If a soft-error counter exceeds a predefined limit, the system management console is informed through its link with the LAN reporting device. The management application can then reconfigure the ring to bypass the faulty node, if in fact the fault can be located. Soft-errors are known as isolating soft errors if a fault domain can be specified. If not, they're called non-isolating soft errors.

Token-Ring Cable Length

If you're installing a token-ring network or you support one, one of the most important rules to follow is that of maximum total distance (MTD). MTD specifies the maximum amount of cable that can be used in a ring without the need for powered, or active hubs. Active hubs regenerate signals that pass through them, while passive hubs do not. The MTD includes all of the physical cable and a factor called equivalent cable length (ECL).

The ECL represents the amount of signal loss that takes place within a hub. The manufacturer of a network hub will provide an ECL for each hub it manufactures. Average ECL figures are approximately 8 feet for STP hubs and 30 feet for UTP hubs. Generally, the MTD when using STP is approximately 1,312 feet at 4Mbps and 590 feet at 16Mbps. If you've specified Category 5 UTP wiring for your token-ring installation, the MTD is approximately 738 feet at 4Mbps and 328 feet at 16Mbps.

On a 4Mbps token-ring network over STP wiring, the maximum distance for a hub to node cable run should be about 150 feet and the maximum overall length between wiring hubs should not exceed 400 feet. In addition, practical experience and industry standards dictate that you try to keep wiring hub cable connections to lengths of 150 feet or less and wall outlet to node cable lengths to 8 feet or less. With STP cabling, it's possible to hang up to 260 nodes off a ring. In reality you'll probably exceed the MTD before you reach this node limit.

Using Category 5 UTP, a main ring will have a node limit of 132 nodes. As with STP, the interaction between cable lengths, the number of hubs and links to the wiring hubs, as well as the number of active nodes on a UTP token-ring network can be quite complex. In addition, many manufacturers now provide active devices claiming reliable operation at up to six times the distance of standard hubs.

With variables such as the signals between wire-pairs, attenuation, temperature, etc., determining the final numbers for your installation can be a nightmare. For example, each time you activate a new node on your token-ring network, the wiring hub inserts the new node's cable segment into the ring, effectively changing the overall size of the network. For reasons like this, your MTD calculations must be done properly to ensure a reliable network.

ARCNET

Attached Resource Computer NETwork (ARCNET) is one of the earliest and most popular local area network technologies. Originally developed by Datapoint of San Antonio, TX, ARCNET is a baseband, token-passing network system that provides connectivity for up to 255 nodes in a star topology. The standard cabling used for ARCNET is 93-ohm RG-62 coaxial cable, with twisted-pair and optical-fiber cable also supported.

A 20Mbps version compatible with 2.5Mbps ARCNET was introduced in 1989 and is called ARCNET Plus. Both versions can exist on the same LAN. ARCNET Plus includes new features such as the ability to connect with Ethernet, TCP/IP (Transmission Control Protocol/ Internet Protocol), and token-ring networks.

> **NOTE** For further information about TCP/IP and other protocols, see Chapter 7.

AppleTalk

AppleTalk is an OSI-based, CSMA/CD LAN technology from Apple, introduced in 1985. It supports Apple's proprietary LocalTalk access method as well as Ethernet (EtherTalk) and token-ring (TokenTalk). The AppleTalk network manager and the LocalTalk access method are built into all MACs and LaserWriter printers, as well as many third-party devices being marketed today. AppleTalk can run on PCs, VAXs, and UNIX workstations.

LocalTalk is Apple's LAN access method that uses twisted pair wiring and transmits at 230.4Kbps. It runs under AppleTalk and uses a daisy chain topology that connects up to 32 devices at a distance of up to about 1,000 feet. LocalTalk can be configured to work in bus, passive star, and active star topologies.

SNA

Systems Network Architecture (SNA) was first introduced in 1974. SNA is an IBM technology used to provide connectivity for the 3270 family of products. SNA includes a suite of networking protocols and was originally designed for centralized IBM mainframe computing environments.

An IBM SNA network is made up of host systems, terminals or workstations running terminal emulation software, printers, cluster controllers, communications controllers, and other components. Nodes connect to cluster controllers which in turn connect to the host or a communications controller if it is not local to the host. SNA is implemented using various transmission media including copper wire or optical-fiber cable.

IBM was concerned about losing SNA users to client/server technologies and in 1985 introduced Advanced Peer-To-Peer Networking (APPN). APPN is a link-layer independent technology, and can run over token-ring, FDDI, Ethernet, and high-speed networks such as B-ISDN and ATM.

NOTE For more information about B-ISDN, see Chapter 5.

FDDI/CDDI

The Fiber Distributed Data Interface (FDDI) evolved from the activities of the American National Standards Institute (ANSI)-X3T9.5 committee, which began its quest in 1982 for a high-speed, optical-fiber based communications network. Copper Distributed Data Interface (CDDI) is a version of FDDI that uses UTP wire instead of optical-fiber cable.

An FDDI network is a dual counter-rotating, optical-fiber ring that operates at 100Mbps and uses a token-passing protocol. Each FDDI node has a chance to transmit frames when a token passes. It is similar to the IEEE token-ring standard, except that an FDDI node can transmit multiple frames successively without releasing a token in between. The IEEE token-ring standard allows token-ring nodes to do this, but IBM has chosen not to allow multiple frames without token release in their implementation of token-ring.

The 100Mbps data rate of FDDI provides organizations with a tremendous channel that can be used to connect multiple subnets distributed across large campus environments. Subnets are separate, smaller networks that are part of a larger network. They are frequently created to improve performance and security. Subnets have their own unique network addresses, which keeps network traffic isolated within a specific subnet. Routers are typically used to interconnect subnets.

NOTE For more information about routers, see Chapter 3.

In the past, using FDDI for the average LAN has not been cost-effective. With the availability of CDDI, however, the cost of using FDDI in high-performance, general-purpose networks has been significantly reduced. UTP wiring, the most popular type of network media in use today, can be utilized to provide CDDI solutions. CDDI networks can provide a high-performance, low-cost alternative to Ethernet and token-ring networks.

FDDI Rings

FDDI uses two rings, one called the primary and the other the secondary ring. Compared to the token-ring, the primary ring is like the main-ring path, with the secondary ring acting like a backup ring path. Nodes or hubs can be attached to either or both of these rings. During normal ring operation, the secondary ring is idle with no user traffic being sent around it, like the backup path in a token-ring implementation.

FDDI Nodes

To differentiate between nodes that attach to one or both rings, two classes of nodes are defined. Class A nodes attach to both of the rings directly, while class B nodes attach to only one of the rings. Attachment of class B nodes can be direct or through a concentrator. Class A nodes should not be powered off. If the node is powered off, the ring will reconfigure around it in order to remain operational.

Gateways, bridges, or routers might be suitable as class A nodes, since you wouldn't normally be powering them down. End-user nodes or workstations, which are frequently powered on or off, make good class B attachments. Concentrators, in addition to nodes, can attach to either or both rings. A dual-access concentrator (DAC), as the name suggests, attaches to both rings. A single access concentrator (SAC) attaches to only one. Only Class B nodes can attach to a concentrator.

Fibre Channel

Fibre channel technology permits high-performance transmissions over optical fiber or coaxial cable. It was originally developed to facilitate communications among mainframes, supercomputers, and high-capacity peripherals. Fibre channel offers throughputs up to 1Gbps.

Fibre channel ports can be connected as point-to-point links, in a loop, or to a switch. Ports log in with each other to trade information about attributes and characteristics. This is done in order to determine if they can work together. If cooperation is possible, they define the criteria under which they will communicate.

A fibre channel switch, or a network of switches, is called a fabric. Information can flow between two ports in both directions simultaneously with data frames being a maximum of 2148 bytes long, each containing a header and a checksum. Headers are the portion of a data packet that contain routing information to ensure the message arrives at its intended destination. A checksum is a value used to reasonably ensure data is transmitted without error. The checksum is created adding the binary value of each alphanumeric character in a block of data and sending it along with the data. At the receiving end, a new checksum is computed and matched against the transmitted checksum. If the two do not match, an error in transmission has occurred.

The Fibre Channel Association (FCA) was formed in January 1993 to encourage the use of fibre channel. The primary objective of the FCA (see netref 2) is to provide a support structure for system integrators, peripheral manufacturers, software developers, component manufacturers, communications companies, and computer service providers.

ATM

Asynchronous Transfer Mode (ATM) is an internationally accepted, high-performance multiplexing and switching technology providing gigabit-per-second throughputs. It has been adopted as the switching standard for Broadband ISDN (B-ISDN).

Because of its ability to transport and route large volumes of data, video, image, graphics, and voice at high speed over local and wide areas inexpensively, ATM promises to revolutionize high-speed data communications.

> **NOTE** For more information about ISDN and ATM, see Chapter 5.

ISOEthernet

Isochronous Ethernet (ISOEnet) is an IEEE 802.9a LAN technology designed to carry Ethernet and Integrated Services Digital Network (ISDN) standard data over Ethernet networks using 10BASET. It is intended to be a lower-cost alternative than ATM.

National Semiconductor (see netref 3) developed the ISOEnet technology to meet the increasing demand for video transmission over the network at video speeds of 16 to 33 frames-per-second (fps). Standard Ethernet only offers 7 to 10 frames-per-second rates. ISOEnet provides 16Mbps over the same 10BASET wiring that today carries Ethernet at 10Mbps by using a more efficient data encoding method.

ISOEnet is backward-compatible with Ethernet, is ATM-ready, and doesn't interfere with standard LAN data because it adds ISDN layers on top of Ethernet's standard 10Mbps transport layer. According to National Semiconductor literature, this results in an additional 6Mbps of available bandwidth.

ISOEthernet can be seamlessly integrated into existing 10BASET Ethernet environments. This is accomplished using an ISOEnet hub in the wiring closet to handle the necessary synchronization between LAN and WAN services. An ISOEnet network adapter card installed in a workstation enables the workstation to connect to the ISOEnet hub using an attachment unit interface (AUI).

The isochronous network communication Alliance (incAlliance) was formed to develop total system solutions for real-time, interactive applications while supporting open standards (Sodergren 1995).

100VG-AnyLAN

100VG-AnyLAN is an IEEE 802.12 technology for transmitting Ethernet and token-ring information at 100Mbps. This technology was jointly announced by Hewlett-Packard (HP) and IBM and has been endorsed by the IEEE standards organization. HP is pitching this technology as the best alternative for upgrading Ethernet and token-ring users to 100Mbps speeds.

100VG-AnyLAN operates over Category 3, 4, or 5 UTP. It supports all the network design rules and topologies of 10BASET and token-ring, allowing enterprises to utilize existing networks and cable infrastructures while upgrading to 100Mbps transmission speeds.

100VG-AnyLAN Operation

According to HP, the key to 100VG-AnyLAN's capabilities is the use of a physical star topology, one of the most commonly used network topologies today. Ethernet and token-ring, while conceptually implemented as shared-media bus and ring topologies, are physically implemented using the star topology with a central hub servicing individually connected nodes.

100VG-AnyLAN uses intelligent hubs to manage network usage and a new, proprietary access method called Demand Priority. With Demand

Priority, nodes wishing to transmit packets signal the request to the hub. If the network is idle, the hub sends an acknowledgment and the node begins transmitting its data packet to the hub. As the packet arrives at the hub, the hub decodes the destination address found within the packet and automatically switches this incoming packet to the outbound destination port.

Since nodes do not transmit packets until an acknowledgment is received from the hub, in theory, Demand Priority networks help avoid packet collisions and provide for prioritization of network traffic. Additionally, Demand Priority is said to move the token-passing process directly into the hub itself, eliminating token rotation delays and reducing latency for nodes on an otherwise idle network.

When using 100VG-AnyLAN to upgrade portions of an existing Ethernet or token-ring network, a speed-matching bridge is all that will be required to connect the subnets, buffering the high-speed packets as they enter the slower-speed network. The same frame types used on the Ethernet and token-ring networks can be used over the 100VG-AnyLAN subnets, eliminating the need for translation bridging.

100VG-AnyLAN may provide a viable migration path. Your token-ring and Ethernet LANs can run over the same four-pair, Category 5 UTP cable your company has been using for the last two years. Hubs are supposedly configurable to support either 802.3 Ethernet or 802.5 token-ring frame types, meaning all the hubs in a given network must be configured for the same frame type.

You can use a bridge to connect a 100VG-AnyLAN network using 802.3 frames to an Ethernet LAN or 802.5 frames to a token-ring LAN. Finally, routers could be implemented to connect the 100VG-AnyLAN net to ATM, FDDI, or WAN connections. Subsequent implementations of 100VG-AnyLAN are intended to support two-pair, two-wire UTP; two-pair STP; and optical-fiber cabling.

REFERENCES

Lumpkin, M. 1991. "Failure Analysis in Token-Ring LANs." In *Handbook of Communications Systems Management, Second Edition*, ed. James W. Conard, pp. 559-565. Boston, MA: Auerbach Publishers.

Sodergren, M. 1995. "Pumping up 10BASE-T with isoEthernet." *Network World.* 12(32):33.

Net References

1. www to http://www.xerox.com/ then browse the Xerox home page.

www to http://www.intel.com/ for the Intel home page.

Information about Digital Equipment Corporation can be found at http://www.digital.com/

2. www to http://www.amdahl.com/ext/CARP/FCA/FCA.html then browse the Fibre Channel Association home page.

3. www to http://www.nsc.com/ then browse the National Semiconductor home page.

Suggested Reading

Sharma, Roshan Lal. 1990. *Network Topology Optimization: The Art and Science Of Network Design*. New York: Van Nostrand Reinhold.

Hegering, Heinz-Gerd. 1993. *Ethernet: Building A Communications Infrastructure*. Reading, MA: Addison-Wesley.

3

Network Components

ABOUT THIS CHAPTER

This chapter describes components that connect nodes, regenerate signals, or route network traffic. These include repeaters, hubs, bridges, routers, and gateways. It also describes other components such as servers (communications, terminal, and print servers), workstations, and personal computers.

INTRODUCTION

Network components are devices connected to a network. Repeaters, which are used to link two LANs of the same type, and hubs, which are devices used to centrally connect wires or cables from workstations and other network components, offer multi-port configurations. They are good examples of intelligent network components.

Repeaters are considered the simplest network components because their only function is to regenerate received signals. Signal regeneration is necessary in order to extend the transmission distance of a medium. Hubs offer additional features and functionality not found in repeaters, such as modular construction, network management, bridging, routing, and switching.

In this chapter, strategic hub features such as the ability to construct virtual networks will be discussed. Virtual networks represent a logical grouping of users regardless of their physical locations on the network. A virtual network can also be an interconnected group of networks that appears as one large LAN to the user. In addition, a virtual network can be centrally managed and controlled. You'll learn about the variety of hubs available today along with important features to consider when evaluating hub components.

Other network components such as bridges and routers are included. A bridge is a device that connects two LAN segments together, while routers are an interface between two networks. Routers can provide more functionality than bridges, and these differences will be discussed later in the chapter.

At one time, workstations were confined to high-powered computer-aided design (CAD) or similar engineering applications. Since the emergence of affordable and very powerful personal computers (PCs), these high-powered workstations are taking a back seat.

This new generation of PC workstations plays an important role in the building of client/server networks. Client/server networks make it possible to divide processing between clients using server-run applications and the servers themselves. Client/server networks also form the basis for creating heterogeneous environments. In a heterogeneous environment, hardware and software from multiple vendors can be shared.

In the "Workstations" and "Personal Computers" sections, popular processor and bus configurations are covered. In the "Servers" section, you'll learn about high-availability servers, technologies such as RAID (Redundant Array of Independent Disks), and strategies for implementing them.

REPEATERS

Repeaters are frequently used to extend the length of a transmission medium beyond its maximum allowable distance. The repeater accomplishes this by amplifying and regenerating received data with no modifications. By regenerating data without modification, repeaters can pass on information very quickly. One drawback to this type of operation is that noise and other interference on the network can be sent along with clean data packets. Repeaters operate at the Data Link layer of the OSI model.

An important rule to remember when installing repeaters is not to use more than four repeaters in succession without a bridge or router in between. If more than four repeaters are installed, the timing scheme of the network can be affected. Thus, it can not reliably handle data packets as they are regenerated and sent out over a medium.

HUBS

Hubs are a central location for the attachment of wires from workstations and other network components. There two types of hubs, active and passive.

Active hubs generally provide more ports than passive hubs and regenerate the signals received from one device to another. Active hubs are similar to repeaters, as they provide an extension of the medium connecting network components.

Passive hubs are usually simple little boxes with a few ports. They can be as simple as a punchdown block or wiring panel. A passive hub does not require an electrical connection, as do active hubs, and does not regenerate the signals it receives.

Modular Hubs

Since the mid-1980s, modular wiring hubs or concentrators have dominated the hub market. These hubs provide network managers and administrators with a convenient way to handle user moves and other organizational changes. For example, if a user must relocate from the marketing department to the accounting department, moving the user's workstation and connecting it to a network outlet is all that is required. Rewiring the LAN is not necessary.

Modular hubs can be configured with multi-port modules inserted into a common backplane. The backplane holds the bus interface and is responsible for the movement of data between installed modules. The design of the backplane is very important to the performance of the hub.

Some hubs are designed for only one type of topology, such as Ethernet 10BASET. Others provide separate physical channels for different topologies such as Ethernet, token-ring, and FDDI.

A new generation of modular hubs support a variety of network topologies and also provide shared bridging and routing. This enables any node connected to the hub, regardless of its topology, to communicate with any other connected node.

Stackable Hubs

Hardware vendors are introducing stackable solutions for smaller or entry-level installations. Stackable hubs offer features such as component management via the Simple Network Management Protocol (SNMP), slide-in bridge modules, redundant power systems, and dial-in remote access units.

NOTE For more information about SNMP, see Chapter 7.

These hubs can provide your enterprise with the benefit of lower cost while at the same time offering more flexibility and fault tolerance than modular hubs. The price-performance ratio of these hubs can be attractive, with newer hub architectures designed to bridge the gap between modular and stackable hardware. At the time of this writing, the per-port cost of stackable hub technology is approximately half that of modular hubs.

Stackable hubs offered by Hewlett-Packard (see netref 1) 3Com (see netref 2), and other manufacturers offer external connectors on the back of each unit which can function like a backplane. Interconnecting hubs in this fashion provides added flexibility to grow your network while the stack appears as a single repeater on the network.

Stackable hubs support Ethernet, token-ring, IBM's Systems Network Architecture (SNA) which is a mainframe network standard introduced in 1974, and FDDI. Support for additional technologies, such as Fast Ethernet and Asynchronous Transfer Mode (ATM), is promised in the future.

Lower pricing on a per-port basis, as well as their relatively compact size, makes stackables a cost-effective way to connect both smaller work-groups and remote offices with minimal difficulty.

Switching Hubs

Switching hubs use a technique called micro-segmentation, which helps reduce contention for bandwidth over a shared medium. By dividing the LAN into separate segments, there are fewer nodes on each segment, resulting in less network traffic.

Dynamic Switching

When a data packet enters a standard, non-switched hub, it enters on one port and exits through all ports. In a switching hub, as each packet enters, the exit port is determined by the data packet's Media Access Control (MAC) layer destination address. This address is commonly found within the first 16 bytes of a data packet, which is about as far into a packet as most switching hubs will look before sending it on.

Most switching hubs employ a process known as dynamic switching. With dynamic switching, data passes through a microchip-based switch-ing fabric that provides dedicated, virtual circuits from port to port. In telecommunications terms, a switch fabric is the facility for connecting two or more transmitting or receiving service providers. Relating this to hubs and data networks, two nodes could be likened to service providers.

Here's an example of how dynamic switching looks in operation: ports 1 and 2 are linked by a virtual circuit. While ports 1 and 2 are communicating, port 3 receives a packet addressed to port 2. The packet waits in port 3's buffer until the data packet being transported between ports 1 and 2 has left the hub. Once the packet is on its way, port 3 creates a virtual circuit between itself and port 2, and the waiting packet is delivered. This is how switching technology helps avoid data collisions and provides wire-speed data rates right to the desktop.

Port Switching

Port-switching hubs are usually the least expensive of the three because of their limited capacity. They typically support only one MAC address per port. A unique MAC address is associated with every Ethernet device on a network.

Port switching lets you divide your LAN into smaller, independent segments and gives you the power to link them at full network speeds. Network managers have the flexibility to assign users to different segments through software control without a trip to the wiring closet. One popular use of this technology is to separate devices, resources, and users into logical workgroups even if they're physically on different LANs.

Segment Switching

Segment-switching hubs are hybrid networking devices that share the attributes of bridges, routers, and hubs. An important characteristic of segment-switching hubs is their ability to provide private network segments to any node attached to a port on the hub. These hubs are becoming very popular for use in imaging and database applications, as well as multimedia and development environments.

Enterprise Switching

The third type of switching hub is known as an enterprise-switching hub. These hubs provide support for linking high-bandwidth technologies like ATM and FDDI. Bottlenecks occur more frequently in traditional, non-switched hubs, because traffic flows through a shared backplane. Each device attached to the backplane competes for a slice of the backplane's total bandwidth.

> **NOTE** For more information about ATM, see Chapter 5. For more information about FDDI, see Chapter 2.

While conventional hubs frequently offer a 10Mbps backplane, enterprise-switching hubs provide high-speed backplanes with the capacity to transmit data at rates exceeding 1.2Gbps. If your company requires support for a network with high bandwidth demands such as multimedia or videoconferencing, these hubs are an excellent choice.

Compatibility

Switching hubs manufactured today will function right out of the box with existing media and network components such as network interface cards (NICs), transceivers, routers, and bridges.

A switching hub can be installed just about anywhere in the network, depending on the type of services you want it to perform. Using management software bundled with many switching hubs, it's possible for you to configure virtual segments that service selected workgroups. Users connected to these segments are assured of privacy, since their data packets will travel over a private path to their destination while communicating with other members of the same virtual segment.

For example, take the accounting group handling payroll and other sensitive services that shares a hub with a software development group. You might not want the developers to have access to the payroll information, and perhaps the new payroll manager shouldn't be able to compile new code!

Using the virtual segmenting capabilities of a switching hub, you could easily accomplish a secure separation of the two groups within the same hub. Strategic deployment of properly configured switching hubs could even eliminate the need for certain router-based firewalls in an organization.

> **NOTE** For more information about firewalls, see Chapter 9.

Hub Features

Here are several key features to consider when evaluating hubs for a network.

Multiple Topology/Media Support

Predicting technologies for future implementation in your organization can be a difficult task. To preserve your initial investment in hub equipment, consider devices that have the capability to mix and match LAN technologies. Ethernet, token-ring, FDDI, as well as emerging technologies like ATM and Fast Ethernet, should be supported. Owning hubs that do not offer this important feature dooms you to owning technology your organization is destined to outgrow.

Fault Tolerance

If a module fails while your system is online, you should have the option of replacing it without bringing the system down and interrupting productivity, and fault-tolerance modules let you do this.

When data passes into a fault tolerant hub, it can be protected by fault-tolerance at the module, power supply, and hub port level. If any component of the hub fails, the nodes attached to it can be automatically switched to a secondary component within the hub.

Slot Independence

Some hubs have specific requirements for slot assignments. For example, a hub may require the power supply in slot 1, the management module in slot 2, etc. Ideally, you should have the flexibility to install a module in any slot you desire. This flexibility is called slot independence.

Here's an example. Suppose you needed an additional multi-port 10BASET module in your existing hub and the hub has one empty slot available. If your hub supports slot independence, it's a relatively easy procedure to install the new 10BaseT module and connect your new users.

If your hub doesn't offer this feature, you may find that the open slot can hold only a specific module, such as a power supply or management unit. Investing in hubs that offer slot independence is a strategic move that can save your company time and money by reducing or eliminating losses due to system down-time.

High-speed Backplanes

Vendors are now starting to offer high-speed backplanes in their hubs. High-speed backplanes can carry a large amount of data, address information, and more. A backplane's capacity determines the overall capacity of a hub. High-speed backplanes, capable of supporting ATM, Fast Ethernet, and other high-speed technologies will be necessary for organizations planning to migrate to high-bandwidth applications in the future.

> **NOTE** For more information about ATM and other network services, see Chapter 5.

Routing and Bridging

Integrating routing and bridging into a hub is a great feature for smaller networks. Router and bridge modules can be installed in the hub itself, eliminating the need for external components.

There are other details such as port density that should be considered when evaluating bridge and router modules for your hub. Port density is the number of LAN, WAN, and communications ports available on the router or bridge modules. Greater port density means more scalability as your network grows.

Whenever possible, secure evaluation units from your vendor. This can provide you with a realistic look at the performance of the module in your environment, not a laboratory.

Latency

Latency is the time it takes the hub to forward a data packet after it's been received. Generally, lower latency translates into faster performance. Some hubs read only the destination address before they transmit a packet. This method may move data through the hub faster, but the hub could end up passing on a damaged packet. In mission-critical environments, dropped packets or corrupted data can be very costly.

For acceptable performance, a good rule of thumb is to look for a maximum forwarding rate of more than 100,000 64-byte packets-per-second. Check to see if this maximum forwarding rate applies between any two ports or just between ports on the same hub module. For best overall performance, the rate should apply to any ports installed in a modular hub chassis.

Management

At the time of this writing, the advanced management capabilities of mid-range and high-end modular hubs offer considerably more control and better flexibility than those of stackable hubs. This should change soon, as manufacturers dash to incorporate new management capabilities into their stackable hubs to allow them to compete with their modular big brothers and sisters.

Differences in management utilities, from support for your current hardware and software platform, to improved monitoring functionality, and even training costs, are key factors to consider when evaluating hubs for your organization.

Scalability

Scalability is the capability to expand your network with minimal changes to accommodate new growth. If your equipment is scalable, products from previous model lines should fit into and function with new product lines. This will allow a company to expand its network hardware base in the future in order to accommodate growth. If they've invested in non-scalable products, they may find themselves lugging obsolete equipment out to the curb. Be sure the hubs you select are scalable.

VIRTUAL NETWORKS

Virtual LANs (VLANs) are growing in popularity because of the flexibility they bring to switched internetworks. VLANs enable network managers to dynamically build and reconfigure logical LANs composed of users on separate physical network segments using virtual circuits or connections.

Virtual circuits are the pathways created between two devices communicating with each other in a switched network or communications environment. These circuits are active only for the duration of the originating data packet. Even though an exclusive connection is established between two devices, it's only temporary and is closed, or taken down, when the communications session is completed. This concept is almost identical to a packet-switching communications network.

VLANs can also help reduce broadcast activity across the network, increase workgroup security, and make it possible to automate network moves, additions, and changes.

One example of a real-world VLAN implementation is a software development company that requires a method of quickly modifying subnets. The subnets could be based on user or project requirements, instead of the typical physical location of each node. Or, in another example, perhaps a law firm would like the flexibility of separately grouping specific LAN segments together. This approach could be used to create secure subnets serving attorneys, paralegals, and legal secretaries. Another option might be to define a VLAN based on protocol or media type.

Because of the absence of VLAN standards, it is sometimes difficult to combine different vendors' equipment on a network. As network use within the organization becomes more important, VLANs will be critical in providing higher performance networks with dedicated bandwidth for each user connection.

BRIDGES

Bridges are used to connect LANs with the same addressing scheme and network technologies such as two Ethernet LANs. Bridges operate at the Data Link layer of the OSI model and can examine a packet's Data Link source and destination address.

NOTE For more information about the OSI model, see Chapter 6.

Many bridges are capable of looking much deeper into a data packet. This ability to look into a packet's data field is known as logical filtering. These added capabilities provide bridges with a method of prioritizing network traffic, allowing them to process protocols more susceptible to delays before they process other traffic.

By examining the packets passing through it, the bridge builds a table containing the addresses of nodes connected to the LAN. When a data packet passes through the bridge, it's checked to determine if its destination address is located on the LAN to which the bridge is connected. If the packet is addressed to a local node, the bridge filters it from the other packets it has received and transmits it to its intended destination. If the data packet contains an address that's not located on the local LAN, it is forwarded to a bridge on the destination LAN, where the process of determining whether the packet needs to be filtered or forwarded would begin again.

Bridges can be translating, encapsulating, transparent, or in the case of IBM token-ring bridges, source routing. Bridges vary in size and configuration. Some offer only a couple of LAN ports for connecting 10BASE2 and UTP-wired LANs, while others provide higher port densities having many LAN and WAN ports.

Popular uses for bridges include splitting overcrowded segments to reduce bottlenecks, expanding the distance or increasing the number of nodes on a network, and linking different network technologies such as Ethernet and token-ring. In this latter case, the two networks must be using the same network protocol.

> **NOTE** For more information about network protocols, see Chapter 7.

Translating and Encapsulating Bridges

The function of a translating bridge is to provide a way for different LAN technologies to communicate by converting packets from one format to another. Translating bridges are most often deployed to bridge Ethernet and token-ring networks.

Encapsulating bridges insert packets, or small pieces of packets, from a sending node's packet type within the packets of a receiving node's packet type. This process is sometimes referred to as tunneling. The encapsulated packet shares a ride with the packet of the native protocol when traveling over the native protocol's network.

An example of encapsulation is a process known as IP tunneling. In this process, NetWare Internetworking Packet Exchange (IPX) packets are encapsulated into Transmission Control Protocol/Internet Protocol (TCP/IP) packets. The resulting hybrid packet is sent over the TCP/IP network to its final destination where it is unencapsulated.

> **NOTE** For more information about network protocols, see Chapter 7. For information about the many layers of protocols described in the OSI model, see Chapter 6.

Transparent Bridging

Transparent bridges were developed by Digital Equipment Corporation (DEC) (see netref 3) and adopted by the IEEE 802.1 committee. The bridge was originally intended to allow devices designed to work on a single LAN to function in a multi-LAN environment.

While the transparent bridge is monitoring all the traffic passing through it, it's dynamically building a routing table that it constantly maintains. To prevent collisions or the possible transmission of duplicate packets, transparent bridges send out special messages described by the IEEE 802.1 standard as configuration bridge protocol data units (configuration BPDUs).

The function of these messages is to provide the bridges with the information they need to configure the attached networks into a logical spanning tree. The spanning tree algorithm is used in bridged internetworks to detect a break in data traffic patterns.

Here's how the algorithm works. From a set of bridges, a root bridge is selected. Once the root bridge is chosen, other bridges in the network determine which of their ports provide a path to the root with the least amount of delay. This is also known as a path cost. The port on the bridges that can access the root bridge with the lowest path cost becomes the root port of the bridge. Other ports are then assigned backup status in the event the primary port fails. The spanning tree algorithm is also used in routers.

Workstations at either end of a transparent bridge can communicate across network segments without actually seeing the bridges. It appears to nodes connected to the bridges on two or more LANs that they're operating on a single LAN, and that each node on the LAN has a unique address. The bridge relieves the workstation of the duty of deciding which nodes are on its physical segment and which ones are on another.

Source Routing Bridging

Source routing was originally proposed to the IEEE 802.1 committee to counter transparent bridging as the proposed standard for joining LANs at the Data Link layer. When the 802.1 committee selected transparent bridging as its standard, champions of source routing went to the 802.5 token-passing standards committee. They successfully convinced the 802.5 committee that source routing was a good way to interconnect 802.5 LANs.

For quite a while, transparent bridges and source routing bridges evolved separately. As time passed and networking further evolved, users voiced a need to interconnect LANs attached via source routing bridges with LANs attached via transparent bridges. This type of bridge became known as the source routing to transparent bridging (SR-TB) bridge.

This approach is a bit complicated, especially when configuring networks that have both types of bridges attached to the same LAN. Eventually, all bridges would offer transparent bridging and source routing would be provided as an optional feature. This type of bridge, able to handle source routing in addition to transparent bridging became known as a source routing transparent (SRT) bridge.

IBM's token-ring networks make use of source routing when they're bridged. With the source routing approach, a workstation sends out an all-routes broadcast frame or discovery packet over the ring. All-routes broadcasting means the packet is sent across every possible route in the network, resulting in as many copies of the frame at the destination as there are all-routes broadcasting bridges in the network. When the packet is returned, it contains a complete set of routing directions, including the identity of which rings the packet has to cross to get to its final destination.

Bridging Strategies

By not allowing data packets to cross a bridge, thus restricting them to local segments, network performance can be improved. Try to keep approximately 80 percent of network traffic confined to local segments for optimal network performance.

You'll also find that the performance of a LAN declines as the number of nodes or media runs increase. Using bridges to implement a number of smaller LANs can often improve network performance, providing devices can be deployed so that intra-network traffic exceeds inter-network traffic.

Another consideration for establishing multiple bridged segments on a LAN might be to segregate workgroup traffic such as creating subnetworks of accounting and personnel groups, for example. Packets from these groups could be restricted to their respective segments, and packets from other segments on the LAN could be rejected completely.

ROUTERS

Routers were designed to filter and forward network traffic and operate at the Network layer of the OSI model. They are frequently used to establish firewalls between subnets and can provide a good defense against broadcast storms. A broadcast storm in a network is an unusual condition most often caused by excessive transmissions of address resolution requests. It can happen when multiple routers come online or synchronize themselves simultaneously, each trying to identify all the connected nodes in the network. Broadcast storms can be controlled by making sure each network segment is properly designed with a balanced number of nodes on each.

Bridges and routers both provide packet routing and forwarding features, but routers can also provide enhanced address filtering functions, as well as packet segmenting, that are way beyond the capabilities of a bridge.

> **NOTE** For more information about firewalls, see Chapter 9. For more information about the TCP/IP protocol, see Chapter 7. For more information about the OSI model, see Chapter 6.

Routers, like bridges, can be used with remote or local connections. With remote connections like T-1 or ISDN lines, routers can balance network usage across multiple links, determine the best data paths, and forward packets to their intended destinations. Deploying routers strategically in local configurations can provide a certain degree of load-balancing and network segmentation, and will often enhance network performance, similar to the segmenting approach of switching hubs.

Brouters

A bridging router, or brouter, operates as a router and a bridge. It combines the dynamic routing capabilities of an internetwork router with the features of a bridge to interconnect different LANs. Operating at the Network and Data Link layers of the OSI model, a brouter can route one or more protocols, routing what it can to other subnets while bridging the remainder of the protocols.

> **NOTE** For more information about network protocols, see Chapter 7.

GATEWAYS

Gateways provide translation services between different protocols like an interpreter provides translation between two or more languages. Gateways are used to connect different devices on the same network and frequently provide connectivity between PCs running terminal emulation applications and mainframes. A gateway can be used as an interface between incompatible e-mail systems, for file transfers from one system to another, or to limit the number of protocols running on a single node.

Gateways work at the Application and Presentation layers of the OSI model, where terminal emulation, file transfer, data formatting, and character conversion functions are handled.

SNA Gateways

Traditionally, connecting to mainframes is accomplished with direct attachment of devices to the input/output channels of a mainframe computer. This is achieved via communications or cluster controllers. These controllers connect multiple communications lines to a mainframe host and perform transmitting, receiving, and numerous message coding and decoding functions.

SNA gateways are easier to install and configure than traditional methods. They provide a friendlier, more cost-efficient growth path and integrate better at the desktop level. Gateways work with a LAN's native transport protocols, reducing hardware expenses and memory requirements. In addition, they provide concurrent availability of LAN and host resources. Major gateway vendors now offer devices supporting all of the IBM connection types, as well as providing connectivity for as many as 254 users per gateway.

In addition to hardware-based solutions, software packages, like Wall Data's Rumba (see netref 4) SNA Gateway, provide users on a LAN or those in remote, off-site locations with the capabilities to connect to SNA machines and access host-based applications and information. Attachmate Corp.'s (see netref 5) LAN-to-SNA gateway supports the attachment of NetWare, TCP/IP, Appletalk, and VINES networks to SNA host computers, and optionally includes Windows-based software that allows PC management of the gateway.

COMMUNICATIONS SERVERS

Also called an asynchronous server or asynchronous gateway, a communications server is a type of gateway that translates the data transmitted over a LAN into asynchronous signals. With asynchronous transmissions, information is transmitted in a stream of bits. These signals are usually used on telephone lines or direct connections to minicomputers and mainframes.

A communications server can handle different asynchronous protocols and it also provides a way for nodes on a LAN to share modems or host connections. Usually one workstation on a LAN will act as a gateway, sharing its serial port connection to a centralized server. All devices on the LAN can use this workstation to get to the modem pool and server. Communications servers are a good remote-access connection point for users who need access to networked files or services when out in the field.

TERMINAL AND PRINT SERVERS

Terminal and printer servers are used to move I/O processes off the system bus and onto the network. This allows serial devices like modems and printers to be utilized as network-wide resources, without affecting the performance of the workstations themselves. Provided a network is not overloaded and is properly designed, terminal servers can transmit and receive data quite reliably.

Terminal servers are often used to extend the capabilities of systems where the availability of serial ports is limited. Terminal servers usually attach to the network using thick or thin Ethernet cable. 10BASET cable can be connected to the terminal server with converters or transceivers.

The two most popular protocols used for terminal sessions are DEC's LAT and Transmission Control Protocol/Internet Protocol (TCP/IP). Both are multiuser protocols that allow users to connect to a host and execute programs as if they were physically connected to that system. The LAT protocol, announced by Digital Equipment Corporation (DEC) in the mid-80s, is one of the industry's most widely used protocols for supporting character terminals over Ethernet networks.

TCP/IP transparently handles the connections between the terminal server and host through telnet or rlogin (remote terminal and login applications) sessions. The terminal server will have it's own IP address with each port appearing as a pseudo serial port. An IP address is a 32-bit address, used in IP routing, that includes a network address identifier and a host ID or end station identifier. Each port on the terminal server can be individually configured as to port speed, flow control, and other features, such as whether it should appear as a modem or printer over the network.

> **NOTE** For information about the TCP/IP protocol, see Chapter 7. For more information about IP Addressing, see Chapter 10.

Support for printers and modems is handled differently by each terminal server vendor. One reliable and popular method of configuring printers and modems is with UNIX daemons, which are usually supplied by the vendor. A daemon is a background process, normally started at boot time, that accepts commands from other processes. Typical daemons include print spoolers, e-mail handlers, and schedulers. The goal of the daemon is to provide access to the ports on the terminal server as if they were local to your machine.

WORKSTATIONS

RISC (Reduced Instruction Set Computer) is the dominant technology for workstations today. The RISC semiconductor was developed by IBM in 1974. A number of internal reasons kept IBM from bringing the technology to market while SUN and other vendors forged ahead with RISC development. Eventually these vendors released their own RISC-based products. IBM's first stable RISC product was the RS/6000, which was introduced in 1990.

RISC provides high performance by doing common computer operations very quickly. In comparison, the microprocessors used in most personal computers (PCs) are based on a design called CISC (Complex Instruction Set Computing). CISC can't execute instructions as quickly as RISC, but has more commands and can accomplish more with each command. Applications written for RISC are normally not compatible with those written for CISC processors.

With prices dropping more than 50 percent over the last few years, many RISC workstations are competitively priced with high-end PCs. One major issue that potential RISC buyers must address is the lack of familiar commercial PC applications that are ported to run under various implementations of the UNIX operating system. For the most part, the products that do run on a wide range of UNIX operating systems are older versions of the software.

> **NOTE** For more information about UNIX operating systems, see Chapter 4.

For the longest time, the biggest advantage of RISC workstations over CISC-based workstations has been their floating-point math performance. However, not many DOS- or Windows-based applications depend on floating-point math. This means you won't see much of an improvement when running general business applications on a RISC workstation.

If your organization uses applications like desktop videoconferencing or computer-telephony integration (CTI), in which fax, voice, imaging, and more all come together, you'll need the fastest chips and multiprocessing power you can get. Features like full-screen images at 30-frame-per-second TV speeds place huge demands on CPUs.

The adoption and implementation of telephony servers to replace aging PBX systems throughout the enterprise is a hot topic at many trade shows and seminars today. RISC technology is well-suited to tasks like this as well as CAD (computer-aided design) and computation-intensive applications.

New developments such as Microsoft's Windows NT network operating system and the Pentium and PowerPC processors are likely to redefine the boundaries that now exist between RISC-based and Intel-based workstations.

> **NOTE** For information about Windows NT, see Chapter 4.

PERSONAL COMPUTERS

Remember when the IBM PC/AT was the personal computer of choice and everyone marveled at the power it brought to desktop computing? With IBM's introduction of the AT in 1984, which extended the original PC bus from 8 to 16-bits, the workstation race was on.

Just about everyone jumped on the bandwagon after that. Beginning in the late 1980s clones were everywhere. Fierce competition at home as well as from manufacturers abroad drove prices down, as the need for more computing power compelled manufacturers to create more powerful, flexible bus architectures and faster microprocessors.

Today, end-users clamor for more speed and power while vendors heed the call with bus technologies like Vesa Local Bus (VLB), Peripheral Component Interconnect (PCI), as well as Pentium, PowerPC, and new RISC-based and proprietary microprocessors.

Bus Architecture

Several PC bus architectures are available. Each offers unique performance and interoperability features that merit consideration.

ISA

The Industry Standard Architecture (ISA) bus is the most common bus architecture. ISA was originally called the AT bus, because it was first used in the IBM AT in 1984, extending the original PC bus from 8 to 16-bits.

Most machines that are ISA compatible will have both 8-bit and 16-bit slots on the motherboard. The majority of PC expansion boards on the market are ISA boards. ISA uses a single bus channel to connect I/O, memory, and processor components. Today, the ISA bus still accounts for a large share of the installed base of PCs.

MCA

In 1987 IBM introduced a proprietary, 32-bit bus MicroChannel Architecture (MCA). With huge increases in clone PC sales, IBM may have had the idea that a proprietary bus like MCA could compete with the clones. MCA, however, wasn't widely accepted by the computer buying public, who didn't embrace its incompatibility with the existing technology, ISA. Nonetheless, MCA is still widely used as the internal bus inside many IBM machines.

EISA

Extended ISA (EISA) was announced in 1988 as an alternative to IBM's MicroChannel Architecture. One of the features of EISA was that it would preserve user investments in existing board-level components such as video and network interface cards.

The EISA bus standard extends the ISA bus to 32 bits and also provides bus-mastering capabilities. Bus mastering is a design that allows board-level components to function exclusive of the CPU and to access system memory and other peripherals independently.

Board-level components that work with ISA motherboards will also function in EISA machines. Even though EISA's data path is 32 bits instead of 16 bits, it still has to operate at the slower 8Mhz speed of the ISA bus to accommodate ISA cards that may be installed on the motherboard. The EISA bus supports sustained transfer rates of up to 33Mbps.

EISA systems are widely known to be hard to configure, with a configuration disk and procedures much like IBM's MCA configuration process. They work well as LAN servers or running a multi-user operating system such as OS/2 or UNIX. DEC, AST, HP, ALR, Silicon Graphics, Compaq and others have incorporated the EISA bus into their workstations.

VESA

The Video Electronics Standards Association (VESA) was formed by a group of manufacturers to address the absence of a standard local-bus interface. VESA defined the VESA Local-BUS (VL-Bus) 1.0 standard, which became popular in 1993, as well as the more recent VL-Bus 2.0, VGA, and Super VGA standards.

VL-Bus 1.0 provided for 50MHz speeds on the motherboard, while add-in, board-level component cards were limited to 33 or 40MHz. The new 2.0 specification, overhauled to attract vendors of Pentium-based workstations, specifies 64-bit data paths, 50MHz timing, and support for write-back caches like those found in the Pentium processor. Write-back caches allow data written into high-speed cache memory from the CPU to be written onto disk or into real memory during idle machine cycles.

There is some speculation that new VL-Bus 2.0 systems will be somewhat faster than comparable Peripheral Component Interconnect (PCI) systems, and that VL-Bus 2.0 will be downwardly compatible with peripherals designed to the older spec. The exception would be the new 50MHz motherboards, in which older VL-Bus cards will not work.

PCI

Peripheral Component Interconnect (PCI) (see netref 6), developed by Intel, is processor-independent and works with any 32 or 64-bit processor. The PCI bus is buffered, allowing the CPU and installed peripherals to function independently, without waiting for one another to transmit or receive data.

PCI is capable of managing a combination of devices, such as high-speed video controllers, SCSI peripherals, and ATM network interface cards, with each offering transfer rates of 100Mbps. This feature makes it well-suited to multimedia and video conferencing applications.

PCI operates independently of the CPU, unlike VL-Bus, at speeds up to 33MHz. PCI is the high-speed bus most utilized with the Pentium processor with an approximate maximum transfer rate of 133Mbps. Other features of PCI are self-configuring expansion cards, automatic conflict resolution, and auto-configuration of the workstation when new components are installed.

Plug and Play

PC manufacturers are constantly implementing new strategies specifically designed to make it tougher for the workstation vendors to peddle their higher-priced products to the corporate information systems market.

One example, The Plug and Play (PnP) (see netref 7) specification, was proposed by companies like Microsoft, Compaq, and Phoenix Technologies in an effort to standardize communication channels between system resources. A system that complies with the specification will include a PnP BIOS, PnP-compatible hardware and applications, and operating systems that recognize the specification.

In PnP systems, the installation of peripheral devices such as CD-ROM drives and sound cards would be easy for users because the system, instead of the user, determines the correct interrupt and direct memory address.

Microprocessors

Since the introduction of the personal computer, there have been several generations of microprocessors manufactured by the leading producers, Intel and Motorola. This section covers two microprocessor families that are notable because of their scalability, interoperability, and performance.

Pentium

In the fall of 1992, Intel decided to call their new 80586 processor Pentium (see netref 8). Originally, it was to be called the 586 and carried the code name of "P5." It was the successor to the 80486 (see netref 9) microprocessor. Intel formally introduced the Pentium in April, 1993.

The Pentium chip is capable of 112 million instructions per second and runs about twice as fast as a 50MHz 486, with its floating-point operations running up to four times faster than a 486. It contains more than three million transistors and is a superscalar chip, which means it can execute two instructions at a time.

Although its integer performance rivals major RISC-based CPUs (Alpha, HP-PA, MIPS, SPARC, etc.), its floating-point performance is generally slower.

The P6 family of processors will be the next generation of Intel's processor technology. P6 processors are designed for complete compatibility with all existing Intel Architecture-compatible software. The P6 is especially designed to deliver optimal performance for 32-bit software.

This includes demanding software like CAD, 3D, and multimedia authoring applications running on performance desktops and workstations, as well as large database and enterprise applications on servers. P6 performance will also enable new PC capabilities like speech recognition. The P6 delivers these features through a technology called Dynamic Execution (see netref 10).

PowerPC

The PowerPC microprocessor was developed under joint agreement between IBM, Apple, and Motorola. It's a combination of the technology found in the RIOS Single Chip (RSC) version of IBM's multi-chip POWER architecture and Motorola's 88110 RISC processor.

The 50MHz, 66MHz, and 80MHz 601s offer a 32-bit superscaler architecture. They are the first versions of the PowerPC chip released and are designed for use in low-cost workstations. Future releases will include the 603, a low-wattage chip intended for portables, the 604, a high-performance chip designed for high-end workstations, and the 620, a server and supercomputer CPU.

Apple has chosen the PowerPC as the platform for their new generation of Macs. IBM is working on porting applications to its PowerPC, especially its compilers and the AIX Workbench/6000 integrated development environment, and SunSoft intends to bring Solaris 2 to the PowerPC.

SERVERS

A server is defined as a shared computer on a local area network. It might be used as a mass storage device, distributor of data, or perhaps as a telephony server. A telephony server is a dedicated, standalone computer that manages telephony activities such as voice, data, imaging, and fax on a LAN.

In client/server computing, the client provides the user interface and performs some or all of the application processing. The server, on the other hand, maintains the databases and processes requests from the client to extract data from or update the database. The server also controls the application's integrity and security.

In a client/server environment, the server is more than just a remote disk drive to the client. Client/server provides applications that are truly distributed in nature, designed for multiple users on a network. For example, if two users attempt to update the same database record at the same time, the update must be reflected instantly on the other user's screen.

Powerful servers and new ways of managing computing resources are necessary to adopt and implement client/server technology throughout the enterprise.

High Availability Servers

Servers required to be continually available for access are called high availability servers. Companies are looking to these high availability servers to support the increasing demands placed on their information technology resources. High-end servers require special design and engineering, usually in the redundancy, hot-swap, and problem anticipation areas.

Even with careful analysis of all the features and benefits these servers have to offer, there is still some uncertainty involved when selecting hardware. Many companies, plunging headlong into the super server hype fail to temper their excitement with a dose of reality.

In the real world, high availability doesn't mean 24-hour-a-day, 7-day-a-week (24/7) uptime. Keeping in mind what your business can and will not endure with respect to a server crash is very important.

Spare Parts

In transaction-based operations, a server housing critical data that becomes inoperable for any length of time could cost the company substantially, both financially and otherwise. In some cases, databases for global operations are stored on a single drive. A failure in this situation could cripple a business if the server could not be accessed for a significant amount of time.

If your business depends heavily on database, application, and other types of servers, consider storing spare parts on-site for emergencies. Service companies offering 24/7 service with 2-hour response times may not be good enough if you're in a critical situation and the system must be functional.

On the other hand, when the cost of downtime necessary to replace failed parts is a major issue, then hot-swap subsystems should be considered. Many servers available today provide redundancy and hot-swap capabilities.

Redundancy

Redundancy is the idea of having a spare part that can take over when a related part breaks. An example of redundancy as applied to mass storage is the RAID disk array; if any disk goes bad, users can continue to access data because of the redundant nature of the array.

Today's high availability servers provide redundancy in critical areas such as power supplies, processors, system boards, network interface cards, and more. When a server detects a failed component, it brings the spare online in place of the defective one. The failed part must still be replaced, otherwise there will be no redundancy for that particular component. Redundancy is a costly tactic, but part of the strategic approach to maintaining as close to 100 percent uptime as is possible.

RAID

The term RAID, which originally stood for Redundant Array of Inexpensive Disks, is also known as a Redundant Array of Independent Disks. RAID subsystems are disk arrays (two or more drives working together) that provide increased performance and various levels of error recovery and fault tolerance.

Does your system require the fault tolerance that RAID provides? The answer depends on factors such as how much revenue your business might lose due to an inability to access mission-critical data if, for example, a drive fails and your systems go down.

The most common RAID implementations are RAID 0, 1, and 5. Level 0, also known as data striping, saves data across multiple disks. While this implementation can substantially increase read/write performance, there is no fault tolerance provided. Level 1 is also known as disk mirroring, and in this configuration, one set of disks is mirrored with a second that is similar in size. In a level 1 implementation, the operating system can only use the capacity of one set of disks. RAID 1 can provide performance increases while also affording a very high degree of fault tolerance.

One of the more widely implemented RAID systems is level 5. This configuration stripes data as well as a parity value over three or more disks. Data and parity info is stored on all of the disks, so that the failure of one disk does not bring the system down. RAID level 4 also stores parity information, with only one drive assigned to hold parity info while the rest handle data.

RAID 5 has excellent read performance but can suffer as far as write performance goes. This makes it a good choice for file and print server environments where files are generally smaller in size. Keep in mind that when a drive fails, both read and write performance are impacted considerably because the system must read data from all of the drives in order to correctly rebuild the drive that has failed. RAID Levels 6 through 10 are proprietary combinations of other RAID levels.

RAID systems usually come in two flavors, software- and hardware-based. Software-based systems, such as the one built into Microsoft Windows NT, are effective but can use up CPU cycles in the host computer in the event one of the drives must be rebuilt. This can cause the host computer or server to become CPU-bound or process-bound, a condition that occurs when excessive processing in the CPU causes an imbalance between I/O and processing.

In a multitasking system, CPU- or process-bound applications can slow down the execution of other applications and the response of the network in general, depending on how the server operating system shares processor time. Today, many manufacturers provide features and functionality that allow you to select the way the RAID system divides its processing capability. A certain percentage can be dedicated to continued storage functions and the rest to the chore of rebuilding your data after a disk fails.

Sooner or later, a hard disk will crash. When it does, no matter what type of RAID subsystem you're using, full recovery will take some time because the data must be rebuilt onto a new drive. In many instances though, a single drive failure will probably not impact productivity too much. Recovering or rebuilding a drive during peak business hours, however, can frustrate even the most experienced systems manager.

Hardware-based systems store RAID firmware in either the host controller or in the RAID cabinet itself. The latter type of system is also known as SCSI-to-SCSI. Controller-based systems are centralized around controller cards with microprocessors and specialized firmware that lives right on the controller card. The controller card in turn fits into an expansion slot of the host system. The SCSI-to-SCSI configuration is a good choice, especially in situations where drivers for the controller-based systems are not readily available for your particular operating system.

A SCSI-to-SCSI RAID system places the intelligence into the disk array cabinet itself and is attached to the host system using a standard SCSI controller. Because there are no special RAID drivers required, this scenario is said to be operating-system-independent. What this means is that the disk array appears as one large drive to the operating system.

RAID Strategies

When choosing as RAID system for your environment, consider the following suggestions:

Try to avoid dependency on proprietary hardware. Some RAID systems comprise cabinets, controllers, software, and hard drives, with a single vendor's name on all the components. In a case like this, your RAID system vendor is known as an original equipment manufacturer (OEM) customer to his suppliers. OEM customers either add value to a product before reselling it, private-label it, or bundle it with their own products. Look for systems that allow you the flexibility to use alternate component brands.

Also, make sure the disk array you select can support large drive capacities. For example, if your RAID system only supports 2GB drives and your cabinet has five bays, the largest capacity you'll achieve is 10GB. On the other hand, if your cabinet can support some of the larger drives on the market today, such as the newer 9GB drives, your capacity can top 40GB in the same cabinet.

Many RAID controllers offer dual channel features, which means they provide multiple SCSI chains with support for at least 14 drives or more. For true redundancy, your RAID system should also support multiple RAID controllers. In this way, your storage capacity grows even more. Selecting a system with high-performance processors provides faster RAID access and can substantially decrease the time it takes to actually rebuild a drive. For this reason, it pays to look carefully at processor specifications when evaluating RAID products.

Your system should provide support for RAID levels 0, 1, and 5. Multiple RAID levels should be supported on the same physical disk array, as well. This provides a convenient way to customize logical drives to suit your applications. SNMP features are important, too, allowing the disk array to communicate with a network management console.

If you're buying RAID systems housed in external cabinets, be sure to select a cabinet with at least six drive bays. Cabinets should also support mirroring/duplexing and other storage devices such as tape and optical drives. Multiple, hot-swappable power supplies with separate power cords are important, too. These can be plugged into separate UPS and power circuits, providing important flexibility when it comes to power management issues. Online spare and hot-swap support is also important for mission critical applications.

Hot Swapping

If you have to shut down your server to replace a failed part, the server obviously becomes unavailable for a period of time. This is where you can benefit from hot-swap features.

Hot-swap means that a component in the server can be replaced while the server continues to run. Some vendors call this a live subsystem. No matter what it's called, the bottom line is continuous uptime.

Troubleshooting

High-end servers with problem-finding hardware and software monitor their installed components such as disk drives and processors. They are constantly looking for indications and patterns of abnormal behavior, such as chronically slower access speeds, that might indicate a failing part.

When the system identifies a potential problem condition, it identifies the part in question, providing you with the option of replacing the part before something major goes wrong. Some of the more advanced units on the market today will even call your pager to alert you to a problem!

Symmetrical Multiprocessing (SMP) Servers

A symmetrical multiprocessor distributes processing tasks such as operating system (OS) functions and applications evenly across multiple CPUs. If the load on the server gets too heavy for a single-CPU system, you can theoretically install a second processor to eliminate performance problems. Many SMP systems, which can cost more than a half-million dollars, can employ up to 32 microprocessors and shared memory that is linked by a high-speed bus.

Conventional services such as file transfers do not realize a significant performance gain from additional processors because their particular bottleneck lies in the system's I/O bus, not in the CPU. For example, database servers perform operations more complex than simple file-retrieval and printing. Because of this, they tend to rely heavily on the server's CPU speed and power to store and retrieve data. In this case, the use of added processors produces immediate benefits in overall system performance.

Pay careful attention when matching system resources with workloads in SMP systems to avoid I/O bottlenecks and the CPU delays that may result. Don't expect performance to increase proportionately with the number of CPUs you install, either. Realistically, you can expect a sizable improvement. Examples of applications that can benefit considerably when executed on an SMP application server are multithreaded database, CAD, and graphics applications.

REFERENCES

Sheldon, T. 1994. *LAN TIMES Encyclopedia Of Networking*. Berkeley, CA: Osborne McGraw-Hill.

Net References

1. www to http://www.hp.com/ahp/Products.html then browse the Hewlett-Packard product information page.

2. Information regarding 3Com Corporation's stackable hub products can be found at http://www.3com.com/0files/products/special/ssadvant.html

3. www to http://www.digital.com/ then browse the DEC home page.

4. www to http://www.walldata.com/rum/rum00.html then browse the Rumba product information page.

5. www to http://www.attachmate.com/attach.htm then browse the Attachmate Corp. home page.

6. www to http://www.intel.com/product/tech-briefs/pcibus.html then browse the Intel PCI technical brief page.

7. www to http://www.intel.com/product/tech-briefs/pnp.html then browse the Intel PnP technical brief page.

8. www to http://www.intel.com/procs/pentium/index.html then browse the Intel Pentium microprocessor product information page.

9. www to http://www.intel.com/procs/pentium/index.html then browse the Intel 486 microprocessor information page.

10. www to http://www.intel.com/procs/p6/dynexec.html then browse the Intel Dynamic Execution technology information page.

Suggested Reading

Perlman, R. 1992. *Interconnections. Bridges and Routers*. Reading, MA: Addision-Wesley.

4

Operating Systems and Environments

ABOUT THIS CHAPTER

All users, system administrators, and network managers depend upon operating system software to provide access to and control of the network environment, its applications, and data. This chapter introduces many popular operating systems, network operating systems, and operating environments.

INTRODUCTION

Operating system software provides access to and control of computer resources. Whether it is how a user manages a laptop or desktop computer, or how a system administrator oversees the operation of a network, this type of software is critical to every aspect of their work.

An operating system, or OS, manages the basic operations of a computer system by controlling the flow of data in and out of the main processor. It determines how a computer's memory is allocated and prioritizes many of the processing tasks assigned to it. Most operating systems available for desktop PCs today are designed to support a single user. Macintosh (Mac OS) and UNIX operating systems offer network and multiuser features.

There are a number of pieces that fit together to make an operating system work, but the key component is the kernel. The kernel handles the management of files, peripherals, memory, and other system resources. It provides processes running on a computer with a way to communicate with each other. In the case of a network operating system, the kernel additionally provides a way for local processes and those running on other devices on other systems to communicate.

Network operating systems (NOS) make shared hardware and software resources available to users, such as printers and e-mail applications. The NOS also provides the user interface to the LAN and communicates with LAN hardware or network interface cards (NIC). In cases where an operating system does not provide network connectivity or multiuser features, a client software component of the NOS must be loaded on the workstation in addition to the OS. The client software is sometimes called the shell or requester.

A NOS differs from an OS in its ability to manage multiple user requests at the same time. It controls the operation of a network by supervising simultaneous requests and providing security that is essential in multi-user environments. For example, there might be a workgroup consisting of 20 users making entries into a database. Several users could require access to the same data file or group of files. The NOS controls read-and-write access to these files to ensure data integrity and reliable access. Security features of a NOS are usually implemented by system administrators and network managers who can determine any user's access to specific servers, directories, and files. A NOS may contain an OS or it may require a separately installed operating system.

> **NOTE** For more information about system administration and network security, see Chapters 9 and 10. For more information about e-mail, conferencing, and collaborative applications, see Chapter 8.

Network operating systems can be used to implement peer-to-peer or server-based networks. Either of these networks can be used to build a client/server environment. In a peer-to-peer network, any workstation can make its resources available for use by any other workstation. Simply put, any computing device on the network can be a server or a client, providing other devices with access to the resources they control. TCP/IP networks operate in a peer-to-peer environment.

In server-based networks, one or more workstations on the network are employed as dedicated servers that run special server software. Server software is generally more complex than the software running on a client, because the server provides specific services to clients that the clients do not provide for themselves. Novell NetWare is an example of a server-based network.

In centralized computing environments, such as familiar mainframe systems, users at dumb terminals communicate with host computers. All processing takes place on the host computer and the results are sent to the terminal for display. Client/server systems operate differently. They can be a mix of peer-to-peer and server-based environments. Typically, a client workstation makes a request to a server. This is done via an application called a requester. The requester's job is to redirect all network-related requests to servers while directing local requests to the operating system installed on the local workstation.

Processing in client/server systems is usually split between the client and the server. The client system might run a database entry application which displays a form-based display, perhaps under a graphical front-end such as MS Windows. The application formats requests for network information and services which are sent by the requester to the server. The server performs back-end processing, such as data lookups and sorting, and sends the resulting information back to the client.

The requester accepts the information from the server and forwards it to the application, which displays the information for the user to view. In this way, network traffic is greatly reduced since the client gets only requested information, not the whole database which would have to be sorted through locally.

Client/server systems are powerful networks that are scalable, interoperable, manageable, and supportable.

NETWORK OPERATING SYSTEMS

Network operating systems are platform-specific. Even when an OS or NOS may be designed for more than one platform, a specific version is required. In the following section, popular network operating systems will be examined.

Windows NT

Microsoft Windows NT Workstation (see netref 1) and Windows NT Server are advanced 32-bit network operating systems (see Figure 4-1). Both NT Workstation and NT Server offer preemptive multitasking and multiprocessing functions, making them powerful server operating systems. The NT Server version also includes centralized security and administration, directory replication, Apple Macintosh services, and RAID support. One major difference between the NT Workstation and NT Server versions is that a machine running NT Workstation cannot be a Domain Controller of an NT Network Domain.

Domain Controllers are servers also known as primary domain controllers (PDC). A PDC allows managers to group users and resources together into a single logical domain. Users log on to the PDC which verifies the user account and provides access to services available across a domain.

NOTE For more information about RAID, see Chapter 3.

Windows NT Server includes all the features of a file-and-print server. This offers a big advantage because the interface to all administrative functions runs through Windows programs, either on the server or on a workstation connected to it. The server can also be used to run applications such as Word or Excel, or just about anything else that runs on a workstation. Using the server in this fashion is okay with small workgroups, but for maximum performance and security you should always use a dedicated server.

Windows NT uses the 64-bit Windows NT File System (NTFS) which provides up to 16 terabytes (TB) of disk space and 4 GB of memory. It can also schedule system and application threads over multiple processors. Thus, it is well-suited to applications such as database and World Wide Web servers that are demanding of processor and Input/Output functions.

> **NOTE** For more information about database applications, see Chapter 8. For more information about World Wide Web servers and applications, see Chapters 10 and 11.

Windows NT is scalable in that it can run on many hardware platforms ranging from a single Intel 486 50MHz chip (see netref 2), to a 100MHz Digital Alpha chip, to a 16-processor Sequent or NCR server. It can also run on symmetric multiprocessing (SMP) machines. SMP systems can provide a significant increase in server performance for much less than the cost of adding additional servers to the network. In addition, an SMP system theoretically reduces administration because there are fewer servers to manage.

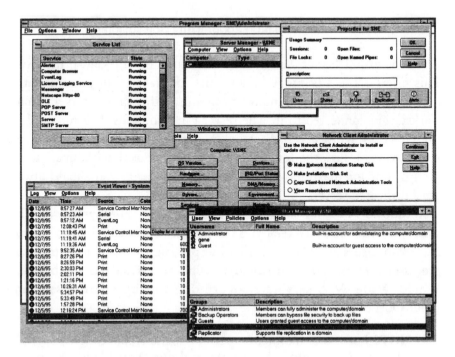

Figure 4-1. Windows NT Operating System (Microsoft Corporation).

Some of the more significant features of Windows NT include peer-to-peer networking features, advanced protocol support for TCP/IP and IPX protocols, remote access services, Apple Macintosh connectivity, uninterruptible power supply (UPS) support, and more. However, while the peer-to-peer capabilities of Windows NT eliminate the need for a dedicated server, installing the NT Server edition would be a good investment if there are more than three or four networked NT Workstations. Windows NT allows developers to easily migrate applications written on one Windows NT platform to another. This is known as portability.

Novell NetWare

NetWare is a family of network operating systems (NOS) from Novell that supports DOS, OS/2, Mac, and UNIX clients. It is one of the most widely used network operating systems available today. NetWare supports assorted network technologies including Ethernet, token-ring, and ARCNET.

> **NOTE** For more information about network technologies such as Ethernet and token-ring, see Chapter 2.

NetWare (see netref 3) runs as a standalone server on Intel 386, 486, and Pentium-based computers. It enables users of the same or different desktop operating systems to share file, print, and other services. NetWare 4.x offers an improved feature-set over NetWare 3.x. The major difference is the introduction of Novell's NetWare Directory Service (NDS) which organizes local and remote users and resources into a hierarchical tree structure, making them easier to manage.

Network administrators and users can easily find objects, which is Novell's definition of a resource, in the NDS system no matter where they're located in a NetWare internetwork. The NDS database is updated regularly to reflect the latest information about objects located throughout the network. NDS is effective at maintaining and managing any network that has more than one server and provides users with the ability to seamlessly connect to objects located throughout the NDS tree.

The NetWare NOS can be integrated with almost any other Novell product to perform a large variety of functions. According to Novell, you can quickly and easily add services such as multimedia, telephony, imaging, software distribution, and more to the NetWare foundation.

NetWare SFT III 3.11

NetWare SFT III 3.11 (see netref 3) is a 32-bit NOS that includes most of the functionality of the NetWare 3.1x NOS, but adds a high degree of fault tolerance. Running on two identical 386 or 486 servers (Novell-certified servers of 25MHz or above are recommended), NetWare SFT III 3.11 helps protect your business against network downtime by integrating two physically separate servers.

The secondary server maintains the same memory image and the same disk contents as the primary server. If the primary server halts because of a hardware-related failure, the secondary server automatically becomes the new primary server. All files, services and applications are continually available to network clients.

Novell recommends using multi-processor systems when running SFT Level III. In this way, one processor can perform the hardware related I/O while the other handles files services and executes other server applications. Mirrored Server Links (MSLs) are also required. These are high-speed 100Mbps Ethernet or optical fiber links that provide close synchronization between duplexed systems.

NetWare for UNIX

A host system running NetWare for UNIX (see netref 3) can function as a NetWare file server and provide file and print services to clients in multiple environments like Windows, DOS, OS/2, UnixWare, UNIX, and Macintosh operating systems. UnixWare is an operating system for 386s and higher and is based on UNIX System V Release 4.2.

NetWare for UNIX preserves the environments of both NetWare client and host users, ensuring that interfaces and commands are familiar to the user. It also maintains the security features of both environments and enables network users to print to host printers.

NetWare for UNIX can be used as an integration tool between supported operating systems and NetWare operating systems. For example, NetWare for UNIX might be a good choice if your business is running critical applications, perhaps an accounting package, on the UNIX platform, and you want to extend access to those applications to desktop computers running other operating systems.

LANtastic

Artisoft's latest release of the LANtastic peer-to-peer LAN operating system (see netref 4) includes significant feature additions and enhancements not found in previous releases. One of the new features is a new universal client technology, which provides seamless desktop connectivity to Novell, Microsoft, and IBM network servers.

The universal client feature includes NetWare Core Protocol (NCP) support that enables LANtastic v6.0 (see netref 4) workstations to access NetWare 2, 3, and 4 servers for file and print services. This support enables users to operate both LANtastic and NetWare networks transparently on the same LAN, while adding flexible networking features to departmental workgroups on existing LANs.

Server Message Block client support gives a LANtastic v6.0 workstation the ability to access any SMB-based server for file and print services. SMB is used to transfer file requests between workstations and servers as well as within the server for internal operations. For network transfers, SMBs are carried within the NetBIOS network control block (NCB) packet.

This feature provides LANtastic v6.0 network users access to servers running Windows NT and Windows for Workgroups, IBM LAN Server, and any other SMB v1.0 compatible system. In this release, Artisoft has incorporated a new, object-oriented groupware system called Artisoft Exchange. It includes advanced e-mail, network scheduling, faxing, and paging features.

LANtastic for OS/2 (see netref 4) is a 32-bit network operating system designed for users of the IBM OS/2 operating system. LANtastic for OS/2 can co-exist with Novell NetWare v.3, v.4, and LAN Server network client software on the same workstation, allowing users to operate on multiple networks simultaneously.

LANtastic for TCP/IP allows a workstation on a LANtastic network to access a wide range of systems throughout the network including DEC VAX, HP, and Sun workstations, IBM mainframes, as well as NCR and AT&T minicomputers.

The Artisoft LANtastic Dedicated Server (see netref 4) is a dedicated server for the LANtastic network operating system. It is a high-performance, 32-bit NetWare Loadable Module (NLM) combined with a run-time version of the Novell NetWare 4.x 32-bit operating system. LANtastic Dedicated Server is designed to provide peer-to-peer functionality along with the performance and expandability of a dedicated server.

Banyan

Banyan VINES (VIrtual NEtwork System) (see netref 5) is a network operating system based on UNIX System V that provides transparent communication across heterogeneous networks (e.g., DOS, OS/2, Windows, and Macintosh). It incorporates mainframe-like security with a global directory service called StreetTalk Global Directory, which supports the X.500 directory services standard, and installs on PC servers and clients. This allows users of popular desktop systems like DOS, OS/2, Windows NT, and Macintosh to share information and computing resources with each other as well as with host computing environments enterprise-wide.

In addition, Banyan now builds its Intelligent Messaging System (IMS), previously available as an option, into the latest release of VINES. As for network services and management, Banyan's Enterprise Network Services (ENS) suite provides a way for network managers to easily identify and locate resources throughout their networks, implement effective security, facilitate messaging, and ensures comprehensive management of the network and attached systems. ENS is available for NetWare, UNIX, SCO UNIX, HP/UX, AIX, and Solaris. Recent versions of VINES also features enhancements in the wide-area network support area, including ISDN and T1 support.

> **NOTE** For more information about ISDN, T1, and other network services, see Chapter 5.

IBM LAN Server

LAN Server (see netref 6) is a network operating system from IBM that runs as a server application under OS/2. It supports both DOS, Windows, and OS/2 clients. LAN Server was originally based on Microsoft's LAN Manager, which was replaced by Windows NT (IBM's implementation of LAN Manager has been replaced, for the most part, by OS/2 2.1), when OS/2 was jointly developed by IBM and Microsoft.

LAN Server is now a full 32-bit network OS both internally and at the application programming interface (API) level and supports the new symmetric multiprocessing (SMP) version of OS/2.

LAN Manager

LAN Manager is a multiuser network operating system co-developed by Microsoft and 3COM that runs as a server application under OS/2 and supports DOS, Windows, and OS/2 clients. Windows NT is the successor to LAN Manager.

It uses the Microsoft File Sharing protocol for file sharing, the NetBIOS protocol for it's transport mechanism, and named pipes to allow data to be exchanged from one application to another either over the network or within the same computer. This process of data exchange is also known as IPC or InterProcess Communication. Examples of IPC are UNIX's named pipes, Windows' DDE, Novell's SPX, and Macintosh's IAC.

DEC PATHWORKS

PATHWORKS (see netref 7) utilizes the LAN Manager protocol to facilitate the creation of multi-vendor client/server environments that can use a diverse set of protocols, network technologies, and applications. There are a number of PATHWORKS versions including PATHWORKS for DOS, OS/2, ULTRIX, TCP/IP, Macintosh, and VMS.

OPERATING SYSTEMS

Operating systems evolved as people needed to solve more complex problems with computers. The first glimpses of what were to become the true operating systems we know today were device drivers or subroutine libraries that were loaded into a computer's memory. These early computers were expensive to use, run, and maintain.

As the operating system evolved, developers wanted to make computers easier to use to improve the productivity of the people using them. File systems were implemented for faster access to data and data storage functions were introduced. It wasn't long before computers became more affordable and it was practical for every user to have one. But these had slow microprocessors and minimal memory. A bare-bones operating system to accommodate these new computers was designed and shipped.

When hardware became more affordable and powerful, computers became more than simply a machine that performed arithmetic calculations. The concept of networking becomes extremely important and operating systems become more sophisticated.

Today, operating systems bring together disparate computing resources and present the user with more convenient abstractions. These resources include devices for processing, storing, and transmitting information, as well as programs that use these devices to deliver services to people.

DOS

DOS (Disk Operating System) is the single-user operating system for the personal computer (PC). It is the most widely used operating system in use today. DOS determines how the PC communicates with peripheral devices installed and attached to it such as video monitors, keyboards, parallel and serial ports, etc.

The DOS operating system originally was developed for the Intel 8088 CPU. Since the 8088 supported a maximum of one megabyte of RAM, the PC was designed to use the first 640K of memory for applications. This 640K block of memory is called base memory. The next 384K or UMA (Upper Memory Area), which is the memory between 640K and 1024K, was designed to be used by the operating system to control peripheral devices.

Because some of the base memory is also used by DOS, only about 500K to 600K is available to user applications. To overcome the PC's 640K memory limit, a variety of third-party memory management products were introduced. Some recent releases of DOS include memory management utilities, eliminating the need for third-party add-ons.

There are a number of vendors offering non-standard brands of DOS. Non-standard can be defined as anything other than Microsoft's version of DOS (see netref 8). Two examples are IBM's PC DOS (see netref 9), which is almost identical to Microsoft MS-DOS, and Novell DOS, an enhanced version of DR DOS (Digital Research DOS). There are features you might consider important for your particular environment which are particular to each vendor's operating system.

Some of these features include PCMCIA (Personal Computer Memory Card International Association) and PEN support. PEN provides the ability to use a stylus instead of or in addition to a keyboard to enter information into a computer. Enhanced media management capabilities include auto-mounting of removable media, advanced disk caching, and the capability to defragment large disk drives. Features like these were absent from earlier DOS releases.

Windows 95

Microsoft Windows 95 (see netref 10) is the new generation of Microsoft Windows products, replacing Windows 3.1 and Windows for Workgroups 3.11 (discussed in the section called Operating Environments). It provides system monitor utilities, remote access, network e-mail, fax capabilities, and file- and printer-sharing for both Windows-based and NetWare-based clients. Plug and Play (PnP) network adapter support is also provided. PnP support provides easier network integration and simplified device installation.

NOTE For more information about Plug and Play, see Chapter 3.

The built-in networking capabilities of Windows 95 are similar to those found in Windows for Workgroups. Windows 95 offers improved reliability due to a new 32-bit architecture and the new systems management architecture enables users to integrate new tools to distribute applications.

Windows 95 includes full 32-bit, protected-mode versions of TCP/IP, IPX/SPX, and NetBEUI, as well as Novell NetWare and Windows NT-based clients. Third-party products are available to provide support for Banyan VINES, DEC PATHWORKS, and Sun's NFS. For users locked-in to the Microsoft suite of products looking for a more powerful, multitasking environment with highly scalable performance, Windows NT Workstation might be worth a look instead of Windows 95.

Following are a few of the improvements the base architecture of Windows 95 provides over previous Windows releases, according to Microsoft:

- A fully integrated 32-bit protected-mode operating system, eliminating the need for a separate copy of MS-DOS.

- Pre-emptive multitasking, and multithreading support—improving system responsiveness and smooth background processing.

- Installable 32-bit file systems including VFAT, CDFS, and network redirectors supporting better performance, use of long filenames, and an open architecture designed to support future growth.

- Thirty-two-bit device drivers available throughout the system, delivering improved performance and intelligent memory use.

- Complete 32-bit kernel, including memory management, scheduler, and process management.

- Improved system-wide robustness and cleanup after an application ends or crashes, delivering a more stable and reliable operating environment.

- More dynamic environment configuration reducing the need for users to modify their system.

- Improved system capacity, including better system resource limits to address issues encountered by Windows 3.1 users when running multiple applications.

OS/2

Operating System/2 (OS/2) (see netref 11) is a multitasking operating system originally developed by IBM and Microsoft for use with Intel's microprocessors and IBM's Personal System/2 (PS/2) computers.

OS/2 Warp and OS/2 Warp with WinOS/2 are designed for home, home office, and mobile environments. The two Warp offerings replace OS/2 for Windows and OS/2 2.1. OS/2 Warp is the third generation of IBM's 32-bit operating system and includes comprehensive Internet access features and utilities such as TCP/IP communications software, Gopher, FTP, Telnet, and e-mail, as well as a World Wide Web tool called WebExplorer.

According to IBM documentation, Warp has all the multitasking and crash-protection power of previous OS/2 releases, runs 32-bit and 16-bit DOS, Windows, and OS/2 applications, and requires as little as 4MB of memory to run. It is available in two editions; one for users who already have DOS and Windows, and one edition for those without Windows.

OS/2 Warp is designed to install over Windows v3.1, Windows for Workgroups v3.1, or Windows for Workgroups v3.11. It works with the Windows code enabling the system to run Windows applications seamlessly with OS/2 and DOS applications on the same desktop. If Windows has not been previously installed, OS/2 Warp will execute OS/2 and DOS programs.

OS/2 Warp Connect combines the core code and user interface of OS/2 Warp with network client technologies from IBM and third parties. OS/2 Connect includes include peer, mobile, and LAN-attached networking products bundled into a single package.

Mac OS

Apple's Mac OS (see netref 12) includes a collection of enhancements over previous versions that are intended to streamline users' interaction with the computer. Some of the new features include improved performance, interactive assistance and customization, DOS/Windows file compatibility, advanced printing functions, enhanced multimedia capabilities, and TCP/IP services.

The upcoming Copeland operating system (also known as System 8) will offer a number of significant improvements over the existing MAC operating environment. Pre-emptive multitasking, protected and demand-paged memory management schemes, multithreading, and hardware abstraction layers are to be included in the System 8 release.

Apple's multitasking technology will help reduce annoying system crashes by improving the way memory is managed. Memory protection will also help reduce crashes by enabling applications to modify only assigned blocks of memory. The memory paging scheme allows blocks of memory not being used by applications to be allocated for virtual memory use. Finally, the hardware abstraction layer (HAL) will separate drivers and extensions from the microkernel, ensuring that errant extensions will not load. A microkernel uses less memory, which makes it more portable and scalable. Another improvement is the replacement of AppleTalk by the Open Transport networking services (see below).

In addition, Apple and Novell are working together to deliver NetWare 4 as a native operating system on Apple's PowerPC microprocessor-based servers. With this strategy, Apple hopes to provide users with the scalability and features of NetWare 4 coupled with the performance characteristics of the PowerPC processor and RISC technology.

Open Transport

Open Transport represents a significant overhaul of the Macintosh networking software, with the final intent being cross-platform compatibility. Open Transport will support AppleTalk, TCP/IP, and serial connections, with Point-to-Point Protocol (PPP) and IPX available as add-on modules. In addition to supporting multiple protocols, Open Transport will provide a means for a Mac to run multiple protocols simultaneously using multiple Ethernet cards.

> **NOTE** For more information about AppleTalk, see Chapter 2. For more information about TCP/IP, PPP, and IPX, see Chapter 7.

Open Transport will also permit developers to use a single Application Program Interface (API) to write Mac networking software for various protocols, instead of having to use a separate API for each protocol. Older Mac software will be compatible with the first release of Open Transport, and developers who create network software for PCs and UNIX workstations will find that Open Transport uses industry-wide network programming standards.

In addition, Open Transport's native Power Mac drivers promise to provide networked Power Macs with a significant speed improvement over the today's emulated network system software.

UNIX

The UNIX operating system was developed in the 1970s at AT&T Bell Laboratories (see netref 13). There are many UNIX versions available today, due in part to AT&T's decision to released the operating system to colleges and universities for use in research and computer science programs. AT&T's open policy paved the way for some of the more popular UNIX systems and features in use today.

In the early 1980s, the Portable Operating System Interface for UNIX (POSIX) standard was defined by the Institute of Electrical and Electronics Engineers (IEEE) (see netref 14) and the American National Standards Institute (ANSI) (see netref 15). POSIX defines a common interface, but leaves the implementation on a specific platform up to the application developer. In addition, POSIX standards are widely accepted today throughout the industry. Operating systems and applications are said to be portable if they can be transferred from one platform to another.

In 1984, the X/Open (see netref 16) group was founded by a group of companies to promote open UNIX standards by testing for integrity and adherence to open standards among products. Bull, Nixdorf, Philips, Siemens, and several other companies were all part of the original X/Open group.

In 1988, the Open Software Foundation (see netref 17) was formed by IBM, Hewlett-Packard (see netref 18), and other members to develop the OSF/1 UNIX distributed operating system and the Distributed Computing Environment (DCE). OSF's DCE is a software environment that allows developers to create applications that can function in distributed client/server environments.

Distributed environments usually consist of products from multiple vendors, along with different operating systems and applications linked to a common network platform (e.g., TCP/IP). Of course, the successful implementation of a distributed environment such as this means that all of these resources must be made available transparently to the end user. Networks such as these are said to be interoperable.

In 1991, an alliance was created between Novell (see netref 3) and AT&T's UNIX Systems Laboratories (USL) called Univel. Their goal was to develop a new desktop UNIX system with native support for Novell's NetWare. The product was to be known as UnixWare. In 1993, Novell purchased USL and formed yet another group called the UNIX Systems Group (USG) that would be charged with managing UnixWare. Interestingly, with the purchase of USL, Novell became the owner of UNIX SVR4.

Because of Novell's desire to move the industry toward a common UNIX operating system, they turned over the UNIX trademark to the X/Open organization. X/Open in turn will now grant the UNIX trademark to UNIX implementations that are compatible with specifications defined by the COSE group. Also in 1993, the Common Open Software Environment was developed by the joint efforts of IBM, Hewlett-Packard, Novell, SunSoft and others. Their goal was to develop a common desktop environment, or graphical user interface, for UNIX.

The main advantage of UNIX is its widespread use as a development platform as well as its portability. Initially, the UNIX OS was popular in engineering, scientific, and computer-aided design and manufacturing (CAD/CAM) environments. Today, it has found a home in business, medical, and other mission-critical environments.

Most UNIX implementations include TCP/IP and Ethernet support, as well as support for distributed file systems such as the Open Software Foundation's (OSF) implementation of the Andrew File System (AFS) and Sun's Network File System (NFS).

> **NOTE** For more information about TCP/IP and other network protocols, see Chapter 7. For more information about Ethernet, see Chapter 2.

While UNIX is an inexpensive, widely-supported, and robust operating system, it isn't without its drawbacks. UNIX can be an unforgiving and sometimes cryptic OS. The learning curve for users as well as administrators can be very long. As with any technology, make sure you've reviewed all the available features and benefits as well as negative implications before making a final decision to use UNIX as your OS. A discussion of some of the more popular UNIX operating systems follows.

System V

In 1989, UNIX Software Operation (USO) was formed as an AT&T division. USO introduced System V Release 4.0 (SVR4), which incorporated XENIX, SunOS, Berkeley 4.3BSD, and System V into one UNIX standard.

The System V Interface Definition (SVID) was introduced, which defined UNIX compatibility. In 1990, USO became UNIX Systems Laboratories, Inc. (USL), a subsidiary of AT&T. In 1993, USL was acquired by Novell and merged into Novell's UNIX Systems Group.

BSD/OS

BSD/OS is an IEEE POSIX-compliant, UNIX-like operating system from Berkeley Software Design, Incorporated (BSDI) (see netref 19). It is based on the 4.4BSD-Lite release of the Computer Systems Research Group at University of California, Berkeley. It includes 4.4BSD's features and capabilities and contains software from many different sources such as MIT's Project Athena, the Free Software Foundation (GNU), Lawrence Berkeley Laboratories, and many other contributors. BSDI's engineers have integrated, improved, and expanded these pieces to create BSD/OS (see Figure 4-2).

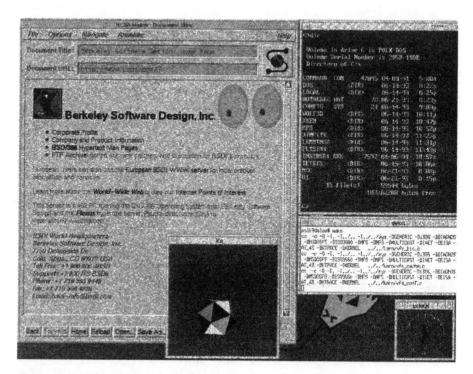

Figure 4-2. BSD/OS operating system (Berkeley Software Design, Inc.)

BSD/OS includes bootable binaries for the base operating system, utilities, X Window System, and numerous software packages. BSDI is able to redistribute source code for just about the entire release (source code for certain X display drivers, certain multi-port serial cards, and the Xircom Pocket Ethernet controllers are not included due to manufacturer limitations). Some of BSD/OS's strengths are its ability to act as a gateway to the Internet (no external router is required), and its complete software development system.

BSD/OS runs on 386, 486, and Pentium PC-compatible systems with ISA or EISA bus architectures. Local bus versions of supported cards also work (for example, local bus IDE controllers or video cards). IBM's Micro Channel Architecture (MCA) is not presently supported. BSD/OS is a multi-tasking operating system, giving you the power to run many programs (also called processes) concurrently.

Licenses for BSD/OS specify no maximum user limit. This means you can connect as many users as you desire and your hardware can support. BSD/OS distinguishes itself from many other PC operating systems in that it operates in protected mode. In protected mode, references outside a program's address space are trapped so that they don't wreak havoc on other programs or the kernel.

Virtual memory is supported, which means you can run a program (or several programs) that requires more memory than the RAM you may have physically installed in your PC. BSD/OS will keep parts of the program's pages in memory and store the rest of them on disk. When disk-resident pages are required, they are paged-in after other pages are paged-out. BSD/OS supports up to 256MB of RAM and virtual memory size can be as large as the sum of your physical RAM plus your configured swap space.

BSD/OS also supports co-residency, meaning several operating systems can share a hard disk. You can boot and run BSD/OS from one part of the disk while reserving another part to boot and run DOS or some other operating system via the boot any program or other boot managers. Native support for the following file system types is provided in the BSD/OS:

- UFS–This is the fast file system developed at Berkeley, achieving very fast disk speeds because of its cylinder groups, careful disk layout strategies, and caching. BSD/OS supports filenames up to 255 characters long, as well as symbolic links.

- NFS–BSD/OS includes an implementation of Sun's Network File System (NFS) with significant performance enhancements. This enables you to export your PC's BSDI file systems (including ISO-9660 CD-ROM file systems) for sharing with other computers on your network that support NFS. It also enables you to access those computers' NFS file systems. The NFS implementation also includes TCP/NFS for use over lower-speed lines or wide-area networks.

- **MFS**–The MFS appears exactly like UFS to programs, but it is optimized for temporary files. MFS gains speed by keeping most portions of its file system in RAM. Actually, MFS stores its data in virtual memory, so its size may be adjusted to suit application requirements. Programs that make extensive use of temporary files (e.g., compilers) see dramatic speedups when the MFS file system is used for /tmp. MFS files are not preserved across reboots.

- **CD-ROM**–BSD/OS also supports the standard CD-ROM file system (ISO-9660), as well as the Rock Ridge extensions which enable a CD-ROM to contain full POSIX file names.

- **MSDOSFS**–mounting MS-DOS file systems directly into a BSD/OS directory hierarchy is supported. Additionally, BSD/OS provides access to MS-DOS file systems, whether they're on a floppy or hard disk.

FreeBSD

FreeBSD (see netref 20) is a state-of-the-art operating system for personal computers based on the Intel CPU architecture, which includes the 386, 486, and Pentium processors (both SX and DX versions). Intel-compatible CPUs from AMD and Cyrix are supported as well.

FreeBSD is based on the BSD 4.4-lite release from Computer Systems Research Group (CSRG) at the University of California, Berkeley. Thousands of additional and easy-to-port applications are available on the Internet. FreeBSD is source-code compatible with most popular commercial UNIX systems. Because of this, most applications require few, if any, changes to compile. FreeBSD provides many advanced features such as:

- Pre-emptive multitasking with dynamic priority adjustment, which ensures fair sharing of the computer between applications and users.

- Multiuser access, which means that many people can use a FreeBSD system simultaneously for a variety of applications. System peripherals such as printers and tape drives can also be shared between all users on the system.

- Complete TCP/IP networking including SLIP, PPP, NFS, and NIS support. This means that a FreeBSD workstation can interoperate easily with other systems as well act as an enterprise server, providing functions such as NFS (remote file access) and e-mail services, as well as putting your organization on the Internet with World Wide Web (WWW) services, FTP, routing, and firewall (security) services.

- Industry standard X Window System (X11R6).

- Binary compatibility with many programs built for SCO, BSDI, NetBSD, and 386BSD. Hundreds of ready-to-run applications in the FreeBSD ports and packages collection.

- Demand-paged virtual memory and "merged VM/buffer cache" design efficiently satisfies applications with large appetites for memory while still maintaining interactive response to other users.

- Shared libraries (the UNIX equivalent of MS Windows DLLs) provide for efficient use of disk space and memory.

- A full compliment of C, C++, and FORTRAN development tools. Many additional languages for research and advanced development are available as well in the ports and packages collection.

- Extensive online documentation.

Linux

Linux (see netref 21) is a 32-bit, multiuser, multitasking UNIX clone that was started as a hobby by Linus Torvalds. This POSIX-compatible operating system includes the X Window System, development tools, and TCP/IP networking services. Linux evolved from not much more than an experimental kernel in October 1991 to a useful operating system by December 1993.

Many users find Linux to be a perfect solution for applications that require a good multiuser operating system but that don't justify spending hundreds of dollars for a commercial UNIX. Linux is used as a platform for World Wide Web, FTP, and X Window System host servers, as well as application development.

Linux runs on PCs and is available free of charge, complete with source code, over the World Wide Web. Many FTP archives also contain Linux applications. Recent releases of Linux have been enhanced with Berkeley networking utilities, tools from the Free Software Foundation, as well as graphics capabilities from the X Consortium.

Linux is also available from several vendors on CD-ROM. Besides saving downloading time, CD-ROM versions such as LinuxWare from Trans-Ameritech Systems provide Windows-compatible installation and access. Applications, documentation, and other components can remain on the CD-ROM and be accessed as needed to save hard drive space.

UnixWare (Univel)

UnixWare (see netref 3) is an operating system for 386s and higher from Novell and is based on UNIX System V Release 4.2. UnixWare was originally developed by Univel, a joint venture between Novell and UNIX Systems Laboratories, Inc. (USL). In 1993, Novell acquired USL and UnixWare is now the trade name of Novell's family of UNIX products.

The UnixWare Application Server runs on a uniprocessor Intel 386, 486, or Pentium-based computer and is a multiuser UNIX operating system designed to integrate with the NetWare network operating system (NOS). In Novell distributed operating environments, NetWare servers provide core networking services to UNIX, DOS, and Windows clients, while the UnixWare server dynamically shares application processing.

According to Novell, the UnixWare Application Server is ideal for businesses that require a high level of NetWare and UNIX platform integration. As a native UNIX operating system, it can also support any of the more than 18,000 applications that run on the UNIX operating system today. In addition, Novell states that the UnixWare platform is excellent for developing business applications that rely on multiple application and database sources.

OSF

OSF/1 is the operating system built around Carnegie Mellon University's MACH kernel. It is a symmetric multiprocessing (SMP) operating system that can run on multiple processors within the same workstation and is compliant with POSIX, XPG3, and SVID base and kernel extensions. OSF/1 provides enhanced security which provides controlled access to the system and its files. OSF/1 also provides dynamic configuration features.

The strategy of OSF/1 is to move various kernel services out of the kernel itself and into user-controlled space in order to provide an OS with innovative features and greater flexibility for the user that's easier to maintain.

SCO

The Santa Cruz Operation (SCO) (see netref 22) markets several operating systems. Open Desktop is a UNIX-based, single-user, client operating system designed to run on Intel-based 386s and higher. It is based on SCO UNIX and includes Motif and X Window System, standard UNIX networking features like TCP/IP, NFS (Network File System), and NIS (Network Information Services), as well as LAN Manager and NetBIOS support. It also includes SCO Merge, which adds DOS and Windows capabilities.

> **NOTE** For more information about TCP/IP and other protocols, see Chapter 7.

The SCO Open Server Network System can be configured as a multiuser server for network users and locally attached character-based terminals. It includes both TCP/IP and Novell connectivity. The SCO Open Server Network System can also be used as a multiuser database or communications gateway server for local and remote users who need access to legacy or external information systems.

According to SCO literature, the SCO UNIX System is the foundation of the SCO Open Server product line and adds increased compatibility, optimized performance, enhanced scalability, configurable security, and simplified installation and administration to the standard multiuser UNIX System.

ULTRIX

The ULTRIX (see netref 7) Operating System is Digital Equipment Corporation's (DEC) native implementation of the UNIX Operating System for their VAX, MicroVAX, VAXstation, VAXserver, and Digital RISC DECsystem and DECstation systems.

It is an interactive, demand-paged operating system that supports virtual memory and multiple processors. Demand paging can copy a program page from disk into memory as required by the application program. The ULTRIX Operating System, according to DEC, provides a high degree of portability among processors running ULTRIX application programs.

The ULTRIX Operating System also offers security features designed to be compliant with the C2 security level (the minimum security level defined by the National Computer Security Center) and includes a set of intersystem facilities to facilitate the communication and networking of multiple systems. It also provides a variety of tools for application development.

> **NOTE** For more information about network security, see Chapter 9.

AIX

AIX (Advanced Interactive eXecutive) (see netref 23) is a scalable UNIX platform from IBM that supports their PowerPC, POWER2, and other POWER-based systems, including IBM RISC System/6000 servers and client workstations.

AIX is based on AT&T's UNIX System V with Berkeley extensions. Some of the more popular features of AIX include:

- The capability to extend the file-system size beyond 2GB, which is a necessity for many companies using large databases, or in transaction processing or environments.

- Disk-striping capabilities, which can be used to improve system performance.

- A new Network Install Manager (NIM) feature, which allows a systems administrator to install applications from a server directly to all AIX client systems on a network. This feature is especially helpful when installing applications and updates.

AIX also offers an integrated desktop based on an implementation of the Common Desktop Environment (CDE). CDE was the first specification, published in 1993, by the Common Open Software Environment (COSE), an alliance of Sun, IBM, HP, USL, Univel, and SCO, dedicated to standardizing UNIX.

A/UX

A/UX (see netref 24) is the Apple Computer version of UNIX for the Macintosh and includes elements from AT&T System V and the University of California, Berkeley, Software Distribution 4.3 (4.3BSD). The Macintosh interface is tightly integrated with UNIX and allows users to choose between a command line interface, X Window System, or Macintosh-style front-end to the standard UNIX commands.

All elements of the popular Mac desktop interface, including menu bars and icons, have been built into the A/UX system. A/UX provides System 7 functionality and gives users easier network access with built-in Macintosh file-sharing, eliminating the need for a dedicated file server. This means that users can share both Macintosh and UNIX files with other users on the network. The A/UX system also integrates the multimedia capabilities of QuickTime, which is a multimedia extension to System 7 that adds sound and video capabilities.

A/UX provides standard UNIX communications features built on the TCP/IP and AppleTalk protocols. MACX, the Macintosh X Window display server, and X11 for A/UX, as well as libraries and a toolkit for X Window System application development, are included with A/UX.

Users can connect to AppleTalk networks through Ethernet (sharing the Ethernet connection with TCP/IP protocols) or LocalTalk networks. With AppleTalk protocols, users can take advantage of AppleTalk printing and AppleShare file services.

> **NOTE** For more information about Ethernet, AppleTalk, and other network technologies, see Chapter 2.

HP-UX

HP-UX is the Hewlett Packard (HP) implementation of the UNIX operating system, and is highly optimized for use on the HP Precision Architecture (PA-RISC) (see netref 25).

HP-UX conforms to X/Open's Portability Guide Issue 4 (XPG4), Federal Information Processing Specification (FIPS) 151.1, POSIX 1003.1 and POSIX 1003.2, as well as AT&T's System V Interface Definition 2 (SVID 2). HP-UX also incorporates selected features from 4.3BSD. Compliance with these standards facilitates portability of applications developed on other standards-based operating systems.

HP-UX also includes a graphical system administration Manager (SAM). It includes software update and install functionality, which makes it easier to update and install software, both from physical media and over the network.

It also features a full suite of ARPA/Berkeley networking services, complete NFS functionality, and a full set of UUCP serial communications facilities. Every HP-UX workstation is capable of acting as a diskless server or a diskless client, potentially saving the enterprise hardware and administration costs. With recent versions of HP-UX, any HP-UX workstation can boot from a server on a LAN and do a cold installation of the operating system onto its local disk.

SunOS/Solaris

SunOS is the multiprocessing operating system component of Solaris from SunSoft Inc. (see netref 26). It is based on UNIX System V Release 4 (SVR4) and provides symmetric multi-processing (SMP) and multi-threading capabilities.

SMP allows all processors in a system to function equally, performing privileged operations (such as I/O) and increasing performance over asymmetrical multiprocessing (ASMP or master/slave) systems. Multithreading is used to process multiple transactions or messages concurrently, and is also the technology most commonly used for creating synchronized audio and video applications.

There's no need to change your applications to benefit from SMP/MT performance, but Solaris 2.2 and above provides user-accessible threads that allow applications to accelerate processing on both uniprocessor and multiprocessor systems. Solaris also has real-time features needed for On-Line Transaction Processing (OLTP) as well as other time-critical applications.

Solaris 2.x also features the OpenWindows graphical user interface and DeskSet workgroup productivity tools. OpenWindows provides users with a powerful desktop environment, complete with remote windows, multi-level menus, drag-and-drop features, and remote usage. The DeskSet windows-based environment features integrated, distributed productivity tools from basic text processing and workgroup time management to multimedia mail.

Solaris uses network services such as NIS+, the naming service from Sun that allows resources to be easily added, deleted, or relocated and NFS to automate routine tasks. (Formerly called Yellow Pages, NIS+ is a redesigned package for Solaris 2.x based on the original NIS.) Software installations and upgrades are automatic, whether you're upgrading a single server or an entire network of Solaris systems.

Solaris 2.x also does away with several system management chores by providing auto-configuration, dynamic driver and module loading, dynamic kernel sizing, self-tuning file caching algorithms, and self-mounting CD-ROM (HighSierra/RockRidge) or floppy (DOS/UFS) file systems.

NEXTSTEP

NEXTSTEP (see netref 27) is a UNIX-based, object-oriented development environment from NeXT Computer. It runs on NeXT computers and 386s and higher and provides an advanced, integrated environment for creating applications with strong graphical user interfaces. Various vendors have licensed NEXTSTEP technology for use in their product lines.

According to NeXT, NEXTSTEP is the first and only UNIX-based operating environment to integrate leading edge object-oriented technology, industry standard networking, and connectivity, as well as a very attractive graphical user interface.

With the addition of NEXTSTEP Developer, users can rapidly develop custom client/server applications that can be seamlessly integrated with shrink-wrapped software to create comprehensive business solutions. NEXTSTEP also includes support for PCMCIA, PCI and ISA Plug & Play, Advanced Power Management, 8-bit color, and assorted peripherals.

IRIX

IRIX (see netref 28) is a UNIX-based operating system for Silicon Graphics, Inc. (SGI) high-end graphics workstations. The latest release of IRIX, which at the time of this writing is v5.2, is an upwardly compatible revision of IRIX 5 and incorporates substantial functionality from UNIX System V Release 4.1 and 4.2. The release of IRIX 5.2 converges all supported Silicon Graphics platforms to the same version of IRIX while preserving SGI customer software investments by providing binary compatibility with applications developed under earlier versions of IRIX 4 or 5.

According to SGI, a new set of system administration tools greatly simplifies a wide range of system setup and administration tasks. For example, the system now informs the user of critical system problems (such as file systems becoming full) via a notifier which appears on the user's current Desk. Whenever possible, solutions are suggested and hyperlinks into the InSight on-line library and system tools are provided.

A feature present in SVR4 and new to IRIX 5.2 is the ability to swap to a regular file in a file system, in addition to a raw swap partition. This allows swap space to be added without shutting down the system or repartitioning your disk.

In addition, the locations of various configuration files and architecture and workstation-independent files have been moved to facilitate sharing diskless systems. This directory reorganization is consistent with releases from other major workstation vendors, and simplifies the administration of heterogeneous networks.

OPERATING ENVIRONMENTS

At one time, operating environments were defined as mainframe software that included the operating system, telecommunications access method, database software, and user applications. As users became more comfortable with computers, a growing need arose to be able to have more than one application active at the same time. Since early operating systems such as DOS were single-tasking in nature, a variety of third-party applications and hardware add-ons were created to address the need for computing flexibility and power.

Terminate and Stay Resident (TSR) applications that remain in memory but can be swapped in and out of view allow users to instantly switch between applications such as a phone directory or notepad. However, many TSRs use important system memory needed for large applications. In many cases, TSRs are not very reliable and can cause regular system crashes.

Expanded Memory (EMS) was created to provide additional system memory beyond the 1MB supported on standard PCs. An EMS board with multiple megabytes of RAM could be installed in an expansion slot on the system board and its memory used directly by EMS applications such as Lotus 1-2-3.

By the late 1980s, the DOS extender was introduced. DOS extenders allow DOS applications to run in, not just reside in, extended memory on Intel 80286 microprocessor-based PCs and up. Borland's Paradox and Lotus 1-2-3 v3.0 were two of the first programs to use DOS extenders.

The Microsoft Windows environment came with its own DOS extender to manage up to 16MB of memory in Windows 3.0 and up to 256MB in Windows 3.1. It allowed users to activate and switch between several Windows and DOS applications simultaneously. This ability to use large amounts of memory in the PC was widely embraced by the technical community and was the technical foundation beneath the IBM OS/2 operating system, Microsoft Windows NT, and other software.

Windows

The original version of Microsoft Windows, v1.0, introduced in late 1985, provided a graphical interface and windowing environment under DOS.

Windows 2.0 was introduced in 1988. It supported overlapping and tiled windows and was later renamed Windows/286. Windows was very DOS-oriented, with programs being launched from an MS-DOS Executive window that displayed directory lists similar to DOS's DIR command. All display elements (windows, scroll bars, etc.) were two-dimensional.

Windows 3.0 was a complete revamping of the Microsoft Windows product and was introduced in 1990. It gained wide support because of its improved interface and ability to manage large amounts of memory. Windows 3.0 ran 16-bit Windows and DOS applications on 286s and above. Windows 3.0 replaced the MS-DOS Executive with Program Manager and File Manager. Display elements in this release were changed to a three-dimensional look.

Windows 3.1 (see netref 29) was the first upgrade of Windows 3.0, and was introduced in 1992. This version provided a more stable environment for running 16-bit Windows and DOS applications than Windows 3.0. It supported multimedia, TrueType fonts, compound documents (OLE), as well as drag-and-drop capabilities. Windows 3.1 also runs 32-bit Win32 applications by translating them into 16-bit calls.

Windows for Workgroups

Windows for Workgroups (WFW) (see netref 29) is a LAN-capable version of the MS Windows v3.1 environment providing integrated file sharing, electronic mail (Microsoft Mail) and workgroup scheduling (Schedule+) capabilities.

Windows For Workgroups also provides Network DDE, which allows users to create compound documents that share data across a network. Windows for Workgroups 3.11 also supports 32-bit disk and file access.

X Window System

The X Window System is a network-based windowing system originally developed by the MIT X Consortium (members of the X Consortium include IBM, DEC, Hewlett-Packard, and Sun Microsystems), and provides an application interface for graphic window displays. X Window System permits graphics produced on one networked workstation to be displayed on another. Almost all UNIX graphical interfaces, including Motif and OpenLook, are designed to work with the X Window System.

The X Window System also provides software tools and standard application program interfaces (APIs) which allows developers to create graphics-based distributed applications. The final application is hardware-independent and functional on any system supporting the X Window System environment. Long time users of the X Window System often refer to the technology as "X."

REFERENCES

Net References

1. www to http://www.microsoft.com/BackOffice then browse the Microsoft Windows NT product information page for specific information.

2. www to http://www.intel.com/procs/index.html then browse for processor information on the Intel processor index page.

3. www to http://corp.novell.com/mkttoc/e1toc.htm then browse the Novell Network Infrastructure page for information about Netware and other networking products.

4. www to http://www.artisoft.com/ then browse the Artisoft Corporation home page for specific product information.

5. www to http://www.banyan.com/ then browse Banyan Systems, Inc. home page for product information.

6. www to http://www.austin.ibm.com/pspinfo/lansrvr.html for the IBM LAN Server information page.

7. www to http://www.dec.com/www-cgi-bin/search-x then browse the DEC search engine. Enter the product or term you want to search for such as ULTRIX or PATH-WORKS.

8. www to http://www.microsoft.com/KB/indexes/msdos.htm then browse the Microsoft Knowledge Base for MS-DOS information.

9. www to http://www.austin.ibm.com/pspinfo/pcdos.html then browse the IBM PC DOS product information page for specific information.

10. www to http://www.microsoft.com/windows/support.htm for the Microsoft Windows 95 product information page.

11. www to http://www.austin.ibm.com/pspinfo/os2.html then browse for more information on the IBM OS/2 product information page.

12. For information about Apple's Mac OS, www to http://www.austin.apple.com/macos/macosmain.html then browse the Mac OS web pages.

13. www to http://www.att.com/timeline/front.html then browse the AT&T Bell Labs home page for more information about UNIX.

14. www to http://www.ieee.org/ then browse the IEEE home page for information about POSIX and other standards.

15. www to http://www.ansi.org/ then browse the the ANSI home page for information about POSIX and other standards.

16. www to http://www.xopen.org/ then browse the X/Open home page for information about UNIX standards.

17. www to http://www.osf.org/general/osf-info.html then browse for information about the Open Software Foundation.

18. www to http://www.hp.com/ then browse the Hewlett-Packard home page for product information.

19. www to http://www.bsdi.com/ then browse BSDI home page for information about BSDI/OS.

20. www to http://www.freebsd.org/ then browse the FreeBSD Organization home page for operating system information.

21. www to http://www.linux.org/ then browse the Linux Organization home page for operating system information.

22. www to http://www.sco.com/ then browse the SCO home page for product information.

23. For IBM AIX product information, www to
http://www.austin.ibm.com/software/OS/VersionInfo.html

24. www to http://jagubox.gsfc.nasa.gov/aux/ then browse this link for interesting AU/X information. Contains tech notes, FAQ's, utilities, etc.

25. For HP-UX product information, www to
http://www.dmo.hp.com/gsy/software/hpux10.html then browse the HP-UX product page on the Hewlett-Packard World Wide Web Server.

26. For information about Solaris, www to
http://www.sun.com/cgi-bin/show?sunsoft/solaris/index.body then browse the SunSoft Solaris information page.

27. For information about NEXTSTEP, www to
http://www.next.com/NeXTanswers/HTMLFiles/1874.htmld/1874.html then browse
the NeXT Computer, Inc., NEXTSTEP information page for specific product
information.

28. For information about IRIX, www to
http://www.sgi.com/Products/software/5.3.announce.html then browse the Silicon
Graphics, Inc., IRIX information page for product information.

29. For information about Windows, www to
http://www.microsoft.com/KB/indexes/windows.htm then browse the Windows section
of the Microsoft Knowledge Base for more information.

Suggested Reading

Adams, S. 1993. *The Rookie's Guide To Unixware: A Major League Operating System*. San
Jose, CA: Novell Press.

Barfield, E. 1995. *PATHWORKS V5: Network Administration and Troubleshooting Guide*.
Ft. Washington, PA: CBM Books.

Bermant, C. 1995. *Windows 95: Microsoft's 32-Bit Merger of DOS and Windows*.
Charleston, SC: Computer Technology Research Corp.

Deitel, H. 1990. *An Introduction to Operating Systems, Second Edition*. Reading, MA:
Addison-Wesley.

Harrington, J. 1994. *Navigating System 7: Understanding The Macintosh Operating System*.
NY: MIS:Press.

Hunter, P. 1995. *Network Operating Systems: Making The Right Choices*. Reading, MA:
Addison-Wesley.

Husain, K. 1995. *Linux Unleashed*. Indianapolis, IN: Sams.

Poole, L. 1994. *Macworld System 7.5 Bible, Third Edition*. San Mateo, CA: IDG Books.

Siyan, K. 1995. *Netware: The Professional Reference, Fourth Edition*. Indianapolis, IN: New
Riders.

Stallings, W. 1995. *Operating Systems, Second Edition*. Englewood Cliffs, NJ: Prentice-
Hall.

Stoltz, K. 1994. *Inside LANtastic 6.0, Third Edition.* Indianapolis, IN: New Riders.

Strobel, S. 1994. *Linux-Unleashing the Workstation In Your PC.* NY: Springer-Verlag.

Switzer, R. 1993. *Operating Systems: A Practical Approach.* NY: Prentice-Hall.

Tennick, A. 1994. *Windows NT: A Practical Guide.* Oxford: Butterworth-Heinemann.

5

Networking Services

ABOUT THIS CHAPTER

Network services are typically offered by telecommunications carriers and used by organizations to provide wide-area connectivity between geographically dispersed sites.

This chapter introduces T-1 and E-1 services and other high-speed technologies such as ISDN, ATM, SMDS, and SONET. Packet technologies including X.25 and frame relay are explained, along with coverage of wireless communications such as cellular, radio frequency, PCS, and satellite systems. A description of European standards organizations is also included.

INTRODUCTION

In the 1960s, there was a global push to upgrade existing public switched telephone systems from strictly analog technology to composite systems that could support both analog and digital signals. This effort resulted in the carrier systems we depend so heavily on today.

The introduction of new high-speed network services such as frame relay, ISDN (see netref 1), and ATM provide a means for organizations to distribute and share a wide range of information between geographically dispersed sites.

However, the ability to transfer data, voice, and multimedia information at high speeds over the network is not without its problems. One of the most important issues that must be addressed with this technology is interoperability.

The term interoperable is an open systems concept that describes how networks and network devices that work on and across multiple platforms. Simply put, it is the ability for one network system to communicate with another, regardless of the vendor.

While newer high-speed technologies such as ATM (see netref 2) try to find their place within the corporate network infrastructure, vendors are busy researching new ways to make older technologies work harder and faster. Take Ethernet, for example. The IEEE (see netref 3) Ethernet 802.3 standard specifies a transmission speed of 10Mbps. Fast Ethernet technologies now promise 100Mbps transmission speeds without the need for companies to deploy new cabling systems. It can work with the existing unshielded twisted pair wiring already installed in most organizations. However, there's more to using this new technology than saying the magic words and loading a new network driver.

> **NOTE** For more information about Ethernet and other network technologies, see Chapter 2.

Most often, there's a big investment necessary in order to gain the full benefit of a new technology such as the high-speed services explained in this chapter. While one part of your existing system is likely to work with a given product, you can bet that most of the other parts won't. This might mean procuring new hubs and routers, network interface cards, cabling systems, or perhaps all of these.

> **NOTE** For more information about network cabling, see Chapter 1.

The question is, how many companies are willing to scrap sizable technology investments made over the past few years on a hunch? Only time will tell. The scalability of these technologies and services is a critical factor in how it can accommodate growth with minimal change, while remaining interoperable and fully manageable. Choosing the right technologies and services is a fundamental part of strategic networking.

Let's examine some of the more popular high-speed network services available.

T-1 AND E-1

T-1 is a term commonly used to refer to a communications link operating at 1.544Mbps. T-1 links are sometimes referred to as DS (digital signal) circuits. The DS refers to the rate and format of the signal, and the T designation refers to the equipment providing the signals. DS and T are used synonymously such as DS-1 and T-1, or DS-3 and T-3.

E-1 is the European counterpart to T1 and operates at a rate of 2.048Mbps. It is a common misunderstanding that T-1 systems are found only in the U.S. and E-1 systems are exclusive to European installations. Actually, this is not the case; T-1 and E-1 merely denote the origins of the communications system standards. The E-1 standards are set by the Conference of European Postal and Telecommunications (CEPT).

How T-1 and E-1 Work

T-1 and E-1 links use digital transmission facilities because of the improved transmission quality and increased reliability they provide over analog facilities. This is partially due to the reduction in the number of lines and equipment required to deliver the increased bandwidths that digital services provide.

Multiple T-1 links can be interconnected to form high-speed T-1 networks. These networks can be used to replace or extend voice services, leased line, or dial-up data networks. A strategic use of high-speed T-1 and E-1 lines would be to create a hybrid T-1 and E-1 WAN link to facilitate international connectivity between stateside and overseas offices.

T-1 and E-1 services can combine voice, data, and video traffic over the same network using a time division multiplexer (TDM). A TDM divides the combined stream of digital information traveling across a link, called an aggregate stream, into equal time slices. For example, consider a company with offices in New York and Los Angeles. The TDM in New York takes the data from each channel in sequence and places it into a time slot on the high-speed aggregate link. In Los Angeles, another TDM receives this aggregate stream and sorts the data back into its original channels. Multiplexers are made up of four separate elements:

- Channel interface units are ports that provide the physical connection of voice and data equipment to the multiplexer.

- Buffers consist of bulk data storage, or memory, within the multiplexer. A buffer can store data that can be read and written between the channels and the aggregate TDM link.

- Frame builder/multiplexers consist of a frame builder (also called a Time Slot Interchanger, or TSI) and a multiplexer, which combines the information from the channel interface units into an aggregate for transmission over a T-1 or E-1 link.

- Line interfaces convert the aggregate stream from the frame builder/multiplexer to a format that is appropriate for T-1 and E-1 transmission.

DSU and CSU

Analog data transmissions require the use of a modem; digital technology uses devices called channel service units (CSU) and data service units (DSU). The Federal Communication Commission (FCC) (see netref 4) requires that every digital circuit be terminated by a CSU. This is because CSUs regenerate received signals and equalize transmitted signals to ensure that data terminal equipment (DTE), such as workstations and other network components, do not send out signals that might interfere with a telecommunications carrier's network.

The DSU handles the actual transmission and reception of a signal and also provides data buffering and flow control. Because of the complementary relationship of the CSU and DSU, they are often merged into the same unit. CSUs and DSUs can perform speed conversions to support fractional T-1 transmissions. Fractional T-1 services provide less than full T-1 capacity and use one or more 64Kbps channels.

CSUs and DSUs have evolved into important network components with advanced features such as network management and diagnostics. These network components enable your business to use new digital technologies to their fullest potential.

ISDN

Integrated Services Digital Network (ISDN) is a communications standard accepted throughout the world. ISDN provides dial-up service, high-speed data transmission, and the ability to send and receive voice, data, and images over end-to-end digital connections. The same twisted-pair copper telephone line that typically carries only one transmission at a time such as voice, computer, or fax, can now handle as many as three separate transmissions simultaneously over the same line.

Some strategic uses of ISDN are telecommuting, video conferencing, remote broadcasting, audio transfer, collaborative CAD/CAM engineering, LAN-to-LAN connectivity, and interactive publishing. ISDN telephones can call to and receive calls from ordinary telephones everywhere. Although the specifics of ISDN implementation are still slightly different from nation to nation, interconnections between any two systems in the world are now possible.

ISDN-BRI

The basic ISDN-to-user connection is called a Basic Rate Interface or BRI (ISDN-BRI). The Basic Rate Interface is defined as two 64Kbps Bearer (B) channels, and one 16Kbps Data (D) channel. Bearer channels transmit user information at relatively high speeds, while separate Data channels carry call set-up, signaling, and other information. The BRI interface is also referred to as a 2B+D connection.

ISDN-BRI provides many new and strategic uses for your telephone lines. For example, the B channels on a single BRI can be used to carry two voice or data conversations, while the D channel is used for simultaneous data packet communications to a third location. The two B channels could also be combined to transmit uncompressed data at rates up to 112Kbps, with rates up to 128Kbps planned for the future.

Depending on the capabilities of your telephone company's central office switch, one ISDN line can handle as many as 8 separate devices and as many as 64 separate telephone numbers through a single ISDN-BRI connection. These devices could be telephones, computers, and fax machines.

ISDN-PRI

The Primary Rate Interface or PRI (ISDN-PRI) in the United States consists of 23 64Kbps Bearer (B) channels and one 64Kbps Data (D) channel. This is also known as a 23B+D connection. PRIs are dedicated trunks that connect medium and large locations to a telephone company's central office. A trunk is a communications channel between two points. The term often refers to high-bandwidth telephone channels between major switching centers. These channels are capable of supporting a large number of simultaneous voice and data signals.

Essentially all modern telephone and computing systems can be connected to ISDN through a PRI. These include PBXs, LANs, WANs, multiplexers, video conferencing systems, and more. ISDN-PRI offers a total bandwidth of 1.544Mbps and is designed for transmission through a standard North American T-1 trunk line.

In Europe and the Pacific Rim, the Primary Rate Interface is supplied through a standard 2.048Mbps E-1 channel, and consists of either 30 or 31 64Kbps B channels and one 64Kbps D channel. This is also known as 30B+D or 31B+D.

Broadband ISDN

Broadband ISDN (B-ISDN) is a second-generation ISDN standard that uses optical fiber as a transmission medium. The term refers to services that require channel rates greater than a single primary rate channel and which support speeds of 155Mbps and greater. ATM will be used as the switching infrastructure for B-ISDN services.

ATM

In 1984, organizations around the world embarked on an ambitious effort to standardize worldwide optical signal levels. This standardization resulted in a series of recommendations for a broadband integrated services digital network (B-ISDN).

The optical data rates, synchronization, and framing format selected for B-ISDN are known as the Synchronous Digital Hierarchy (SDH) in Europe and the Synchronous Optical Network (SONET) (see netref 5) in North America. In 1988, Asynchronous Transfer Mode (ATM) was named as the switching and multiplexing technique for B-ISDN. It is expected that by the next decade, most of the voice and data traffic generated in the world will be transmitted by ATM technology.

Networks carrying real-time data, such as high-resolution video and voice, have high peak bandwidth requirements. ATM is a scalable technology and supports data rates into the multi-gigabit range. This makes ATM a good candidate for delivering these types of service.

Some vendors have announced new technologies to allow users to begin using multimedia applications over existing infrastructures without disruptive and expensive network upgrades. It will be interesting to see how these technologies evolve through real-time delivery of collaborative applications combining text, voice, images, and video across LANs and WANs.

ATM LANs

An ATM LAN consists of a set of ATM switches connected to hosts or mainframes, routers and gateways, and interfaces to public carrier networks. Each of these components has several interfaces that allow them to be interconnected in various ways. For example, a host could be connected to one or more ATM switches while simultaneously connecting to a public ATM network. An ATM switch has three interfaces:

- A host computer interface

- A point-to-point link interface that allows the switch to be connected to other ATM switches

- A public ATM network interface for connecting to carrier-based public networks

ATM Switches

ATM switches can accept input from a variety of input devices, including digitized or digital video. These switches convert the data received into ATM cells which can be comfortably transported across large and small networks. Many manufacturers are offering ATM hardware to help system managers connect their Ethernet and token-ring LANs to ATM networks.

> **NOTE** For more information about Ethernet and token-ring, see Chapter 2.

Here's a look at some of the technologies used to facilitate ATM connectivity:

- Campus LAN backbone switches can connect several servers and routers using high-speed point-to-point ATM links.

- A LAN-to-ATM converter is a newer ATM technology that provides for almost transparent connectivity to equipment on existing LANs.

- ATM workgroup switches can be used to connect high-end workstations directly to an ATM network and are comparable to campus backbone switches, except they don't require the redundancy of a backbone switch.

- Enterprise ATM switches are aimed at wide-area networking, using private leased lines as well as carrier ATM services.

- ATM data service units (DSU) are implemented in instances where you'd like to use ATM as a wide-area transport for a router that doesn't have an ATM interface.

- Carrier ATM switches are used in the central offices of your telephone company or public carrier.

ATM Cells

The information in a data packet is segmented into fixed-length cells of 53 bytes. The small size of the ATM cell keeps the maximum delay caused by the transmission of a single cell over the network relatively short. This is called low latency. Applications can use as many cells as necessary to move data over the network.

Each ATM cell is composed of a header and an information field. The header contains all of the information needed to route a packet to its destination. Thus, the data tells the network where it should be routed rather than vice versa. The ATM switching hardware extracts routing information directly from the cell header.

In addition to the flexibility provided by the header information, ATM provides asynchronous transmission of packets. This avoids the need for signals to be perfectly timed, or synchronous, as they move throughout the network. Asynchronous means that packets can arrive at random and not be tied to a set time. This is one way ATM differs from technologies like frame relay, which reassembles received packets in their proper order before sending them to their final destination.

Some of the more popular scenarios include using ATM networks for distributed network computing, digital medical imaging, delivery of real-time collaborative medical consultations, and scientific visualization. ATM is favored for high-bandwidth applications such as these because of its ability to support data traffic with widely varying service requirements. ATM does not require much network node functionality, since most of the work is done within the switches. This provides a way for very high data rates and low latencies to be attained.

Standards governing the interoperability of ATM components are forthcoming. When purchasing ATM hardware for your organization, make every effort to buy all of the equipment from a single vendor, or a group of closely aligned vendors. The strategic approach in situations such as this is to use turnkey solutions where interoperability usually isn't an issue.

LAN Emulation

As networks are migrated to ATM services, users must often continue to use existing LAN applications. A new standard called L-UNI (LAN Emulation User-to-Network Interface), pronounced "looney," provides for the operation of existing networked applications across an ATM network.

LAN Emulation (see netref 6) is implemented by three network components. The LAN Emulation Client (LEC) is a software driver that runs on a network client. Through the driver, the ATM network appears as a regular Ethernet or token-ring LAN. The LAN Emulation Server (LES) maintains lists of ATM and LAN addresses for all network nodes. When the LES receives a query from an Ethernet or token-ring LAN destined for an ATM node, it looks up the appropriate destination address and loads the Ethernet or token-ring packets into ATM cells for transmission to devices on ATM LANs.

ATM carries messages to a single node only and does not support multi-point broadcasts. If the LES can't respond to a query, such as a broadcast, the message is directed to the Broadcast Unknown Server (BUS). The BUS maintains lists of virtual LANs on the ATM network. When a BUS receives a broadcast message, it retransmits the message to every member of the sender's virtual LAN.

NOTE For information about Virtual LANs, see Chapter 3.

With LAN emulation, everything above the Media Access Control (MAC) layer is supposed to work the same way it does on an ordinary Ethernet or token-ring network; standard 802.3 or 802.5 MAC specifications are supported. Network interface cards (NICs) and drivers do not have to be replaced and protocol stacks that are loaded on top of network drivers stay the same, as do end-user applications. However, IPX and IP, the two protocols used most over LANs today, must be modified to work over ATM without LAN emulation.

NOTE For information about the IP and IPX protocols, see Chapter 7.

SMDS

Switched Multimegabit Data Services (SMDS) (see netref 7) is a high-speed, switched data communications service offered by local telephone companies and frequently used to interconnect LANs. It uses the IEEE 802.6 Distributed Queue Dual Bus (DQDB) MAN networking technology and supports data rates up to 45Mbps.

DQDB is IEEE's standard 802.6 for Metropolitan Area Networks (MAN), formerly known as Queued Packet and Synchronous Exchange (QPSX). DQDB technology operates by maintaining a queue at each workstation or device to resolve when the device can access its dual buses. Dual buses provide bi-directional transmission between each station.

The DQDB topology includes two parallel runs of cable, typically optical fiber, linking each node. This provides for full-duplex operation between any two devices at speeds in excess of 155Mbps. Like ATM, SMDS has a 53-byte cell format. Included in the header of an SMDS cell are control, priority, and error-checking information.

SONET

The Synchronous Optical Network (SONET) (see netref 5) provides high bandwidth, high reliability and manageability and is well-suited for use as a wide-area backbone to interconnect LANs. For the next few years the primary use of SONET will be in large telecommunications carrier backbone networks.

SONET requires the use of optical fiber from end to end. However, local fiber capacity can be a real issue because of the expenses associated with providing fiber to the desktop. The synchronous in SONET stems from the requirement that all SONET nodes on a network be kept in tight time synchronization. Second-generation digital transmission techniques, such as those used with 1.5Mbps T1 and 45Mbps T3 copper links, are asynchronous.

Asynchronous links do not provide the synchronization between nodes that SONET requires. Until local fiber infrastructures are further developed, there is no practical way for organizations to connect directly to a carrier's SONET network. It is possible to connect to a SONET network using copper T1 or T3 lines, but SONET's higher bandwidth and end-to-end management features will not be available.

SONET Standards

The absence of a full set of standards to permit the interoperability of different vendors' equipment means that any point-to-point SONET solution would require a single vendor. This limits its usefulness outside of a carrier's own network. It also makes it impossible for users to implement wide-area SONET networks using public network facilities, even when fiber access is available. According to industry sources and trade publications, fixing SONET standards to include and implement the right management pieces might take another two to four years.

It is difficult for most companies to justify the expense associated with using the features of a SONET network. With future SONET capacities specified at more than 13Gbps (622Mbps is available at the time of this writing), there should be plenty of bandwidth to spare for most applications.

PACKET TECHNOLOGIES

Packet technologies send data in packets over a network, usually to a remote location. Transmitted data is divided into individual packets of data, with each packet having a unique identification, carrying its own destination address. Thus, each packet can travel a different route to its final destination. It is possible for the packets to arrive in a different order than the one in which they were originally transmitted, but a packet ID allows the data to be reassembled in proper sequence.

X.25

X.25 (see netref 8) is a low-speed packet-switching technology that is widely used today for interactive, transaction-oriented applications such as order entry and credit card verification. Most X.25 networks operate at top speeds of 56Kbps

It is perfect for sending e-mail and small data files across wide area links. AT&T and Sprint use worldwide X.25 networks to support their AT&T Mail and SprintMail global electronic messaging services. To establish a session between workstations or other data terminal equipment (DTE), X.25 can use Permanent Virtual Circuits (PVC) or virtual calls.

Virtual Connections

A PVC is like a leased line. It ensures a connection through a packet network between transmitting and receiving devices. PVCs are set up by prior agreement between an organization (the user) and a packet network provider. At that time, a logical channel number is established for the user.

A logical channel is a virtual connection operated over a physical connection, like copper or fiber cabling, that can support one or more concurrent virtual connections. Thus, when a device sends a packet out onto the network, the logical channel number within the packet verifies that the sending device has a PVC connection to the receiving device. PVC's require no call setup or breakdown procedures.

A virtual call, which is also known as a switched virtual call, is similar to a regular dial-up call, since it requires setup and breakdown procedures. Here's how it works: The calling device will issue a special X.25 packet over the network known as a call-request packet. This packet contains a logical channel number as well as the address of the device that is being called. The network uses this address to route the call-request packet to a remote device, usually a Data Communications Equipment (DCE) device, which supports the call on the remote side of the connection. A DCE device establishes, maintains, and terminates sessions on a network.

If the receiving device accepts the call request, it transmits a call-accepted packet back to the network. The network then sends this packet as a call-connected packet. Finally, the channel enters into a data transfer state, establishing an end-to-end virtual circuit.

To conclude the session, one of the devices sends a clear-request packet which is received as a clear-indication packet and then confirmed with a clear-confirm packet. After the call is cleared, the logical channel numbers are made available for another session.

Frame Relay

Frame relay service (see netref 9) has been viewed as one of the more versatile packet-switched technologies available for efficiently linking geographically separate organizations. Bridge, router, and other network hardware vendors are commonly supplying frame relay interfaces for their devices. A router supporting a TCP/IP network uses each of the Permanent Virtual Circuits (PVC) in a frame relay network the same way it uses dedicated links. The overall network is still TCP/IP, but instead of a dedicated circuit, the link is established using two PVCs, one for each network, leased from a frame relay service provider.

For more information about TCP/IP and other network protocols, see Chapter 7.

The public frame relay network is made up of a collection of switches. This means that packets traveling from your London LAN to your Hong Kong LAN could each take a different route through the public frame relay cloud. The router at the destination LAN would reassemble the packets in their proper order and send them to their intended destination.

Frame relay is generally deployed in bandwidths from 56Kbps to about 1.30Mbps. It can be implemented over dedicated T-1 lines, but the widespread application has been toward public networks and ISDN because of the benefits it offers over T-1 based services, with the biggest advantage being cost. According to some users, the cost advantage of frame relay increases with distance. For the most part, you'll find frame relay services follow a flat rate schedule, with slight increases for long distances, while the cost of private lines is entirely conditional on the distance of the link.

One major appeal of fast packet technologies like frame relay is their ability to cost-effectively manage bursty LAN traffic. Because packet networks statistically multiplex traffic from many sources, they can handle bursts of traffic on lines where bandwidth is adjusted to accommodate average traffic flow. This means you're able to achieve higher-than-average data rates over a link. In statistical multiplexing, a channel is assigned to communicating devices like telephones, modems, faxes, etc., only when it actually has data to send or receive.

Pricing of frame relay service is based on several conditions. The first is the number of access points, or PVCs, your company requires. For example, if your New York location wants to connect to four other offices around the country or the world, you'd need five PVCs on your frame relay service at your New York office.

Second, each PVC is assigned a guaranteed throughput rate or committed information rate (CIR). CIRs are a measure of the average data rate used by the customer over a period of time. The PVC user is allowed to send bursts above the CIR once in a while, while charges for the service are based on the assigned CIR. Finally, a port speed has to be assigned to the connection (the PVC) between your site and your carrier's nearest point-of-presence (POP). A POP is also known as a LATA, or Local Access and Transport Area. It is a geographic region set up to differentiate local and long distance telephone calls. It is also the place your long distance carrier, called an IntereXchange Carrier (IXC), terminates your long distance lines just before they're connected to the local phone company's lines or to your own direct leased lines. All long distance phone connections go through POPs.

Bursting is popularized by vendors as a way to increase the cost-effectiveness of frame relay networks and can be a very attractive feature, especially if your company usually moves small chunks of data. As an example, a 256Kbps port speed might offer a CIR of 128Kbps. This configuration would allow you to transfer data at speeds up to the full port speed of 256Kbps, while paying for a CIR of only 128Kbps. However, keep in mind that if your site bursts more regularly than the service provider feels comfortable with, they might request that you increase your CIR. The higher the CIR, the higher the costs.

WIRELESS COMMUNICATIONS

The wireless communications and data services market, while growing in popularity, is still in its early stages. Vendors have a number of technological obstacles to conquer before broad adoption by the general and business public takes place.

Wireless vendors like RAM Mobile Data, Ardis, Metricom, CDPD providers, and analog cellular networks all operate in neighboring portions of the 800Mhz to 900MHz bands. The issue here is that each one uses a different modulation scheme and transmission protocol. Thus, it is necessary to use proprietary modems to access each service.

The Portable Computer and Communications Association (PCCA) is working on a set of common extensions to the familiar TIA-602 AT (Hayes) modem command set. These extensions are based on the +W command prefix from ANSI/TIA/EIA. Wireless extensions to NDIS and ODI, two popular LAN device driver interfaces, are also being developed.

NOTE For information about NDIS and ODI, see Chapter 7.

These extensions, which the PCCA is developing in conjunction with the WINSock Forum, will provide a means of integrating established LAN-based applications with wireless networks such as RAM and ARDIS while streamlining integration with existing Windows applications and protocol stacks.

One example of this is Oracle Corporation's client-agent-server product, Oracle in Motion, which provides a network-independent platform for developing Windows-based wireless applications. Using an agent that resides on the LAN to query information from the host, it minimizes round-trip packet traffic, which is a common cause of reduced throughput when using remote applications.

Cellular Digital Packet Data (CDPD)

Wireless data transmissions currently travel concurrently with analog cellular voice, but cellular service providers are moving to adapt digital technology to data communications. One of those technologies is Cellular Digital Packet Data (CDPD) (see netref 10).

NOTE For information about CDPD, see Chapter 1.

CDPD was developed by eight major telecommunications carriers, working toward the goal of one integrated, nationwide CDPD network: Ameritech Cellular (Chicago), Bell Atlantic Mobile Systems (Bedminster, NJ), Contel Cellular (now part of GTE Mobilnet), GTE Mobilnet (Atlanta), McCaw Cellular Communications (Kirkland, WA), NYNEX Mobile Communications (Orangeburg, NY), Pacific Telesis Cellular (San Ramon, CA), and Southwestern Bell Mobile Systems (Dallas).

In analog cellular services, the transmission channel has to remain idle for a certain period between each voice call. CDPD works along with the analog cellular system and allows users to send data packets in between voice calls during these idle periods. CDPD can use the cell sites, transmission towers, and some radio-frequency (RF) equipment of existing voice cellular networks to provide these services. Many analog cellular carriers are building and testing CDPD networks for future deployment.

NOTE For information about RF technology, see Chapter 1.

Connectionless Network Protocol

CDPD uses OSI's Connectionless Network Protocol (CLNP) to access a backbone of routers that keep track of users' locations as they move in and out of specified cell sites. CLNP is an OSI network layer protocol that doesn't require a circuit to be established before data is transmitted. CLNP is the OSI equivalent to Internet IP, and is sometimes referred to as ISO IP.

> **NOTE** For information about the seven layers of the OSI model, see Chapter 6. For more information about protocols, see Chapter 7.

Cell Sites

Radio links are established between the cellular carrier and your cell phone or cellular modem by means of cell sites. The area served by a cell site is referred to as a cell. Cell sites are arranged in sets of three, or tri-sectors. A trisector is a set of three cell sites, each with 19.2Kbps of bandwidth (or 56Kbps per trisector) available for CDPD services.

One router services approximately 60 trisectors. Routing updates are conducted as users move from cell to cell. The router network provides key network attributes such as address resolution, roaming, intersector and intrasector routing, and interconnection into corporate internets, the Internet, or other online services.

Digital Sense Multiple Access (DSMA) will allow multiple users to share a single cellular frequency. The difference is that instead of managing 10Mbps, such as when it is used over Ethernet, DSMA will handle 19.2Kbps. Once connected to the CDPD network, a wireless device competes for part of the available 19.2Kbps bandwidth, similar to the way your workstation contends for LAN bandwidth.

CDPD will use the SubNetwork Dependent Convergence Protocol (SNDCP) and a Data Link protocol called Mobile Data Link Protocol (MDLP). This combination will give the user a direct connection to a router backbone. The MDLP uses MAC frames and sequence control to provide error detection and recovery, while the SNDCP provides segmentation, header compression, encryption, and authentication.

The Virtual Office

You boot up your notebook computer with its CDPD wireless modem enroute to your office in Los Angeles. The ride from Las Vegas to Los Angeles will take several hours, but you can't wait. You've got to check your e-mail for an important message regarding your biggest client. Let's look at the concepts that allow you to do this.

When your wireless modem initiates a connection, a registration process is started that provides your remote device with access to your carrier's wireless network. Your wireless modem is homed to a specific router that will keep track of your location and all messages intended for you will be forwarded to that router.

When you move out of your home trisector, this home router will forward your packets to another router, which in turn directs traffic within the group of trisectors you are in at that particular time. This method keeps routing updates to a minimum and allows you to roam freely, from cell to cell or city to city.

According to McCaw Cellular, due to the number of router transitions that have to take place in the network, a CDPD network has a typical delay of about 75 ms. When the length of the transmission is more than a few packets, idle time between bursts can bring transmission rates down as low as 1200bps. This makes CDPD more appropriate for sending small messages and transactions instead of larger files.

CDPD Applications

Applications CDPD might be well-suited to include credit card verification, point-of-sale (POS), vehicle dispatching including package delivery and tracking, service calls, and factory inventory control. General information, such as news, weather and traffic advisories can also be delivered to mobile users via CDPD.

Another example of the versatility CDPD provides is that a small police department in Connecticut uses CDPD-capable police cars. This provides officers with access to state and national crime databases and enables the officers to check a vehicle's registration without using the police radio, which can be scanned by possible offenders.

Radio Frequency (RF)

Wireless WAN services are based on radio transmissions, with different parts of the radio spectrum assigned to various services. The quality of wireless channels fluctuates, however, and can cause data loss as well as high error rates. One of the most common wireless technologies relies on radio frequency, or RF signals. These RF signals send and receive data using low-power transmitters and receivers.

> **NOTE** For information about radio frequency technology, see Chapter 1.

Strategic Applications

As noted in Chapter 1, RF equipment is often used to facilitate remote pager communications, but RF coverage isn't limited to paging alone. There are certain services using RF technology that broadcast pager messages as well as wireless copies of *The Wall Street Journal* or *USA Today* directly to your desktop.

Using wireless RF modems, you might connect a portable computer to your workgroup LAN, opening the door to e-mail exchange with other users while you're on the road as well as the possibility to share files remotely and print to LAN-attached printers.

What's in store for the future? Specialized Mobile Radio (SMR) services, a two-way radio dispatch service used for years by taxi fleets, should become widely available. A number of SMR operators are converting their SMR networks to digital technologies to deliver both voice and data to a single device, allowing them to compete with cellular service providers.

SMR systems have less radio spectrum than analog cellular systems do, but the signal can reach 25 times farther, reducing the providers' costs when building a national network. In addition, call-handling capacity is said to be fairly high and costs are estimated to be 10 to 15 percent less than the cost of cellular service.

Enhanced Specialized Mobile Radio (ESMR) digital technology offers improved capacity over SMR networks, with EMSR devices providing users with cellular-quality, voice-enhanced dispatch capabilities, messaging services, and wireless data transfer speeds from 4.8Kbps to 9.6Kbps.

PCS

Personal Communications Services (PCS), which operate in the range of 1.8 to 2.2GHz, are being introduced by a number of vendors. PCS is a lower-power version of cellular and is one of the most recent offerings in the realm of wireless communications. It is expected that PCS will receive and send data, faxes, voice, and eventually video, and is expected to be less costly than cellular services.

In the future, devices and applications supporting a wider variety of services will be widely available from PCS phones with built-in paging capabilities, to telemetry applications that can change the messages on electronic signs through the airwaves.

The PCS derivative of CDMA, known as PN-3384, has been approved for ballot as an ANSI standard by the Telecommunications Industry Association (TIA) and the Standards Committee T1 Telecommunications. CDMA is a North American digital cellular standard that is being installed by cellular carriers in the U.S. It has also been adopted and is scheduled for deployment by carriers in Argentina, Hong Kong, and the Philippines. Korea has also chosen CDMA as the national cellular standard and plans to deploy systems in the mid-1990s.

Satellite

Since its introduction in the early 1980s, Very Small Aperture Terminal (VSAT) technology has enjoyed consistent growth in many industries. VSAT networks provide a way for remote locations to communicate with a centralized computing facility (i.e., a company's headquarters).

VSAT uses a star configuration to provide an efficient means for distributing throughout an enterprise data, audio, video, voice, and fax, maintaining the same level of performance at each site regardless of the site's location.

> **NOTE** For more information on transmission topologies, see Chapter 2.

The VSAT Network

VSAT networks are made up of several components. First, there is a central hub or earth station. The hub consists of a satellite antenna, usually five to nine meters in size, usually located at headquarters or another company location. A switching element within the hub provides the capabilities to route data from one point on the network to another. It is the switching element that connects to data terminal equipment (DTE), which are computers or other network equipment.

A network control system, or NCS, provides network management capabilities by allowing the network manager to configure, download, monitor, or troubleshoot the whole network from the central hub location. Radio Frequency (RF) and Intermediate Frequency (IF) equipment are integral to the VSAT network because these signals are used to transmit the data to and from the satellite.

At the remote location, small antennas up to about two meters in size are installed, along with an outdoor RF unit (ODU) and an indoor digital processing unit (IDU). A cable connects the ODU to the IDU. It is the IDUs job to carry out the necessary functions related to data transmission and reception. The IDU features two to four RS-232 ports and can support multiple protocols. This provides a way to connect a variety of equipment to a VSAT network.

Installing a Remote VSAT Node

Installing a remote VSAT node is a fairly simple process. First, an ordinance review is usually performed to determine local licensing and permit requirements along with a site survey to verify site conditions and map out the installation.

Be sure to consult your landlord when performing the site survey. The landlord's approval of antenna location and mounting is vitally important!

Next, the antenna is installed and positioned for a clear line of site to the satellite. Finally, communications are established with the central hub at headquarters to confirm proper operation of the VSAT.

How VSAT Technology Works

VSATs send and receive data between the hub and remote stations via Ku-band or C-band geosynchronous satellites which orbit the earth at the same speed as the earth's rotation. In this way, the satellites maintain a constant position relative to the network's antennas (or dishes), eliminating the need for constant repositioning.

Private VSAT networks are those that have their own central hubs, usually set up in organizations with more than 200 remote sites. These central hubs may cost millions of dollars. The alternative to private networks and hubs are shared hub services. Shared hub service providers offer access to a centrally located hub that is generally shared with several clients.

Communications between the shared hub site and your company can be achieved through land-based (terrestrial), microwave, or satellite connections, to name a few. By making use of shared hubs, your company could eliminate the significant cost associated with the implementation and management of a private hub facility while gaining the advantages and benefits of satellite-based networking.

VSAT Strategies

Retail stores gather and process financial data daily and transmit this information to headquarters. Point-of-sale (POS) and credit card verifications as well as daily item pricing for merchandise sold in the stores is also transmitted in a cost-effective, timely fashion using VSATs.

Because of VSATs ability to transmit a variety of data, including audio and video information, they are a popular means of distributing music, advertising and other programming designed to reach consumers while they're in the store and ready to buy. Some companies use the video capabilities of VSATs to provide training, facilitate remote buying, and other corporate communications.

The automobile industry finds VSATs a good way to facilitate interactive dealer-to-manufacturer communications. This includes warranty services and inquiries, order entry, credit check and authorization, as well as vehicle and parts locator applications. There has been an increased demand for manufacturer-to-dealer communications including video training for sales and service personnel, new car introductions, and in dealership music, as well.

The banking industry, with it's dependence on using and distributing information and electronic data interchange (EDI), appreciates the capabilities of VSATs. Today, with banks and financial institutions handling more and more transactions via high-volume automatic teller machine (ATM) as well as a constant flow of new products and services, VSATs play an important supporting role in helping to move this data globally.

Since VSATs offer numerous backup systems, including disaster recovery and other fail-safe systems that can automatically re-route communications in the event of failure, it is a perfect match for the mission-critical business requirements of the financial industry.

NOTE For information about disaster recovery, see Chapter 12.

ACQUIRING SERVICES

When exploring your options in the world of network services, keep in mind that everything is negotiable. Factors such as the size of your organization and the amount of business you're willing to commit to the vendor can help determine your strength at the bargaining table. Regardless of this, you should feel confident that the price your vendor quotes can be negotiated; sometimes at a substantial discount.

For professionals dealing with the design and deployment of a global network infrastructure, negotiating network service contracts can be a nightmare. Often these professionals haven't a clue to winning the best overall deal in terms of cost and flexibility, while avoiding the pitfalls and one-sided provisions often found in these contracts.

If terms like MRC, site limit, discontinuance with liability, CIR, and floating rates sound like a foreign language, keep in mind that these terms are second nature to your vendor. You're swimming with the sharks here, and the best way to avoid being eaten is to turn to an expert to help structure your network services deal. There are companies whose sole purpose is to negotiate telecommunicatons contracts. The savings to your organization could amount to thousands, possibly millions over the life of a contract.

Of course, there's no substitute for proper planning. Before contacting a telecommunicatons vendor familiarize yourself with the terms and conditions found in these type of contracts as well as the network services themselves. Whether you're shopping for material goods or high-speed network services, being an educated consumer can help when you implement your wide area network.

EUROPEAN TELECOMMUNICATIONS STANDARDS

This section is intended to provide an overview of the more well-known European telecommunications standards bodies and organizations. These organizations are responsible for developing standards, protocols, and many professional and educational activities.

CEPT

The Conference des administrations Europeenes des Postes et Telecommunications (CEPT) or European Conference of Postal and Telecommunications Administrations, is a standards-setting body. Its membership includes European Post, Telephone, and Telegraphy Authorities (PTTs). CEPT participates in relevant areas of the work of CEN/CENELEC and was originally responsible for the NET (Normes Europeenes de Telecommuncation or European Telecommunications Standards) standards. That responsibility was later passed on to ETSI.

CEN/CENELEC

Comite European de Normalisation/Comite European e Normalisation ELECtrotechnique (CEN/CENELEC) are two committees that have combined to address the standardization of information technology.

The focus of their work is aimed at the development of functional standards for OSI and related standards. Its membership comprises national standards bodies such as the UK's BSI (British Standards Institution, the UK standards body that is responsible for input to European and international standards-setting bodies like the ITU-T), as well as other European standards bodies.

NOTE For information about the OSI standard, see Chapter 6.

ETSI

The European Telecommunications Standards Institute (ETSI) is the European counterpart to ANSI, the American National Standards Institute.

ETSI's main focus is telecommunications integration in the European community as part of the single European market program. ETSI is a self-funding organization that has progressively merged since 1990 with both CEPT and EBU (European Broadcasting Union).

ETSI was founded in 1988 as a result of an in initiative of the European Commission. It was established to produce telecommunications standards by democratic means for users, manufacturers, suppliers, administrations, and PTTs (Postal, Telegraph & Telephone). PTTs are governmental agencies responsible for combined postal, telegraph, and telephone services in many European countries.

CCITT

The CCITT (The Consultative Committee on International Telegraphy and Telephony) is one of the four permanent parts of the International Telecommunications Union (ITU) based in Geneva, Switzerland. The scope of CCITTs work is much broader than just telegraphy and telephony. It includes data, new services, systems, and networks such as ISDN.

ITU

The International Telecommunications Union (ITU) (see netref 11) is an organization established by the United Nations with membership from practically every government in the world.

The ITU's mission is to set telecommunications standards, allocate frequencies to various uses, and hold trade shows every four years. The organization has its origins in Union Telegraphique which was formed in 1865 with the specific aim of developing standards for the telegraph industry. In 1947, under a United Nations charter, Union Telegraphique was reformed as the ITU.

NOTE For information about ITU conferencing standards, see Chapter 7.

REFERENCES

Net References

1. www to http://www.bellcore.com/ISDN/ISDN.html and browse for information about ISDN on the Bellcore ISDN home page. This site was established in response to the many requests received by the Bellcore National ISDN HotLine staff to make certain ISDN public documents are available electronically. You'll find some very good ISDN references here.

2. www to http://www.atmforum.com/ then browse The ATM Forum home page. The ATM Forum is a worldwide organization, aimed at promoting ATM within the industry and the end-user community. There are a number of good ATM resources here.

3. www to http://www.ieee.org/ then browse the Institute of Electrical and Electronics Engineers, Inc. (IEEE) home page for information about the IEEE and IEEE standards.

4. www to http://www.fcc.gov/ then browse for news releases, events, speeches, public notices, and more.

5. www to http://www.adc.com/~don/sif/remote.html then browse the SONET Interoperability Forum Executive Interest Group home page for information concerning SONET management, interoperability, and deployment issues.

6. www to http://www.atmforum.com/atmforum/LANE.html for a press release from the ATM Forum describing the ATM LAN Emulation Specification.

7. www to http://www.cerf.net/smds/smds-bgr.html for a very good overview of SMDS provided by the SMDS Interest Group.

8. www to http://www.cis.ohio-state.edu/htbin/rfc/rfc-index.html then browse the RFC index list for the RFC by number. Click on the link to access the RFC source document. This index list contains the most recent RFCs. If you prefer to use ftp to access RFC documents, then ftp to ds.internic.net then log in as anonymous and search for an RFC in the /rfc directory.

9. www to http://www.mot.com/MIMS/ISG/tech/framerelay/resources.html then browse for specific information about frame relay on this excellent frame relay resource page.

10. www to http://www.cdpd.net/ then browse the CDPD Forum Web Server for information about CDPD.

11. www to http://www.itu.ch/ then browse the ITU home page. The home page is part of the ITU Telecom Information Exchange Services (ITU TIES) which also includes Gopher and FTP servers. You can search this Web server, or follow links on this page (see "About this Web").

Suggested Reading

Black, U. 1994. *Frame Relay Networks: Specifications and Implementations.* NY: McGraw-Hill.

Black, U. 1995. *ATM: Foundation For Broadband Networks.* Englewood Cliffs, NJ: Prentice-Hall PTR.

Bocker, P. 1992. *ISDN, The Integrated Services Digital Network: Concept, Methods, System. Second Edition.* NY: Springer-Verlag.

Cuthbert, L., and J. Sapanel. 1993. *ATM: The Broadband Telecommunications Solution.* London: Institution of Electrical Engineers.

Kessler, G. 1993. *ISDN : Concepts, Facilities, and Services, Second Edition.* NY: McGraw-Hill.

Klessig, R. 1995. *SMDS: Wide-Area Data Networking with Switched Multi-Megabit Data Service.* Englewood Cliffs, NJ: Prentice-Hall.

Lewis, S., and R. Hermes. 1995. *ATM/SONET Explained.* Fremont, CA: Numidia.

Pruitt, J. 1988. *T-1 Networks, Design To Installation: Handbook For Managing Voice & Data Systems.* Tulsa, OK: PennWell Books.

Stallings, W. 1992. *ISDN and Broadband ISDN. Second Edition.* NY: Macmillan.

Stallings, W. 1993. *Networking Standards: A Guide to OSI, ISDN, LAN, and MAN Standards.* Reading, MA: Addison-Wesley.

6

Designing and Implementing Networks

ABOUT THIS CHAPTER

This chapter shows how network software, hardware, and skills come together when planning, designing, and implementing a network. It's a birds-eye view with lots of references to information contained in this book and elsewhere.

Creating network solutions means applying innovations that are specific to your business and taking into account the technical and organizational needs that exist there. With the strategic and tactical information in this chapter, you will understand how to concentrate your efforts toward a network infrastructure that serves your organization.

INTRODUCTION

Creating or modifying a network is a complex activity. Whether the network is a local area network, a wide area network, or links to global public networks, these projects require extensive planning, resources, and commitment by any organization.

The complexity of these tasks can be broken down into manageable pieces by a systematic approach. The first step is realizing the nature of this work. Building networks is a process that has the following attributes:

- It requires planning and allocation of resources.

- The plan should include several stages and many steps in each stage.

- The work is continuous in that it must proceed expeditiously until it is completed.

- It requires action at every stage and step.

- It is an iterative process which allows for contingencies and stepwise refinement to plans as field effects are encountered during execution.

The nature of your organization and the goals and objectives you seek should determine the shape of the project, including how you conceptualize this process.

For purposes of presenting this information, we break down the whole process into three stages: planning, design, and implementation. Although we will include discussion of planning, the focus of this chapter will be on the latter two stages where specific understanding of networks is needed.

Planning, as we present it here, is largely what the organization does prior to specifying the actual shape of the network. This planning stage should result in a business plan and a clear understanding of the needs and requirements of the organization and how the network project should achieve them.

The design stage is where the architecture of a network takes shape in conformance to the objectives of the business plan. The architecture of a network is defined by the selection of transmission media and the technologies, protocols, software, and hardware that place data onto the medium and transport it from one network device to another.

In the implementation stage, the time and effort put into the planning and design stages come together to create a physical network that serves the needs of the organization and the people who use it.

You may choose to break down the entire process into two stages, named, for example, planning and implementation or design and implementation. You might add a stage after implementation to account for maintenance and future planning. No matter how many stages you select, there should be at least two, but not too many. Instead, you should break down each major stage into several steps. Each step should be defined as a distinct activity that can be assigned and managed independently, but also fit into the overall sequence of tasks.

Before we take a look at the different networking environments and network technologies, it is important to discuss the standard that makes it possible for networks to function in an open environment. It is called the Open Systems Interconnection. We have referred to it throughout this book as the OSI Reference Model. It was invoked as a means of conceptualizing the nature and interrelationships of network components, technologies, and techniques. A brief description is presented here as a means of conceiving of the network as a complete entity, providing a common ground for discussion, and offering a shared goal for achieving interoperability in a global and heterogeneous environment.

THE OSI REFERENCE MODEL

The Open System Interconnection (OSI) is a set of standards developed by the International Standards Organization (ISO). These standards and the OSI Reference Model that conceptualizes them provide a common framework to which manufacturers can adhere. This lets you purchase hardware and software components (referred to as open systems) from your favorite vendors with some degree of certainty they'll work together without huge incompatibilities. An open system can be defined as a computer and associated software and peripherals that conform to standards based on the OSI model. By adopting these standards, open systems can communicate with each other over a network regardless of the manufacturer of the hardware or software.

Many widely used protocols have a structure that is based on the OSI model. This model organizes the communications process into seven different categories, or layers. Layers seven through four deal with end-to-end communications between the message source and the message destination, and layers three through one deal with network access.

> **NOTE** For more information about network protocols, see Chapter 7.

This layered structure provides a way to prepare data for transport over a network. The data is "chunked" and passed through the layers with each layer adding its own information to the data packet with a final result being a packet that can be sent to any user at any time over any type of transmission medium.

The Physical layer, Data Link layer, Network layer, Transport layer, and the upper Application, Presentation and Session layers comprise the model. The Physical and Data Link layer functions are normally handled in hardware while higher layer functions are performed in software or firmware.

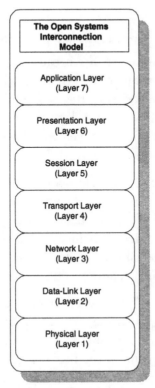

Figure 6-1. The OSI Reference Model.

Here is an explanation of each of the seven layers and their respective functions:

- **Physical (layer 1)**—The Physical layer specifies the physical medium used in the network, such as UTP, optical fiber, or coax. It also addresses the functions necessary to send and receive data over the particular medium. The Physical layer is the lowest layer in the OSI model and is the layer where repeaters operate.

- **Data Link (layer 2)**—The Data Link layer, or Link layer, tries to make the physical link reliable by controlling access to the medium. Low-level error detection and recovery is performed here, as well. In IEEE standards, this layer is further divided into 2 sublayers, the Media Access Control (MAC) layer and the Logical Link control (LLC) layer. While the MAC sublayer deals with the actual physical medium, or network cabling, the LLC sublayer handles logical connections over the cable. Bridges function at this layer.

- **Network (layer 3)**–The function of the Network layer is to control routing across the network. Because the route from one node to another might require a path through yet another node, the Network layer makes sure that a virtual path exists between any two nodes. If a link should fail, the Network layer is responsible for selecting another route. As you may have already guessed, routers function at this layer.

- **Transport (layer 4)**–The Transport layer performs error recovery of data and makes sure reliable communications exist over the network. In the case of garbled data or lost packets, the Transport layer would request a retransmission. It also regulates the flow of data, preventing the possibility of data overruns in instances when one machine sends packets faster than another can receive them.

- **Session (layer 5)**–The Session layer establishes and manages sessions between application programs. As an example, if your PC communicates with a mainframe, software in this layer would actually set up and maintain the network connections between the two machines. Password verification, login and logout procedures, and network monitoring and reporting are some of the other activities carried on at the Session layer.

- **Presentation (layer 6)**–The Presentation layer focuses on defining the format of the data that is exchanged between applications (i.e.; protocol conversion between different nodes using different formats, etc.).

- **Application (layer 7)**–Application layer services such as e-mail, remote logins, and file transfers are used by the user or application program directly.

Thus, for planning networks, the OSI Reference Model provides a unifying and functional description of all aspects of networking. Besides providing a conceptual tool for the planning, implementation, and trouble-shooting of networks, it is also a standard by which diverse products can be evaluated, especially in how they achieve interoperability.

NETWORKING ENVIRONMENTS

There are two basic types of network environments: a centralized environment in which a large, powerful computer handles the processing and storage needs of many users, and a distributed environment where these duties are balanced between centralized systems and more powerful computers which access them.

Centralized Networks

A centralized network system is often referred to as a legacy system. This term describes centralized computers such as mainframes that have been used by an organization over a long period of time. Mainframes have been around since the 1960s and have been used for software development and data warehousing.

Connectivity to mainframes is provided via serially connected terminals. This is typically referred to as a host-terminal environment because the mainframe acts as a host system which is accessed by display devices called terminals. These devices are often called dumb terminals, because they have little or no independent internal processing capability.

Although the use of older, more centralized systems has been waning in comparison to distributed systems, they are far from becoming obsolete. One reason is that many companies that deployed early client/server systems have not realized the performance and stability they require for their mission-critical business applications.

Many organizations choose to integrate their legacy systems into newer client/server environments. These companies create new applications that run on client/server platforms and are used to access data residing on the mainframe, where it functions as a file server. This strategic approach provides interoperability between the legacy systems and modern networks, preserving investments in technology.

> **NOTE** For information about mainframe connectivity, see Chapter 8.

Distributed Networks

There are many types of distributed network environments. Some are dedicated to one of the popular types described below, but many large or geographically dispersed systems actually employ a hybrid of distributed and centralized systems. In many instances, organizations turn to outside help to create and manage their distributed networks because they lack the time, capability, or financial resources to do it themselves.

Take backups, for example. In distributed environments, information is generally stored in multiple locations. However, the various departments throughout an organization may use incompatible backup systems and may not have technologists on staff with the multi-platform training needed in environments like these. While certain backup systems available today move information from different client and server operating systems automatically to a central location, these systems are few and very expensive to implement.

What about support? Traditional help desks are generally reactionary. For example, when a server or shared printer malfunctions, the solution is often a quick fix to remedy the immediate problem so that users can continue with their tasks. However, when problems arise in distributed networks, they usually involve multiple systems as well as the networks connecting them. Diagnosing problems in this environment requires the ability to analyze and troubleshoot all of the components involved, including transmission media, network servers, workstations, and applications.

Peer-to-Peer

In peer-to-peer networks, any computing device connected to the network can function as a server or a client, providing other devices on the network with access to the resources they control. Peer-to-peer networks involve direct communications between clients without a dedicated server. They are generally easier to use and administer than other networks. Since there's no dedicated server, issues like security, backups, and traffic congestion are not easily managed on standard peer-to-peer systems. For example, in an imaginary peer network with 25 nodes, each workstation has a 2GB hard drive installed. If each user simply used half of the drive's available disk space to store data, backups of the 25GB would take quite awhile, not to mention the amount of time required to restore the data in the event of a failure or other emergency.

Peer-to-peer networks are ideal for small organizations because they are relatively inexpensive and, in most cases, do not require someone to do the full-time work of network administration. Peer networks can also encourage a more natural social working environment. People move about the organization sharing files, memos, and other information. Peer networks function in the same way, allowing users to share their local resources with everyone else connected to the network. examples of peer-to-peer networks include networks based on Microsoft Windows for Workgroups, Windows 95, or Artisoft's LANtastic network operating systems.

> **NOTE** For more information about network operating systems, see Chapter 4.

Client/Server

Client/server networks distribute resources and services throughout the network instead of being centralized, as in traditional mainframe environments. They are the networks most often designed and implemented today.

Early client/server systems were established to provide graphical front ends to mainframes or other centralized resources. The host provided file and database services, while the client PCs or workstations presented the graphical user interface (GUI). This model essentially substituted workstations for dumb terminals.

As these systems grew more popular, organizations developed client-based applications that did more than simply act as a graphical front-end. Unfortunately, as clients were added, hosts were overwhelmed by the increased processing demands. Each new client connection demanded additional memory and CPU resources. Moreover, as client-based applications grew more complex, they became more difficult to deploy and maintain. The result was reduced network performance and increased operating costs, leaving users and management very frustrated. Recent advances in client/server technology have adjusted for distributed systems and heterogeneous environments by using scaleable, portable, and interoperable systems that can respond and grow with demand.

NOTE For more information about servers, see Chapter 10.

Novell's NetWare is an example of a server-based, client/server network. In this type of network, dedicated servers running special server software provide services to network clients. In server-based environments it is the server's responsibility to provide services such as file access, which includes opening and closing files, reading and writing data, security, resource allocation tracking, and print services. In NetWare networks, the workstations handle much of the processing load, which frees the server to perform server-specific tasks more efficiently.

TCP/IP, which stands for Transmission Control Protocol/Internet Protocol, is increasingly being used to implement LAN to LAN and LAN to WAN internetworking. In this open and distributed environment (typically called an internet) any computer on the network can function as a server and provide services to any other system running the TCP/IP client software.

Client/server networks should be planned and designed based on organizational fit, or an organization's need for interoperability, not a specific technology or collection of technologies. If the implementation of technology is driven by the needs of the business, organizations can assemble standards-based networks that interconnect to form integrated, scaleable systems.

Heterogeneous Networks

Distributed environments can include legacy systems as well as new technologies that span multiple hardware and software platforms. Environments like this are known as heterogeneous networks. Heterogeneous networks are the result of assembling network devices and software from a variety of vendors, configuring them and attaching them to the network, with the end result being a seamless enterprise network.

An example of a heterogeneous network would be an organization with mainframe systems used for database applications and several business units. Macintosh workstations are used in the marketing group for client presentations, PC workstations and servers in the administrative group for accounting and word processing tasks, and UNIX workstations and servers in the development group for cross-platform application development. In a heterogeneous network, any of these devices would be able to utilize computing resources throughout the organization, regardless of the platform or operating system.

Heterogeneous networks in some instances are also known as enterprise networks. Enterprise networks can encompass both the local and wide area network domains in scope. They integrate all of the systems within an organization, no matter what the platform or operating system.

NETWORKING TECHNOLOGY

One way to distinguish computer networks is by the distance the technology is intended to cover, such as a local area network (LAN), a metropolitan area network (MAN), and a wide area network (WAN).

Local Area Networks

A LAN provides a way for a number of independent devices to communicate, typically at data rates between 1Mbps and 16Mbps. With the introduction of high-speed network technologies such as Fast Ethernet and ATM, 100Mbps to gigabit speeds are becoming achievable.

> **NOTE** For more information about Fast Ethernet, ATM, and other network technologies, see Chapter 2.

LANs are most often found in a single building or a group of buildings that are close together. However, a LAN does not cover a distance of more than a few miles. LANs can provide network users with access to data distributed throughout the network on workstations or servers. Depending on the network operating system used, it may be possible for several users to access the same data at the same time. There are several types of LANs in use today, including peer-to-peer and client/server types described previously.

> **NOTE** For more information about network operating systems, see Chapter 4.

There are many reasons for an organization to implement a LAN. For example, resource sharing across the network can include printers, modems, and mass storage devices. Sharing resources can reduce the cost of technology implementation since every user does not have to have a printer, modem, or hard disk connected to his or her workstation. The ability to centrally manage the network and its resources provides a secure environment, as well as a convenient means of creating standard computing policies throughout the organization.

Networks also change the way people work. By bringing together different departments and workgroups, the social and organizational structure of an organization becomes more focused. This approach also provides a way for users and managers enterprise-wide to work more closely with one another.

> **NOTE** For more information about organizations and societies, see Chapter 13.

Metropolitan Area Networks

Metropolitan area networks (MANs) typically interconnect two or more local area networks within a campus, city, or Local Access and Transport Area (LATA). A LATA is a geographical area within which a local telephone company may offer local or long distance telecommunications service up to a range of 20 or 30 miles. This means that MANs are technically confined to local calling areas. However, MANs can stretch to cover hundreds of square miles, linking to other telecommunications providers' networks.

MANs operate at higher speeds than LANs and can achieve transfer rates up to 155Mbps. MANs provide an integrated set of network services for real-time data, voice, and image transmission. The IEEE 802.6 standard defines an optical-fiber, dual-bus architecture in which two fiber cables provide data transmissions in opposite directions simultaneously. Failures in the network are automatically reconfigured until repairs can be made.

Wide Area Networks

Network services provided by local and long distance communications carriers link geographically remote LANs or MANs. These interconnected networks are collectively known as wide area networks (WANs).

WANs can use private or public networks. Private networks consist of switching and communications equipment that is owned by the organization. This can help maintain a certain level of security and control over traffic that is transmitted over the network. Public networks are operated by telecommunications carriers and switching is handled directly by the carrier's network equipment. When there is not enough data traffic to justify dedicated leased lines and a private network, public networks can efficiently and cost-effectively serve the organization.

Deployment of LAN internetworks over WANs to branch offices and remote sites introduces many challenges. There are numerous issues to be considered when linking LANs to form wide area networks, including, but not limited to, bandwidth availability for applications, protocol conflicts, management of the enterprise-wide network, and the impact of the technology on corporate culture.

Internetworks

Internetworks can be workgroup or departmental LANs using different network operating systems that are connected together to form larger networks such as private, enterprise networks. Internetworks can also be made up of WANs using public telecommunications networks such as the Internet. These networks, when managed by a single organization, are also referred to as enterprise networks. Two examples of large internetworks that are being designed, tested, and implemented are the National Information Infrastructure (NII) and the Global Information Infrastructure (GII). These are often referred to as information super-highways.

> **NOTE** For more information about network operating systems, see Chapter 4. For information about the Internet and information superhighways such as the NII and GII, see Chapter 11.

PLANNING

The planning stage is vital when implementing a new network or upgrading an existing one. To effectively establish a technology strategy, you need a clear understanding of the needs and requirements of the organization that the technology will serve. Just as important is your ability to recognize the objectives in using the technology.

The end result of the planning stage should be an integrated business and technology plan and budget. The plan and budget should closely match technology requirements against defined needs and capabilities. In addition, the risks and benefits of the technologies themselves must be clearly defined and understood.

There are five important stages in this discovery process we call planning a network. The first stage establishes the project agenda and defines the planning team and its leadership. The next two stages assess the needs and capabilities of the enterprise. The third stage balances the needs against the capabilities. The final stage compiles, analyzes, and documents all of this information in a project plan and combines it with a project budget and schedule.

Establishing the Project

Networking projects do not arise out of thin air. They arise downstream in the chain of events and decisions that proceed from the recognition of organizational needs by management for which the solution is defined in terms of a networking innovation or change.

The old adage often holds true for network planning: if it ain't broke, don't fix it. This is especially true if the problem is inappropriately defined purely in terms of not having the latest technology. However, determining the problem in organizational terms does not always fit the adage. Certainly, there are improvements to networking infrastructure that arise from aging or obsolete technology that cannot meet the demands for which it was designed.

There are also many other problems that are identified by management as part of the change and growth of the organization for which networking provides a solution. This is becoming increasingly true in an era where information is the service and networking is its infrastructure. For example, it may be the need to reach new markets through electronic commerce on information superhighways or expanding the communications and productivity for a globally dispersed workforce.

However the problem is discovered and defined, the determination of the solution generally proceeds from upper management and involves internal or external technology consulting.

Before the networking project can be officially initiated, a project leader and team must be established. Many case studies have shown that the project and team must also have the clear endorsement and commitment by upper management. This can be communicated through internal publications, meetings, and special events, but it also must be sustained throughout the entire length of the project.

Once these initial steps have been made, the networking project can get under way by assessing the needs and capabilities of the organization with respect to a networking solution.

> **NOTE** For more information about networking as an innovation and other organizational issues, see Chapter 13.

Assessing Needs

By evaluating the feedback gathered during this step of the planning process, it is possible to fully assess the needs of individual users, workgroups, and other organizational groups. This helps ensure that the resulting network infrastructure and network applications will provide the tools and methods of communication that are compatible with users and, thus, likely to be used.

Conduct User Interviews

The best way to determine the needs of the organization is to talk to the people who will actually be exposed to the changes associated with the networking innovation. Sure, meeting with executives and managers is just as important, but the people who will use the network most should be your main focus when performing a needs analysis.

Computer users in organizations are often frustrated with access and performance of their networks and applications. They express this frustration among themselves, but also by expressing tacit compliance, by resisting certain changes related to the network innovations, or in the extreme, by avoiding the use of computing resources completely. One reason is because they are often not allowed to be part of the solution. Too often, top-down innovations avoid their feedback and participation during the planning stages of network design. Of particular importance is getting advice and gaining support from opinion leaders, no matter what their formal status may be within the organization.

> **NOTE** For more information about organizational and social issues, see Chapter 13.

Define System Requirements

Defining system requirements is accomplished by detailing the technical and organizational requirements of the project. This is similar to creating the functional specification described in Chapter 1. This document becomes an important plan that should be reviewed by all members of the design and implementation team.

These requirements also form the basis for later acceptance testing and can be used to provide vendors with the information they need to properly bid on the project.

Perform Site Surveys

The site survey is a procedure that provides important information about the physical location where a new network is to be implemented. Space requirements for wiring closets, computer rooms, and office and cubicle locations can be gathered from the site survey.

When planning for upgrades in existing networks, the site survey becomes an analysis of the current network's status as well as an opportunity to examine possible strategic improvements. Questions such as the number of workstations requiring hardware and software upgrades for new applications, building modifications to accommodate new computing resources, or network services requirements for WAN connectivity can be answered after the site survey is performed.

Determine Security Requirements

Today's network environment is much different than those of 20 years ago. Security threats came from within the organization by way of authorized users who misused accounts, theft, vandalism, etc.

Breaches in network security can occur for any number of reasons. However, they happen most often because the important step of creating security policies and procedures is skipped. These policies and procedures should conform to the organizational and business needs of the organization to be truly effective. The following steps should be considered when creating a security policy and implementation plan:

- Determine what must be protected and from whom or what.

- Determine how likely security threats are and what the risk and costs of a breach in security would be to the organization.

- Determine how the organization will prevent and respond to security threats.

- Review the above steps continuously, improving the process every time a weakness is found.

    NOTE For more information about security, see Chapters 9, 10, and 12.

Develop Contingency Plans

As already mentioned, planning a networking project must allow for iteration that is both a refinement and a means of contingency for field effects that occur when the plan is implemented.

These contingencies should outline events that may influence this change and what the anticipated responses will be. These must be expressed not only in specific actions, but also in terms of financial, time, and resource expenditures.

Assessing Capabilities

Understanding the capabilities of the enterprise provides a way to leverage existing as well as future assets. Too often, technology is deployed before an organization's capabilities are clearly defined. Yet when capabilities are understood, it is much easier to assess the costs and benefits associated with design and deployment of new technology.

Many companies have organizational assets they may not be aware of, such as remote access capabilities, underutilized qualified technical personnel or network resources. With patience and a little detective work, these capabilities can be brought to light, providing new insights into the development of strategic technology and business plans. Can you think of any hidden capabilities in your organization?

Balancing Needs and Capabilities

Once the assessment of needs and capabilities is completed, approved by the necessary authorities, and documented, business and technical plans can be developed.

Sharing Knowledge

It is important for technical personnel to be closely involved with executives and managers forging the business plan. One benefit of this is the expertise technical team members can bring to the table.

Technical team members are a good source for information about specific technologies and the costs for procurement and implementation.

They can also be of great help when defining specific risks associated with certain technologies. Evaluating information from both technical and non-technical team members can help determine how the technologies in question suit the needs of the organization This can be immensely helpful when developing a strategic networking plan.

Creating a Project Plan

The design and implementation of a new network infrastructure or upgrade cannot succeed without a detailed project plan.

The project plan is a formal document that identifies the business plan that has been formulated prior to and during the planning stage. The wording of this plan should be expressed in organizational terms and should be authored or at least approved by upper management associated with its development.

This document should initially define the project goals and schedule in business terms, including start and end dates for specific tasks and the resources assigned to carry them out.

Plan the Design and Implementation

With the planning stage nearly completed, with respect to identifying the problem and initially defining the solution, specific plans must be made for the crucial design and implementation stages. One of the most important components of the project plan is the determination how certain tasks will be accomplished in terms of resources and personnel.

Project Management

Because of the iterative nature of network design and implementation, the timeline between different stages of a project's life cycle can change frequently. Project management software can help organize projects of any size and offers powerful resource-handling, costing, and scheduling capabilities. More recent project management applications offer networking features that let managers share information about projects and coordinate employees and other resources assigned to those projects, including schedules, milestones, reporting, etc.

Most important, though, is communication and teamwork. If everyone involved with a project communicates issues and concerns on a regular basis, the chances of projects being on time and within budget are increased.

Create an Acceptance Plan

This acceptance plan forms the basis of testing that occurs during the subsequent stages of the project. It is based on the technical and organizational requirements gathered during the needs assessment stage.

Defining a Budget

The project budget should be the result of financial planning and coordination with internal and external technology consultants. It should be a written document which specifies all of the anticipated costs and contingencies associated with the project: manpower, construction (physical, electrical, environmental, etc.), network hardware and software, network services for WAN, etc.

It should be subject to analysis and approval by upper management and all financial and technology decision-makers associated with the business plan.

Final determination and approval of the budget should follow the design stage. The final document should record any changes that were made from the initial to final form of the budget for auditing and other purposes.

DESIGN

Networks that can grow with increased demand (scalable) and function across different hardware and software platforms (interoperable) are the result of good planning and design strategies.

Design strategies are shaped from information gathered during the planning stage. It is at this stage of the network design and implementation process where network technologies and components are selected and quantified.

All vendors from which the organization would like a quote, including support and maintenance providers, are presented with functional specifications and requests for quotes (RFQs) are submitted. Network services for wide area connectivity are evaluated and security requirements are developed at this stage. Cost analysis and budgeting are performed as a final step.

NOTE For more information about RFQs, see Chapter 1.

Logical and Physical Designs

The logical design is the conceptual model of the organization's requirements for network hardware and software, network applications, and interconnectivity options (e.g., WAN). It can include data flow-charts and high-level network diagrams. These tasks can be performed with any of the graphics and network drawing packages such as Visio, NetViz, ClickNet, and others.

If the project involves a network upgrade, this is the point in the process where existing network technologies are identified and evaluated for use in the new network. The logical design will serve as a foundation for the physical design.

The physical design includes detailed construction plans, network diagrams, descriptions of network components, financial estimates for each piece of the network (e.g., media, network hardware, software, services, etc.). Electrical and environmental requirements (e.g., telephone/wiring closets, grounding information, uninterruptable power supply (UPS) specifications, air conditioning and heating requirements, etc.) are included in the physical design as well.

Network Design Tools

Network design tools are instrumental in helping to create the physical design of a network. These software tools run on several platforms and addresses a broad range of network planning tasks. With the aid of network design tools, design strategies can be developed to identify possible enhancements in network performance and reliability and can help provide insight into possible solutions to other complex network design problems.

One example of network and workflow simulation design tool is Prophesy, from The Abstraction Software Company (see netref 1). Prophesy allows users to simulate their respective LAN and WAN environments for day-to-day management optimizations and to make educated guesses on ways to improve or solve performance issues before making expenditures. These tools can help answer the following types of questions:

- What will be the response time of a workstation if an additional server is not installed?

- How many workstations can be serviced by the current server configuration?

- What is the impact on the system if one or more network components fail?

Documenting the Installation

A complete set of documents and diagrams keeps track of how the network is built. Flow charts, detailed network diagrams, equipment spreadsheets, and network wiring diagrams should be part of the installation documentation set. This is where the project manager and members of the network design and implementation team keep track of how the project is progressing.

As equipment and services are installed and completed, it is noted in the log that is part of the documentation set. This documentation can also be used to conveniently track unfinished tasks as the project progresses and build a maintenance log for the network, its components, and services.

IMPLEMENTATION

The implementation stage is where all the planning and design work is put into action. There are quite a few steps involved in the implementation process. If the planning and design stages revealed that structural modifications were necessary to accommodate a new or upgraded network, once the necessary permits are obtained, construction can begin.

In the planning and design stages, the selection of vendors takes place. Since it is unusual for a single vendor to supply all of the equipment and services for a network project, there are usually several vendors under consideration. In the implementation stage, a specific vendor or vendors will be selected based on their responses to the RFP. Hardware, software, and services should be ordered from them at this point. Remember to build the lead-times required for shipment of hardware and software as well as installation of network services into the project schedule.

Once construction is completed, hardware and software and network services are scheduled for delivery and installation, the process of building the physical infrastructure can begin. Frequently, the project can progress while construction is actually going on.

Installing and Testing Transmission Media

The installation and testing of transmission media is an important step in the implementation process. Installation is usually performed by one cabling contractor while testing and certification are handled by another. Two contractors should be used to ensure unbiased testing of the cabling system.

At this time, it is also necessary to begin training network managers and administrators in the operation and management of the network. The physical layout of the network, including wiring closets and computer rooms, as well as network management platforms and user applications, must be fully understood by the technical managers and staff to properly support the network and the users. While training takes place, installation of the network hardware begins.

> **NOTE** For more information about transmission media, cabling contractors, and cable testing and certification, see Chapter 1. For more information about system administration and network management, see Chapter 9.

Installing and Testing Network Hardware and Software

Installing the network servers, workstations, and other network components such as bridges and routers is the next step in the implementation process. Network software and services are also deployed at this time.

The installation and testing of network services can be time-consuming, so it's best to get these carrier services in-house as soon as practical. This approach can help reduce the possibility of running past the closing date of the project because network services were not installed and tested on time.

Network Components

Typically, network components consist of servers, workstation, bridges, and routers. Often, the vendor can pre-configure workstation and server hardware so it reflects the desktop and server configurations the company requires. This can be done off-site or at the time of installation. Preloading and configuring the software can substantially reduce the time required to deploy servers and workstations. The same holds true for network components such as bridges and routers.

> **NOTE** For more information about network components, see Chapter 3.

Network Software

Depending on the network operating system being installed, there may be a requirement to separately support operating system and network operating system software on clients and servers. This is true for networks based on Novell's NetWare, for example.

Operating systems such as Microsoft's Windows NT and many UNIX-based offerings provide built-in networking functions and do not require a separate operating system to function. Enabling enhanced features, such as domain name systems (DNS) or shared file systems, is a matter of loading and configuring the required software modules included with the software.

NOTE For more information about operating systems and network operating systems, see Chapter 4. For more information about DNS, see Chapter 10.

Network Services

Network services such as frame relay and ATM provide ways to interconnect remote sites or access outside service companies, such as market data or payroll services. Network services require careful planning as well as installation lead time and testing.

For example, while data terminal equipment (DTE) on an analog network usually consists of a modem, things are slightly different when using digital services. Digital systems require the use of a channel service unit (CSU) or data service unit (DSU), depending on line speed. In most installations, integrated CSU/DSU's are commonly used.

NOTE For more information about frame relay, ATM, and CSU/DSUs, see Chapter 5.

It is critical that desired bandwidth is matched to network application requirements when planning and designing the network. For example, a database application performing hundreds of reads and writes to compile a report might use a good portion of the available bandwidth on a digital line. The telecommunications carriers supplying network services can be of great help in this area if the organization lacks the technical expertise to perform these analyses.

NOTE For more information about bandwidth, see Chapter 1. For more information about network applications, see Chapter 8.

Acceptance Testing

Once the network implementation is completed, the network has to be tested to ensure it meets the expectations of management and end-users, performs properly, and fulfills the goals of the organization as defined in the planning stage.

Administration and Maintenance

This step determines how the network is taken care of once it has been installed.

Network Administration

As the network implementation progresses, it is imperative that the network managers and administrators trained early on in the implementation phase are ready and able to assume responsibility for the day-to-day operation of the network.

> **NOTE** For more information about system administration, see Chapter 9.

Maintenance Services

While administration of day-to-day items such as backups and network infrastructure support is usually handled by in-house technical personnel, hardware and software maintenance services are usually outsourced to a third-party maintenance provider. There are several approaches to securing outside maintenance services.

Basic maintenance programs help ensure consistent system availability by providing all the parts and labor needed to restore malfunctioning new or used equipment to proper operating condition. This service is usually contracted at a fixed yearly cost. With time and materials programs, the company pays only for the specific services performed by service provider's technicians, systems engineers, and consultants. Some organizations contract for on-site technicians from a maintenance provider. This approach places a full-time or part-time technician employed by the service provider at the company's location to provide on-going service.

Training

Training users and technical staff to use and support the network and network applications maximizes the company's investment in information technology. It can also improve efficiency.

Training can be provided by in-house systems staff or peer-to-peer programs. It can also be supplemented using training providers and consultants to meet high-demand training needs. These needs are often realized with the implementation of a network innovation and its associated change.

Documenting the Network

Documenting the network infrastructure of an organization is one of the most important but often-forgotten steps in the process of network design and implementation.

Using the set of documentation developed during the implementation stage as a foundation, a complete reference of the network hardware, software, components, and services should be assembled. This reference serves as a user guide, technical support manual, and maintenance record for users, management, and technical staff.

As with training, the documentation can be provided to some degree by in-house systems personnel, but unless there are trained technical writers on staff, this work should be subcontracted to technical writers.

REFERENCES

Net References

1. www to http://www.csn.net/abstraction/ then browse for more information about Prophesy, the Windows-based network and workflow simulation system.

Suggested Reading

Miller, Mark. 1995. *Internetworking: A Guide to Network Communications LAN to LAN; LAN to WAN, Second Edition*. NY: M&T Books.

Schatt, S. 1993. *Understanding Local Area Networks, Fourth Edition*. Indianapolis, IN: Sams Publishing.

Madron, T. 1994. *Local Area Networks: New Technologies, Emerging Standards, Third Edition*. NY: Wiley.

Martin, J. 1994. *Local Area Networks, Second Edition*. Englewood Cliffs, NJ: PTR Prentice-Hall.

7

Protocols

ABOUT THIS CHAPTER

Protocols define the nature of network communications. When they
become widely adopted by vendors and developers, they become de facto
standards. When you employ them, you achieve interoperability. This is
a key to strategic networking.

Some of the most popular protocols are described in this chapter:
transmission, management, messaging, Internet, and routing protocols.
These are the rules and standards that are used to move information over
the network.

INTRODUCTION

Protocols are a collection of rules and procedures that control the transmission of data between devices. Network devices that need to communicate must use protocols to understand each other and exchange data,
just as two people speaking different languages use an interpreter.

The essence of a protocol is that two computers follow an agreed-upon
set of rules for sending and receiving electronic messages to minimize
transmission errors (Myers, 1995).

Selecting Protocols

Selecting protocols when designing networks is a serious issue. In today's
fast-paced business world, many networks are often deployed without
strategic planning in this area. Similarly, software that requires specific
protocol support must be implemented with regard to the effects these
added protocols may have on the organization or network. Skipping
these important steps produces networks that are essentially a tangle of
protocols that are difficult to manage and support.

When planning a network, make sure you've matched the features,
benefits, and risks associated with selected protocols to the needs and
capacities of the organization, as well as those of the network users. This
approach helps build networks that are used instead of avoided.

> **NOTE** For more information about needs assessment, see
> Chapter 6.

TRANSPORT AND NETWORK PROTOCOLS

To transmit data over a network, protocols split data files into small
blocks, or packets. When a packet is transmitted, the receiving device
checks the arriving packet to make sure it is not damaged (e.g., lost or
changed data). If the packet is good, an acknowledgment is sent to the
workstation that originated the data packet and the session terminates.

However, if the packet is checked by the receiving device and found to be damaged, the sending device is instructed to retransmit the packet until it has been received error-free. Protocols keep errors in check using a mathematical technique that measures the data packets to make sure they've arrived perfectly.

Transport protocols provide end-to-end data exchanges where network devices maintain a session or connection with each other. This is done to ensure a reliable exchange of data. Network protocols handle addressing and routing information, error control, and requests for retransmission. These protocols function at the Transport and Network layers of the OSI model.

Routable and Non-Routable Protocols

Routable protocols are used primarily to move data beyond the boundaries of a single LAN. They use a layering structure that is very close to the OSI model, specifically the Network layer. Routable protocols learn about network connections and select the most efficient path or link for data to travel between any two network devices. They can also dynamically choose an alternate path if one should fail. Routable protocols include TCP/IP and Novell's IPX/SPX.

> **NOTE** For more information about the OSI model, see Chapter 6.

Non-routable protocols use a layering structure that is different from the OSI model. They do not use Network layer addresses when identifying network devices. Thus, they can not directly manage the flow of data between LANs. Instead, non-routable protocols are used when traffic is confined to a single network or LAN. There are techniques available that make it possible to route the data associated with non-routable protocols over interconnected LANs. Non-routable protocols include NetBIOS and SNA/APPN.

TCP/IP

Networks using the TCP/IP (Transmission Control Protocol/Internet Protocol) were designed in the 1970s to provide a method of communication between different hosts participating in the government's Advanced Research Projects Agency Network (ARPANET). This network was the foundation for the Internet.

NOTE For more information about the Internet, see Chapter 11.

TCP is a connection-oriented Transport layer protocol that uses the connectionless services of IP to ensure the reliable delivery of data. Connection-oriented services establish a link between two devices on a LAN. This link stays active for the length of a data transmission and can be closed when the transfer is finished. With connectionless services, there is no requirement to establish a link between a source and destination device before data transmission can begin. Connectionless services are capable of sending data packets to multiple destinations, while connection-oriented services can not.

TCP/IP caught on very quickly mainly because it provided important services such as file transfer, e-mail, and remote login across a large number of distributed client and server systems. TCP/IP was introduced with UNIX and then it was later incorporated into the IBM environment.

To ensure that multi-vendor, multi-platform systems could communicate, the original design of TCP/IP was based on Open System Standards. Because of this design, TCP/IP is platform independent in that it operates in a similar manner no matter what the platform. This is synonymous with interoperability, a key strategy for choosing and using protocols.

Novell IPX/SPX

The Internetwork Packet Exchange (IPX) is a NetWare protocol used to move data across a Novell (see netref 1) network. The IPX packet deals directly with routers to move data across Novell NetWare internetworks. IPX is a result of Novell's efforts to add new services and features to the original Xerox XNS protocols.

IPX uses the Sequenced Packet Exchange (SPX) protocol to provide applications with a reliable, connection-oriented data transport service. In the OSI model, IPX conforms to the Network layer and SPX the Transport layer.

The terms reliable and unreliable are often associated with connection-oriented and connectionless services, but this shouldn't be taken to mean one is good while the other is bad. Let's look at an example to clarify this. A connection-oriented service is said to be reliable because it guarantees the delivery of data. Yet, if a high number of transmission failures caused the connection to be frequently terminated, the data would still be transmitted reliably, but delays from these interruptions would make the overall use of the service unreliable.

On the other hand, with an unreliable connectionless service, the delivery of data is not guaranteed. Even though the service might deliver nine out of ten data packets successfully, none of the deliveries are officially checked so you would never know if the data actually arrived. Protocols are sometimes paired, such as TCP and IP, to provide for reliable deliveries that ensure data integrity.

IPX is available on a wide variety of platforms today and is fairly easy to implement. Several UNIX products, including Univel's UnixWare, now support IPX.

> **NOTE** For more information about the OSI model, see Chapter 6. For more information about UnixWare, see Chapter 4.

Multiple Protocols

A network interface card (NIC) can accept input from only one hardware driver at a time, which means that a NIC can only support a single protocol at any given time. However, separating the hardware operations of the NIC from the protocols themselves allows software to be developed that enables several protocols to share the NIC's resources simultaneously.

Vendors such as Microsoft, Novell, and 3COM recognized the need for multi-protocol support on a single NIC and developed device drivers to address this need. A device driver is a software application that extends an operating system's ability to work with peripherals.

ODI

The Open Data-link Interface (ODI), developed by Novell and Apple, provides concurrent support for multiple protocols on a single NIC. It also allows network devices to communicate with other devices throughout the network, such as file servers and workstations, without rebooting.

A strategic use of ODI is a workstation that connects to a Novell NetWare network running IPX/SPX as well as a UNIX network running TCP/IP. ODI provides the capability for one transport protocol to run over different network adapters. Thus IPX/SPX could be run over both Ethernet and token-ring topologies, creating an interoperable network out of two independent ones.

> **NOTE** For more information about Novell NetWare, see Chapter 4. For more information about Ethernet and token-ring, see Chapter 2.

NDIS

The Network Driver Interface Specification (NDIS) was developed by Microsoft and 3COM. NDIS offers support for up to four NICs in a single workstation and each NIC can support up to four protocol stacks. A protocol stack is a group of drivers that work together to span the layers in a network protocol hierarchy such as TCP/IP and OSI. Thus, multiprotocol stacks can address a single NIC or individual protocols can address their own NIC. ODI and NDIS are used frequently in Novell and other PC-based networks.

NetBIOS

NetBIOS (Network Basic Input/Output System) is a network protocol designed exclusively for use in LANs. It was originally designed by IBM and Microsoft for the IBM PC LAN program as an API (Application Programming Interface). NetBIOS, along with its API, provide support of peer-to-peer network functions and a simple interface for writing network applications.

There is no routing layer in NetBIOS (or NetBEUI, described below). This means that NetBIOS cannot provide internetworking capabilities. Other protocols such as IP or IPX must be used for internetworking. NetBIOS provides session and transport services (layers 4 and 5 of the OSI model), thus NetBIOS is often used to establish a connection between devices.

The frame format of NetBIOS was never standardized for transmission over a network. This lack of interoperability prevented communication between different network vendors' products and resulted in proprietary implementations of NetBIOS being created such as the version used by Artisoft's LANtastic, for transmission between clients and servers. The NetBIOS frame format was later formalized in NetBEUI.

NetBEUI

NetBIOS Extended User Interface, or NetBEUI (pronounced net-booey), is the native network protocol used by Microsoft's Windows NT (see netref 2) and Windows 95 (see netref 3). NetBEUI is an enhanced version of the NetBIOS protocol used by network operating systems (NOS) such as LAN Manager and LAN Server.

NOTE For more information about NOS, see Chapter 4.

Systems that use NetBEUI, such as Windows NT, can communicate with other Windows NT systems as well as workstations running Windows for Workgroups. Windows NT uses NetBEUI to handle services such as disk and printer sharing over the network. It also supports NetBEUI in Microsoft's Win32 and Windows 95 API (Application Programming Interface). This allows developers to use network communications in their applications.

SNA/APPN

System Network Architecture/Advanced Peer-to-Peer Networking (SNA/APPN) is IBM's proprietary networking protocol. SNA was introduced by IBM (see netref 4) in 1974 and was designed to operate at the Data Link layer of the OSI model. Originally, SNA networks were centralized architectures with a host computer controlling many terminals.

APPN was announced as an enhancement to SNA to provide support for distributed applications in IBM networks such as such as mainframes, AS/400s, and PS/2s. APPN enables direct communication between users anywhere on the network, a feature SNA could not provide.

> **NOTE** For more information about SNA servers, see Chapter 10.

SDLC

The Synchronous Data Link Control (SDLC) protocol was defined by IBM to facilitate communication over WAN links to IBM hosts in SNA environments. SDLC is the primary serial link protocol for SNA and is a superset of the High-level Data Link Control protocol (HDLC).

The primary station is responsible for establishing and maintaining links. Thus, in SDLC, a primary station controls the operation of secondary stations. Secondary stations are periodically polled by the primary station to see if they have data to send. If a secondary station has data, it transmits when acknowledged by the primary station.

An example of a typical SDLC configuration would be remote dumb terminals in a bank branch connected to cluster controllers. The cluster controllers connect to the host (mainframe) system at headquarters via a dedicated communications link.

MANAGEMENT PROTOCOLS

SNMP/SNMP-2

The Simple Network Management Protocol (SNMP) is an industry standard network monitoring and control protocol. Data is passed to network management consoles by way of SNMP agents. These agents can be hardware or software processes that report activity occurring in network devices such as hubs, bridges, and routers. The management console is the client side of network management software that provides the user interface and in-depth views of a network.

The information the agents forward to network management consoles is contained in a Management Information Base, or MIB. A MIB is a configuration that defines what information can be obtained from a network device and what functions can be controlled, such as turning the unit on and off.

SNMP 2 provides enhancements to the original SNMP, such as security and an RMON (Remote Monitoring MIB), which provides continuous feedback without having to be queried by the SNMP console. SNMP is widely deployed in TCP/IP networks. SMTP is transport independent, however, because it is not limited to TCP/IP networks.

> **NOTE** For more information about network management consoles and system administration, see Chapter 9.

MESSAGING PROTOCOLS AND INTERFACES

Mail protocols determine the way e-mail is sent and received. There are standard protocols that are used for internetworks and proprietary protocols used by vendors for LAN and enterprise messaging.

E-mail systems are made up of four components: the mail client, the message store, the message transfer agent (MTA), and directory services. E-mail enabled applications usually work with the message store part of an e-mail system via an application program interface or API. Mail enabled applications provide features such as forms routing, work flow, and scheduling, and use mail functions to actually route the forms or to send meeting requests to users on a network (see netref 5).

> **NOTE** For more information about e-mail, see Chapter 8.

Leading APIs for PC-based e-mail include Microsoft's Messaging Application Programming Interface (MAPI), Lotus Development Corp.'s Vendor Independent Messaging (VIM), Common Messaging Calls (CMC) from the X.400 API Association, and Novell's Standard Message Format (SMF) from NetWare MHS.

Mail Protocols

POP

POP, the Post Office Protocol (currently POP3), is used largely to read mail from a POP mail server. The mail server stores any mail directed to the user until the mail client software requests it.

SMTP

SMTP, the Simple Mail Transport Protocol, is an Application layer protocol designed to transfer mail from a sending client to a receiving server. SMTP can relay mail between servers on different systems, providing an SMTP server exists on those systems.

SMTP does not define how mail is sent from a mail application to SMTP, the actual format of the mail message, or how the mail is delivered to an intended receiver. SMTP is concerned only with the transfer that occurs between two SMTP processes (the sending client and receiving server).

> **NOTE** For more information about the seven layers of the OSI model, see Chapter 6.

SMTP manages transactions in three steps. First, a connection between the client and server is established. Next, mail is transferred across the connection. Finally, the connection is closed. Here's how a typical SMTP exchange might look:

The transaction begins with a MAIL command that delivers the sender's identification. One or more RCPT commands follow the MAIL command. The RCPT command provides receiver information. Finally, a DATA command delivers the actual mail data. The transaction ends with an end of mail data message, confirming the end of transmission. Request for Comment (RFC) 821 describes this procedure in detail (see netref 6).

Mail Interfaces

MAPI

Microsoft's MAPI (Mail API) is a programming interface that enables an application to send, address, and receive messages, integrating applications with electronic messaging systems. MAPI is part of Microsoft's WOSA (Windows Open Services Architecture) and can be used only on the Windows platform.

VIM

The VIM (Vendor-Independent Messaging) interface is a cross-platform protocol and interface that supports Windows, OS/2, DOS, and Macintosh. The VIM interface definition is the charter of the VIM consortium. Lotus, Apple, Borland, IBM, Novell, and WordPerfect are current members of the VIM consortium.

CMC

CMC, or Common Messaging Calls, is an Application Programming Interface (API) that provides the three fundamental capabilities required to add messaging functionality to an application. They are the ability to send messages, read messages, and translate names into messaging addresses.

CMC was developed by XAPIA, the X.400 Application Program Interface Association, which introduced the first CMC interface in 1993. It is designed for applications that rely on the store-and-forward features provided by many messaging systems. CMC can be used to develop cross-platform, interoperable applications. This is because applications written to CMC standards operate independent of a particular operating system or messaging system.

MHS/SMF

Message Handling Service (MHS) is a native messaging system from Novell that provides support for multiple operating systems and messaging protocols. MHS uses a standard directory structure for sending and receiving messages called the Standard Messaging Format (SMF).

An SMF message consists of three parts: the envelope, the message heading, and the message body. The envelope tells the Message Transfer Agent (MTA), which is the store-and-forward part of a messaging system, how to process the message. The message heading is used to pass important information to the receiving application, such as where the message came from and where it's going. Finally, the message body consists of plain text or structured text, depending on the application used to create the message.

Ordinarily, an organization running e-mail services on a LAN dedicates a workstation to function as a MHS gateway. The gateway can be configured to exchange e-mail with users on different e-mail systems that implement MHS. This approach simplifies the exchange of e-mail between organizations using different e-mail platforms and is a good example of interoperability.

Conferencing Protocols

The T.120 Protocols for Audiographic Conferencing (see netref 7) were ratified by the International Telecommunications Union (ITU). They are a standard series of communication and application protocols and services that provide support for real-time, multi-point data communications. These protocols also ensure that different applications can communicate and that they can coexist on the same machine.

In essence, it means that many users can simultaneously communicate. It also means that software and hardware products ranging from conferencing software, telecommunications devices and bridging services, video digitizers, and data projectors can be interoperable with each other if they all conform to this standard.

INTERNET AND APPLICATION PROTOCOLS

These protocols provide application-to-application data exchanges. They function at the Application, Session, and Presentation layers of the OSI model.

SLIP

SLIP (Serial Line Internet Protocol) is an Internet protocol designed to transmit IP (Internet Protocol) packets over a serial link, such as a private telephone line. Using SLIP to connect to the Internet provides dial-up users with a way to have their own Internet location or domain name (see netref 6).

Thus, a SLIP user's Internet address would look the same as if he or she were directly connected. For example, the workstation called station1 connects to an Internet provider with a domain name of sne.com. The SLIP user's Internet address becomes user@station1.sne.com.

> **NOTE** For more information about Internet addressing and domain names, see Chapter 9.

While SLIP has become very popular over the years, it has not been adopted by a standards body. In addition, SLIP does not offer multi-protocol support or other important features as does the more recent PPP (Point-to-Point Protocol) described next. When a network is built on an IP-only foundation, SLIP is a good choice. However, if a network runs more than one protocol, PPP is a better choice because of its ability to support multiple protocols such as DECnet, IPX, IP, and AppleTalk.

PPP

PPP (see netref 6) is the Internet Standard for transmission of IP packets over serial lines. The Point-to-Point Protocol (PPP) was developed by the Internet Engineering Task Force (IETF) in 1991. More advanced than the earlier SLIP protocol, PPP is used over low-speed dial-up lines as well as high-speed T-1 links. PPP provides password-protection using the Password Authentication Protocol (PAP) and the Challenge Handshake Authentication Protocol (CHAP).

PPP can also be used to encapsulate common Network layer protocols in specialized Network Control Protocol packets. It effectively replaces the network adapter driver that allows remote users to log on to a network as if they were locally connected. Standards for transporting protocols such as IP, AppleTalk, and IPX over PPP are publicly available.

PPP is becoming widely accepted by users and vendors alike. For example, Microsoft provides PPP implementations in Windows NT and Windows 95.

> **NOTE** For more information about Windows NT and Windows 95, see Chapter 4.

HTTP

The HyperText Transport Protocol (HTTP) (see netref 8) is the protocol used since 1990 as the basis for the World Wide Web (WWW). The World Wide Web (see netref 9) is a distributed hypermedia system and is enjoying enormous popularity among Internet users.

HTTP was originally conceived by an organization called CERN (Conseil Europeen pour la Recherche Nucleaire). It is widely used in distributed, collaborative, hypermedia information systems. CERN's formal name is now the European Laboratory for Particle Physics, based in Geneva (see netref 10).

The HyperText Markup Language (HTML) is used to create the hypermedia documents transmitted by HTTP. HTML documents can include graphics, audio, formatted text, and even video (see netref 11).

NOTE For more information about the Internet and World Wide Web, see Chapter 11. For more information about hypermedia and HTML, see Chapter 8.

Although designed for use over the Internet, HTTP can provide distributed information services for use within an organization as well as externally. For example, a company could produce a training guide complete with hypertext links to related training materials or a sales brochure with links to more detailed product and service information. This approach provides a low-cost method of distributing information that is easy to update.

Using an Internet browser, such as Netscape Communications Corp.'s Netscape Navigator (see netref 12), a user could request a specific Web server and page. This is done using a Uniform Resource Locator, or URL. URLs represent different documents, media, and network services on the Web.

MIME

Once a link is established between the browser and Web server the browser passes information to the server about the types of data, called MIME (pronounced Me-Me) types, that it can handle. MIME stands for Multipurpose Internet Mail Extensions, which are simply extensions to SMTP that allow it to carry multiple types of data (e.g., audio, video, binary, etc.). The requested information is transmitted and the link is terminated. These activities are all controlled by HTTP.

S-HTTP

HTTP offers many functional features. However, one of the most important features, security, is lacking. Modifications to HTTP are being introduced to address this shortcoming, such as the Secure HyperText Transport Protocol (S-HTTP) (see netref 13).

S-HTTP is an extension of HTTP that provides much needed security services for transaction confidentiality, authenticity, and integrity between HTTP clients and servers. This is particularly important to organizations and users wishing to transact business over the Internet.

Secure HTTP authenticates a client's identity through digital signature verification and other features and only works with transactions that use the HTTP transfer protocol. S-HTTP is endorsed by the IETF and the World Wide Web Consortium.

When a S-HTTP-capable browser requests access to a secure document on a server, the server sends the browser what's known as a public key. The browser issues a second encrypted request to see the document with that public key and then returns it to the server. The server then decodes the encrypted request with its private key. The server's private key is the only key that can decrypt the browser's request. Using this method with online forms provides a secure means of sending sensitive information, such as a credit-card number, to a server.

NNTP

The Network News Transport Protocol (NNTP) is an extension of TCP/IP that provides a network news transport service for the distribution, inquiry, retrieval, and posting of Usenet news articles over the Internet. It is designed to be used between a news reader client such as NetManage's NewtNews and a news server.

NNTP-compatible servers exchange and update items for all or selected newsgroups across LANs and WANs. This process usually occurs at night, and provides users with the latest news articles in over 10,000 newsgroups each morning.

NNTP is an ASCII text protocol. Thus, a newsreader application is not necessary to connect to a news server. For example, using the telnet utility, you can connect to the news server by entering commands in the following format: telnet servername.

The term servername in this example should be replaced by the name of your news server. Typing HELP fetches a list of additional commands. The original NNTP standard proposal was published in RFC-977 (see netref 6).

ftp

ftp (File Transfer Protocol) (see netref 6) was first developed in the early 1970s at MIT. It provides a way to log in to another Internet site to retrieve or send files via TCP/IP. Files can contain binary or ASCII text. They may be transferred one by one or in multiples. ftp also provides the user with various functions such as changing, creating, deleting, and listing the contents of directories.

There are many Internet sites that have established publicly accessible repositories of material that can be obtained using ftp. This is accomplished by logging in using the account name anonymous. Thus, these sites are known as anonymous ftp servers.

ROUTING PROTOCOLS

Routers operate at the Network layer of the OSI model. Therefore, they must be able to recognize the protocols they are designed to route. A router will ignore protocol traffic it has not been assigned to handle.

Routing gateways are routers (or sometimes workstations) that join individual networks. They route data through a network by examining the destination addresses contained within data packets. These addresses are checked against entries in the device's tables. Routing tables indicate the best route to the next network or gateway. There are two types of gateway protocols: interior and exterior.

> **NOTE** For more information about the OSI model, see Chapter 6. For more information about routers, see Chapter 3.

Interior Gateway Protocols

Interior gateway protocols, or IGPs, operate within network domains or autonomous systems. An autonomous system is defined as a collection of hosts and routers that use the same routing protocol and are managed by a single organization, such as a corporation, university, or government agency.

RIP

RIP, or Routing Information Protocol, was developed by Xerox Corporation in the early 1980s for use in Xerox Network Systems (XNS) networks. Today, many PC networks use routing protocols based on RIP. While RIP functions well in smaller environments, it has limitations that must be considered when used in larger systems.

For example, RIP limits to 16 the number of router hops between any two hosts in an autonomous system. This might not be practical for an organization with hosts deployed in many locations spanning numerous internetworks. RIP is also slow to converge, which means that it takes a long time for routers to become aware of network changes. This can be troublesome, especially in situations where users make requests for critical data that is unavailable immediately because of convergence delays.

Finally, RIP decides which route is the best through an internetwork by looking at the number of hops between the two end nodes. This technique does not take into consideration factors such as link utilization, variations in line speed, and other important factors that can be considered when selecting the best path between two nodes.

OSPF

The OSPF protocol was developed by the OSPF working group of the Internet Engineering Task Force (IETF) as a replacement for RIP. Every major IP routing vendor supports OSPF.

Using information gathered from devices connected to it, a router using OSPF builds a network topology map. Periodically, these routers check to make sure their neighbors are still connected to the network and then broadcast information concerning the status of the links.

OSPF is a dynamic routing protocol that can quickly detect changes in a network, such as router failures, and calculate new routes after a period of convergence. This period of convergence is generally acceptable and involves a minimal amount of traffic re-routing.

IGRP

Cisco Systems (see netref 14) created the Interior Gateway Routing Protocol (IGRP) in the early 1980s to enable more diverse internetworks to be deployed. IGRP determines the best path through an internetwork by examining the bandwidth and delay of the networks between routers. IGRP converges faster than RIP and does not suffer from RIP's hop count limitation. Cisco's newer Enhanced IGRP is capable of handling AppleTalk and Novell IPX routing information, as well as IP routing information.

Exterior Gateway Protocols

Exterior Gateway Protocols, or EGPs, provide routing between autonomous systems.

EGP

The first widely used exterior routing protocol was the Exterior Gateway Protocol (EGP). EGP does not utilize hop-counts to make routing decisions. Hop-counts indicate the number of routers a data packet has to pass through to reach its final destination.

EGP updates specify what networks can be reached through a particular router. EGP is limited for use within complex internetworks and is being phased out in favor of routing protocols such as BGP, which endeavors to address the most serious of EGP's problems.

BGP

BGP is an inter-domain routing protocol co-authored by a Cisco Systems founder. It employs a more sophisticated routing algorithm than EGP. Cisco Systems continues to be involved in BGP development. Later revisions of BGP are designed to take on scalability issues of the growing Internet.

REFERENCES

Myers, M. 1995. "Lions, Tigers and Networks." *Data Based Advisor* 13(2):120.

Net References

1. www to http://www.novell.com/ then browse for more information about IPX on the Novell home page.

2. www to http://www.microsoft.com/BackOffice then browse for information about Windows NT and Microsoft BackOffice products.

3. For information about NetBEUI and Windows 95, www to http://www.windows.microsoft.com/windows/tryitout.htm then browse for information about NetBEUI and Windows 95.

4. www to http://www.ibm.com/ then browse for information for SNA/APPN on the IBM home page.

5. www to http://www.ema.org/ema/ema-home.htm then browse the Electronic Messaging Association home page. The Electronic Messaging Association exists to promote the development and use of secure global electronic commerce. Timely information about what's going on in the electronic messaging arena can be found here.

6. www to http://www.cis.ohio-state.edu/htbin/rfc/rfc-index.html then browse the RFC index list for the RFC by number. Click on the link to access the RFC source document. This index list contains the most recent RFCs. If you prefer to use ftp to access RFC documents, then ftp to ds.internic.net then login as anonymous and search for an RFC in the /rfc directory.

7. www to http://www.csn.net/imtc/t120.html then read and use the links (to download text in MSWord or PostScript format) in the HTML document entitled, "Overview of the T.120 Protocols for Audiographic Conferencing."

8. www to http://www.ics.uci.edu/pub/ietf/http/ then browse for information about HTTP on the IETF Hypertext Transfer Protocol (HTTP) Working Group home page.

9. www to http://www.w3.org/ then browse Web pages on the World Wide Web consortium. A huge repository of information relating to the World Wide Web can be found here.

10. www to http://www.cern.ch/ then browse for more information about CERN and its support of collaborative research and the World Wide Web.

11. For information about HTML, www to http://www.w3.org/hypertext/WWW/MarkUp/MarkUp.html then browse this document.

12. www to http://www.netscape.com/ then browse for information about Netscape Navigator on the Netscape home page.

13. For information about security on the Web, www to http://www-ns.rutgers.edu/www-security/wts-wg.html then browse the Web Transaction Security working group home page. The WTS working group is specifically tasked with developing requirements and specifications for the provision of security services to HTTP.

14. www to http://www.cisco.com/ then browse the Cisco home page for more information about Cisco products, routing protocol information, and more.

Suggested Reading

Black, U. 1993. *Computer Networks: Protocols, Standards, and Interfaces: Second Edition*. Englewood Cliffs, NJ: Prentice-Hall.

Black, U. 1995. *TCP/IP and Related Protocols, Second Edition*. NY: McGraw-Hill.

Comer, D. 1995. *Internetworking With TCP/IP, Third Edition*. Englewood Cliffs, NJ: Prentice-Hall.

Feit, S. 1995. *SNMP: A Guide To Network Management*. NY: McGraw-Hill.

Goralski, W. 1995. *TCP/IP Applications and Protocols*. Charleston, SC: Computer Technology Research Corp.

Guruge, A. 1984. *SNA: Theory and Practice—A Comprehensive Guide To IBM's Systems Network Architecture*. Maidenhead, Berkshire, England: Pergamon.

Kapoor, A. 1992. *SNA: Architecture, Protocols, and Implementation*. NY: McGraw-Hill.

Martin, J. 1994. *Local Area Networks, Second Edition*. Englewood Cliffs, NJ: Prentice-Hall.

Perlman, R. 1992. *Interconnections: Bridges and Routers*. Reading, MA: Addison-Wesley.

Randesi, S. 1992. *SNA: IBM's Systems Network Architecture*. NY: Van Nostrand Reinhold.

Stallings, W. 1993. *Networking Standards: A Guide to OSI, ISDN, LAN, and MAN Standards*. Reading, MA: Addison-Wesley.

8

Network Applications

ABOUT THIS CHAPTER

Not so very long ago, the experience of many computer users was largely defined by host-terminal or standalone applications. Even when LAN and WAN networks and applications took hold, they consisted of core business applications such as word processing, accounting, and databases. It took several years before client/server applications and internetworking reached the desktop.

This chapter takes a high-level look at some of the more popular client software applications and their underlying technologies: remote connectivity, e-mail, publishing and graphics, multimedia and hypermedia, databases, and groupware.

INTRODUCTION

One of the most important of recent trends in networking is the emergence of the network-savvy power user. Though not necessarily capable of pulling cable or administering networks, these users are becoming increasingly capable of defining and managing their work through software that exploits networking.

This trend has its roots in an underlying objective of this technology: the distribution of computing and communications resources to each user through client/server technology. It can also be traced to the need of organizations and their users to seek greater access to information that is critical to their needs. Although there will always be novices, gone are the days where every user is arbitrarily relegated to that status.

Developers have been responding to this demand by placing more emphasis on usable design and organizational fit in their software development plans and testing. Although the client/server model of network software inherently delivers more power to the user's desktop, even this distinction is being redefined in many ways. Due to changes in the workplace and the increasing demands and capabilities of users, client software features are becoming more robust and in some cases taking on functions typically associated with server applications. In other cases, developers are providing servers that, although they are not industrial-grade, can still meet the needs of users who need more control of applications through running personal servers.

> **NOTE** For information on personal and high-performance servers, see Chapter 10.

This chapter focuses on several popular categories of client applications that exploit internetworking through the use of open standards, and common formats and languages.

REMOTE CONNECTIVITY

Connectivity is an issue for any user who needs access to network resources. Although this is a given with direct connection to networks, there is need for additional support when internetwork and remote access is needed. The needs and situations of these users are varied and can change. Software and hardware that provides flexible network access must conform to open standards to accomplish interoperability with remote computers in a variety of protocols, platforms, and wired and wireless communication links.

The users may be calling from home, on the road, or through another LAN. The communications can range from plain old telephone service (POTS) to Switched 56 or ISDN, or even ATM or SMDS from fixed sites. Their need for applications and resources can range from e-mail and file transfer to full Internet access or video-conferencing.

> **NOTE** For information about network services, see Chapter 5.

Connectivity to different network environments requires the use of compatible protocols for communication. To access a NetWare LAN, you need to use the IPX protocol. To communicate with networks and systems connected through the Internet, you must employ the TCP/IP protocol suite. Although these popular protocols can provide connectivity to many systems, there are many other network protocols, such as SNA networks serving IBM mainframes, AS/400 minicomputers, and PCs.

> **NOTE** For more information about TCP/IP, IPX/SPX, SNA, and other network protocols, see Chapter 7.

There are several ways that connectivity can be provided. One or more protocols can be supported directly in the operating system (such as IPX and TCP/IP support in Windows 95), or through third-party software that is compatible with your operating system, such as with TCP/IP protocol suites.

TCP/IP Connectivity

TCP/IP has become a standard for many enterprise internetworks and the Internet. It not only provides connectivity, but it achieves interoperability through its use of open standards. Because of its wide adoption, it achieves this on a global scale among a wide diversity of software and hardware platforms.

Connectivity through Operating Systems

UNIX was the first operating system that provided native support of an internetworking protocol. TCP/IP was implemented in the UNIX operating system in the 1970s by the University of California at Berkeley and a consulting firm named Bolt, Beranek, and Newman. The U.C. Berkeley version of UNIX was the first to support popular TCP/IP utilities. Other versions of UNIX that have been developed since then all provide native support of TCP/IP.

Microsoft Windows operating systems provide direct support of TCP/IP. Windows NT server and client software and Windows 95 provide both IPX and TCP/IP connectivity. Third-party vendors such as NetManage (see below) provide compatible software for Windows 3.1 and Windows for Workgroups.

The Macintosh operating system can support TCP/IP protocols through applications such as MacTCP that executes whenever a compatible application requires TCP/IP connectivity. The OS/2 operating system with its Warp Connect versions also provides native support of TCP/IP.

> **NOTE** For information about TCP/IP support in UNIX and about operating systems, see Chapter 4.

Connectivity through Protocol Suites

Protocol suites are integrated packages of software that provide network connectivity and applications. These suites are typically designed for operating systems that do not provide full support for the TCP/IP protocol or utilities.

One of the most popular TCP/IP protocol suites is NetManage's Chameleon (see netref 1). Chameleon provides a comprehensive

Windows-based solution to the demands of multi-vendor and heterogeneous networking environments. It provides direct connection for Ethernet and token-ring networks and remote connection via SLIP and PPP. It works concurrently with Novell NetWare, Microsoft LAN Manager, Banyan VINES, and other network operating systems.

Chameleon uses a winsock stack. A stack is a program that allows Windows-based programs to operate within TCP/IP. Applications in this suite include an integrated SNMP agent, server and client for NFS, ftp, World Wide Web, and many TCP/IP client applications, including: telnet, SMTP/Mail, News Reader, Archie, TN3270 and TN5250 terminal emulators, gopher, network chat and conferencing applications, and a host of internetwork diagnostic tools.

TCP/IP protocol suites are typically included with Internet access packages. Compuserve's Internet Office (see netref 2) includes TCP/IP support in a set of applications which also provide secure LAN, WAN, and Internet connectivity. Its Network File Manger and SPRY Mosaic Web browser provide secure data transfer by supporting Internet firewalls. It is available in a family of products that vary in the number and type of applications, including those formerly available in SPRY's Air Series and Wall Data's Rhumba connectivity packages. An additional feature includes the use of the CompuServe network for international access by remote users.

Mainframe Connectivity

There are two ways to achieve remote access with mainframe and other legacy systems that employ host-terminal communications: use a server with a compatible protocol or use terminal emulation. Terminal emulation allows PCs and similar workstations to communicate as a "dumb" terminal with a host. Terminals are display devices that don't have the processing and storage features of personal computers and thus, are often called dumb terminals.

Client/Server-to-Mainframe Connectivity

Systems Network Architecture (SNA) is the predominant protocol for remote access to IBM and compatible mainframe systems. Using an SNA server provides compatible communications with a remote host while reducing demand on individual computers and the host. It achieves this by distributing the workload onto the SNA server(s).

For example, Microsoft's SNA Server provides mainframe connectivity within a client/server architecture (see netref 3). It provides communication with remote computers such as IBM mainframes, AS/400 minicomputers, and PCs on a network using the Systems Network Architecture protocol. Concurrent access is possible with more than one host (or peer).

> **NOTE** For more information about SNA and other types of servers, see Chapter 10.

Terminal Emulation

Terminal emulation can be achieved with hardware, such as adapter cards that emulate the IBM 5250 or 3270 terminals. It can also be performed strictly through software emulation.

Terminal emulation software provides direct and dial-up connections to host systems, especially legacy systems such as IBM mainframes. It displays remote host sessions complete with terminal mode functions that are adapted to workstations and PCs. These functions include the assignment of certain keys to delete or insert characters, break connections, and issue commands to the host. Terminal emulation is available in standalone software or included with data communications and protocol suite software (e.g., NetManage's Chameleon).

Rumba for the Mainframe by Wall Data (see netref 4) provides mainframe connectivity software for Windows. It lets a PC access 3270 mainframe applications and information. Network connection types include: async, SDLC, coax, and LANs. It also includes 3270 graphics terminal emulation and a graphical front-end to IBM's PROFS application. Rumba is also included in CompuServe's connectivity package, Internet Office Professional (Rumba) version.

PC and X Window System Connectivity

Interoperability is needed to communicate between popular, but distinct environments such as Microsoft Windows on the PC and the X Window System on UNIX workstations. However, because these are graphical environments, terminal emulation is not useful. A separate breed of emulator is needed.

The X Window System is a network windowing system for UNIX. In a client/server environment, an X client application on one computer can display on another computer on the network. The X Window System can support different graphical interfaces. Windows to X Window connectivity and control software provides a PC with this capability. For example, eXodus from White Pine Software (see netref 5) provides X server capabilities to a PC running Windows. eXodus is also available in a Macintosh and Power Macintosh version.

Cosession PC2X, from Triton Technologies and available through Unipress Software (see netref 6), provides X Window System to Microsoft Windows remote display and control. Using this software, you can run Windows and DOS applications from an X Window on a UNIX workstation or X terminal on a TCP/IP network. For UNIX-based systems, this can be used by system administrators and help desks to remotely service any PC on the network.

Remote Node

Remote node access software allows a remote computer to function as if it were directly connected to the network. This is achieved with a remote node server equipped with several ports to handle incoming calls from remote users.

> **NOTE** For information about remote node servers, see Chapter 10.

Each remote user must be equipped with networking software on his or her PC. The remote user dials, connects to a host, and performs a login procedure. Except for the speed of the connection, operations are the same as a direct connect to the LAN.

Remote node access can be made with modems through basic telephone or ISDN service. Remote node software converts the asynchronous single stream of data to network packets using the native protocol of the network operating system.

Multiple protocol support (IPX, TCP/IP) and high speed (through compression and high baud rate) are important features of the server. For example, having many simultaneous users or the need to process a high volume of data can slow down the system. Software that supports the use of "traps" allows the host to indicate progress of data transfer and other statuses to the remote client.

Remote Control

Remote control software is another way to provide remote access to network resources. Instead of connecting as a node, this method lets you remotely control a computer that is connected to the network via a dial-up telephone line, a direct cable connection, or from a remote, internetworked LAN.

This type of software can also be used for remotely controlling a computer that is not connected to a network. One-to-one remote control can be achieved through serial port or dial-up modem connections.

The process involves the use of remote control software installed and running on two machines: the caller and the receiver (or the remote and host computer). When using telephone lines, remote control software on the calling machine uses a modem to dial the number of a remote PC.

Once connected, keystrokes sent over the modem will control the distant PC and the software on the receiving PC will send back the corresponding changes in screen images. The actual program is executing on the receiver PC. Its capabilities and resources (including the network, if it is accessible through the receiver PC) are available to the calling PC. Over a LAN or internetwork, the remote control software uses network addressing to access a host.

A communications server is needed if more than one remote-control user needs to simultaneously access the network. Essentially, it is a single chassis that contains many PCs in the form of plug-in modules supported by a large power supply and multiplexed modem ports.

Remotely Possible/Sockets by Avalan Technology, Inc. (see netref 7) is a Windows application that operates remote systems over LAN, WAN, and Internet TCP/IP-based networks by using the Windows Sockets interface standard. It provides remote file transfer, chat mode, and printing. Besides working with direct connections, it also operates over SLIP and PPP connections.

Remote control of PCs over LANs with IPX, NetBIOS, or NetBEUI protocols is supported by the Remotely Possible/LAN version. For dial-up connectivity to control PCs via modems or other asynchronous devices, you can use the Remotely Possible/Dial version.

Symantec's pcANYWHERE (see netref 8) is a popular remote control application for DOS and Windows.

It provides remote access via network (NetWare IPX, NetBIOS, and Banyan VINES) or dial in/out through gateways. Both remote caller and host capabilities are available for computers running DOS or Windows. pcANYWHERE supports a wide variety of terminal emulation, offers security features, and can also be used as a data communications program to access a BBS or online information system.

Cosession/PC2X (mentioned above) provides connectivity, display, and remote control of a PC from an X Window System workstation or terminal on a TCP/IP network. Other products in the Cosession series provide PC-to-PC and Windows-to-Windows connectivity and remote control.

Wireless network solutions are ideal for a wide range of situations where PCs are in close range, but not amenable to cabling. These tasks can range from temporary or emergency peer networks to backups and transfers between laptops and desktop PCs. AirShare from Traveling Software (see netref 9) is composed of Remote Access software and two spread-spectrum radio transmitter/receivers that connect to the serial port of each machine. With three frequency bands to choose from to avoid interference, PCs within 30 feet can transfer files at speeds up to 115,200 bps. The Remote Access software provides drag-and-drop file management and transfer through a File Manager view of each machine.

E-MAIL

E-mail, short for electronic mail, was one of the first communications services provided on networks. As it satisfies a basic social need to communicate ideas and feelings, primarily through words in the form of messages, it is also the most popular and ubiquitous network application for this purpose.

Unlike more traditional technologies such as the mail, phone, or fax, e-mail has unique benefits for network users. As electronic messaging became widely accepted and used, the need for more enhanced messaging applications grew. Outgrowths of e-mail include network applications such as mailing lists, newsgroups, conferencing, and groupware. Thus, e-mail is an integral component of these and many other network applications.

> **NOTE** For information about mailing lists, newsgroups, and other internetwork messaging applications, see Chapter 11.

Message Format

The message format of e-mail has a two-fold purpose: it determines how message routing takes place, and it forms a record of the interactions among the machines and people through which it passes. Understanding this can help you gain more control of how you send and receive messages, and how you can examine it when problems occur.

Like a word processor document file, an e-mail message is divided into two separate sections: the body and the header. The body of an e-mail message is the content of your message. The basic format for the body of e-mail messages is readable text with only standard ASCII text-formatting symbols such as carriage return and tabs. Although many mail clients with a graphical interface allow a variety of proportional and mono-spaced fonts, this feature is largely preserved for reading. Mono-spaced text is used to accommodate a wide range of e-mail applications on diverse computing platforms.

Mail Addressing

The header of an e-mail contains addressing information that is used by the mail client to create, edit, and manage it as a document and by mail servers that direct it to its destination. The header precedes the message body and contains routing information. The header data is recognized by the applications in which it is created, as well as those to which it is transmitted and received.

It is composed of several lines that begin with a header name followed by a colon, such as To: for the destination. The information in the field that follows the colon specifies the address or other information implied by the header line. Some of this information is automatically supplied by the e-mail program and some of it is supplied by the user.

Although the exact composition of this routing information can vary among applications, the basic header information must be fairly consistent for e-mail to be recognized by various mail programs.

This is achieved by following a standard. Mail headers for internetwork e-mail generally conform to the format defined in the Internet Request For Proposal (RFC) document named RFC 822 (see netref 10). E-mail on UNIX machines and many mainframe and mini-computers generally conforms to this standard, and it is required of any mail transmitted over the Internet.

Generally, e-mail addresses take the form of user name followed by host name and other network information as needed. These names are typically assigned by a system administrator. When it comes to the exact syntax of e-mail addressing, there are important differences in format to observe between distinct network operating systems (e.g., NetWare and UNIX) and between mail protocols used by e-mail applications. SMTP (Simple Mail Transfer Protocol) is a messaging protocol used in TCP/IP networks such as the Internet. Other major messaging protocols are the international X.400, IBM's SNADS, and Novell's MHS. However, some widely-used messaging products such as cc:Mail and Microsoft Mail use proprietary messaging protocols.

NOTE For more information about e-mail protocols, see Chapter 7.

Thus, whether or not the system requires only the user name or both user name and host information depends on the protocol(s) used by your network operating system and mail application. For example, an Internet domain address takes the form of username@host, whereas addressing mail within the same LAN could be accomplished by simply addressing mail to the name of the user. UUCP (UNIX-toUNIX-CoPy) is an older mail system that is still used with UNIX systems. UUCP addressing can be identified by a format that includes each host computer in the message path to the user separated by exclamation character symbols (i.e., host!host!user).

The Internet is a resource for continuous learning about LAN and internetwork messaging. There are World Wide Web sites such as the home page of the Electronic Messaging Association (see netref 11) and an interactive Web site with an online form that provides information about internetwork mail addressing (see netref 12).

A mail gateway is software that assists in the conversion of diverse addresses and message formats between different operating systems, network protocols, and mail applications.

Additional considerations are needed to address users at the diverse information services that have gateways to the Internet. For example, to address e-mail from the Internet to a CompuServe user, you have to replace the comma in the user ID number with a period and put the ID number before compuserve.com which is the Internet domain name. Using 123.456@compuserve.com as the destination address would reach a user with 123,456 as the CompuServe ID. For other information services, you put the user name before the domain name of that service, such as username@aol.com for an America Online user.

> **NOTE** For more information about e-mail addressing and domain names, see Chapters 9 and 11. For more information about mail servers and gateways, see Chapter 10.

Header lines that indicate destination of the message include e-mail address information about one or more primary recipients (To:), and (optional) secondary recipients as carbon-copy (Cc:) and blind carbon-copy (Bcc:). E-mail addresses in To: and Cc: are (automatically) not included in the e-mail message to Bcc: recipients.

The address information that goes in the field following a header line can be the actual address of a user, an alias (or substitute for an actual name), a mailing list name, or even a program that processes the mail. An example of a recipient indicated in all three destination fields might look as follows:

```
To:  pdh7555@is.nyu.edu
Cc:  gene@sne.com
Bcc: johndoe@aol.com
```

One or more e-mail destination addresses must be supplied in the form that is recognized by the sending and receiving mail program. Multiple addresses on the same header line are usually separated by commas.

A recipient of an e-mail message can use an e-mail program to redirect it to one or more other people. In these cases, the destination header lines are preceded by Resent-, such as Resent-To: for a message redirected to another primary recipient.

Subsequent header lines indicate the origin of a message. These include the primary author (From:), the person or program that sent it (Sender:), and the address for any replies (Reply-To:). Additional header lines are used to indicate the date the message was sent (Date:), the path back to the original address (Return-Path:), an ID for the message (Message-ID:), and optional header information about the subject (Subject:), comments (Comments:), and keywords (Keywords:) that describe the contents of the message.

During the transport of the message, additional headers are added that describe the route the message took, including information about what machines received it (Received from and Received by) along with the associated time and date of receipt. This information can be helpful in tracing the path of the message, especially when there are problems.

Here is an example of a mail header and body in a message received from an automated reply mailer:

```
Received: from cice.uunet.ca by is.NYU.EDU
(5.61/1.34)
id AA11175; Mon, 3 Jul 95 13:09:25 -0400
Received: from sq.sq.com ([192.31.6.128]) by
cice.uunet.ca with SMTP id <174343-3>; Mon, 3
Jul 1995 13:09:12 -0400
Received: by sq.sq.com (Smail3.1.29.1 #3)
id mOsSowF-OOOHFmC; Mon, 3 Jul 95 13:05 EDT
Message-Id: <mOsSowF-OOOHFmC@sq.sq.com>
Date: Mon, 3 Jul 1995 13:05:00 -0400
To: pdh7555@is.NYU.EDU
From: ll@sq.com (automated reply)
Subject: Re: Product Information.O
Vacation mailer for Lucky Lindy <ll@sq.com>
I have received your email but am away on
vacation until the end of July. If you need
immediate assistance, please contact
info@sq.com. Thank You. This is a recording.
```

Mail Extensions

When formatted text, images, or other media (including data) are transmitted via e-mail, the associated file can sent with the e-mail message as an attached file. One or more attached files can accompany the text-based e-mail message by using a standard encoding method supported by the e-mail program. It converts the binary data into encoded text used by the transmitting mailer. This coded file is then decoded by a compatible mechanism in the e-mail program of the receiver.

The Multipurpose Internet Mail Extensions (MIME) (pronounced Me-Me) format is a widely supported standard for sending multiple files with a single e-mail message and encoding one or more binary files so that they can be sent with e-mail over the Internet. Older encoding mechanisms such as BinHex for the Macintosh and UUencode for UNIX are also popular standards that are supported in many e-mail programs. The MIME protocol is defined in the Internet RFC 1521 (see netref 10). It specifies how multiple objects can be included in e-mail, the use of alternate character sets, and the means of defining future types of Internet mail.

NOTE For more information about MIME and related e-mail protocols, see Chapter 7.

When you need to send a large file as an e-mail attachment, you should consider its size and the relative transmission time it would take for you to send it and for the recipient to receive it. Sending a large file not only extends transmission times at both ends, but also adds cost and may increase the likelihood of transmission errors. If the sender or receiver is using dial-up connectivity, this can add considerably to phone charges. Many e-mail programs let you specify the largest file size that can be automatically downloaded from a POP server.

Mail extensions such as MIME only encode the file so that it is converted to text. To significantly reduce the sizes of files to transmit, you should use a file compression program prior to sending an attached file.

> **NOTE** For more information about file compression, see Chapter 11.

E-mail Software

With the growth of networking and client/server technology, e-mail applications have developed as three basic types: mail servers, mail clients, and e-mail software that includes both server and client function. In some cases, a user may run a mail client to prepare, store, and manage e-mail and also employ a SMTP mail server running in the background (as a daemon) to handle direct transmission and receipt without requiring a middleman such as a POP server from their network service provider.

> **NOTE** For more information about mail servers, see Chapter 10.

Eudora Pro from QUALCOMM (see netref 13) is a full-featured e-mail client available for the Mac and PC platforms (see Figure 8-1). Originally offered as shareware over the Internet, it has grown to be the most popular e-mail package with over 2 million users. It uses SMTP to send mail to designated SMTP mail server which delivers it to the mail server of the recipient. On the receiving side, Eudora uses the POP protocol to receive mail that is stored on a POP server. It creates and recognizes mail that meets the RFC 822 Internet mail and RFC 1521 MIME attachment standards.

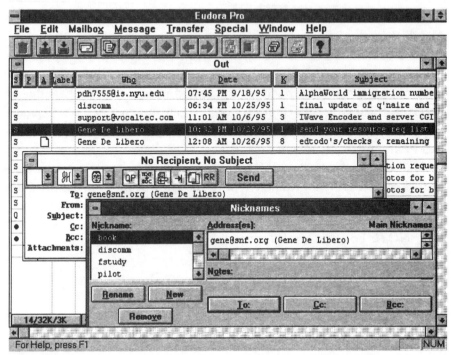

Figure 8-1. Eudora Pro e-mail client software (QUALCOMM Inc.).

Besides providing the standard functions to create, edit, search, and store text files for messages, Eudora Pro provides advanced features. A signature is composed of text which users can create to add contact and other information automatically to the bottom of any message. A filter can be created to automatically identify and process elements of incoming or outgoing mail messages according to certain rules. For example, you can specify that incoming mail with a particular e-mail address in the From: header line can be automatically stored in a special mailbox.

Attachments such as formatted text files, graphics, programs and other data files can be sent and received in encoded form with e-mail in any of three popular formats: MIME, BinHex, and UUencode. Eudora offers direct connectivity through TCP/IP networks and dial-up with SLIP or PPP protocols. Eudora Pro also includes TCP/IP connectivity software.

Z-Mail from Network Computing Devices, Inc. (see netref 14) is a mail client with cross-platform capability (UNIX, Windows, and Macintosh) and open system mail protocols (TCP/IP, SMTP, UUCP, POP-3). Some of its unique features include: support for serial connections to mail host using a serial (dial-up) line, a spelling checker, the ability to send mail from within MAPI-enabled applications, and mailbox synchronization between your PC or laptop and your network mail host.

Pegasus is another popular mailer that can be downloaded as freeware from the Internet (see netref 15). It offers flexible mailing services locally, through NetWare MHS, and via the Internet (using the POP3 and SMTP protocols). A unique feature called Noticeboards allows other mail users to examine collections of specified messages and post new messages to them.

Some e-mail programs like IMail from Ipswitch (see netref 16) offer both server and client functions. Having server capability is important if you want to extend control over the manner in which you transport and manage mail. IMail is a complete TCP/IP mail system with versions for Windows and Windows NT. The package includes SMTP and POP3 clients and servers, multiple mailboxes, MIME support, personal and shared address books and aliases, and compatibility with any Winsock 1.1-compliant TCP/IP product.

NOTE For more information about e-mail servers, see Chapter 10.

Privacy and Encryption

Accompanying the free exchange of information through e-mail is the risk of interception and monitoring by people other than the recipient. The e-mail message might contain highly personal information that should remain private, such as credit card numbers used in electronic transactions or strategic information passed between business contacts.

The problem with the interception of mail is due to the journey it takes from sender to receiver across internetworks. As revealed in the mail header of a message sent through the Internet, e-mail can be routed through many systems before reaching its destination. As the mail is passed from one mail server to another, anyone with privileged access to that system can read and even alter the contents of a message without the sender or receiver being aware of it. The interceptors of that mail could be anyone or any organization and their purposes could vary from harmless mischief to damaging espionage.

Not only does this problem undermine the social benefits of personal communication, but it undermines confidence in electronic commerce. Another problem is authentication, the use of a personal signature to verify a transaction or communication. For network communications, a digital·equivalent of a signature is needed. Fortunately, the process of encoding information for computer storage or communication can also be used to create digital signatures.

Encrypting, or scrambling the character codes, can prevent anyone from deciphering them who doesn't have the right to do so. There are several methods of achieving this level of privacy and authentication. Some are built-in functions of mail programs and others are implemented as standalone software programs which are used before sending or after receiving encrypted mail.

PGP, or Pretty Good Privacy, is a program that uses public key encryption. PGP creates a public key using a secure algorithm developed by RSA Laboratories (and made available under a non-export license). Public key cryptography can provide both privacy and authentication.

The software and documentation are copyrighted by its original author Philip Zimmermann, but it is available as a standalone program in both freeware and commercial versions which can be downloaded from the Internet. PGP is also available as software that provides secure audio via modem-to-modem "phone" communications (originally for Macintosh, subsequently for Windows). It uses speech compression and strong cryptography protocols to achieve real-time secure telephone conversations (see netref 17).

When sending a message, you use the PGP software to sign with your own secret key and also encrypt the signed message with the public key that belongs to the recipient of the encrypted message. When the message is received, the recipient must first decrypt the message with a personal secret key, then check the enclosed signature with the sender's public key.

Thus, this system does not require a secure channel to send the message, which means it can be used over the Internet or other public networks. However, it relies on the availability of PGP public key servers on the Internet and UUCP mail systems, which allow exchange of public keys. Keys are sent to these servers in the body of e-mail messages. The USENET newsgroup (alt.security.pgp) provides information about this system and a listing of new sites.

PEM, or Privacy Enhanced Mail, is another public key encryption system. It is embodied as a standard in Internet documentation RFC 1421 through RFC 1424 (see netref 10). It is used by developers as a means of incorporating public key encryption features in e-mail and other data communications software.

> **NOTE** For information about Internet documentation, see
> Chapter 11.

PUBLISHING AND GRAPHICS

Publishing and graphics applications are fairly recent arrivals to network applications. Besides the high-bandwidth demands that images place upon networks, exchange of formatting text, images, and page layouts have been a challenge to both developers and users. With this growing need for interoperability, several document and page description languages have become standards by which inter-format and internet-work exchange can be accomplished.

Page Description Languages

Page Description Languages (PDL) provide an elegant means of describing the contents of a page for output devices such as display monitors, printers, and imagesetters. Instead of using a memory-hungry bitmap description of a page, these languages communicate with a series of commands that describe the page image for output devices that are equipped with a matching PDL. Besides reducing memory requirements, a PDL provides a standard by which hardware and software can communicate. This is called device-independence. One benefit of this is the ability to use the same file for a network laser printer, high-resolution imagesetter, or a network file server.

As all objects and their positions on a page can be described with commands, a PDL can be used to write, modify, or troubleshoot the page output. Generally, graphics, word processing and other software applications provide an interface by which the programming is made easier. Through the use of PDL commands, a wide variety of visual effects can be performed, such as rotation, slanting, clipping, and fountain effects.

Printer manufacturers often provide a proprietary PDL which is employed in software drivers. One of the more popular of these PDLs is Hewlett-Packard's Printer Control Language (PCL) that is used by its line of laser printers.

PostScript is the most popular PDL because it is the oldest, most robust language and is widely supported among computer platforms, hardware devices, and software. For example, PostScript is the PDL employed in the Adobe Acrobat Portable Document platform and the widely used Adobe Typefaces.

Document Markup Languages

Document markup languages provide a means of defining the structure of documents by embedding standardized, readable text codes in the body of the text. In turn, publishing, database, and other applications which recognize the markup language can display and print documents that contain these codes.

Another advantage of the use of document markup language codes is the portability of a document in the form of storage, indexing, and retrieval in a consistent format to multiple media. The same document definition can be used in CD-ROM, special display monitors, various types of print and online applications, etc.

Many word processing and desktop publishing software programs use embedded codes to format documents. But these formatting codes are proprietary, however, and not as fully specified or as widely supported as a markup language.

Document markup languages define the distinct structure of a document by building blocks called elements. Once defined, headings, bullet lists, and other elements can be defined within the document by inserting tags, which are readable text codes.

For example, first-level heading tag codes surrounding the word Introduction might look like this:

```
<H1>Introduction</H1>
```

SGML

SGML, or Standard Generalized Markup Language is an international standard (ISO 8879) for document interchange, distribution, and publishing. SGML-compliant applications have been traditionally used in high-production environments such as in government and the computer industry. The application of SGML is expanding to specialized environments such as the World Wide Web, Braille, CD-ROM, and many other multimedia applications

SGML functions like the grammatical rules that are used to determine the construction of writing in a language such as English. It does not specify the actual format of a document, however, but rather how to create one or more Document-Type Definitions (DTD) which in turn specifies the formatting elements.

Applications that are SGML-compliant recognize the structure of these documents and perform the task associated with the application. For example, Panorama Pro by SoftQuad (see netref 18) is an SGML browser for the World Wide Web. It recognizes, displays, and lets the user navigate SGML documents that are accessed on the Web. It also includes features that let you publish SGML files for the Web, and create and edit style sheets.

Author/Editor by SoftQuad uses a word processor interface and built-in templates to facilitate the creation and editing of SGML documents. It provides multi-platform support, multiple media formats, SGML parsing, and macro capabilities. It also checks and validates existing documents for conformity to SGML.

HTML

HTML stands for Hypertext Markup Language. Although it is described as a subset of SGML, it is technically a DTD (Document-Type Definition) that describes the formatting structure for hypermedia documents as used on the World Wide Web (Berners-Lee and Connolly, 1993).

As HTML support has become common in word processors and browsers, this has supported both standalone and LAN use of HTML-based internal publishing and document systems.

HTML includes commands for formatting, heading levels, inline graphics, links to other HTML documents, and links that execute external programs through the Common Gateway Interface (CGI). CGI (see netref 19) allows scripts written in any programming language and stored on Web servers to be accessed by HTML browsers. CGI scripts can be used to collect and return data from online forms or execute other applications. Essentially, this wide range of commands allows a Web site or local HTML environment to use text, graphics, sound, video, or execute other programs. This can transform a computer screen image into an online shopping mall, a virtual reality game, or a virtual bank.

As a subset of SGML, a standard HTML file can be recognized by any SGML application. However, like any standard, HTML is constantly changing and new standards are always playing catch-up to extensions made by vendors in support of their products. For example, Netscape may implement several new commands in its popular Web browser which can be read by only this browser and compatible applications. Which, if any, of these local extensions will be absorbed in the next HTML standard is uncertain. Thus, you may encounter HTML documents on the Web that will not appear or operate completely the same for all browsers.

Proposals and the current draft of the HTML standard are coordinated by the Internet Engineering Task Force (IETF) Working Group on HTML. Documents related to the HTML standard can be accessed on the Internet (see netref 20).

Different levels of functionality and features have been associated with each version of this evolving standard. HTML Level 0 supported character-based browsers, HTML 1 supported inline images, and HTML 2 supports scripts and forms.

HTML 3 (in progress at the time of this writing) will likely incorporate extensions associated with popular browsers such as Netscape. These extensions include style sheets, table support, wrap-around text and a figure tag for images, dynamic document support to refresh images or pages, and other new elements for more sophisticated typographical control and page design. It should also include the HTML+ extensions proposed by Hewlett-Packard. Future versions are likely to include formatted document and interactive multimedia extensions already being used in PDL, Java applet, audio streaming, and Director movie support.

Fortunately, each new HTML standard supports previous levels. Thus, users with character-based browsers can access pages coded according HTML 2.0, but cannot view images or other unique features. Updating Web documents is required in situations where the new features are desired. Many HTML editors provide an automatic rules-checking feature that alerts you to HTML incompatibilities.

HTML files can be created and edited in any text editor or word processor by directly typing HTML commands along with the text. There are two basic types of HTML editors: some are standalone HTML editors and others are integrated into word processors. Most editors ease Web page production by including template pages which already contain typical HTML coding.

Hot Metal Pro by SoftQuad (see netref 18) is a standalone HTML editor (see Figure 8-2). It lets you create original HTML documents or edit existing ones. One view lets you see all the HTML tags and URL links, and the other view shows the document as it would appear in a browser. HotMetal contains many word processor features, including a spell checker, a thesaurus, and search and replace. Web page features include standard templates, a table editor, and the ability to create and display forms and inline graphics. It can also check and validate any existing HTML document for conformity to HTML rules and compatibility with Web browsers.

Figure 8-2. HotMetal Pro editor with a home page template created by SoftQuad Inc. (SoftQuad Inc.).

WebAuthor by Quarterdeck (see netref 21) is an example of an HTML editor that is integrated within a popular word processor to take advantage of its familiar functions; in this case, it's Microsoft Word for Windows (as of version 6.0). It installs itself into Word so that it can be run as a menu command or by clicking on a toolbar icon. It uses Word style lists to embed HTML tags and can also import and edit existing HTML documents. Creating links is done by highlighting text (or selecting a graphic image) and then defining the link in a dialog. Links can be made within the same document, to another HTML document, or to an Internet service such as gopher, telnet, ftp, etc.

> **NOTE** For more information about HTML and the World Wide Web, see Chapter 11.

Document Viewers

Document viewers provide the ability to transmit and view formatted text and graphics over internetworks and between diverse computer platforms. Even with graphical and cross-platform environments such as the World Wide Web, there is no assurance that the document will appear exactly like the original. Web browsers typically let users adjust page elements such as fonts to their preferences, whereas document viewers preserve the layout of the original.

Another important benefit of this type of software is that users can view documents without using the exact software or hardware that was involved in their creation. All that is required is a reader program which is available for most computer platforms (Windows, DOS, UNIX, and Macintosh) and which can be freely distributed.

The Acrobat software series (see Figure 8-3) by Adobe (see netref 22) employs their widely recognized standard called Portable Document Format (PDF). It uses the PostScript page-description language which is the basis for its wide support. Adobe typeface packages such as the 65 PostScript screen and printer fonts in Adobe Type Basics and the Adobe Type Manager are widely used for PostScript font support and management.

Adobe Acrobat is actually composed of several programs. Acrobat PDF Writer creates PDF files from within word processors and other applications. Acrobat Exchange lets you add navigational links in PDF files. Acrobat Search provides full-text search of PDF files indexed with Acrobat Catalog. Acrobat Reader is used to view, navigate, and print PDF files. The Acrobat Pro series also includes Acrobat Distiller which converts PostScript files into PDF.

Envoy by WordPerfect and Novell (see netref 23) provides portable document publishing and viewing for the Windows and Macintosh platforms using its proprietary technology. It provides additional features, such as electronic sticky notes, highlights, and bookmarks. Annotations can be personalized by name and style to allow collaborative annotation.

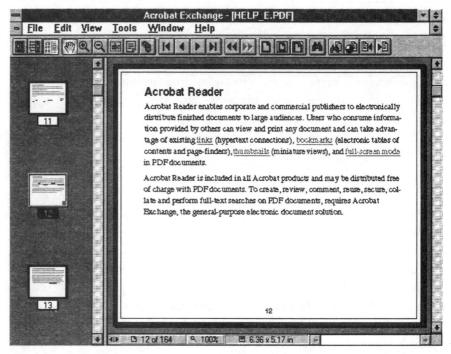

Figure 8-3. PDF document in an Acrobat viewer (Adobe).

Desktop Publishing

There are many network-capable applications that perform a wide variety of vital desktop publishing and graphics production tasks. Strategic choices for these applications should include interoperability among major computing platforms and document and graphic formats. One of the most important trends in desktop publishing in a network environment is strategically employing a document interchange standard such as SGML in the final product for Web publishing or multimedia.

FrameMaker (see netref 24) is an integrated publishing application that provides sophisticated word processing, layout, and graphics functions. Interoperability is achieved through program versions and file compatibility between Windows, Macintosh, and X/Motif platforms.

To provide greater interoperability with SGML, the widely-supported cross-media and platform standard, a separate product named

FrameMaker+SGML allows users to create, edit and publish structured and SGML documents using a graphical interface. It combines page composition, text editing, graphics, interactive structure validation, and SGML support.

Products such as SGML Composer provide a high-speed batch composition system. It reads SGML document instances, DTDs, and FOSI (Formatting Output Specification Instance) files and then automatically builds fully paginated documents.

Corel Draw by Corel (see netref 25) provides a complete publishing environment, including Draw vector graphics, Paint for bitmap graphics, Ventura Publisher desktop publishing, and many other applications and clip art.

Visio by Shapeware (see netref 26) is a business graphics package that provides drag-and-drop creation of drawings, diagrams, and charts through more than 750 shapes from 22 job-specific stencils. Network diagrams and flow charts are among the many templates included with this package.

Document template software provides a useful publishing function by automating document assembly. For example, HotDocs from Capsoft Development Corp. (see netref 27) builds intelligent templates for a wide array of business documents and lets users interactively customize them within a word processor. Repetitive documents are then quickly assembled by other users by simply filling out forms as they are presented.

Clip art resources are abundant and accessible through search engines on the Internet. There are many ftp and gopher sites which contain directories that store images in many formats as well as audio, animation, and video clips. The multimedia viewing capabilities of the World Wide Web make it especially useful for clip art repositories (see netref 28).

MULTIMEDIA AND HYPERMEDIA

Networked multimedia applications fall into a few basic categories, each of which will be discussed separately in this section. From the easiest to use to the most complex, these include: document-conferencing, image retrieval, hypermedia, and audio- and video-conferencing.

Document-Conferencing

Network-capable document-conferencing applications let two or more users work interactively online with documents composed of text and images. To the degree that this type of software supports collaborative activities such as annotations and editing, it can fit under the larger category of groupware (discussed later in this chapter). However, not all of these applications go that far in what they offer. Typically, they operate on the familiar metaphor of the whiteboard, in which a document is displayed on the screen and users are given tools to mark up the document and visually communicate.

Documents composed of text and images can be any of the familiar products of everyday computer applications, such as desktop-published pages, spreadsheets, database forms, graphics, or screens from programs in which these documents are produced.

The real world equivalent of whiteboarding would be a case in which two people examine a paper document and place notes and make suggested changes, but without speaking or seeing each other. Although that would be artificially restrained in the real world, across a network it's just another type of virtual exchange with its own share of tradeoffs. For example, although audio-video conferencing can support whiteboarding, the added types of media raises the storage and bandwidth toll.

Whiteboarding without audio-video support is the least demanding of networked multimedia applications because it only uses typical screen images that are updated and manipulated by a shared set of interface tools. This type requires the least storage and peripheral equipment, uses the least network bandwidth and generally costs the least to purchase, operate, and maintain.

Conferencing Standards

Generally, document-conferencing and other collaborative products have been proprietary in that they require each user to operate the same software, but emerging standards will allow products from separate vendors that comply with these standards to work together.

For example, the T.120 document-conferencing standard (see netref 29) that was ratified by the International Telecommunications Union (ITU) establishes a standard series of communication and application protocols and services that provide support for real-time, multi-point data communications.

This standard ensures that different applications can communicate and that they can coexist on the same machine. For example, if one conference user is running a T.120-compatible program like FarSite (described below) and another site has a different T.120-compliant product, they can still communicate. Other examples include the use of a T.120-compliant document-conferencing projector, or the use of T.120-compatible bridging services from companies such as ConferTech and MCI (see netref 30), which allow multi-point conferencing over telephone connections.

> **NOTE** For more information about T.120 and other network protocols, see Chapter 7.

Conferencing Products

Document-conferencing products vary in their support of users and network access. Abilities range from support for a conference between two users (point-to-point) over a LAN up to support for multi-party (multi-point) conferences over a LAN or WAN. Direct connect or dial-up access can be supported.

Creating a conference is initiated by a single user who can use a phone book feature to look up IPX or IP addresses of other users. In some cases, the software lets a user search for existing conferences in various subnets.

Some packages only display bit-mapped images of documents and files, a feature in which annotations cannot be applied to the original file, whereas more advanced features allow users to view an actual file and make changes to it during the conference.

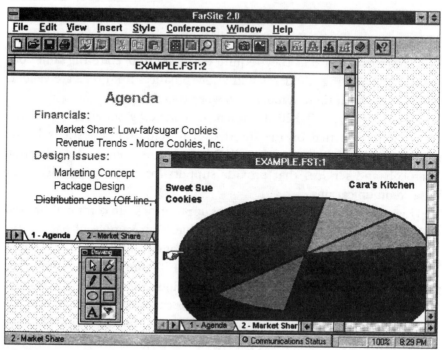

Figure 8-4. Farsite document-conferencing (DataBeam).

FarSite by DataBeam (see netref 31) is a Windows-based, T.120-compliant, conferencing software (see Figure 8-4). It can accommodate conferences using a mixture of IPX, TCP/IP, and (async) modem links. Point-to-point (one-to-one) or multi-point (many to many) conferences can be created using MODEM, IPX, TCP/IP or any mixture of the three.

A conference user can select materials to be either private or shared. You must explicitly share (using a command) for it to be transmitted to the other conference participants. Having private items on your screen allows you to view other materials from multiple sites without disrupting the conference.

Multimedia Conferencing

CU-SeeMe is video-conferencing software (see netref 32) that was developed at Cornell University and is licensed commercially through White Pine. Although it initially supports gray-scale video, it is an evolving product with new features being added regularly through its beta program. Concurrent text and audio support are available, making it an increasingly attractive platform to experiment with low-entry TCP/IP internetwork conferencing.

> **NOTE** For more information about CU-SeeMe and video-conferencing, see Chapter 11.

The ComputerEyes line of products by Digital Vision (see netref 33) provides video digitizer hardware and software in support of multimedia and video-conferencing products such as CU-SeeMe. They offer a wide range of black-and-white and color digitizers and software for PC and Mac platforms. The software includes image capture, editing, and storage functions, and support for CU-SeeMe video transmission.

Person to Person conferencing software by IBM (see netref 34) supports a wide range of network conferencing functions, including whiteboards, file transfers, and chat. It can also transmit and view video images using the ActionMedia format. Other features include an address book, still-image capture, and clipboard. It is available for Windows and OS/2. It can be used over modem, ISDN, LAN, and WAN.

Hypermedia

As the reliability and popularity of the World Wide Web illustrates, networked hypermedia provides a robust delivery platform for applications and a powerful medium for rich interaction. Hypermedia is more than the rich mix of text, images, audio, and video associated with multimedia. It also uses a linking mechanism to jump from one object to another as found in hypertext. With hypermedia, these links can be not only made with text, but with other objects such as images. This flexibility offers the cross-referencing power of hypertext with the richness of virtual reality, where audiovisual objects and environments can be manipulated by the user. If the hypermedia application is implemented on a network, the added access and real-time interaction of simultaneous users can augment and enhance its objectives.

As with other types of network-capable applications, you can use off-the-shelf software or you can develop your own hypermedia applications using authoring systems available for most major platforms or programming languages like C++ or Visual Basic.

Despite useful models for hypermedia design developed by Douglas Engelbart, Theodor Nelson, Tim Berners-Lee, and other leaders in this field, the effort and expense that usable design requires often takes a back seat to quick development. Fortunately, documentation on hypermedia design and production is abundant on the Web. For example, the August 1995 issue of the *Communications of the ACM* journal is devoted to articles on hypermedia design by leading researchers (Bieber and Isakowitz, 1995). It is available in print and as a hypermedia environment on the Web (see netref 35).

DATABASES

New software and hardware technologies are bringing the traditionally text-oriented database to life with multimedia, imaging, and visualization. This offers new ways for users to view and manipulate data, and also allows users to construct and manage databases across networks using diverse platforms.

Data Types

Information in its stored and transmitted form has a rich history and development. Tied to the growth of culture and technology, multiple sources of media are part of our symbolic legacy. Similarly, the storage and manipulation of information as computer data has been tethered to the capabilities of computer and network technology. Until recently, database applications were largely limited to text.

With the development of imaging and multimedia technologies, database applications expanded to embrace more forms of data representation. One direction was the development of dedicated applications, such as image databases for picture storage and to manipulation of the data through graphical interfaces. More recent trends in database design integrate multimedia capabilities into traditional database applications to store text, still and moving images, and sound. Using client/server based, graphical operating systems such as Windows NT and OS/2, a natural and efficient connection between the database server and the operating system results in greater efficiency and ease-of-use.

Database Models

As there are many types of data, databases should be designed to reflect the rich and varied sources of information that the data represent. Several models are presented here: freeform, relational, and hypermedia. Although these distinctions can be made among the various types of database products, there is a growing trend to integrate these functions into single, hybrid database application that operates in a client/server network environment. Examples of this trend are briefly covered under the last section, "Emerging Models."

Freeform

Information has varied forms. In text formats such as memos, notes, letters, reports, and articles, the data structure is inherently flat, sequential, and generally unstructured.

Flat, sequential database applications have been available for some time to handle simple lists and tables. Many text-based applications such as word processors, e-mail, operating systems, and programming languages have traditionally managed text through increasingly powerful formatting and search functions.

There are limitations, however, because database is not a primary function in these applications. For example, word processors and e-mail programs have limited search capabilities that are generally restricted to single files. Information managers and similar applications are generally adept at organizing information, but from a limited range of sources and formats such as notes, memos, and contact data.

Database software such as askSam from askSam Systems (see netref 36) addresses the varying demands of a freeform database by working with native data, whether it is unstructured or structured, or in one or more files. Available for DOS and Windows in standalone and network versions, it uses import and export filters and templates to handle the varied data formats. You can also create hypertext links and bookmarks for active jumps between related data. Varied search functions include full-text, wildcard, Boolean, proximity, numeric, date, and hypertext.

Relational

Entering information in structured form (i.e., many fields per record and many records per file) is more suitable to enterprise and mission-critical data.

However, in larger, more dynamic applications, the relational database model works more efficiently by using tabular data from many database files. RDBM, short for Relational Data Base Management, was developed in the 1980s in response to this need, and has become the predominant model for managing complex and dynamic information.

Besides being well-suited to representing the most common entities and their relationships in a structured format, it can also represent data independent of data structure or access. A standard means of querying databases is achieved by using the Structured Query Language (SQL). It has the advantage of interoperability in that it is recognized by many database applications, including those by Sybase, Oracle, Microsoft, and many other vendors.

> **NOTE** For information about database and SQL servers, see Chapter 10.

Hypermedia

A hypermedia database can store, manage, and display information as multimedia data and it can make links between these data items. Specialized image databases or video server technologies are varied examples of this type of database application. The World Wide Web and its platform-independent, global client/server environment is a good candidate for database applications, especially for interactive transactions in electronic commerce.

The HTTP protocol and its Common Gateway Interface (CGI) (see netref 19) allows script processing, which can be used to send and receive data between a Web browser client and a database server. This feature, combined with HTML support for fill-in forms, lets users type data in fields that can be sent via CGI scripts to a query a database. This information can then be returned via the script to update the Web page with information retrieved from the database.

However, hypermedia systems such as the World Wide Web are stateless systems that do not process more than one transaction per connection. That's why a Web browser will re-attempt connection to a host when you click on a link that makes a request. This limitation is acceptable for one-pass transactions such as submitting data after filling out the fields in a form or requesting specific data stored in a database using a search engine. For more complex and multiple requests that require maintaining the state, CGI scripting must return state data or issue commands to keep the database open until another CGI command closes it.

A growing number of organizations that need to provide interactive and selective access to information from their large databases are using CGI scripting in this manner on their World Wide Web sites. For example, companies such as Federal Express (see netref 37) support customer tracking of shipments through a Web page. It lets them enter information in a form with scrollable fields from which they can select existing data. When the user completes the form, a CGI script then queries the shipment-tracking database. It then retrieves the requested data and dynamically prepares a Web page that is customized to the information they have requested.

The Web is a convenient interface that is platform-independent and globally accessible. Using it for interactive data querying of large databases and creating personalized Web pages from the returned data is a strategic solution for electronic commerce. Searching and ordering from online retail catalogs, conducting consumer marketing surveys, and many other interactive database applications can be achieved with this type of hypermedia system.

NOTE For more information about the World Wide Web, HTML, and CGI, see Chapter 11.

Emerging Models

The relational database model is by no means fixed in its development. One of the more recent enhancements is the Open Database model as developed by Pick Systems. While the relational model is designed to store data in a two-dimensional table, the Open Database model accommodates more complex data relationships by allowing multiple values to be stored in fields.

Handling multi-dimensional data represents another enhancement or challenge to the traditional RDBM model. Less-structured data such as transactions, events, or measurements can be represented as objects or events with two or more attributes. Some dimensions are associated with a factual representation of a measurable aspect of the object or event and the other dimensions are descriptive of the fact dimension. For example, an event such as a network broadcast storm can be described in terms of its duration, impact, and other aspects.

A typical application for this type of data representation is data mining, in which trends are observed and described in collections of data. For example, the multidimensional data can be a series of observations by a help desk about the amount of times a network bridge fails per network segment per day. Data warehousing is a related application in which distributed data can be accessed to report trend information for decision-support.

NOTE For information about the HTTP protocol, see Chapter 7.

GROUPWARE

Groupware is a category of software that employs networks to share information among groups of people working on one or more projects. It employs one or more familiar applications such as e-mail, conferencing, project management, word processing, and database, and integrates several of these as functions within a single product.

It uses a consistent interface to produce, organize, view, and communicate information in a useful format among users in the group. Groups determine the tasks they perform with this software, whether it is inventory management, client tracking, minutes of meetings among remote users, and other tasks associated with their work.

As this genre of software presumes collaboration among its users, it often presents challenges to organizational cultures where individual control of information is often valued higher than the benefits of team effort. Groupware represents more than saving paper, filing, and time; it presents a novel and expedient way for ad hoc groups to manage one or more projects simultaneously without excessive meetings, telephone tag, or interruptions. A strategic approach to implementing groupware employs these and other tactics:

- Seek the endorsement and initial use by opinion leaders and top-level executives.

- Conduct pilot testing with small groups and well-defined tasks.

- Slowly gain consensus through increasing the size and number of workgroups.

- Create incentives and recognize achievement that specifically address collaborative workgroups.

- Be prepared to support quickly rising demand with a reliable and well-administered network infrastructure.

Most important is the recognition that successful implementation of groupware in an organization is more than a technology fix. It represents a challenge to existing business practices and social norms among the people who are using it and the clients who are served by it. Any benefits that arise will come through a sustained commitment to constructively change these norms to achieve the desired outcomes. Collaboration is not a goal, but a process. The rewards are found in the effectiveness and efficiency that it can bring to the organization that supports this process.

Lotus Notes (see netref 38) deserves the distinction of single-handedly popularizing this genre of collaborative software. Ray Ozzie began development as early as 1984 and its release in 1989 by Lotus marked a new way of tying together messaging and database applications. It lets users create documents that contain text, graphics, and other media whether these are in freeform structure such as memos, and notes, or more structured such as reports, inventory items, etc. These documents can also contain hypertext links which jump to related information when selected. Templates are available for quick creation of databases according to typical tasks such as inventory or contact lists.

Documents are stored in separate databases according to categories created by a user. One or more databases can be grouped together in a visual organizer called a workpage. Each workpage appears as a tabbed folder which displays the name and icon of each of its component databases. Although users can name and arrange workpages as they see fit, the first and uppermost workpage in a cascaded series is usually called Mail. It contains one or more databases that act as mailboxes for the user. Mailboxes receive mail from a Mail Router at a specified interval in the store and forward method. The incoming messages are stored as documents in a specified mail database.

Documents stored in any of the databases can be shared with others through electronic mail over the network that supports Lotus Notes and to other networks through mail gateways. It can use front-ends to share data with Sybase and Oracle databases, the Internet, AT&T's Network Notes and other public-access networks.

Another groupware solution is provided by GroupWise by Novell (see netref 39). This revamped groupware version of WordPerfect Office provides a collaborative networked environment by integrating e-mail, scheduling, and task-management software.

Besides typical mail features that include support for attachments, GroupWise offers many other tools. The Calendar provides planning and time management. The Schedule tool is a personal and group appointment tool. Assign Task identifies tasks, people, and the time frame needed to achieve stated goals. The Write Note tool posts reminders and memos to other users and yourself. The Phone Message tool sends "while you were out" memos.

The future of groupware, database, and other network applications is hard to predict. Technologically, these applications are increasingly being revamped for portability and interoperability on global internetworks, where we increasingly do our work. In doing so, will these unique functions become fused along with multimedia, desktop publishing, and graphics into the ever-popular Internet services such as the World Wide Web?

As far as organizational fit, there are many challenges that remain. For example, will the inherently collaborative and flattening effect of groupware technology come into conflict with more rigid hierarchical organizational cultures that reward personal achievement? These trends are likely to continue and so are the associated challenges. Solutions can be found in a more strategic approach that takes all these factors into account when planning and implementing network applications.

REFERENCES

Berners-Lee, T. and D. Connolly. 1993. "Hypertext Markup Language: A Representation of Textual Information and Meta-information for Retrieval and Interchange." IETF Internet Draft. To access this and related documents on the Internet: ftp to ds.internic.net then login as anonymous and search for documents from the IETF in the /ietf and /iesg directories.

Bieber, M. and T. Isakowitz. 1995. "Designing Hypermedia Applications." *Communications of the ACM.* 38(8): 26-29. This is the introduction to a series of articles on this topic by leading researchers. Also available on the World Wide Web (see netref 34).

Net References

1. www to http://www.netmanage.com/ then browse the Chameleon product listing on NetManage home page.

2. www to http://www.compuserve.com/ then browse the CompuServe home page for Internet access information.

3. www to http://www.microsoft.com/ then browse the Microsoft home page for the SNA server product information.

4. www to http://www.walldata.com/ then browse the Wall Data home page for Rumba product information.

5. www to http://www.wpine.com/ then browse the White Pine home page for eXodus product information.

6. www to http://www.unipress.com/ then browse the Unipress home page for Cosession and other product information.

7. www to http://www.ultranet.com/~dtemple/ then look for information about Avalan Technology remote control software products such as Remotely Possible.

8. www to http://www.symantec.com/ then browse the Symantec home page for pcANYWHERE product information.

9. www to http://www.travsoft.com/ then browse the Traveling Software home page for AirShare product information.

10. www to http://www.cis.ohio-state.edu/htbin/rfc/rfc-index.html then search the RFC index list for the RFC by number. Click on the link to access the RFC source document. This index list contains the most recent RFCs. If you prefer to use ftp to access RFC documents, ftp to ds.internic.net then login as anonymous and search for an RFC in the /rfc directory.

11. www to http://www.ema.org/ then browse the Electronic Messaging Association Web pages for information about electronic mail and related applications.

12. www to http://www.nova.edu/Inter-Links/cgi-bin/inmgq.pl then complete the form to find out how to send Internet mail from one type of network to another.

13. www to http://www.qualcomm.com/ then browse the QUALCOMM home page for information on Eudora and to download the light version or order the full-featured commercial version.

14. www to http://www.ncd.com then browse the NCD home page for product information about Z-Mail.

15. ftp to risc.ua.edu/pub/network/pegasus/ then download the most recent version of the Pegasus mailer in compressed format.

16 www to http://www.ipswitch.com/store/ then select the IMail product link for product and ordering information from Ipswitch.

17. www to http://web.mit.edu/network/pgp then read the information about PGP on the MIT distribution site for PGP page. Clicking on the link for obtaining PGP will display instructions for filling out a form and downloading the freeware software developed at MIT. The freeware license is restricted to non-commercial use and an RSA license prohibits export. An audio version of PGP software is also available through a link on this page or by www to http://web.mit.edu/network/pgpfone/ then follow a similar procedure for downloading the software. For a commercial version from Viacrypt Inc., www to http://www.getnet.com/viacrypt/ then read about its features and instructions for ordering.

18. For SGML and HTML information and products, www to http://sq.com/ then browse the SoftQuad home page for information about its SGML browser, Panorama Pro and the SGML editor, Author/Editor. Look also for its HTML editor, Hot Metal Pro, and other publishing software.

19. For an overview of CGI and links to more information, www to http://www.w3.org/hypertext/WWW/CGI/Overview.html

Also, www to http://www.yahoo.com then use the menus to select Computers and Internet, then World Wide Web, then Internet, and finally GGI, or you can add the following to the URL:
/Computers_and_Internet/Internet/World_Wide_Web/CGI_Common_Gateway_Interface/
The yahoo.com Web site is a good starting point for information about CGI scripting for a variety of computer platforms and languages.

Also, for a magazine article about CGI, www to http://www.zdnet.com/~pcweek/navigator/nav_0522.html then read the article and follow the links to other sources of information about CGI.

20. For the current draft of HTML 3.0 from IETF, www to http://www.w3.org/hypertext/WWW/MarkUp/html3/CoverPage.html

For documents covering Netscape's HTML extensions, www to http://home.netscape.com/assist/net_sites/html_extensions.html

21. For information about the WebAuthor editor and other products including browsers, Internet suites, and utilities, www to http://www.qdeck.com/ then browse the Quarterdeck home page.

22. www to http://www.adobe.com/ then browse the Adobe home page for information about the Acrobat software series, Adobe fonts, and PDF.

23. www to http://wordperfect.com/ then browse the WordPerfect home page for information about Envoy and other software. Also www to http://www.novell.com/ then browse the Novell home page.

24. www to http://www.frame.com/ then navigate from the Frame Technology home page to information about its multi-platform line of publishing products. Also, www to http://www.adobe.com/ for additional information.

25. www to http://www.corel.com/ then navigate from the Corel home page to information about its line of publishing and graphics products.

26. www to http://www.shapeware.com/ then navigate from the Shapeware home page to product information about the Visio business graphics product.

27. www to http://www.itsnet.com/home/capsoft/public_html/ then browse the Capsoft HotDocs product page.

28. The following Web sites contain clip art for use in desktop publishing and Web projects:

http://www.cs.yale.edu/HTML/YALE/CS/HyPlans/loosemore-sandra/clipart.htm then select from Sandra's Clip-Art Collection.

http://wisdom.uwex.edu/ceclipart/ then select from the Univ. of Wisc. Cooperative Extension Clip Art Collection.

http://www.mindspring.com/~guild/graphics/clipart.htm then select from Clip Art Images for Use in HTML Documents.

http://www.yahoo.com/Computers/Multimedia/Pictures/Clip_Art/ then select from the Yahoo.Com Computers: Multimedia: Pictures: Clip Art collection.

http://www.wellesley.edu/Gifs/ then select from the Wellesley.edu Clip Art collection. Images are mostly in GIF format.

http://www.wellesley.edu/Gifs/buttons.htm then select from the Wellesley Collection of Buttons.

29. www to http://www.csn.net/imtc/t120.html then read and use the links (to download text in MSWord or PostScript format) in the HTML document entitled, "Overview of the T.120 Protocols for Audiographic Conferencing."

30. www to http://www.mci.com/ then access the links on the MCI home page, among which is provided a tour of services through an online tour of a fictitious company named Grammercy Press.

31. To reach DataBeam, the makers of Farsite, e-mail to support@databeam.com. You can also contact them via dial-up at their conference site by using the Join Conference dialog within Farsite, or call them at 606-245-3500, or fax to 606-245-3528.

32. For information about the licensed, commercial version of CU-SeeMe, www to http://www.wpine.com/ then browse the White Pine home page for CU-SeeMe product information.

For information about CU-SeeMe software, mailing list, and links to other CU-SeeMe sites where it is used, www to http://www.jungle.com/msattler/sci-tech/comp/CU-SeeMe/

33. www to http://www.digvis.com/digvis/ then browse the Digital Vision home page for information about the complete line of ComputerEyes video digitizer hardware, software, and other products.

34. www to http://www.ibm.com/ then browse the IBM home page and submit a customer feedback form requesting information about Person to Person and other products by IBM.

35. www to http://www.acm.org/siglink/ then click on the bullet item: Communications of the ACM–August 1995 Special Issue on Designing Hypermedia Applications. This links to a Web page for this online issue. A graphical overview (concept map) appears containing the names of all the articles. Click on a corresponding block that contains the title of the article you want to read. You can return to this map at any point while navigating through the articles. The hypermedia design for this online version includes over 150 links with labels (in different formats) that describe their interrelationships. Link types include text, figures, footnotes, citations, and external works on the Web.

36. www to http://199.44.46.2/askSam.htm and browse the askSam Systems Web page for information about askSam freeform database and electronic publisher software.

37. www to http://www.fedex.com/ then browse the Federal Express home page for links to its Web-based air-bill tracking system.

38. www to http://www.lotus.com/ then browse the Lotus Development Corp. home page for information and links on Lotus Notes. Also, www to http://www.ibm.com/

Also, www to http://www.cs.gmu.edu/lotus/ then access the Lotus Notes home page of the George Mason University Dept. of Computer Science. It describes ongoing Lotus Notes projects and provides information about the setup and use of Notes.

39. www to http://wordperfect.com/ then browse the home page of WordPerfect Corporation for information about WordPerfect GroupWise and other publishing and groupware products.

Also www to http://www.novell.com then browse the home page of Novell for information on about network and groupware products.

9

System Administration

ABOUT THIS CHAPTER

In the first five chapters, we discussed many of the components used to implement networks, from transmission media to high-speed network services. In Chapter 6, we introduced network planning, design, and implementation. In this chapter, we cover the management, security, and administration of networks. This chapter also covers management and security issues related to supporting an internetworking presence such as an integrated Web site on the Internet.

INTRODUCTION

Networks need a good deal of care and feeding to function reliably. In the case of a small organization with a LAN supporting small workgroups, system administration is frequently performed by one or two people. These networks are commonly built on a single platform, such as using Intel-based PCs for the hardware and Novell (see netref 1) NetWare for the network operating system.

> **NOTE** For more information about NetWare and other network operating systems, see Chapter 4.

In larger organizations, the need to support enterprise networks through a WAN and through public internetworks requires the cooperation and skills of many administrators. These large networks are often heterogeneous in nature. Heterogeneous networks are environments that consist of different hardware and software platforms which run unique operating systems and protocols.

Technology downsizing is essentially the process of shifting processing resources from centralized mainframes to servers on LANs. With downsizing and the resulting staff reductions occurring more frequently, some administrators find themselves managing several platforms simultaneously. The mindset is that giving more responsibility to fewer people reduces operating costs and streamlines the operation of the business. Experience has taught us that this approach doesn't always work. The usual result is an organization lacking technical focus with temporary solutions implemented as problems occur.

The concept of network management means different things to different people. When we talk about network management in this book, we mean the methods and procedures associated with maintaining a fully-functioning network environment. For example, when connecting a network to the Internet, it is necessary to have a fully qualified domain name and network number registered with the InterNIC. This is done to ensure that every IP address and domain on the Internet is unique. This is a task that falls to system administrators or managers.

When networking the enterprise meant terminals connected to mainframes or a small LAN within an organization, the most system administrators and managers had to worry about was making sure the door to the computer room was locked. Networks today are a far cry from that description. More and more organizations are building global internetworks that at some point connect to the Internet. Connecting an organization to the Internet provides a way to take its business right to the heart of global interaction with more than 30 million users and their respective organizations.

> **NOTE** For information about the Internet, see Chapter 11. Information about building an integrated Internet presence can be found in Chapter 10.

However, connecting corporate information technology resources to public networks does not come without security risks. A large part of administering and managing internetworks is keeping them safe. To effectively do this, there must be a clear understanding of what network resources must be protected (e.g., files, hard drives, communications gateways, databases) as well as who and what they must be protected from. Having this understanding can reduce the associated risks considerably.

Administration of the network encompasses the day-to-day chores of backups, software and hardware inventory control and licensing, virus protection, and other tasks. It also includes service and support. The term, service, is normally associated with the support of hardware and software throughout the enterprise. Service can be arranged through independent third-party service providers or through the vendors of the products themselves. Support brings together help desks, documentation of the network and its use, as well as user training.

MANAGEMENT

Effective network management is based on how organizations work. If the functionality of the network management system does not properly address business issues, such as the need for the network to be consistently available, it becomes a liability instead of an asset. Network management policies and procedures must be a combination of business and technical requirements that are defined by senior management and technical leaders. They clearly define how and why, through management tools and other methods, the organization's network infrastructure is managed and supported.

Thus, network management means using management tools, policies, and procedures together to effectively manage a network. When we talk about management tools, we mean software-based products that run on different hardware platforms. These products collect and display information about devices connected to the network and monitor their performance. Network management architectures often comprises of several parts:

- Devices and services that must be managed such as routers, bridges, servers, workstations, and high-speed network services.

- Management applications that manage specific portions of the network, such as SNMP manageable devices, by collecting information and storing it for later retrieval.

- High-level applications that consolidate and process the stored information collected by the management applications.

Once consolidated and processed, the information is made available through a user interface. This final step allows administrators and managers to make educated decisions regarding network optimization and functions.

Management Tools

Network management tools provide a means of monitoring and controlling network configuration, and system status, and issuing network alerts when problems occur. Proper network management is absolutely essential to ensure consistent uptime whether your network environment is based on a single protocol or platform, is department-wide or enterprise-wide. To effectively manage your network, you'll need solid network tools and training. Keep in mind that even the best tools can be useless if they're not used correctly!

Most network applications and components available today support SNMP, which is an industry standard network monitoring and control protocol. Using SNMP, you can collect and evaluate network performance data. SNMP agents, which can be hardware or software processes, report on activity occurring in network components like hubs, routers, bridges, network interface cards, etc. This activity is reported to the workstation running the network management platform, such as SunNet Manager, HP OpenView, IBM NetView, etc.

While SNMP was developed by the Internet Engineering Task Force (IETF) (see netref 2) primarily for TCP/IP networks, the Common Management Information Protocol (CMIP) became part of the Open Systems Interconnect (OSI) protocol suite. CMIP is an ISO (International Standards Organization—see netref 3) network monitoring and control standard for managing heterogeneous networks. CMIP has not fared as well as SNMP, but is supported by a number of network management vendors.

> **NOTE** For more information about open systems and the OSI model, see Chapter 6.

These agents return information contained in a MIB (Management Information Base), which is a directory used by SNMP that specifies the names, status, and location of all information resources residing on a network. SNMP-2 is an updated version of SNMP designed to provide enhancements over SNMP and offers improved security, protocol operations, and file management.

Windows SNMP is an industry specification that defines how SNMP network management products interface with a TCP/IP protocol stack. Windows SNMP allows SNMP products to be developed independently from the protocol stack and the SNMP.

> **NOTE** For more information about SNMP/SNMP-2 and other network protocols, see Chapter 7.

As networks are interconnected to form internetworks, the ability to perform remote monitoring becomes very important. Using remote monitoring, network problems can be identified and often resolved from a management console. This eliminates the need to send a technician to a remote location, which can be expensive and time-consuming. With the introduction of SNMP's Remote Monitoring Management Information Base (RMON MIB) standard, it is easier to monitor the performance of remote network devices and LAN segments.

RMON allows network administrators and managers to monitor heterogeneous networks at the Data Link and Physical layers of the OSI model. By installing RMON-compliant devices on network segments, all data packets that are sent to and received from these devices can be monitored. RMON enhances the monitoring capabilities of standard SNMP MIBs by keeping a record of performance statistics (also known as events) that can be used for functions such as performance tuning, network planning, and problem diagnosis.

Management Applications

Network management applications are available directly from many hardware vendors or as add-on products from independent vendors. These applications can manage an assortment of network components regardless of the manufacturer. Previously, network management applications managed only one type of device from a selected vendor, such as a router or a bridge. This provided a very limited means of managing an environment.

Some of these applications are modular in design and highly customizable, relying on third-party network management platforms like Solstice SunNet Manager from SunSoft and OpenView from Hewlett-Packard (see netref 4) for basic monitoring and control functions. Higher-end network management systems can handle huge amounts of management data, storing information in a Relational Database Management System (RDBMS).

NOTE For more information about databases, see Chapter 8.

Network management tools can be used to troubleshoot some of the more common problems administrators face daily. These might include network congestion, alarm floods, broadcast storms, bad cabling, excessive collision rates, failed adapter cards, and overloaded segments, just to name a few.

Because of the availability of state-of-the-art network components, planning and design tools, and management software, it's easier than ever to design and implement efficient network infrastructures. By properly designing and balancing the number of nodes residing on each network segment (also known as segmenting), problems such as broadcast storms can be reduced or eliminated altogether. Design tools can help you do this.

In the past, our understanding of what was actually happening on the network was limited, since there were no readily available, competent products to measure and report application traffic loads and network usage. Without the proper tools, finding solutions to some of the problems we face every day would be like asking a doctor to diagnose a medical problem in a patient they can't examine!

Management Consoles

A network management console functions like a control panel that allows you to monitor and control the components and applications that make up your network. Most consoles are based on software applications and utilize SNMP. By using SNMP, the console can communicate with any other SNMP-capable device. Components that implement these features are known to be SNMP-manageable. Management consoles are used for several functions:

- Configuring network devices.

- Analyzing network resource performance.

- Identifying and resolving network faults.

- Simplifying and automating network management tasks.

In addition, a variety of specialized management applications provided by console vendors or by third parties can be launched from the management console. For example, a hub or router vendor might offer a management application that executes as an add-on to one of the popular console packages available today.

One of the more popular network management packages available today is Solstice SunNet Manager (SNM) from SunSoft (see netref 4). SNM software is a network-based, multiplatform performance and fault-management tool. According to Sun literature it is the leading network management platform for single domains. SNM is available for both the SPARC and x86/Pentium platforms, providing coverage on popular RISC and CISC systems.

SNM is used to monitor and control network and system resources (see Figure 9-1). Integrated tools provide fault, configuration, accounting, performance, and security management services. In addition, SNM provides an integrated development environment that allows vendors as well as users to build custom tools to address unique requirements.

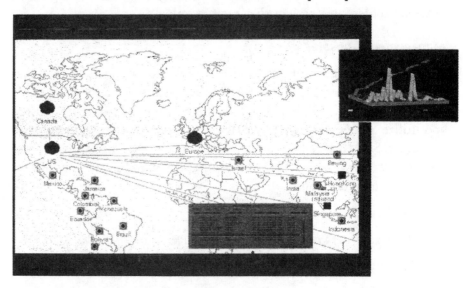

Figure 9-1. Solstice SunNet Manager (SunSoft).

Another approach to managing Internetworks uses the World Wide Web. WebManage technology from Tribe Computer Works (see netref 5) capitalizes on the distributed nature of the Internet, allowing its family of network products to be managed using standard Web browser software. For users in smaller environments where on-site technical support is not always available, the process of handling basic setup or port configurations using a graphical interface such as a Web browser can be quite appealing. The possibility of managing of routers, switches, remote access servers, and more using this type of technology can give non-technical users more control over managing their networks.

Out-of-band network management is used in situations where a router or other network component cannot be accessed via the main internetwork links (e.g., leased lines are temporarily down). Most routers or bridges provide serial ports that provide for the attachment of a modem. This allows you to dial directly into the unit to configure or troubleshoot. One of the main advantages of out-of-band network management is that if a system failure occurs (which may be severe enough to bring your LAN or WAN down completely), you can use a standard telephone link and modem to reach a bridge, router, or other network component to diagnose possible problems.

Hardware Tools

A network protocol analyzer is a hardware device that lets you look inside your network to help you determine what's going on or going wrong. It can capture individual data packets or streams of packets which can be time-stamped to help you diagnose time-out problems or examine network components that may not be responding to requests. It can also track network utilization levels and save the collected information for later review. An example of this would be collecting information to determine if a specific network segment is overloaded. Most network analyzers can also generate traffic, so you can see how a segment might behave when it's under a simulated load.

While some companies offer standalone network analyzers that require considerable expertise and more than just a basic understanding of network protocols and troubleshooting, others provide all-inclusive expert analyzers that require only minimal experience required (see netref 6). Connect the system to a power supply and your network, and you're off and analyzing. Some products even offer suggestions to help you correct problems on your network. With additional software, these products can take the data collected by these expert analyzers and automatically generate a model of your company's network. The model could include topology, protocols, applications, and LAN and WAN traffic.

Domain Names

There are two addressing schemes used on the Internet. An IP address is a unique numeric representation of a computer's location within a network. It comprises four sets of numbers separated by periods. A domain name is a unique alphabetic representation of a computer's location within a network. IP addresses can change, whereas domain names usually stay the same. Domain names are also easier to remember. Thus, the domain name is more commonly used when describing an Internet address.

The first segment of the domain name indicates the host computer name. The last segment identifies the top-level domain (see netref 7). Any items in between identify subdomains, which are networks or individual machines within the top-level domain. Domain names provide an organization with a unique identity that is used over the Internet and allows Internet users to find each other.

For example, snf.org identifies Strategic Networking Forums as an organizational domain, and paris.snf.org would be a host named paris at that domain, whereas is.nyu.edu would be a host at a university in the educational domain. Other domain categories are described below. A user receiving e-mail through a mail server at newyork.snf.org might use an e-mail address of gene@newyork.snf.org to represent a person named Gene who can be reached at that domain.

> **NOTE** For more information about e-mail and e-mail addresses, see Chapters 8 and 11.

Domain Name System

DNS, or domain name system, handles the translation from domain names to IP addresses. It is a distributed system, composed of a hierarchy of name servers and databases that handle address resolution requests.

There are two types of domain name servers: primary and secondary. Primary name servers store host name and IP address information while secondary name servers replicate this information. Unless network users are comfortable using raw IP addresses in place of host names, a name resolver such as DNS must be used. DNS is used extensively in the Internet as well as in larger private enterprise networks.

In the Domain Name System, there is a hierarchy of generic names called top-level domain names (TLDs). Five of these generic domains are international and two are restricted to use by organizations in the United States.

Worldwide Generic Domains

- COM–The COM domain was established for commercial organizations.

- EDU–The EDU domain was originally intended for all educational institutions. Many universities, colleges, schools, and educational service organizations are registered in this domain.

- NET–The NET domain is intended for registration of the computers of network providers. Customers of the network provider would have domain names of their own (not in the NET TLD).

- ORG–The ORG domain was instituted as the miscellaneous TLD for organizations that didn't fit into the other domains.

- INT–The INT domain is for organizations established by international treaties or international databases.

United States Only Generic Domains

GOV–Originally intended for government offices or agencies, only agencies of the U.S. Federal government may register in this domain.

MIL–The MIL domain is used exclusively by the U.S. military.

In smaller private networks, simple host tables are sometimes utilized instead of DNS. A host table is simply a list of host names along with their IP addresses. The downside to using host tables is that they must be replicated on each workstation, unless a naming service such as Sun's NIS (Network Information Services) is used. Formerly known as Yellow Pages, NIS is a de facto UNIX standard (see netref 8).

How DNS Works

Imagine an address book that contains the names and IP addresses of several domain name servers. To use this address book, you randomly contact one of the servers listed and request the IP address or domain name of the network device with which you want to communicate. If the server can't provide the requested address, it provides the name or address of another name server that might be able to service your request. This process will repeat itself until you get the address you're looking for or a message stating that the address doesn't exist.

The Windows NT Server uses domain-based directory services, not DNS. This provides a way for network managers to logically group users and resources into a domain controlled by a server called a Primary Domain Controller (PDC). The PDC validates user accounts upon login and provides a way for all servers in a domain to share the same user security database. Under this system, each domain must be managed separately. However, Windows NT Server (see netref 9) also offers the ability to create interdomain trust relationships. Thus, network administrators and managers in one domain can grant access privileges to users from other domains.

For administrators wishing to implement domain naming services within the Windows NT environment, DNS from MetaInfo (see netref 10) is a good choice. It offers good usable design for organizations operating an integrated Web site under NT because of its many features and low entry investment. Bind software, which is a popular UNIX DNS server implementation, is available free over the Internet (see netref 11). MetaInfo's DNS for Windows NT is a direct port of Bind 4.9.2 to

Windows NT. It is a true 32-bit multithreaded application and runs as a NT system service.

NOTE For more information about Windows NT, see Chapter 4.

Registering a Domain Name

Currently, the RIPE NCC (Réseaux IP Européens Network Coordination Centre) is the regional registry for Europe and the APNIC (Asia Pacific Network Information Center) is the regional registry for the Asia-Pacific region. The InterNIC administers the North America region and all as-yet-unappointed regions (see netref 12). The InterNIC Registration Services is located at Network Solutions, Inc., Herndon, VA, and is funded by a cooperative agreement from the National Science Foundation (NSF). The InterNIC provides assistance in registering networks, domains, Autonomous System Numbers (ASNs), and other Internet-related services to individuals and organizations.

As the Internet is growing so rapidly, there has been a huge increase in domain name requests. For domain name registration, you must submit an application via e-mail (see netref 13) that verifies that the chosen domain name does not conflict with one that is already in use or is someone else's trademark. Additionally, registrants are now limited to one domain name each and must pay a fee to register a domain.

Verifying a Domain Name

To verify if a domain name has been previously registered with the InterNIC, Whois can be used. Whois is a utility that provides an electronic white pages of Internet network entities such as domains, network numbers, ASNs, and their associated contacts.

To access Whois, use the telnet utility to connect to host RS.INTERNIC.NET. When greeted by the registration host, type WHOIS and press Return or Enter. Use the command WHOIS HELP for further information on how to use Whois. To perform a Whois query to see if the domain name SNE.COM has been previously registered, for example you could type WHOIS SNE.COM and press Return or Enter.

> **NOTE** For more information about Internet basic services and applications such as Whois, see Chapters 10 and 11.

IP Addressing

Network devices in a TCP/IP network need a unique IP address that is specified in dotted-decimal format. An IP address is a 32-bit binary number usually represented as four fields (sometimes called octets) with each field containing an 8-bit number in the range 0 to 255 separated by decimal points. An example is 198.181.149.23. This notation is commonly known as a dotted quad. Network administrators usually provide IP addresses.

An IP address consists of two parts: one identifies the network and one identifies the node. The Class of the address determines which part belongs to the network address and which part belongs to the node address. Classes can also be distinguished in decimal notation. If the first octet is between:

- 1 and 126–Class A address. Class A network numbers are reserved for the largest organizations.

- 128 and 191–Class B address. Class B network numbers are appropriate for fairly large organizations. There can be 16,394 Class B networks, each with up to 65,536 devices.

- 192 and 224–Class C address. Class C network numbers are assigned to most organizations requesting a network number. There can be approximately four million Class C networks, each supporting up to 254 devices.

- 225 and 240–Class D address (reserved for multicasting).

- 241 and 255–Class E address (reserved for future use).

The value 127 is reserved for loopback and is used for internal testing on the local network device.

Network Masks

Enterprise networks are often built by interconnecting workgroup and departmental LANs. These LANs (and sometimes WANs) that are interconnected with bridges and routers are known as subnetworks. A network mask, or netmask, is specified in decimal notation similar to an IP address. The netmask determines which part of the IP address specifies the subnetwork number and which part specifies the host on a subnet.

> **NOTE** For more information about bridges and routers, see Chapter 3.

Using the proper netmask is critical for correct routing. For example, if your workstation can communicate with network devices outside your network but not to devices within your network, chances are that an incorrect netmask has been specified. The most popular IP networks are Class C subnetworks which use 255.255.255.0 as their netmask. Class B subnetworks use 255.255.0.0.

IP addresses can be allocated in two ways: by static or dynamic addressing.

Static Addressing

Static IP addresses provide a consistent and reliable means of identification. This type of address is typically used by a server so that it can be accessed by other servers, workstations, and other types of network components. If the server's IP address was dynamically assigned, workstations might not be able to reach the server because the address would change each time it was booted.

Dynamic Addressing

Through dynamic addressing, a network server automatically provides IP addresses to machines when they boot. This eliminates the need to constantly change local configuration files. Because the addresses are assigned at boot time, all machines can share the same configuration.

An example of strategically using dynamic IP addressing is with remote users that access the network via a SLIP or PPP dial-up connection. It is common for mobile users to need access to data in several locations. By dynamically allocating a remote user's IP address, the organization can use a small block of IP addresses, a kind of dynamic address list, which can be solely dedicated to the mobile user base.

Dynamic Host Configuration Protocol

Dynamic Host Configuration Protocol (DHCP) provides a way for workstations on an IP network to get their configurations from a server, called a DHCP server. The DHCP servers have no knowledge of the workstations up to the point where they connect and make a request for configuration information. DHCP is designed to help reduce the amount of overhead involved when managing a large IP network. DHCP is particularly useful for network applications that require an IP address.

DHCP is based on BOOTP, or the bootstrap protocol. The major difference between the two is that BOOTP requires pre-configuration of host information in a server database, while DHCP allows for dynamic allocation of network addresses and configurations to attached hosts as well as automatic recovery and reallocation of unused IP addresses. For further information about DHCP, refer to the specifications in RFC1541, RFC1534, RFC1533 (see netref 14).

NOTE For more information about protocols, see Chapter 7.

New Protocols

The rapid and extensive growth of the Internet has brought about a number of difficulties relating to the management of IP network numbers. The overhead associated with the allocation of IP network numbers for global Internet users has placed a great burden on the organizations that perform this function. In addition, the volume of IP network numbers that are now reachable through the Internet has taxed the capabilities of many routers to manage forwarding tables. Also, poor utilization by organizations of allocated IP network numbers has threatened to deplete the Class A and Class B network address space.

Over the past few years, agreement among the Internet community in favor of a number of possible solutions to these problems has emerged. Essential changes to the Internet protocols to ensure the Internet's continued long-term growth and well-being are being considered. Two of these proposed changes are CIDR and IPng.

CIDR (Classless Inter-Domain Routing)

Classless Inter-Domain Routing (CIDR) allows routers to group routes together in order to cut down on the quantity of routing information carried by core routers (see netref 15). Coupled with BGP-4 (Border Gateway Protocol Version 4), CIDR will allow the Internet to grow until the eventual deployment of new protocols, such as IPng.

IP Next Generation

The Internet Engineering Task Force (IETF) has proposed a new protocol called IP Next Generation (a.k.a., IPng or IPv6) to extend the present IPv4 version and help accommodate this extraordinary growth of Internet users and IP address requests (see netref 16). The IPv6 protocol replaces the present version's limited 32-bit addresses with 128-bit addresses.

NOTE For more information about protocols, see Chapter 7.

SECURITY

Security breaches occur every day. We read about them in newspapers. We hear stories of exotic high-tech espionage as well as hacker attacks. Although many of these assaults are foiled, some succeed in stealing vital government and business secrets or fleecing electronic cash out of secure accounts. However, there are a number of ways to prevent and confront security breaches.

One example is to implement a strict policy of explicit rights and privileges to data and other resources. These rights center around certain management functions such as adding and removing devices, reformatting mass storage devices, and changing the protections or ownership of directories and files for example.

As the system grows, more privileges can be added or revoked. We do not mean to imply that the actual task of managing rights and privileges on a network is an easy task. At some point, the management and control of managing rights and privileges can become a full-time obligation.

The reality of today's internetworked society is that any node attached to the network is vulnerable to attack and can be compromised, even if the attacker has no idea where the machine resides or the nature of its configuration. To ensure critical business data is protected, it's important to carefully develop and follow a security plan.

Security Planning

The first step the security-conscious, networked organization must take is to develop policies and procedures which become the foundation for a comprehensive security plan. The security plan is driven, much like the implementation of technology itself, by the requirements of the business. Balancing the need for a secure network environment with the high availability and accessibility that users demand can be difficult, but not impossible.

Determining what must be protected and from whom is a good first step. Generally, security can be divided into three areas: account, network, and data security. Account and network security address the need to keep unauthorized users from gaining access to the system. The third area, data security, is concerned with preventing unauthorized access to data.

Let's take a look at these three issues. While we've presented three possible approaches to addressing them, these suggested solutions do not contemplate policies or procedures for their use or implementation, which should be specific to each organization.

Account Security

Authentication is a procedure in which a user must prove they are who they claim to be. This process is typically associated with account logins when a password known only to the user, and linked to the user's network account, is used to verify the authenticity of the user. Sometimes, in systems requiring very high security, additional authorization procedures such as voiceprinting and fingerprinting are implemented.

Network Security

Certification provides a way to authenticate clients who wish to access resources in distributed environments when logging in to the system. The verification process is performed by trusted third-party called a certification server. The certification server lets other servers in the network know that the user is who she or he claims to be. At that point the user is cleared to use a secured service such as an application, file, or database server.

The certification procedure was developed at the Massachusetts Institute of Technology (MIT) and is implemented in the MIT Kerberos security system (see netref 17). Kerberos is implemented in e-mail packages such as Eudora Pro (see netref 18) to provide added security features when sending e-mail.

Data Security

An encryption system, also known as a cryptographic system, provides a way to transmit data across an untrusted network or communications system without fear of disclosing the content of the information to anyone who might come into possession of the information during its journey. There are two types of encryption services: private and public.

In private systems, information is converted using an algorithm based on a private key that is held by both the sender and receiver of the data. The converted data is meaningless and can be transmitted over untrusted networks. The recipient can decrypt the received data with the private key he or she owns. The issue with this type of system is getting a copy of the private key to the recipient while ensuring the key has not been compromised.

In a public system, users own private keys and make public keys available in public locations. Users wishing to send confidential data encrypt the data with the recipient's public key. Once this data is encrypted with a public key, it only be decrypted using the private key owned by the recipient.

NOTE For more information about privacy, see Chapters 8 and 13.

Security on the Web

If your organization operates an integrated Web site, there are a number of specific security issues that must also be addressed in the security plan.

CIAC (see netref 19), established in 1989, is the U.S. Department of Energy's Computer Incident Advisory Capability. Using these general guidelines as a starting point when implementing a Web site is a good idea:

- The information server should reside on a system dedicated solely to information distribution. Only information to be distributed should reside on this system. Assume that any information placed on the system will be made available to the Internet userbase, should the Web server be compromised.

- Servers should run with as little privilege as necessary. If at all possible, server software should not run as root on UNIX systems. This limits possible damage if an intruder discovers a vulnerability.

- Whenever possible, server software should be executed in a restricted file space (chroot environment in UNIX), thus restricting files to which the server has access and making it more difficult for users to access unintended information.

- System administrators should closely monitor the integrity of the system and the information to be distributed.

Using the filtering features of bridges and routers a network boundary, or firewall, can be created. Information packets are filtered to prevent certain types of data from passing through the bridges and routers. Packets are typically filtered based on their type, e.g., IPX or AppleTalk, or destination address.

> **NOTE** For more information about bridges and routers, see Chapter 3. For more information about protocols, such as IPX and AppleTalk, see Chapter 7.

Firewalls

An Internet firewall is one of the best ways to protect a network against unauthorized access. The main purpose of a firewall is to guarantee that the communication between an organization's internal networks and the Internet conforms to the organization's security policies. Thus, firewalls allow networked users to access the Internet while keeping unknown or untrusted users out. For example, a firewall can be constructed to protect against unsecured remote login (rlogin) access which would allow intruders to enter the network. Internet firewalls are generally built around routers or gateways, functioning as a one-way door to the Internet.

Physically, a firewall is a combination of computers and software that is strategically deployed between a company's network and the Internet. More complicated firewalls can block traffic traveling from outside the network to the inside, but could permit users on the inside to communicate freely with the outside world. Firewalls are also important in the sense that they can provide a central point where security and auditing can be imposed. The conceptual model of the firewall is a pair of devices: one that is deployed to block traffic, and another that exists to allow traffic.

Authentication and other privacy enhancements are good complements to firewalls, but stopping intruders from getting into your company's private network is the first and most important step. Firewall implementations should adhere to the following basic structure (Cheswick and Bellovin, 1994):

- Traffic to and from the network must pass through the firewall.

- The firewall itself must be resistant to penetration.

- Only authorized traffic is allowed to pass through the firewall.

Internal firewalls can also be implemented when there is a need to segregate certain domains from others within an organization. Let's use the administration, accounting, and product development workgroups at a commercial applications development organization as an example. Corporate policy might dictate that public access to accounting records is restricted. The development group might want to keep its source code highly confidential. Firewalls, strategically situated between these domains could help accomplish these goals.

By detecting unauthorized or unusual access attempts to the network, a firewall helps network administrators and managers identify hackers and respond proactively instead of reactively to possible network break-ins. A well designed firewall should provide detailed reports and analysis features, including alarms that signal possible security breaches, analysis of unusual traffic, and overall Internet utilization reports, to name a few.

Firewalls can't protect against attacks that don't go through the firewall. Many organizations are concerned about proprietary data flowing out of the company through Internet as well as internetwork connections. In cases like this, it is just as likely that internal sources could copy data to magnetic tapes or disks, and the like, to export data. To be successful, a company's firewall policies must be realistic and should conform to the security policies and procedures of the organization. In addition, to properly maintain installed firewalls, administrators and managers must keep pace with advances in security procedures, technologies, and hacker techniques.

Packet-filter Gateway

A packet-filter gateway acts as a router between two networks and functions at the Transport layer of the OSI model. It usually consists of a series of simple checks based on source and destination IP addresses and ports. As packets flow from their source to the destination, the packet-filtering gateway either forwards or blocks them. Packet filters are often implemented on routers, with most major router vendors supplying packet filters as part of the router's default operating system distribution.

Application Gateways

Application gateways function at the Application layer of the OSI model. In most application gateway implementations, additional packet filter machines are required to control and screen the traffic between the gateway and the networks. A typical configuration includes two routers with a host in the middle, which serves as the application gateway.

NOTE For more information about the OSI model, see Chapter 6.

Instead of a list of rules that define which packets or sessions are allowed through the firewall, a program or application accepts the connection. It then performs strong authentication on the user, such as requiring a one-time password. After this password check, it often prompts the user for information on what host to connect to. Application gateways and packet-filtering routers can be combined to provide higher levels of security and flexibility than if either approach were implemented alone. Application gateways are used to protect telnet and ftp sessions, e-mail, X Windows, and other services.

For example, an outside user who has opened an ftp session (via the ftp application gateway) to an internal system (such as an anonymous ftp server) might then try to upload files to the server. The application gateway can filter the ftp protocol and deny all puts, or uploads, to the anonymous ftp server. The application gateway ensures that nothing can be uploaded to the server. It provides a level of additional security, versus sole reliance on file permissions being set correctly at the anonymous ftp server.

For most environments, these gateways provide much higher security because, unlike the other types of gateways, it can perform strong user authentication to ensure that the person on the other end of the IP connection is really who they say they are.

Circuit-level Gateways

A circuit-level gateway relays TCP connections but does no extra processing or filtering of the protocol. An example of this would be where an NNTP (Network News Transfer Protocol) server connects to a firewall. The internal systems' NNTP clients would connect to the firewall as well. The firewall would simply pass the NNTP information through from the NNTP server to qualified clients. The clients see the packets as originating from the firewall instead of the NNTP server.

SOCKS (see netref 20) is a popular de-facto standard for automatic circuit-level gateways. It allows hosts behind a firewall to gain full access to the Internet without requiring direct IP reachability. It works by redirecting requests to talk to Internet sites to a server, which authorizes the connection and passes data back and forth.

> **NOTE** For more information about NNTP and other protocols, see Chapter 7. For more information about USENET news and newsgroups, see Chapter 11.

Hybrid Gateways

Application gateways are combined with circuit-level gateways or packet filters. When different gateways are combined, they are known as hybrid gateways. Hybrid gateways allow internal hosts unobstructed access to unsecured networks while implementing strong security on accesses from unsecured or untrusted networks.

Proxies

A proxy gateway (also referred to as a proxy server) serves as a gateway between a local network and the outside world (see netref 21). The primary use of proxies is to allow access to the World Wide Web from behind a firewall. Proxies typically run on firewall machines.

The proxy typically waits for a request from inside a firewall, forwards the request to a remote server beyond the firewall, then reads the remote server's response and forwards it back to the client. Proxies also perform document-caching services, enabling clients to obtain remote Web documents via the server instead of from the original site. When the proxy gets a request, it either fulfills the request from the cache or gets it from the original site (while caching it locally). Thus, any future requests for the document would be answered with a local copy of the document.

The result of this is that each document is downloaded only once, saving time and network bandwidth. Clients do not lose any functionality when going through a proxy, which understands most of the important World Wide Web protocols such as HTTP, WAIS, ftp, and NNTP. For example, let's look at a user on a workstation situated behind a firewall who wants to browse the Web.

The proxy gateway has been configured to allow specific connection requests from the user's workstation to be redirected to other ports on the proxy. If the workstation tried to open port 80 (the standard HTTP server port) on the proxy, for example, perhaps the proxy would redirect the request and allow the workstation to connect to its port 8080. In this way, the proxy actually makes the request over the Internet and retrieves the requested documents, not the workstation.

> **NOTE** For more information about protocols, see Chapter 7. For information about implementing integrated Web sites, see Chapter 10.

Secure Transactions

The Secure Sockets Layer (SSL) protocol, was developed by Netscape Communications Corp. and is implemented in certain commercial releases of their Web server and browser applications. It was developed to provide privacy over the Internet and allows client-server applications to communicate in a way that cannot be eavesdropped. Servers are always authenticated and clients are optionally authenticated. At the time of this writing, the SSL protocol has been submitted to the IETF as an Internet Draft (see netref 22).

SSL replaces networking subroutine calls used by Web server (or browser) software with modified, secure versions of these subroutine calls. These modified calls make use of encryption and digital signatures which are transparent to both the user and the Web software. The SSL routines control the collection of a public key from a server operated by RSA Associates' (see netref 23) certificate services department, the creation of a unique session key, and then encrypt communications using a strong encryption algorithm, RC4, which is licensed from RSA.

Secure HTTP (S-HTTP) is the scheme proposed by CommerceNet (see netref 24), a coalition of businesses interested in developing the Internet for commercial uses. It is a higher level protocol that works only with the HTTP protocol. S-HTTP is used in several commercially available Web server and browser products.

Unlike SSL, S-HTTP requires that the Web browser or server software understand and negotiate the details of choosing a method for encryption, exchanging encryption keys, and handling digital signatures. SSL can coexist with S-HTTP because S-HTTP is quite flexible.

Although both companies would like to see their secure transaction protocol adopted as an international standard, the use of two security methods raises interoperability issues. Businesses with a desire to perform online credit card transactions must approach customers differently, based on which Internet browser they're using.

For example, companies using SSL software can't guarantee the security of Web transactions initiated by browsers other than Netscape Navigator. Because of this and other compatibility issues, at the time of this writing the companies have agreed to a unification effort. The agreement paves the way toward universal, secure Internet commerce by offering a new standard that's essentially a hybrid of S-HTTP and SSL, and which would be compatible with both.

> **NOTE** For more information about how SSL and S-HTTP are used with Web servers, see Chapter 10.

ADMINISTRATION

System Administrator, Technical Support Specialist, Network Manager, LAN Manager, Systems Manager, Information Technology Specialist, and more recently, Technologist are some of the titles being applied to technical personnel whose duties involve the management of computer networks. There are probably dozens more, but in reality, it's hard to find many clearly defined boundaries in a technical environment, especially for roles that interact with non-technical users and management. What follows are some of the less glamorous, but very important functions left to system administrators to perform.

Backup

In most organizations, the topic of network backups does not get the attention it deserves. Let's get right to the point; backups are the heart of your organization. It's a simple rule. No backups, no organization. Many companies with well-designed backup policies and procedures recovered from the terrorist attack on the World Trade Center fairly quickly. Those without backup policies and procedures didn't have it so easy. But simply having a backup plan isn't enough. Our experience (and the experiences of many others) shows that, along with a plan, the backup application must be able to perform flawlessly. After all, what good is a backup if it can't be restored?

Implementing a backup strategy is not something you can get from a book or your backup software's instruction manual. A backup plan must be specifically designed to meet the requirements of the organization. These include the level of strategic benefit the data to be archived has to the company, the impact the backup process has on normal operations, and the ability to backup other operating systems. Centralizing the backup process allows the administrator to break up the network into smaller domains, which can represent remote sites or subnetworks within a local site. Backups can then be scheduled, executed, and managed from a single console.

There are a multitude of backup solutions for every platform available. Our advice is to check the trades for reviews and evaluations and ask your peers what they use. Be sure and obtain an evaluation copy from a prospective vendor before you buy. Make sure the product works within your infrastructure and can successfully backup and restore your sensitive data.

Virus Protection

Although many organizations consider themselves lucky to escape the increasing number of computer virus outbreaks in recent years, one of the only ways to really protect the network from the threat of infection is to proactively protect the network and its resources against viruses.

Virus software can be installed on servers and nodes to provide for virus scans at system startup, on demand, or when files and directories are accessed. Features such as pager, console, and network broadcast notification services allow administrators to quickly respond to virus threats. Selecting products that support fast execution and scanning times make daily virus prevention tasks less intrusive on server resources and users.

Inventory

Inventory and asset management packages can help keep track of network hardware and software, letting you know if you're in compliance with software licensing agreements. They can also help spot configuration changes that may cause problems. Some products also include support for software distribution.

One example is The Norton Administrator for Networks (NAN) from Symantec (see netref 25). NAN provides a single solution that automates the often repetitive administration tasks of software distribution, hardware and software inventory, and software metering over a heterogeneous environment. NAN supports DOS, Windows, Macintosh, and OS/2 workstations and includes reporting, charting, and exporting capabilities.

Service and Support

Service and support is big business. There are many companies that specialize in providing these technical services to organizations large and small. Some of the more popular services available include standard service packages where the vendor agrees, for a certain fee, to provide technical repairs and services onsite. Other programs include hot swap programs, hot spares, help desks, and disaster recovery and contingency services.

Maintenance

Many companies hire service companies to provide consistent system maintenance and repairs to their organizations throughout the country or the world. Regardless of the hardware problem or branch location, administrators can make a single phone call to the service provider's hotline. Relationships such as, these help to ensure that systems stay up and running and also reduce downtime. This approach gives the company specialized technical expertise in areas where they chooses not to use its in-house staff.

Help Desks

What's the ultimate goal of the help desk? Ideally, a fast, accurate resolution for each question or problem. This approach requires an investment in qualified personnel as well as applications designed to provide timely information on a variety of technical subjects, from workstation configurations to network cabling specifications (see netref 26).

For example, The Micro House (see netref 27) Technical Library on CD-ROM provides technical specifications and configuration information from over 1600 manufacturers. According to Micro House, this information includes details on PC clones, outdated, unsupported, and unidentified system boards, network interface cards, hard drives, controller cards, peripheral cards, and more. A tool like this can save administrators many hours of unproductive downtime searching for answers to the technical problems that commonly plague companies of all sizes.

Help desk applications provide a way for you to actually manage the network management process itself. Some help desk software allows you to assign trouble orders or tickets as well as technicians to specific problems. This provides a way for support managers and staff to efficiently track the problem-solving effort to a successful close. The ability to track your technical problems from start to finish is one of the keys to maintaining a successful help desk.

Other strategic uses of the help desk include searches through records of past incidents to see how specific problems have been resolved. Managers could use the reporting features of some help desk software to generate reports to analyze whether manpower levels meet the requirements of the enterprise. Artificial intelligence is becoming more widespread in help desk applications, with some applications even providing popular solutions to a problem while you're entering the symptoms! If your business depends on computers and information technology to compete in today's global economy, help desk technology provides your enterprise with a tactical approach to solving problems more efficiently.

Documentation and Training

Systems documentation is critical to the development and maintenance of a network. Technical writers, whether in-house or outsourced, should have specific experience in describing procedures and software associated with computer and network systems. Administrators, programmers, and managers should support, but not assume, this highly-specialized work.

When it comes to training as a function of network management and system administration, there are two distinct groups: the network management and operations staff and the users. Staff should regularly receive training on new procedures and equipment through vendor and in-house programs. This is especially true for new hires and also when the system undergoes an upgrade. Changes to the network and staff are innovations which must be strategically managed so that changes are successfully made. The appropriate timing and selection of training topics and methods can have a profound effect on the bottom line of the organization.

User competence is perhaps the most critical component of a smooth-running network. Adequately trained users place much lower demands on network support staffs, and network managers with proper skill sets can head off or resolve problems more quickly. Training providers can be an important resource to network managers.

Using the vast amount of information and expertise available on the Internet is a strategic way to leverage your time and financial resources. Newsgroups and mailing lists (see netref 28) are plentiful on such topics as system administration and networking, and managers can effectively filter and moderate how these resources are used within the organization to keep knowledge and skills current, to troubleshoot, and plan change.

Training is an important issue that should be addressed when considering a Web site, too. Must the technical support staff be trained to support the Web site? Perhaps new hires will be necessary. Whatever the situation, management must be practical about the level of support they can expect from their technical staff as well as from the Internet service provider (ISP). While many ISPs provide excellent technical support, the reality is that the level of technical support offered by most ISPs is basic, at best.

Users must also be conscious of the limits of the technology in terms of how it meets the needs of the business. Many users new to the Internet expect instant gratification when seeking information and services. Unfortunately, while the Internet is rich in content, knowing where to look for information and services requires time and patience. As with any new technology, there is a certain learning curve associated with using the Internet.

REFERENCES

Net References

1. www to http://www.novell.com/ then browse the Novell home page for information about Novell products.

2. www to http://www.ietf.org/ then browse the IETF home page for information about the IETF.

3. www to http://www.iso.ch/ then browse the ISO home page for more information about the ISO.

4. www to http://www-dmo.external.hp.com/nsmd/ov/main.html then browse this page for information about OpenView. Information about SunNet Manager can be found at http://www.sun.com/cgi-bin/show?products-n-solutions/sw/solstice/network/snm.html

5. www to http://www.tribe.com/ then browse the Tribe home page for information about their products.

6. http://www.ngc.com/
This is the home page for Network General Corporation. Specific information about the Sniffer Analyzer can be found at http://www.ngc.com/product_info/

7. ftp to ftp://ftp.isi.edu/in-notes/iana/assignments/country-codes then browse this page for a list of top-level domain names.

8. www to http://www.eng.auburn.edu/users/doug/nis.html then browse this text on securing NIS. Background information about the latest version of Sun's Network Information Service Plus (NIS+) is located at http://www.Sun.COM/cgi-bin/show?sunsoft/solaris/Solaris-datasheets/NISplusTechnicalSpe.html

9. www to http://www.microsoft.com/NTServer/ then browse the Microsoft Back Office page for more information about NT Server.

10. www to http://www.metainfo.com/ then browse the MetaInfo home page for more information about DNS and other products.

11. ftp to ftp://ftp.uu.net/networking/ip/dns/bind/ then download the specific version of Bind you want.

12. www to http://rs.internic.net/registration-services.html for more information about the InterNIC registration services. The RIPE Network Coordination Centre can be reached at http://www.ripe.net/

A copy of the RIPE Database Template for Networks and Persons can be found at ftp://ftp.ripe.net/ripe/docs/ripe-119.txt

ftp to ftp://ftp.apnic.net then search the /apnic/info/articles directory for more information about APNIC.

13. ftp to rs.internic.net then change to the /templates directory. Transfer the file /templates/domain-template.txt for a domain name registration template.

14. www to http://www.cis.ohio-state.edu/htbin/rfc/rfc-index.html then search the RFC index list for the RFC number you want. Click on the link to access the RFC source document.

15. www to http://cio.cisco.com/warp/public/582/18.html then browse this page for more information on CIDR.

16. www to http://ganges.cs.tcd.ie/4ba2/ipng/ then search this page for more information about IPng.

17. The Kerberos page at MIT can be found at http://www.mit.edu:8001/people/proven/kerberos/kerberos.html

www to http://nii.isi.edu/publications/kerberos-neuman-tso.html then browse the document, "Kerberos: An Authentication Service for Computer Networks" for a good overview of Kerberos. Further Kerberos links can be found at http://www.yahoo.com/Computers_and_Internet/Security_and_Encryption/Kerberos/

18. www to http://www.qualcomm.com/quest/QuestMain.html then browse this page for more information about Eudora and Eudora Pro.

19. www to http://ciac.llnl.gov/ then browse this page for more information on Internet security.

20. www to http://www.socks.nec.com/ then browse this page for more information about SOCKS.

21. www to http://www.w3.org/hypertext/WWW/Proxies/ then browse this page for more information about World Wide Web proxies.

22. www to
gopher://ds.internic.net:70/00/internet-drafts/draft-hickman-netscape-ssl-01.txt then
browse this page for the full text of the SSL Internet draft document.

23. www to http://www.rsa.com/ then browse the RSA home page for more information
on RSA data encryption products.

24. www to http://www.commerce.net/ then browse this page for for more information
about CommerceNet and S-HTTP.

25. www to http://www.symantec.com/lit/util/netut/nan20.html then browse the NAN
page for more information about NAN.

26. www to http://bos_npa.silverplatter.com/cdref.htm then browse this page for more
information about Network Support or Network Reference applications on CD-ROM.

27. www to http://www.microhouse.com/ then browse this page for Micro House
product information.

28. ftp to ftp://ftp.uu.net/uunet-info/ then download the file newsgroups.Z or
newsgroups.gz for a good sampling of available newsgroups. Under Windows, an
application such as WinZIP can uncompress these files.

Suggested Reading

These additional net references are provided to help you find additional information on
topics described in this chapter:

For a glossary of network management terms, www to
http://www.netcreations.com/fibercorp/glossary.htm

http://smurfland.cit.buffalo.edu/NetMan/index.html is a good reference for Network
Management sites and information on the Internet.

http://www.wp.com/lowens/ is the Network Management Resources Home Page. Good
links to the latest developments in network management technology, products, and
standards.

Links to Network Management information and related sites can be found at
http://www.yahoo.com/Computers_and_Internet/Networking_and_Communications/Network_Management/

Northeast Consulting Resources, Inc. (NCRI) offers an online discussion group on network and system management moderated by Jim Herman. The purpose of this discussion group is to better understand how to accelerate progress in solving the problems of managing complex multivendor networks and distributed systems.

www to http://www.ncri.com/NM_Forum.html for additional information.

The document SNMP & CMIP: An Introduction to Network Management can be found at http://www.undergrad.math.uwaterloo.ca/~tkvallil/snmp.html

This Network Management page presents an unbiased evaluation of network management products that enable administrators to manage their networks more efficiently. www to http://yoda.semcor.com/~yarbroug/ for more information.

www to http://snmp.cs.utwente.nl/iso/ then browse this page containing references to existing literature, software, and other information sources related to network management.

www to http://usenix.org/about_sage.html for information about the System Administrators Guild.

www to http://www.first.org/tools/tools.htm#firewall then browse a comprehensive listing of network security tools and sites where they can be obtained.

www to http://www.ncsa.com/fwpd1.html then browse the FireWall Product Developers' (FWPD) Consortium page. Links to FWPD Consortium members are here, too.

www to http://www.netins.net/showcase/fidonet/sysadmin.htm for a Tribute to System Administrators.

www to http://www.nmf.org/home.htm then browse the Network Management Forum home page for information, publications, and other information related to network management. The NMF is an organization that attempts to promote and accelerate the worldwide acceptance and implementation of a common, service-based approach to the management of networked information systems.

www to http://www.wp.com/LOWENS/ then browse The Network Management Resources home page for comprehensive links to the latest developments in network management technology, products, and standards.

www to http://wwwsnmp.cs.utwente.nl/int/ for the Internet Management Navigator.
The network management information in this section is primarily based on European-
related network management matters.

Several of the following titles were the result of a search of the Library of Congress
records. You can do this by using telnet to connect to locis.loc. gov. Select the first
option, "Library of Congress Catalog," then follow the instructions for searching.

Baker, R. H. 1995. *Network Security: How to plan for It and Achieve It*. NY: McGraw-Hill.

Devargas, M. 1993. *Network Security*. Manchester, England: NCC Blackwell.

Goralski, W. 1995. *Internetworking: Building and Managing   Enterprisewide Networks*.
Charleston, SC: Computer Technology Research Corp.

Kaufman, C. 1995. *Network Security: Private Communication In A Public World*. Englewood
Cliffs, NJ: PTR Prentice-Hall.

Miller, M. 1995. *Internetworking: A Guide to Network Communications LAN To LAN, LAN
to WAN, Second Edition*. NY: M&T Books.

Shaffer, S. L. 1994. *Network Security*. Boston, MA: AP Professional.

Stang, D. J. 1992. *Network Security, 6th Edition*. Washington, DC: International
Computer Security Association.

10

Internetwork Servers and Gateways

ABOUT THIS CHAPTER

Internetwork servers and gateways are the software engines that deliver your presence on information superhighways and throughout your enterprise. Look here for individual coverage of setting up and using Web, network news, mail, file transfer, search engines, multimedia, and other types of servers and gateways. Establishing an Internet presence? Look here for an overview of building an integrated Web site with multiple servers working in harmony. Descriptions of enterprise servers are also included.

INTRODUCTION

As organizations grow, LANs are frequently interconnected to form WANs. These WANs, also known as internetworks, are the infrastructure that provides organizations with the ability to communicate, operate, and transact on a global scale.

Shared information contained on servers throughout the enterprise can help organizations expand new markets while advancing communications with management and employees. There are many different kinds of servers, from file servers that provide LAN data repository services to World Wide Web servers (see netref 1) supplying documents, audio, video, and other digital information and services to a global userbase.

Servers are computers that run specialty software to operate, such as database or Web server software. They are the foundation for client/server networks. Also known as distributed environments, client/server networks allow the organization to strategically locate resources and services throughout a network instead of centralizing them, as in traditional mainframe environments.

> **NOTE** For more information about internetworks and client/server networks, see Chapter 6. More information about the World Wide Web can be found in Chapter 11.

Servers can be deployed departmentally as part of a local workgroup, such as a document file server, or for access by an entire organization such as a database server. While servers are essential for delivering content over an internetwork, gateways are also necessary. They protect the organization from unwanted access, like a firewall can when tactically placed between an internal network and the Internet. They can also perform services such as the exchange of electronic mail between internal systems and those outside the organization. An example of this type of gateway would be a cc:Mail to SMTP gateway, allowing users on an internal LAN using cc:Mail to communicate with systems outside the organization who use SMTP-based mail applications, and vice versa.

NOTE For more information about electronic mail, see Chapters 8 and 11. For information about firewalls, see Chapter 9. Information about SMTP and other protocols can be found in Chapter 7.

With the convergence of telecommunications, television, and computer technologies into the digital realm, organizations with a desire to learn about and exploit current network technologies can gain an important edge. Part of that edge is establishing an Internet presence. Whether the organization is a small art gallery that wants to display and sell paintings, a school that wants to promote its educational services, or a well-established company with a global operation, a presence on the Internet is essential (see netref 2). A presence on the Internet equates to having an address and performing a service or producing products there in the same way that organizations do at their physical sites.

NOTE For more information about Internet addresses and domains, see Chapter 9.

The importance of having an address on the Internet is due in part to the fact that the Internet is already a useful model for interoperability. UNIX, Macintosh, PC, and mainframe computers all share space on the Internet. As of Spring, 1995, use of the World Wide Web exceeded e-mail and file transfers on the main backbone of the Internet. The World Wide Web provides an unprecedented opportunity to do business with millions of customers. Thus, more and more companies are finding the Web to be a strategic focus for an Internet presence because it provides a robust and globally accessible development and delivery platform.

It is robust because there are currently as many as 30 million users, with a large and growing number of organizations providing products and services on the Web. The Web is a blending of platforms, applications, and services that interoperate to comprise one of the largest internetworks on the planet. Organizations can use the Internet and future information superhighways to leverage their expertise in marketing and technology against the relatively low entry costs that are associated with connecting to and using the Internet.

As many organizations are already discovering, we believe that building an integrated Web site is a strategic networking solution. As we use the term, an integrated Web site uses many different servers in harmony to provide the right mix of content and services.

BUILDING AN INTEGRATED WEB SITE

Let's imagine the results of your work after building an integrated Internet presence. For example, upon accessing your organization's home page with their World Wide Web browser, people may see an attention-getting animation with sound created with Java. The applet actually recognizes who they are based on data obtained from a previous visit. As they browse the page, there are links to internal and Internet sites where mailing lists covering topics from company benefits to world politics are described. There are forms presented that allow them to subscribe and unsubscribe to the lists of their choosing.

Wide Area Information Servers (WAIS) comb through enterprise file server archives as well as Internetwork servers searching for requested information. Links to the organization's own gopher space (see netref 3), as well as gopher sites around the world are available, where information is displayed in a familiar menu format. Virtual Reality "worlds" are spawned, where three-dimensional worlds can be navigated for remote conferencing and site walk-throughs. Links to multimedia servers providing audio and video broadcasts of live and archived events can be found on the integrated Web site as well.

Links to news servers housing USENET newsgroups are also there, where more than 10,000 discussion forums exist on an incredible range of subjects from technical support issues to human sexuality. Vendor links to sites providing sales and product support are a mouse-click away, as are file transfer (ftp) sites where users can download the latest software patches, images, video, and sound from vendors, conferences, and archives.

There are also hyper-links to other helpful and interesting sites using various internetworking tools. Can't remember the title of the book a friend mentioned, such as Strategic Networking? Try the link to the

Library of Congress (see netref 4) via telnet. Need a phone number for a vendor or perhaps a friend at a university? Use the Ph server link or finger request form (see netref 5). Requests for information about a specific user will be returned by these servers.

NOTE For more information about Internet applications, see Chapter 11.

Establishing an Internet Presence

By establishing a presence on the Internet through a Web site, organizations and individuals can gain access to a market of global magnitude. The model of electronic commerce can be found on the Web, whether to advertise, sell products, publicize the organization, or to offer information. The foundation of that presence is a Web site. Here is a high-level blueprint for its construction.

NOTE For more information about the Internet, see Chapter 11.

Choosing an Internet Provider

An Internet Service Provider (ISP) will be necessary to access and communicate via the Internet. When considering a connection to the Internet, you must decide whether or not full-time connectivity is required. Around-the-clock availability involves dedicated links to an ISP, which can be expensive to install and maintain. Pricing from local and long distance carriers can change frequently and vary from site to site. While it is possible to operate a Web site using high-speed modems, this type of connection will be relatively slow and multiple connections will most likely overload the link. In addition, when using dial-up SLIP or PPP connections, the Web site is available only when a connection is made to the provider.

NOTE For more information about SLIP, PPP, and other protocols, see Chapter 7.

For most Web sites, a 56Kbps dedicated link to a service provider is the minimum acceptable configuration. If the organization anticipates a large amount of traffic or intends to serve complex documents with audio and video included, they may require more bandwidth than a 56Kbps connection can provide for decent performance. In this case, a T1 line (1.54Mbps) or fractional T1 would be a better choice.

NOTE For more information about T1 links and other network services, see Chapter 5.

Many telecommunications companies offer Internet connectivity services as well as high-speed network services. If the organization already uses high-speed network services, these existing assets can be leveraged to facilitate an Internet connection. Some ISPs also offer Web home page design and management services. They will help design HTML pages, and will also store, and manage the content right on their Web servers. While costs vary among ISPs, setting up a Web site in this manner requires little or no capital investment.

When selecting an ISP, consider the level of technical support the organization requires. Many ISPs have come a long way in providing quality technical support, while others may not measure up.

NOTE For more information about ISPs and Internet connectivity, see Chapter 11. Information about HTML can be found in Chapter 8.

Establish an Internet Address

A unique domain name and IP address are needed to establish an Internet connection for a Web site. In many cases, especially in non-UNIX environments, TCP/IP software will also be needed. TCP/IP is part of the UNIX operating system and is often bundled with certain operating systems and network operating systems, such as Windows NT. In the case of Windows NT, TCP/IP is included but not automatically installed when NT is installed.

NOTE For more information about domain names, registration, and IP addressing, see Chapter 9. For more information about TCP/IP, see Chapter 7. For information about operating systems and network operating systems, see Chapter 4. Information about protocol suites can be found in Chapter 8.

Determining System Requirements

The next step is to determine the hardware platform and operating system. Many Web server products can operate on platforms as basic as an Intel 386-based computer running DOS and Windows 3.1 (see netref 6). For interoperability and supportability, the operating system you choose should be based on the company's existing hardware and software infrastructure.

Web servers are available for most software platforms, including UNIX, Windows 3.1 and Windows 95, Windows NT, OS/2, Mac OS, VMS, AmigaOS, and OS/400 (see netref 7). Web sites anticipating considerable activity should seriously consider dedicating a host computer to be used exclusively as the Web server. However, under low loads it would be possible to use the host for other tasks in addition to its Web server duties.

NOTE For more information about operating systems and network operating systems, see Chapter 4.

As content is added to the server over time, it will eventually exhaust hard disk storage space on the host computer. Of course, this depends on the Web server software as well as the content that is being served. Content that is rich in graphics and other multimedia information will take up considerably more room than text-based HTML files. When building a Web server the rule for hard disk storage is the bigger the better. The main idea is to have enough archive space available to reduce the possibility of downtime and expense related to a hard disk upgrade as the Web server and its contents evolve.

Selecting and Configuring a Web Server

Next, the actual Web server software must be selected, installed, and configured. According to a survey conducted by Paul E. Hoffman (see netref 8) in October 1995, the most popular Web servers were the free UNIX-based servers from NCSA and CERN, as well as Apache, a spin-off from the NCSA server (see netref 9). The next most popular category was commercial software led by Netscape's. UNIX-based software, MAC-based WebSTAR, and PC-based WebSite (see netref 10). There were over a dozen other server packages found, each of which had only a small percentage of the server market.

The selection, installation, and configuration of Web server software can be different for each organization. While one would expect Web server applications to come with an interactive installation program and strong documentation, this is not always the case, especially when obtaining free server software via the Internet. In most instances, the installation procedure often requires steps such as modifying a configuration file, which includes information such as the name of the server, the server port (the standard port for HTTP servers is 80), and the top-level directory or folder from which files will be served. Depending on the operating system, this process can be very simple or somewhat involved.

Once these steps are accomplished, the remainder of the Web server configuration process entails more rudimentary tasks, such as setting up base-line HTML documents and maintenance options. One of the HTML documents will be designated as the home page, which is usually the first page to appear when a Web site is visited. It contains high-level information about the organization and what is found on the other pages. Considerable planning, design and testing should be made for each of the pages and for how all of them work together.

If the Web server is UNIX-based, the installation and configuration could be a bit more involved. Besides editing configuration files, there may be a requirement to edit and compile source code. Server installations on other platforms, such as UNIX, can be quite complex, requiring technical knowledge above and beyond that of a typical user.

Supporting the Web Site

Ongoing support and maintenance is an important part of keeping the integrated Web site running smoothly and efficiently. This includes training users, verifying HTML documents, and checking the integrity of links to other sites and information on the Internet. This is necessary because hypertext links can become outdated as sites evolve, server content is changed, and servers become unavailable. Typographical errors inadvertently entered into a URL (Uniform Resource Locator) can render a link useless, returning annoying server error messages to the client. Thus, a major part of maintaining a Web site consists of finding and fixing a variety of possible HTML and link-related errors.

> **NOTE** For more information about publishing and graphics and document markup languages such as HTML, see Chapter 8.

While smaller Web sites can be maintained with relative ease, sites that serve a large volume of frequently changing data can be almost impossible to support and maintain. The level of available technical support within the organization, or from an outside source such as an ISP, is an important consideration. The issue of support must be addressed before the Web site is implemented. After all, there's really no way to provide a stable Web site that meets acceptable performance and availability standards if there is no one qualified to address technical problems.

> **NOTE** For more information about managing internetworks, see Chapter 9.

INTERNETWORK SERVERS

Internetwork servers provide many services, from serving HTML documents over the World Wide Web to providing USENET news across enterprise networks. This sections describes popular internetwork servers and their unique functions.

> **NOTE** For more information about newsgroups, see Chapter 11.

Web Server

A Web server provides a presence on the World Wide Web from which Web client applications (called browsers) can access information. This type of server is technically known as an HTTP (Hypertext Transfer Protocol) server, because it is used for distributing HTML (Hypertext Markup Language) information over the World Wide Web. Web servers run HTTP as a service under Windows NT or as a daemon under UNIX. Both of these terms refer to the background operation of the server.

However, Web servers are not confined to Internet use. They can be used for internal applications, such as distributing information within an organization. Human resource policies, procedures, and training information, and marketing materials such as fact sheets, catalogs, and price lists can be easily distributed. Online multimedia presentations can be made available to hundreds or even thousands of users. In addition, workgroups could document their projects using a Web server to share schedules, data, and other artifacts of their work.

Web server software is available for most operating systems, with many packages freely available via the Internet. Keep in mind, however, that a good portion of this freely available software was rapidly developed in research or university environments where rigorous security testing is not always given great significance.

For a guide to Web server software that is available via the Internet, start with the W3 Consortium home page (see netref 11). The links on this page provide further information about various Web server packages and can also be used to download the software. The W3 Consortium is an industry consortium run by the Laboratory for Computer Science at the Massachusetts Institute of Technology (MIT). Another good source of Web server software information can be found on the Web Servers Comparison page (see netref 12).

> **NOTE** For information about Web browsers, see Chapter 11. For information about HTTP, see Chapter 7. For information about HTML, see Chapter 8.

Personal and High-Performance Web Servers

There are two types of Web servers presently available for publishing information on the Internet: personal servers and high-performance servers (sometimes referred to as high-end servers).

A personal Web server is a low-cost, low maintenance Web server. It is generally used by individuals and small groups or organizations as an easy and quick way to establish a home page on the Internet and does not require any UNIX or advanced technical experience to install and maintain. However, this type of server also has limited features, provides minimal security, and does not generally offer the same capacity to service many simultaneous clients as a high-performance server.

The benefit of the personal Web server is that it can provide important flexibility to organizations because of the power it gives people to publish or read information—right from their desktops. The key is remembering that it's not how big you are or how big your Web site is, but it's your ability to have the flexibility and agility to serve and access servers without incurring the penalties of cost, complexity, and other factors frequently associated with high-performance Web servers. If an organization is considering secure and high-volume transactions over the net (e.g., electronic commerce), then a personal Web server wouldn't provide good organizational fit. For smaller workgroups, however, the ease of installation and use of personal Web servers is an example of usable design, and their application makes for good organizational fit.

A personal Web server (and client browser) is bundled with the NetManage Chameleon TCP/IP suite (see netref 13). It can be quickly installed and configured with Windows-based dialogs and immediately used with sample HTML files. Forms and image mapping are supported as well as some access control: only the default document root directory or one that you specify can be accessed by Web clients.

The Quarterdeck Web Server (see netref 14) is a Windows-based personal server that falls somewhere near the higher end of this class without the hassles associated with many high-performance servers. It can be set up in minutes within a Windows-style graphical configuration and runs in the background without using much memory. This server can handle up to 16 simultaneous connections and up to 25,000 requests per hour. Although its security features are limited, it still provides some control. It can determine access by users or groups and log server access. It supports image maps, CGI forms, and MIME.

High-performance servers provide secure communications and advanced performance to organizations and individuals who want to create or access information services on global networks. They enable electronic commerce and secure information exchange over the Internet, as well as private TCP/IP-based networks. Netscape Web servers, from Netscape Communications Corp., use Netscape Navigator's graphical interface to provide a simple, forms-capable interface for point-and-click server installation, configuration, and maintenance (see Figure 10-1). Forms are used for the initial configuration and management of server functions including user authorization, transaction logging, and process configuration (see netref 15). Netscape Web servers are available for many platforms including Windows NT, OSF/1, HP-UX, AIX, IRIX, SunOS, Solaris, and BSDI/OS.

> **NOTE** For more information about security and secure transactions over the Internet, see Chapter 9. Information about operating systems and network operating systems can be found in Chapter 4.

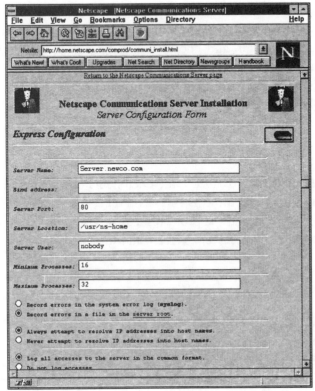

Figure 10-1. Configuring the Netscape Commerce Server™ (Netscape Communications Corporation).

Another high-performance Web server is the Internet Office Web Server from CompuServe (see netref 16). It offers built-in SQL support and allows users to create dynamic HTML pages that have the ability to connect directly to databases. The server offers secure transactions with support for both S-HTTP and Secure Sockets Layer (SSL) protocols. Versions are available for Windows NT, Sun Solaris, SunOS, HP-UX, AIX, and BSDI operating systems.

WebSTAR from StarNine Technologies, Inc. (see netref 17) is a Web server for Macintosh computers. It is based on Chuck Shotton's popular MacHTTP. WebSTAR allows organizations to publish hypertext documents on the Web, including GIF and JPEG images and QuickTime movies. WebSTAR is compatible with all Web clients including Mosaic, Netscape's Navigator, as well as Prodigy. An optional Security Toolkit provides authentication and encryption using SSL to ensure that Web connections are completely private. This enables WebSTAR to verify the identity of users and to encrypt transmitted data. Another optional toolkit called the Commerce Toolkit also includes SSL, which adds support for commercial transactions over the Internet.

How Web Servers Work

Using HTTP and HTML, electronic documents can be created that can use powerful Internet protocols such as SMTP, ftp, gopher, WAIS, and more. Let's look at how these protocols and services work together under the auspices of the Web server to create an integrated Web site.

> **NOTE** For more information about network protocols, see Chapter 7.

When a request is made by a browser, the HTTP service or daemon on the Web server responds to the request by sending a HTML-formatted Web document back to the browser for display. Most Web servers now support the Common Gateway Interface (CGI), which allows an application or script to be run on the server as part of the original HTTP request for a Web document. CGI applications can be developed in Perl, TCL (Tool Command Language), C++, Visual Basic, and other languages.

Here's an example of a typical session between a browser and Web server. A prospective customer accesses the company's home page using a browser. The Web server returns an HTML document that the customer sees. It offers a menu of products and services. The customer chooses "Browse Catalog" from a list of hyperlink choices. In seconds, the server returns another page with descriptions, pictures, and pricing information about the products contained in the selected catalog.

> **NOTE** For more information about CGI and HTML, see Chapters 8 and 11.

Another choice from the menu of products and services might allow the customer to download a formatted product catalog (frequently in ASCII unformatted text, PostScript, or popular word processing formats). Often, e-mail addresses are provided on the page which are used to contact the sales department or a particular salesperson. Yet another choice might be to fill out an order form to purchase products. Choosing to order a product returns a form to the browser which the user completes and submits, usually by way of a "submit form" button somewhere on the form.

This is where the CGI application comes into play. Submitting the form to the server triggers a CGI application or script that could parse information submitted by the browser and link to an inventory database to confirm product availability. If the product is available, it updates tables in the inventory database to reflect the quantity remaining. Next, the CGI script starts another application that submits the credit card number to a transaction processor for verification. If the charge is approved, the script generates an invoice, and an HTML document is returned to the browser and displayed. If the charge is not approved, the CGI script might return an HTML form advising the user to try another credit card. This is a simple example, but offers a glimpse into the possibilities and power of external processing with CGI.

What if the customer clicked on the button labeled "feedback"? In this case, the browser would forward the resulting document as an e-mail message and SMTP (Simple Mail Transfer Protocol) would carry the message to the server. If a copy of the product catalog was requested, it could be sent from the server via ftp. With many of the powerful HTML and SGML authoring tools available today, it's possible to build customized documents that provide enhanced views of Web content using powerful search engines like WAIS.

NOTE For information about SMTP, see Chapter 7. For information about HTML and SGML, see Chapter 8.

WAIS Server

A Wide Area Information Server (WAIS), houses databases containing mostly text-based documents, although WAIS documents may contain sound, pictures, or video as well. The WAIS server is a program that services client search requests. Anyone on the Internet can easily read the information published via WAIS by using a wide variety of browsers or viewers such as WAIS, Netscape, Mosaic, a gopher client, etc. WAIS servers are available for several platforms (see netref 18).

A WAIS server generally runs on a machine containing one or more information sources, or WAIS databases. The WAIS protocol is used to connect WAIS clients and servers and is based on the NISO Z39.50 Information Retrieval Service and Protocol Standard (see netref 19). This protocol suite allows WAIS to speak with multiple search clients.

> **NOTE** For more information about databases, see Chapter 8. For more information about protocols, see Chapter 7. For more information about Internet client applications, see Chapter 11.

Mail Server

A mail server comprises a host computer and software that together provide electronic mail reception and forwarding services. The mail server makes it possible for network users to send e-mail messages to, and receive messages from, any other user on the network.

An SMTP server uses the Simple Mail Transfer Protocol (SMTP) protocol which is the de facto standard for the Internet. It provides store and forward mail capabilities between host mail systems on a network. Working in conjunction with a client mail program, such as Eudora Pro by QUALCOMM Inc. (see netref 20), SMTP servers send mail created by the mail application and receive mail from other hosts on a network. After receiving e-mail, they pass messages to a local e-mail application. SMTP is a standard feature on UNIX platforms.

A POP server uses the Post Office Protocol (POP) to provide store and forward services. POP servers are intended to move mail on demand from an intermediate server, or mail collection point, to a single destination machine, usually a PC or Macintosh. Once delivered to the destination machine, the messages are typically deleted from the POP server.

IMail, from Ipswitch, Inc., (see netref 21) is an Internet e-mail product for Windows that includes both client and server software for SMTP and POP. These servers allow users to receive mail directly at their workstation. A single PC can be implemented as an IMail POP server where multiple IMail users can store and retrieve mail from their PCs using IMail's POP client. It supports MIME encoding and mailing lists.

IMail's Mail Server for Windows NT uses the NT services to receive, store, and forward mail via SMTP, and receive and transmit mail via POP3. It supports the use of four types of alias that can point to mail addresses on local or remote systems, a file containing a list of mail addresses, or to an executable program on the host system. User information can be provided with built-in finger and Whois services. Vacation processing allows an automatic response that is mailed once to each user who sends mail. A separate list server program provides the creation, management, and distribution of automated mailing lists. This package also includes a Windows Mail client.

Internet Shopper LTD's (see netref 22) NTMail for Microsoft Windows NT (Intel and Alpha) provides Internet standard SMTP and POP mail services. NTMail's 32-bit multi-threaded services take advantage of the scalability of Windows NT and provide support for single user systems, private corporate LANs, or LANs with local dial-up access to the Internet, as well as large WANs processing tens of thousands of messages per day. Mail servers use MX records. They can either forward or hold mail for those destinations that are currently unreachable. MX records indicate the host names and IP addresses of e-mail servers residing on a network. NTMail can act as an intelligent mail server for Microsoft Windows 95's Exchange Mail System, giving Windows 95 complete access to Internet mail.

Microsoft Mail Server offers a messaging infrastructure that supports users on the Windows, Windows NT Server, Windows NT Workstation, Windows for Workgroups, Windows 95, MS-DOS, Macintosh, and OS/2 operating systems. It is a popular choice for enterprise networks.

WinSMTP from Wildbear Consulting, Inc. is another flexible SMTP/POP3 server with auto-responder and mailing list features. WinSMTP is currently available in Windows 16- and 32-bit versions (see netref 23).

Auto-Responders

An e-mail auto-responder (also referred to as a mail reflector or mailbot) is another program that runs on a server. Auto-responder features are often part of SMTP server applications, such as NTMail (see Figure 10-2).

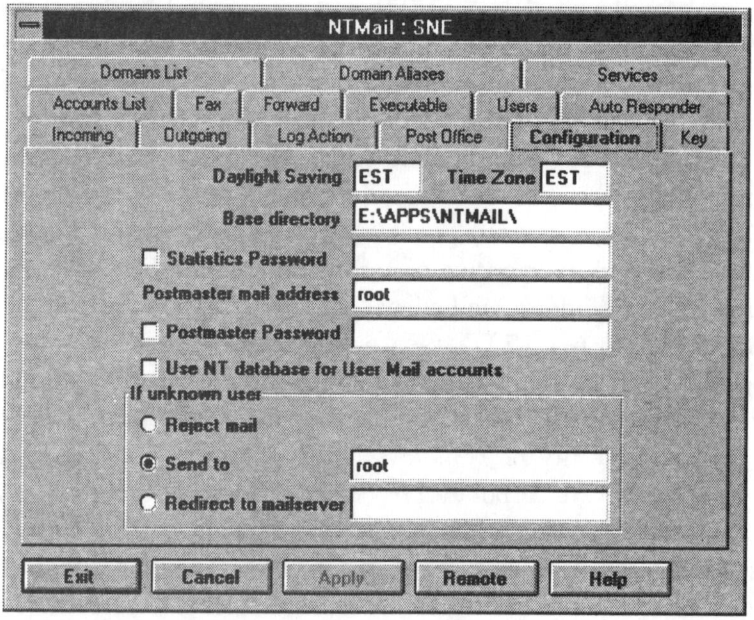

Figure 10-2. NT Mail configuration screen (Internet Shopper Ltd.).

An auto-responder will automatically send a document to any user who sends an e-mail request to the auto-responder's e-mail address. For example, immediately prior to publication, we set up an auto-responder to provide information about this book and related Strategic Networking Forums (see netref 24). We configured the auto-responder to return a corresponding document to the reply-to address it finds in your e-mail message. You send an e-mail request to the e-mail address that we assigned to the mailing list. The message doesn't need a subject or any body text.

The e-mail request is received by our SMTP server. We have defined a document that resides on our mail server such as one called book.txt. The auto-responder knows to send this text as an e-mail in response to any incoming e-mail addressed to it. Thus, the ASCII file called book.txt is processed and sent as a reply to your reply-to e-mail address. This process usually takes from a few seconds to a few minutes, depending on the workload of the mail server.

List Server

A list server, also known as a listserv, is an application running on a server that receives incoming mail messages, interprets them, and takes action based on them. For example, several tasks a list server might perform are handling subscriptions to mailing lists (see netref 25), redistributing messages sent to the lists, and delivering files to users based on incoming requests.

Some of the more popular standalone listserv packages run under UNIX and require Perl or C compilers to create the executable application. They are available over the Internet and include Majordomo and Listproc (see netref 26). Many of these high-performance, dedicated listerv applications are being ported to Windows NT and other platforms. Some Windows NT mail servers (such as NTMail and IMail, see above) include useful listerv applications.

If you want to run a moderated list, which means that you check each message to be sure it's acceptable before distributing it to the list, you can use a standard e-mail application instead of a full-blown listserv. When a message arrives, you simply forward it to the list. Using sendmail on a UNIX system, you can set up a special list under an alias. By editing the file to which the alias points, mail sent to the alias will be re-sent to the whole list.

These approaches are fairly simple to implement, but are not without problems. If you want automatic distribution of messages, you should look into using a dedicated list server application.

NOTE For more information about mailing lists, see Chapter 11.

News Server

Internet news, or USENET news, is distributed using a protocol called the Network News Transfer Protocol (NNTP). NNTP servers must be configured with the address of at least one other server with which it can exchange news. The servers can exchange any one or more USENET discussion groups, called newsgroups, or limit the exchange of news to certain newsgroups. Articles are passed in both directions, and the News servers compare message-id headers to see whether they have updated news for each other.

News servers enable users to participate in a remote dialogue by posting (sending to the newsgroup) and reading messages (from the newsgroup) on various topics of interest. USENET newsgroups can support multiple conversations, or threads, on a given subject. This provides a way of displaying postings in the context of the prior discussion, which allows the reader to follow an entire discussion from its inception, though they may join well after the discussion has started.

Individual sites establish policies and procedures to oversee the huge quantity of incoming messages, and to decide how long messages can be kept before they must be removed to make room for new ones. Typically, messages are stored for less than a week. The average daily accumulation of new USENET messages can occupy more than 60MB of hard disk space.

Setting Up a News Server

In order to become a USENET site, another site or sites on USENET must be willing to provide news and/or mail. For higher reliability, it is advisable to locate more than one such site. A News server application must be secured, installed, and configured. Several companies and organizations offer News server software (see netref 27).

As for hardware requirements, a complete USENET server system carrying all of the standard 8 USENET hierarchies, a majority of the alt newsgroups, and various regional newsgroups should plan to have at least 3GB of hard disk storage available. News servers are often set up on UNIX machines, but can also work on Intel-based PCs.

Newsgroups

Because discussion groups provide a unique vehicle for interactive group collaboration, they have become popular for internal workgroup tasks as well as for ad-hoc public forums. There are now over 8,500 public newsgroups in the Internet (see netref 28).

To create a newsgroup (see netref 29), there are certain procedures that must be followed. First, a request for a discussion on creating a new newsgroup must be posted to a newsgroup called news.announce.newgroups. The name and charter of the proposed group, whether it will be moderated or unmoderated, and the name of the moderator (if it is in fact a moderated newsgroup) is usually determined during this discussion period. After the discussion period, a vote is taken. If there are no serious objections to the creation of the newsgroup and the required amount of votes have been received, the newsgroup is created.

NOTE For more information about newsgroups, see Chapter 11.

Multimedia Server

High-end multimedia servers provide high-performance multimedia services over a wide variety of computer platforms. These specialized servers are designed to store and distribute sophisticated, interactive multimedia information to large numbers of simultaneous clients over LANs and WANs. Applications include video on-demand, audio on demand, video teleconferencing, interactive learning, and more.

The hardware-independent, multimedia software RAID, a feature of the Oracle Media Server from Oracle Corporation, is an example of a multimedia server that employs portable features. This type of multimedia server guarantees not only the ability to read data as in traditional RAID systems, but to continue delivering data from failing hardware subsystems with no delay of continuous, real-time presentations (i.e., streams).

NOTE For more information about multimedia, see Chapter 8.

MBONE Tunnels

The MBONE is a virtual network (see netref 30) made up of LANs capable of directly supporting IP multicasts which are joined by virtual point-to-point links called tunnels.

The tunnel endpoints are typically workstations whose operating systems support IP multicasting and can run the multicast routing daemon, mrouted. The daemon monitors multicast groups to which the LAN is subscribed for reception and transmission of audio and/or video data. The Distance Vector Multicast Routing Protocol (DVMRP) is the multicast routing protocol implemented by the mrouted program.

Internet Service Providers (ISP) wishing to participate in the MBONE provide one or more IP multicast routers to connect with tunnels to other MBONE participants and to its customers. The multicast routers are typically installed separately from a network's production routers because most production routers do not presently support IP multicast. Most sites would simply use workstations running the mrouted daemon (as mentioned above). RFC1112 describes the recommended standard for IP multicasting in the Internet (see netref 31).

> **NOTE** For more information about MBONE and multimedia conferencing, see Chapter 11.

Chat Server

Chat servers run the Internet Relay Chat (IRC) protocol, which is designed for use with text-based conferencing. They provide a connection point where clients can connect to talk to each other, and also provide a point for other servers to connect. This forms an Internet Relay Chat (IRC) network.

IRC is a real-time conversational system similar to the talk command available on multiple platforms. Unlike network-based talk applications, IRC allows more than two users to communicate at once and provides access to the global Internet. New chat servers are being developed by commercial software companies that allow users to communicate and interact in fully navigable 3-D, virtual environments with other real people who are represented by graphical avatars.

NOTE For more information about IRC and Virtual Reality, see Chapter 11.

Audio Server

Audio on-demand (AOD) delivery systems allow publishers of news, entertainment, business, and educational content to deliver audio through the Internet to users of multimedia computers. They do this by providing compressed audio files that are sent in a stream from a Web server to multimedia-capable workstations equipped with compatible browsers. Usually, these compressed audio files are served by the Web server itself, requiring no external AOD server. The player application (defined as a helper application when configuring a browser) continuously decompresses the audio and plays it in real time, even over modems. This is known as audio streaming.

NOTE For more information about audio on-demand and Web browsers, see Chapter 11.

Internet Wave (IWave) from VocalTec (see netref 32) allows for the encoding of standard .WAV files into one of two proprietary formats that can be streamed from Web servers. Minor modifications to the Web server configuration files are required to allow it to serve VocalTec audio files. These modifications are necessary in order for the Web server to recognize the encoded sound file formats (similar to configuring a browser to use helper applications). A CGI script is provided that allows the client to fast-forward the audio content.

TrueSpeech is a family of speech compression and decompression algorithms developed by DSP Group, Inc. of Santa Clara, CA (see netref 33). TrueSpeech audio content can be added to Web documents and served by Web servers by encoding sound files with the TrueSpeech encoder and modifying the configuration of the server. This is similar to the IWave product mentioned above. The TrueSpeech encoder is available for free in the Sound System of Windows 95 and Windows NT. These two products offer good usable design and organizational fit for small as well as larger organizations.

An example of an actual AOD server is the RealAudio Server from RealAudio Technology and Progressive Networks (see netref 34). The RealAudio Server runs on the Windows NT and UNIX platforms. Instead of the Web server, the RealAudio Server handles the serving of the on-demand audio files. However, using a standalone server instead of a Web server to distribute audio on-demand files increases the investment and support costs required to implement and run a Web site.

Figure 10-3 represents an example of a Web site serving three popular and stratified audio streaming technologies at one site.

Figure 10-3. A netcaster site featuring Internet Wave audio on-demand (VocalTec and Jeff Pulver).

Video Server

A video server uses specialized software that treats video images as data so they can be stored on disk. The software also provides a way for the server to supply stored video images to workstations. Supplying video to client workstations requires huge volumes of data to be moved around the network as well as very large storage capacities.

For example, a Moving Pictures Experts Group (MPEG) feature-length movie needs between 3 and 4GB of hard disk space. MPEG is a standard for compressing full-motion video. MPEG provides a resolution of 320x240 at 30 frames-per-second (fps) with 24-bit color and CD-quality sound and is used in CD-ROMs and Video CD.

Because of the size of the information being transferred over the network, bandwidth issues must be carefully considered. The industry is somewhat divided on the best transmission medium for video and multimedia services, with asynchronous transfer mode (ATM) on the high-end and Ethernet on the low-end.

An example of a video server is the Oracle Corp. (see netref 35) VideoServer. It supports storage and playback of all popular video compression formats, providing centralized storage of gigabytes of video material. The VideoServer can support thousands of concurrent users.

Reflectors

CU-SeeMe reflectors are an example of video servers that allow for multi-party conferencing over the Internet using CU-SeeMe video-conferencing software. CU-SeeMe (see netref 36) is a video-conferencing program available to anyone with a Macintosh or PC running MS Windows and a connection to the Internet.

Reflectors have the ability to send multicast but not to receive. Without reflectors, only point-to-point connections connecting two CU-SeeMe users are possible at the time of this writing. The CU-SeeMe reflector program available from the CU-SeeMe development team is written in the C language for UNIX systems.

> **NOTE** For more information about enhanced Internet services and applications, such as audio, video, and conferencing, see Chapter 11.

ftp Server

An ftp server, such as the one included with NetManage's Chameleon products, allows Internet users access to local files and directories. Access to the ftp server can be restricted by defining users and assigning passwords. You can also configure the server to define the server's time-out value and specify how many users can be connected to the ftp server simultaneously.

Only authorized users may have access to the ftp server. The ftp server daemon is supplied with many UNIX operating systems. For example, an anonymous user may be defined. This is generally the username invoked when accessing any public ftp site over the Internet. Once an anonymous user has been defined, connection attempts for anonymous are accepted. The anonymous user must then enter a valid Internet mail ID in the form user@company.dom when asked for a password. The use of the anonymous login identifier is referred to as anonymous ftp.

A user may have permission to see all local drives, directories, and files or be restricted to a certain directory and its subdirectories. For example, users with read-only permissions can retrieve files, but not send them to the ftp server. In addition, read-only users cannot create or rename directories or files. With many ftp server applications, a log is created which contains information about client operation, such as login, logout, and files-accessed activity.

An example of an FTP server for Windows NT that is easy to install and administer is WFTPD from Texas Imperial Software (see netref 37). WFTPD is provided in 32-bit and 16-bit versions to allow use on all Intel x86 Windows platforms and is compliant with RFC959 and RFC1123. It supports multiple logins and simultaneous transfers and works with Mosaic, Netscape, and Cello browsers. With WFTPD, secured access is facilitated with the use of password authentication, address-based host authentication (restricting certain hosts), and the ability to restrict specific users to named subtrees of a directory structure (see Figure 10-4). Further security is implemented by means of user rights, which may be set easily on any directories in a system—including those that don't yet exist.

NOTE For more information about ftp, see Chapters 7 and 11.

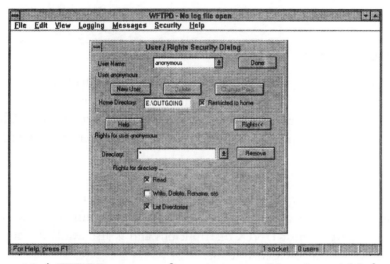

Figure 10-4. WFTPD access configuration screen (Texas Imperial Software).

Gopher Server

Gopher servers store files containing text or binary data, directory information (called phone books), images or sound. Links to other gopher servers result in network wide cooperation to form what is called gopherspace. These gopher servers are accessed by gopher clients which can search for and retrieve files from gopher servers anywhere on the Internet.

Gopher clients also provide gateways to other information systems (World Wide Web, WAIS, Archie, Whois) and to network services (telnet, ftp). The freeware GOPHERS software (see netref 38) from the European Microsoft Windows NT Academic Centre (EMWAC) allows a Windows NT machine to serve information using the gopher document delivery system.

The gopher client presents information to the user as a series of nested menus (resembling the organization of a directory with many subdirectories and files). However, the subdirectories and the files may be located either on the local gopher server or on gopher servers situated at remote sites. As far as the user need know, all information items presented on the menus appear to come from the same place.

NOTE For more information about gopher, see Chapter 11.

Special Services

The following servers and services are very useful, as many Internet users already know. They are often included in TCP/IP connectivity suites, operating systems, and network operating system distributions. Clients for these services can be found in abundance on the Web (see netref 39).

Telnet Server

A public telnet server allows anyone to use the telnet application to login to a remote machine and run a client program to obtain data. Telnet is part of most UNIX distributions and is also available for DOS, Windows, and Mac-based systems.

Using telnet makes it as easy to connect to a machine on the other side of the world as it is to connect to one across the office. To use telnet to connect to a remote host, you type the command telnet followed by the address of the site you wish to connect to. For example, telnet locis.loc.gov would enable a telnet connection to the Library of Congress.

Finger Server

A finger server is a daemon, application, or service that provides information about a user, which is generally found in a plain ASCII file created and edited by the user. The finger client application is used to access a finger server.

For organizations with many hosts, a single host may be designated as the finger server host. This host collects information about who is logged on to other hosts at that site. This provides a convenient means of getting information about network users at any given time.

For example, if a user at site X wants to know about users logged on at site Y, the user simply queries the server host instead of each host at that site. If a user on host X wants to know about a user on host Y, finger must make a network connection to host Y. If host Y is running a finger server program, that program is asked to relay information about the selected user back to host X where the client finger application displays it.

A finger server can deliver information about users in different formats, depending on how the server is invoked. The term, finger, invoked without any options performs a site-wide finger request, regardless of which machine it is invoked. Switch arguments can be used for getting the long form of finger information and for getting information only about the local machine.

A freeware finger server for Windows NT is available from the European Microsoft Windows NT Academic Centre (EMWAC). It implements the finger protocol defined in RFC1288 (see netref 40). This server runs as a Windows NT service, just like the ftp server that comes with Windows NT.

Ph Server

The Ph server, also called nameserver, provides a database for the storage and retrieval of telephone and e-mail directories, but it can be used to store any type of information.

The Ph server maintains the actual data and runs a query interpreter program that receives requests and sends back information. The client runs a program (often called Ph) that sends requests to the server. The Ph client has been ported to most major platforms in use on the Internet. Client functions are also built into many programs, such as Eudora Pro by QUALCOMM Incorporated (see netref 20).

> **NOTE** For more information about Internet searching, see Chapter 11.

Whois Server

The Internet Registration Service maintains an important database of networking information called the InterNIC database. The names of the administrative and technical contacts for registered domains are entered into the database when domain or IP number applications are processed by the InterNIC. Individual Internet sites also maintain databases that contain information about their specific site.

The information held in these databases is made available by Whois servers that receive requests from Whois clients, using the Whois protocol.

Some mail servers, such as the IMail Mail Server for Windows NT, provide built-in Whois (and finger) services.

ENTERPRISE SERVERS

File Server

A file server handles the storage of files and data on a LAN. Its main function is to process requests to read and write file data to disk. File servers usually comprise a computer and large hard disk subsystem providing very fast access. RAID protection is often implemented on the file server. The RAID level you need depends on the performance required, the usage of the data, and how important the data is to the operation of the organization.

In some networks, many users requesting access to servers can create performance bottlenecks. An underperforming file server can slow network performance to a crawl. Because of this, it is important that the server be able to comfortably handle large transaction loads. Unfortunately, many organizations don't take the time to properly test and tune servers. The result of this is often frantic fire-fighting to resolve bottlenecks as they occur.

Software tools are available to gauge server performance. By employing these tools and carefully evaluating the CPU, memory, mass storage, and network interface cards installed in the server as well as their configuration, performance can often be increased. However, if the server simply facilitates the sharing of files over a network, adding additional CPU's brings minimal performance gains.

The strategic approach is to purchase disks with lightning-fast access speeds and make sure the hard disk controller installed in the server provides high transfer rates. Anything that can be done to generally improve the all-around configuration of the disk subsystem should be considered. In many cases, servers are simply overworked. Segmenting and distributing the workload among several file servers is often the best tactical solution to performance issues. This segmenting approach applies not only to servers, but to network components in general.

> **NOTE** For more information about RAID and network components, see Chapter 3.

Application Server

Application servers provide for the centralized storage and access of networked applications. This approach simplifies management as it is much easier for system administrators to configure access rights and permissions and apply updates to application when they're all in one place. Application servers can be deployed to run specific applications or simply provide centralized storage and access for networked applications (much like a file server). In some instances, such as in client/server systems, both the front-end and back-end systems perform processing.

Application servers are frequently deployed in rightsizing projects. Rightsizing means porting enterprise computing applications, which traditionally have been deployed on host systems, to distributed computing systems. Application servers are generally high-performance computers. Models offered by computer manufacturers today provide fault tolerance and redundancy as standard features.

> **NOTE** For more information about client/server systems, see Chapter 6. Further information about fault tolerance and redundancy can be found in Chapter 3.

Database Server

Database servers store data and other information that is accessed by users following client/server access methods. The database server is a central repository for data, much like file and application servers. However, unlike these other servers, most of the data processing occurs on the database server itself. Front-end clients and back-end database applications can also split the processing load. A large number of database servers in use today are accessed using commands that conform to Structured Query Language (SQL) standards.

Software is also part of a database server. Through server software applications, database servers can support many simultaneous users, providing not only database storage and retrieval capabilities but features such as transaction management and logging, automatic index and record locking, and full data security. Many of the database server applications available today are multithreaded in design. This approach can exploit Symmetrical Multi-Processing (SMP) and uniprocessor architectures to deliver database scalability, manageability, and performance.

> **NOTE** For information about SMP servers, see Chapter 3. Information about databases can be found in Chapter 8.

Print Server

Print servers allow users to share printers and plotters by connecting them anywhere on a network. All users can print to the printers and plotters as if they were directly connected to the host. This can increase printing resource utilization while reducing the costs associated with deploying printer hardware. Many print servers offer simultaneous multi-protocol support for IPX/SPX (for Novell NetWare), TCP/IP, AppleTalk, and other protocols.

> **NOTE** For more information about protocols, see Chapter 7.

Fax Server

Network fax servers manage incoming and outgoing faxes for network users. They do this by storing and forwarding faxes via the telephone system or LAN.

A fax server can also be a specialized interactive voice response system. When a caller contacts the fax server, it answers and reads a menu of options that usually includes a list of documents it can send the caller. A caller can choose which documents they want to receive via his or her touch-tone phone. Finally, the caller designates the fax number where the documents are to be sent.

Delrina WinFax PRO for Networks from Delrina Corporation (see netref 41) is an example of network-based fax software for Microsoft Windows and Windows 95 users. It enables network users to send and receive faxes directly from their workstation by sharing one or more standard fax modems. WinFax PRO for Networks can access up to 16 fax modems in a workgroup and can operate in a dedicated or non-dedicated server environment. WinFax PRO for Networks also includes additional features including routing options, e-mail, and management capabilities.

Remote Node Server

Using a remote node server, the caller uses network resources as if his or her workstation was directly connected to the LAN. Remote-control means the caller controls and works within the environment on the callers own computer. Processing happens on the remote machine and all data (word processing documents, spreadsheets, etc.) created during the session stay on that machine.

Remote node servers are a good choice for telecommuting users who work out of their homes or travel with portable laptop computers and need to be in touch with the office. The remote node servers would assign the calling workstation a LAN-connected node via modem, allowing the remote user to access disk drives, printers, and other network components.

> **NOTE** For more information about remote node and remote control, see Chapter 8.

Backup Server

Backup servers provide backup and archiving services to enterprise networks. Ideally, backup servers are highly interoperable, supporting heterogeneous networks comprising NetWare, Macintosh, and UNIX systems. They also support a variety of backup devices.

Typically, backup servers perform automatic, network-wide full, incremental, and differential backups. They provide for the management of assorted media and maintain indexes of previous backups and associated media volumes. Backup servers very often have the ability to do live file system backups as well as simultaneous backups of multiple clients. These features ensure that all networked data is reliably archived.

> **NOTE** For more information about backup utilities and disaster recovery and contingency, see Chapter 12. For information about internetwork management, see Chapter 9.

SNA Server

Using an SNA server provides compatible communications with a remote host while reducing demand on individual computers and the host. It achieves this by distributing the workload onto the SNA server(s).

For example, the Microsoft SNA Server provides mainframe connectivity within a client/server architecture. It provides communication with remote computers such as IBM mainframes, AS/400 minicomputers, and PCs on a network using the Systems Network Architecture protocol. Concurrent access is possible with more than one host (or peer).

> **NOTE** For more information about SNA, see Chapter 7.

GATEWAYS

A gateway is a software application that acts as a translator between disparate computer network systems. These systems may use different protocols, languages, or architectures. Gateways repackage information they receive to match the destination system. Most gateways operate at the Application layer of the OSI model.

Gateways can also be checkpoints through which information must pass on the way to its final destination. These are called security gateways. If certain pre-determined criteria are not met, the data is rejected and not allowed through the gateway. This could include login or file transfer requests. Several examples of gateways are mail, Internet, and security gateways.

> **NOTE** For information about the OSI model, see Chapter 6.

Mail Gateway

Frequently, there are several e-mail systems employed in enterprise networks. In these instances, mail gateways must be established to provide interoperability between different mail systems. An e-mail gateway centralizes e-mail collection and distribution to hosts and users. Mail gateways are also useful for synchronizing user directories or mailing lists across two or more messaging systems.

An example of a mail gateway is the Microsoft Mail Gateway to SMTP, which links its Microsoft Mail e-mail system to UNIX and other systems supporting SMTP. It can also link multiple Microsoft Mail networks transparently over an SMTP backbone such as the Internet.

> **NOTE** For more information about SMTP, see Chapter 7. For more information about e-mail, see Chapter 8.

Internet Gateway

Many online services are now offering Internet connectivity to their users, including America Online, CompuServe Information Service, Delphi, the Microsoft Network, and Prodigy. By providing access to the Internet, these commercial online service providers are also known as Internet gateways.

Security Gateway

The explosive growth in both Internet user and Web server categories makes sensitive data increasingly more vulnerable to compromise and corruption. This creates a strong need for security gateways. Firewalls and proxies are two of the more popular types of security gateways implemented. These are covered in detail in Chapter 9.

REFERENCES

Net References

1. For a list of registered WWW servers, www to
http://www.w3.org/hypertext/DataSources/WWW/Servers.html then browse alphabetically by continent, country, and state.

2. www to http://www.lvalue.com/ for an example of the Lvalue Art Gallery.

www to http://www.nyu.edu/ for the The New York University home page.

To access an example of a business presence on the Web, www to
http://www.fedex.com/.

3. www to gopher://gopher.micro.umn.edu/ then select the directory called "Other Gopher and Information Servers." This link will allow you to search gopher servers and throughout the world.

4. telnet to locis.loc.gov then follow the instructions to access the Library of Congress information system.

5. www to http://www.mi.cnr.it/finger.html then complete the finger form which returns information about the user.

6. www to http://www.city.net/win-httpd/ then browse this page for more information about Windows httpd.

7. For an index of available Web servers, www to
http://www.yahoo.com/Computers_and_Internet/Internet/World_Wide_Web/HTTP/Servers/
then browse the page and follow the links for additional information.

8. www to http://www.proper.com/www/servers-survey.html then browse the server survey page.

9. www to http://hoohoo.ncsa.uiuc.edu/docs/ then browse for more information about NCSA HTTPd. Specific information about the CERN httpd can be found at http://www.w3.org/hypertext/WWW/Daemon/Status.html. Information about Apache can be found at http://www.apache.org/

10. For information and downloading Netscape products, www to http://www.netscape.com/comprod/server_central/index.html then browse for information about Netscape Web server products. Information about the WebSTAR Web server can be found at http://www.starnine.com/webstar/

WebSite Web server information is located at http://website.ora.com/

11. www to http://www.w3.org/pub/WWW/Servers.html then search for information about the server package of your choice. There is a also a link here to a list of servers in the Web Developer's Virtual Library.

12. www to http://www.proper.com/www/servers-chart.html then select the links of interest. The list includes all Web servers that seem to be currently supported.

13. For more information about Chameleon, www to http://www.netmanage.com/netmanage/products/cham.html then browse the NetManage Chamelon page.

14. www to http://www.qdeck.com/qdeck/products/WebServr/ then browse this page for more information about WebServer.

15. For information about configuration, www to http://home.netscape.com/comprod/communi_install.html then browse the configuration form.

16. www to http://ipa.spry.com/info.html then browse this page for more information about the Internet Office Web Server.

17. www to http://www.starnine.com/webstar/ then browse this page for more information about WebSTAR.

18. www to http://www.tucows.com/softwais.html then browse to select and download Wide Area Information Server software for MS Windows.

19. For information in an article entitled, "An Overview of the Z39.50 Information Retrieval Standard," www to http://www.nlc-bnc.ca/ifla/pubs/core/udt/occasional/udtop3.htm

20. www to http://www.qualcomm.com/quest/QuestMain.html then browse for more information about Eudora and Eudora Pro.

21. www to http://www.ipswitch.com/store/apps/imail/ then browse for information about IMail.

22. For information about the NTMail server, www to http://www.net-shopper.co.uk/software/ntmail/index.htm then browse the NTMail page for links to specific information.

23. ftp to ftp://ftp.metrics.com/smtp/ then search for the particular version of WinSMTP you want to download.

24. For more information about Strategic Networking Forums, send e-mail to info@snf.org. No subject or body text is necessary.

25. www to http://www.cuc.edu/cgi-bin/listservform.pl then search for the list server you'd like to register with. This page allows users to subscribe and unsubscribe to list servers around the world.

26. ftp to ftp://ftp.greatcircle.com/pub/majordomo/ then download the latest release of Majordomo. Majordomo requires Perl. If you don't have Perl, you can get it from ftp://ftp.netlabs.com/pub/outgoing/perl5.0/

Information about Listproc can be found at http://www.cren.net/listproc/info.html

27. For information about DNEWS, www to http://world.std.com/~netwin then browse the FAQ.

www to http://home.netscape.com/comprod/news_server.html then browse for more information on the Netscape News Server, an NNTP server for Windows NT.

28. ftp to ftp://ftp.uu.net/uunet-info/ then download the file newsgroups.Z or newsgroups.gz for a good sampling of available newsgroups. Under Windows, an application such as WinZIP can uncompress these files.

29. For information about creating a newsgroup, ftp to ftp://rtfm.mit.edu/pub/USENET/news.announce.newusers/ then login as anonymous and download the file (with a very long name):
How_to_Create_a_New_USENET_Newsgroup

30. www to http://www.best.com/~prince/techinfo/mbone.html then browse the MBONE Information Web page for additional information about the MBONE.

31. www to http://www.cis.ohio-state.edu/htbin/rfc/rfc-index.html then search the RFC index list for the RFC number you want. Click on the link to access the RFC source document.

32. www to http://www.vocaltec.com/ then browse the VocalTec home page for more information about IWave.

33. www to http://www.dspg.com/ then browse the TrueSpeech page for more information about TrueSpeech.

34. www to http://www.prognet.com/index.html then browse the RealAudio home page for more information about the RealAudio player, encoder, and server products.

35. www to http://www.oracle.com/ then search for information about VideoServer.

36. www to http://CU-SeeMe.cornell.edu/ then browse the CU-SeeMe project page for more information about CU-SeeMe.

37. ftp to ftp://papa.indstate.edu/winsock-l/Windows95/Daemons/ then download the latest version of WFTPD for NT (presently 32wfd202.zip).

38. www to ftp://emwac.ed.ac.uk/pub/gophers/ then download the GOPHERS server for Intel-based systems, MIPS, and DEC Alpha systems.

39. www to http://interserve.com/ then search for links pointing to suggested DOS, Windows, and Mac client software.

40. For information about a finger server, www to http://emwac.ed.ac.uk/html/internet_toolchest/fingers/contents.htm then browse and download the software from this link.

41. www to http://www.delrina.com/ then search the Delrina home page for information about WinFax PRO for Networks.

Suggested Reading

There is a lot of information about the World Wide Web and its services located throughout the Internet. While you may have to spend some time wading through it to determine its value to you, it is free and often represents the thoughts of people closest to the inner workings of the topics they discuss.

Aside from the official Internet documentation mentioned in the beginning of this chapter, here are some references to lists and documents with accompanying links that bring the documents into your Web browser for viewing, saving, and printing. Many of these sources are virtual or online libraries sponsored by associations, schools, and vendors with a strong commitment to the growth of the Internet.

A list of Internet servers for the Mac OS can be found at http://www.freedonia.com/ism/

For a list of frequently asked questions (FAQ) about the Web, access the Sunsite online library via www to http://sunsite.unc.edu/boutell/faq/

For examples of audio-on-demand broadcasts, access any of these Web pages: www to http://town.hall.org/, www to http://nothcoast.com/~savetz/voice-faq.html, www to http://www.intel.com/pc-supp/nsp.html

For information about about setting up a World Wide Web service, check the following link: http://www.leeds.ac.uk/ucs/people/BKelly/aberdeen_paper.html

The paper describes the client and server software tools that are used to access the World Wide Web. A summary of tools that can assist information providers is given.

For information about the Internet and Web, access online documents in the Web Developer's Virtual Library via www to http://WWW.Stars.com/Vlib/

For information about the Web servers, www to http://WWW.Stars.com/Vlib/Providers/Servers.html for an overview of various Web servers and other Web server-related information.

Information about running a WWW service can be found at http://www.leeds.ac.uk/ucs/WWW/handbook/handbook.html

To download documents called FAQs (frequently asked questions) relating to newsgroups, ftp to ftp://rtfm.mit.edu/pub/USENET/news.answers/

www to http://hoohoo.ncsa.uiuc.edu/ then browse the NCSA HTTPd Home Page for information about the latest versions of NCSA HTTPd. Information about the Secure NCSA HTTPd can be found at http://www.commerce.net/software/Shttpd/

www to http://sunsite.unc.edu/chris/daemons/ for WWW terms defined, server etiquette, a link to the WWW FAQ, descriptions of what servers do, and a collection of tools for server administrators.

www to http://wsk.eit.com/ then browse the Webmaster's Starter Kit page for more information about the process of installing a basic Web server and optional extensions.

www to http://www-swiss.ai.mit.edu/wtr/ then browse the Web Tools review page, an online journal for developers of World Wide Web sites.

www to http://www.catt.ncsu.edu/~bex/tutor/index.html then browse the page for a tutorial to teach you how to write simple cgi-bin scripts and their associated forms. The CGI FAQ can be found at http://www.best.com/~hedlund/cgi-faq/faq.html

The CGI newsgroup is called comp.infosystems.www.authoring.cgi

For the CGI Virtual LIbrary reference, www to http://www.charm.net/~web/Vlib/Providers/CGI.html

www to http://www.lbl.gov/ctl/vconf-faq.html then check the software section under the heading "Getting Started with Videoconferencing."

www to http://www.primenet.com/~buyensj/ntwebsrv.html then browse the Windows NT Web Server Tools page for links to helpful NT Web server applications.

Armstrong, L. 1995. "Setting Up a Web Site." *LAN Times* 12(8):96.

Ellsworth, J. 1995. "Three Routes to a Web Presence." *PC Magazine* 14(9):224.

Gonzalez, S. 1995. "Building a Web Presence." *PC Magazine* 14(9):205.

Gonzalez, S. 1995. "Turnkey Solutions: One Stop Shopping." *PC Magazine* 14(17):253–271.

Magid, J. 1995. *The Web Server Book: Tools & Techniques for Building Your Own Internet Information Site*. Chapel Hill, NC: Ventana Press.

Morgan, E. 1994. *WAIS and Gopher Servers: A Guide for Internet End-users*. Westport: Mecklermedia.

Reichard, K. 1995. "A Site of Your Own." *PC Magazine* 14(17):227–228.

Reichard, K. 1995. "Windows NT-Based Servers: What's the Rush?" *PC Magazine* 14(17): 229-252.

11

Internet Services and Applications

ABOUT THIS CHAPTER

The Internet is more than a global internetwork with millions of host computers. It connects people and organizations around the world and makes them as close as a local phone call. The Internet is the information superhighway in the present and the likely model for its future. It is all part of an unprecedented change in the way we communicate and work and play. Here, you'll learn about its roots, its growth, and how to access it for yourself.

Services and associated client applications are described: World Wide Web, WAIS and other search engines, e-mail, Whois, mailing lists, newsgroups, file transfer, gopher, and more. Enhanced and emerging services and applications are covered as well: Internet Relay Chat, MBONE, audio and video streaming, multimedia, virtual reality, and the budding of electronic commerce with secure transactions, virtual banks, and electronic cash.

THE INTERNET EXPLAINED

In many ways, describing the Internet is like shooting at a moving target. At best, what you read here can be considered a brief introduction and partial list of a highly dynamic environment consisting of computing and communications resources.

The recipe for making sense of the Internet requires that you consider equal parts of the following ingredients: lab bench, test bed, scholar's haven, global platform for electronic commerce, and grand social experiment. Nonetheless, the Internet can be initially understood by looking at its short history (see netref 1), concentrating on some of its more popular services, and considering the directions that things seem to be taking.

Roots of the Internet

Following the development of early computer networks that operated in isolation on government, military, and educational facilities, the U.S. Advanced Research Projects Agency (ARPA) developed ARPANET, the first single, global network to connect computers among these remote networks.

The firm of Bolt, Beranek, and Newman, Inc. (BBN) was contracted to develop a network protocol by which diverse and remote machines could communicate. Out of this work emerged packet-switching, a network transmission technique that ensures delivery through a common transmission line. Instead of sending one continuous stream of data, it breaks down the data into smaller chunks called packets, each of which contain information about its source and destination.

Several important developments took place during the 1970s which set the stage for the emergence of the Internet: the development of TCP/IP (Transmission Control Protocol/Internet Protocol), and the adoption of the UNIX operating system, which provided many of the network communications tools that are used today.

In 1973, ARPA conducted research programs to extend packet-switching to ships at sea via satellites in synchronous orbits (SATNET) and ground mobile units via ground mobile packet radio (PRNET). This effort to link users of different packet networks together became known as "Interneting," and the "Internet" (and ultimately, the Net) became a term used to describe this global, public internetwork.

By the mid-1970s, researchers became interested in doing more than exchanging computer data between machines. They also began satisfying their need to communicate with other researchers about scholarly and social matters. Several types of network communications emerged during this time: e-mail, computer mailing lists, and file transfers to and from central data repositories.

During the 1980s the National Science Foundation (NSF) established several supercomputer facilities dispersed across the country, but accessible by researchers through a network backbone named NSFNET. The funding and management of this network was awarded to Merit (a non-profit organization managed by a consortium of eight Michigan universities) and also supported by MCI (telecommunications) and IBM (routers). During this time, limited commercial traffic was allowed under the stipulation that it would support the growth and maintenance of the network.

In 1991, the High Performance Computing Act was enacted to support research and development of the National Research and Education Network (NREN), a high-speed national computer network. NSFNET is the backbone of NREN and provides links between other government networks, including NASA's NSINET, the Department of Defense MIL-NET, and the Department of Energy ESNET.

By 1993, the NSFNET had become the largest TCP/IP network and was ready to subcontract the wide range of support services that had become necessary for operation. Registration services went to Network Solutions, list maintenance of ftp (file transfer) sites was assigned to AT&T, and reference materials were assigned to General Atomics. Collectively, these services and their respective providers became known as InterNIC, which stands for the Internet Network Information Center. It now represents the central source of information about the Internet.

Statistics from the InterNIC (see netref 2) are available online for a wide variety of networking topics, including the growth of the Internet.

For example, the number of host computers on the Internet has been doubling every year from 1989 to 1995. Although it is hard to accurately assess the overall number of users, growth figures for popular services such as the World Wide Web indicate a five-fold jump from 2 million in 1994 to 10 million in 1995. The overall number of Internet users is estimated by various sources at two to three times this figure as of 1995. With the addition of host computers from large corporations and online information services providing Internet access, this growth trend is likely to continue for many years.

Telephone and cable services represent another important factor in the growth of the Internet and other global networks. Both plan to support high-speed and high bandwidth data services through upgrades of their existing infrastructures. Telecommunications companies can provide dedicated connections to Internet providers over telephone lines through ISDN modems. Cable operators can provide continuous connections to shared cable-LAN services over hybrid fiber and coaxial cable systems. These service providers will provide tremendous growth for the Internet as these markets become deregulated and the networking infrastructures are upgraded to provide reliable, two-way interactive services.

> **NOTE** For more information about network services, see Chapter 5.

From Internet to Information Superhighways

The Internet represents the first and currently foremost model of a public, global internetwork. However, if its relatively short history is any guide, there are likely to be significant changes in the coming years as both network services and subscribers increase in variety and numbers. Some of the broad bandwidth and wide access aspects of what are called information superhighways of the future are already being planned.

National Information Infrastructure

The National Information Infrastructure, or NII (see netref 3), is a plan for a national internetwork of computers and telecommunication networks, services, and applications. One of the founding principles and goals of the NII is that it must promote interoperability and open standards. As originally planned, the private sector builds, owns, and operates the NII, whereas the United States government works in partnership with the private sector in developing an advanced NII. The NII can be viewed as three layers of functions: applications, services, and bitways:

- Applications are information technologies that are used to complete tasks across a variety of application areas.

- Services provide the building blocks for applications and the interfaces for displays and other input and output devices. For example, a library retrieval system would require at least two services to complete an information exchange: a text search service and a file transfer service.

- Bitways, or physical infrastructure, provide a means of transmission (e.g., cable, optical fiber, etc.) plus controlling software to transmit data from one place to another.

Global Information Infrastructure

The GII, or Global Information Infrastructure, is a plan to interconnect local, national, regional, and global networks (see netref 4). This worldwide "network of networks" could provide a global information marketplace and encourage broad-based social discourse among people in all countries.

The concept of the GII extends beyond hardware and software. It recognizes the people involved in the creation and use of information, development of applications and services, construction of the facilities, and training necessary to realize the potential of the GII. Thus, the GII can be defined as a system of applications, activities, and relationships.

There are many important issues to resolve for public-access national and global networks. A central goal that has been articulated by the government and many action groups is the notion of universal service. Although there can be premium channels or restricted access on global information systems, many believe that there should always be some basic level of public access and related information such as for education, health, etc. Other issues include private versus public access and the right to privacy. Technical issues include delivery of multimedia information with adequate bandwidth and support for as many as hundreds of separate channels of communication (or one very big one).

Internet Organizations and Documentation

The Internet is more than a physical interconnection of computer networks. It is also a largely decentralized but collective effort to define and document its operation. The success of the Internet is largely due to the open standards that have been adopted for its services and applications. As a result, users of diverse hardware and software platforms can interoperate and scale their systems and applications within a global internetwork.

> **NOTE** For information about the related topic of open systems, see the OSI Reference model in Chapter 6.

This work is performed informally by its users and formally by organizations assigned to these tasks. The results usually take the form of policies, procedures, and standards (see netref 5). Most of this output is stored at designated repositories in the form of online documentation.

Founded in 1992, the Internet Society is the organization (see netref 6) that is given the authority by vote of Internet users to handle administration. Within this organization are three principal bodies that perform its separate tasks.

The Internet Architecture Board (IAB) (see netref 7) is in charge of development of network protocols, the associated standards, and resources such as network addresses. On-line information that describes Internet research and development is available in the form of Request for Comment (RFC) documentation. RFC documents are named with a number code after the letters RFC, such as RFC822. An RFC document is never revised, so the higher the number code after RFC, the more recent the documentation.

Subsets of RFCs describe specific areas. For Your Information (FYI) documents cover topics related to the Internet, including descriptions of protocols, applications, statistics, and even tutorials. Standards (STD) are one or more RFCs that cover specifications that have been approved as standards on the Internet. RFC, STD, and FYI documents can be found at several sites on the Internet and are accessible through many of its services, especially the World Wide Web and the ftp file transfer services (see netref 8).

The Internet Engineering Task Force (IETF) (see netref 9) develops technical specifications that lead to standards. It identifies technical problems and specifies protocols and standards to solve them. It also promotes technology transfer and discussion among the Internet community of users. Online documentation includes reports on its meetings and activities.

Accessing the Internet

The choice of network services for establishing Internet connectivity should reflect the use of appropriate technology that is geared to your needs and capabilities. Not every individual or organization needs a continuous, high-speed connection. Plain old telephone service (POTS) with high-speed modems can suffice for occasional access to the Internet through an enterprise WAN or Internet provider. It is also appropriate for branch office and mobile users who need to access the central office through an Internet connection. The advantage is global reach for the cost of a local call. The disadvantage is that dial-up connections are subject to varying availability of shared lines and modem pools.

Although it requires the most commitment of resources, dedicated links through T1 or T3 lines offer the greatest bandwidth, throughput, and uninterrupted service. If you are setting up Internet connectivity for a large organization, a 24/7 (24 hours a day/7 days a week) connection can support mission-critical operations that require uninterrupted service. These operations can include database access, transactional services, or providing Internet access services to subscribers. At thousands of dollars per month for line charges alone, this option is reserved for organizations that require premium service.

Situated by cost and quality between the dial-up and dedicated lines are high-speed digital services such as frame relay and ISDN. These are increasingly being considered by organizations and individuals as an affordable, yet high-quality alternative to dedicated lines.

NOTE For more information about network services, see Chapter 5. For information about establishing an Internet presence, see Chapter 10.

Internet Service Provider

An Internet Service Provider (ISP) is in the business of providing a variety of Internet access and other value-added services such as Web page design to individuals and/or businesses. Some are large, online information services such as CompuServe, America Online, and Prodigy. They offer gateway services to the Internet for their subscribers.

NOTE For information about gateways, see Chapter 10.

Choosing a provider is probably the most important step you can take. Although large Internet providers with toll-free numbers, many local points-of-presence (POP), and flat fees are generally desirable, bigger is not always better. A smaller Internet provider that offers access through a local phone call may be just as good or better for your needs. You should compare both the type and quality of services that are provided. For example, in many local dialing areas, local calls are part of the basic service and can be quite economical.

A good provider should be able to support a wide range of Internet services and provide reliable connectivity. That means not getting busy signals because modem pools are tapped, or having disruptions in the service due to malfunctions at the provider's end. You should also check for any hidden fees, such as rates that kick in after exceeding a given allotment of connect time or setup fees. Keep in mind that the availability and response of their customer and technical support is also critical.

As with any other purchase, you should get all the information, check with other users, and make feature and cost comparisons prior to signing up with an Internet provider. Although there are sometimes difficulties and delays in changing providers, the only way to test their services and fees is to actually sign up for a trial period. Usually, you will know within a month or so whether the reality matches the promises. If the provider doesn't measure up, you can cancel your service and try another one.

There are many organizations and small businesses springing up that offer access to the Internet using their computers on a hourly-fee basis. This can be a great way to test-drive the Internet or to access it when you are on a trip or in an area where dial-up is not practical. Some of these services are geared for walk-in traffic. Some even provide a cafe-like atmosphere with hot java (the drink), the daily paper (in print), and real-time chat (face-to-face).

Software from online information services, network operating systems (e.g., Microsoft Windows 95), and connectivity packages (e.g., Internet Chameleon by NetManage) have text files or help systems that can be searched for an Internet provider (prior to going online). In some cases, sign-up procedures can be activated from this software. Also, ads for Internet providers are often listed in newspapers and magazines.

Although you must already have Internet access to use this method, the World Wide Web has several sites that list Internet providers and contact information (see netref 10). For example, while researching this book, we consulted these lists to find and use Internet providers (GTI, see netref 11, and Network-USA, see netref 12).

Following a trend in enhanced support, these and many other Internet providers offer varied dial-up (SLIP, PPP, and ISDN) and 24/7 services (dedicated connections), and expanding local points-of-presence through new sites and access through toll-free numbers.

In Europe, PIPEX (see netref 13) is one of the leading Internet providers. Through an arrangement with other providers and resellers on the continent, they provide many points-of-presence throughout Europe, a variety of direct connect and dial-up services, software, and training. They also provide Internet access software (PIPEX Dial), which gives the individual or mobile user the means to access the Internet. It includes a PIPEX dial-up connection, a PPP dial-up TCP/IP stack, Mail-it (e-mail software from Unipalm), Netscape (Web browser), and a simple telnet client.

BASIC SERVICES AND APPLICATIONS

The distinction between Internet services and applications can be thought of as what is available and how you can use it. The term, services is used to describe a range of features that are made available on the Internet through its protocols, basic utilities, network sites, databases, and supporting organizations. Common examples are e-mail, file transfer protocol, newsgroups, mailing lists, and real-time audio and video services.

The term applications is used to describe the software, hardware, and procedures that exploit these services. Common examples are server and client software for various platforms, such as an e-mail program. The term, applications is also discussed in more general terms to consider how we actually use these services for our individual and organizational needs.

World Wide Web

In the spring of 1995, the World Wide Web (a.k.a., the Web, WWW, or W3) became the most popular Internet service on the NFSNET backbone, which is often used as a estimator of overall use on the Internet.

It was originally conceived in 1989 by Tim Berners-Lee as a means of linking documents so that researchers could share information at the CERN Physics Lab in Switzerland. Since then, it has become a flexible hypermedia service that is interoperable and ubiquitous on the Internet (see netref 14).

Besides linking hypermedia objects such as documents, images, audio, and video, it can launch other Internet services as well as external applications. By virtue of its popularity and flexibility, it has established itself as a de facto service of emerging information superhighways and electronic commerce.

The protocol that governs Web client/server communications is called the HyperText Transfer Protocol (HTTP).

> **NOTE** For information about HTTP and other protocols, see Chapter 7.

Web documents are formatted according to the Hypertext Markup Language (HTML). It is a standard markup language that is used to display text, images, and other objects on Web pages.

The Uniform Resource Locator (URL) is an addressing mechanism for the Web. It describes the means of retrieving information (http://), the Internet address (www.snf.org/), and the name of a directory and/or HTML document (info/index.html). When joined together, the previous examples in parentheses form one URL that indicates the address of a page with information about Strategic Networking Forums (http://www.snf.org/info/index.html).

For more examples of URLs, look at the Net References at the end of this chapter. Note that a URL using Web access begins with http://, whereas ftp access begins with ftp://, and so on for each service.

URLs are entered into Web documents at specific points in the text or image which should link to another Web document (or section of the same document) whether it is located on the same server or on any other web server throughout the Internet.

Although Web documents are associated with displaying static text and graphics, these links can also activate other applications which can display video or sound. HTML version 2.0 introduced support of a forms feature which provides the retrieval and processing of user-supplied information. HTML 3.0 is currently under consideration. It may include many features that are associated with a proposed extension named HTML+ and well as popular, but still proprietary, features found in Web browsers such as Netscape Navigator.

Using the Common Gateway Interface (CGI), information can be dynamically produced "on the fly" based on user interaction. CGI is a mechanism that allows external scripts to be executed from within an HTML document. For example, clicking a button link in a Web document can trigger a CGI script which contains a series of executable commands. These commands can then direct procedures or execute applications which perform one or more tasks, such as returning information from a database.

NOTE For more information about HTML and CGI, see Chapter 8.

Web Browsers

Web browsers are World Wide Web client applications that can navigate and display documents and other objects on the Web. There are two basic types of browser interfaces: character and graphical.

Character-based browsers show Web information only in text format. Links are indicated by underlined or highlighted text. Links are activated by moving the cursor over the link and pressing a designated key. Lynx is a popular character-based browser that can be used online via telnet to a host that supports it (see netref 15) or run as a PC-based client that can directly access the Web (see netref 16).

Users who have a UNIX shell account with their service providers cannot use SLIP or PPP or TCP/IP services. For these users, SlipKnot emulates a Microsoft Windows-compatible graphical Web browser (similar to Mosaic). SlipKnot is published by MicroMind Inc. as restricted shareware (see netref 17). It is designed for modem or direct serial line users.

Graphical browsers are available in a wide variety of packages and can vary in their features, but all offer text, images, video, and sound on computers that support multimedia. A direct, PPP, or SLIP dial-up connection to the Internet is required for this type of browser.

Mosaic was the first graphical Web browser. Its reliability and rich features were responsible for the quick interest and ultimate growth of the Web. Mosaic was developed by the National Center for Supercomputing Applications (NCSA) in Champaign, IL, and was made freely available through the Internet (see netref 18).

Netscape Navigator (see Figure 11-1) by Netscape Communications Corporation (see netref 19) was the first commercial browser. It is available in standalone and integrated browsers. Newer versions of the browser include features such as: secure electronic mail, threaded newsgroups, and Live Objects support for interactive multimedia content such as Java applets, frames, and Netscape inline plug-ins.

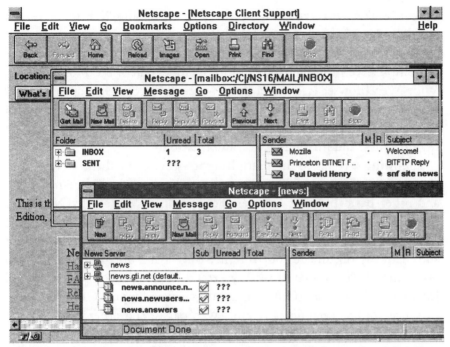

Figure 11-1. Netscape Navigator™ graphical Web browser with integrated mail and newsgroup clients (Netscape Communications Corp.).

Netscape Web products for Web content development include:

- An integrated Web tool (Navigator Gold) to create, edit, and navigate live online documents and publish content in real-time that can include Live Objects.

- A professional visual development environment (LiveWire) for creating, deploying, and maintaining entire online application systems. It can maintain live content or live online applications for use within an enterprise or across the Internet. A professional version of LiveWire adds relational database connectivity for creating online applications with transaction and information management capabilities and integration with existing databases.

Several TCP/IP Internet connectivity suites bundle Web software. For example, NetManage's Chameleon suite includes an easy-to-use, graphical browser (as well as a personal Web server).

CompuServe's Internet Office suite includes the SPRY Mosaic World Wide Web browser (see netref 20). It uses Terisa System's open security standard to support secure transmission (with any S-HTTP server) of sensitive data such as credit card numbers, accounting records, human resource files, and mission-critical information.

Following a trend to integrate Internet services in client/server applications, a new breed of Web browser applications include e-mail, ftp, and other basic Internet services. For example, Mariner by NCD (see netref 21) is a Web browser that integrates applications for several basic Internet services (ftp, newsgroups, etc.). Intuitive tools such as AutoPilot automatically document your Internet travels and organize the sites you visit into folders. Search capability extends from these custom folders to Internet-wide searches. Online graphics viewers support GIF and JPEG. Advanced online caching of e-mail, Web pages, and other data provides on-demand retrieval of this information whether online or offline.

There are many software products that provide functions that complement Web browsers. Some of these are available through Web browser software producers like Netscape. Other Web utilities are standalone applications. For example, some products convert text to HTML, others automatically copy Web addresses, create and manage bookmark lists, and paste them as active links into HTML pages, such as the URL Grabber by Brooklyn North Software Works (see netref 22).

NOTE For information about Web servers and integrated Web sites, see Chapter 10.

WAIS

WAIS is an acronym for Wide Area Information Server (see netref 23). The multimedia content of WAIS databases are made available on the Net through WAIS servers and accessed by using browsers or viewers such as WAIS, Netscape, Mosaic, gopher, etc. It can search textual and binary data in databases on the Internet, including USENET newsgroups and BITNET archives.

> **NOTE** For information about WAIS and other servers, see Chapter 10.

Web Search Engines

There are many search engines on the Web. You can use them to find information on Web pages. Some of these services are free and some are commercial services that provide limited function or a limited amount of searches for free.

Web search engines (which often use WAIS) typically scan indexed databases on the Internet using terms and categories that you supply as one or more keywords. The order of keywords and their separation through special characters such as commas are some of the ways that syntax can be used to further specify the nature of the search. The search rules are often provided with examples at any of the Web pages that act as search engines. Key terms are typically entered in a form that contains a submit or reset button to execute or clear the current search keywords.

INFOSEEK is a Web search engine created and operated by a company of the same name. They use WAIS services within a form-based Web search. You can conduct an INFOSEEK search directly through a Net Search button on Netscape Navigator Web browser or by accessing it at infoseek.com. There are many other popular Web search engines on the World Wide Web (see netref 24).

Web Learning and Information Sources

The Web and its underlying standards and practices are subject to constant change through refinement and revision. Following the continuous learning strategy that we recommend for networking topics throughout this book, learning more about all aspects of the Web can be achieved by strategically exploiting the Net.

In short, you have to employ strategies for riding the crest of these changes. When using the Net for continuous learning, we recommend two specific strategies: learning by example and building a personal web of learning. These strategies apply whether you seek to exploit Web use for yourself or your organization or if you plan to create HTML content and publish it on the Web.

We recommend that you learn by example. Visit Web sites that can benefit you by using or emulate in the creation of your own Web pages. Find these sites by using categorized lists and Web search engines under keywords that relate to your intended use of the Web. Then follow these links and visit the Web sites.

If you like what a Web site offers, add the home page and selected pages of that site to the bookmark lists in your Web browser. As you build up this list of personal links, place them under unique categories or separate bookmark lists.

If you plan to experiment with Web page design, you should also save selected examples of the HTML coding by using a Save (Source) option that includes the source HTML tags of that page. By loading this HTML file in a text editor or an HTML editor, you can modify the data and/or tags on that page to suit your needs and then test it in your browser using the Open file command. When you have it right, you can let others test it by loading on the Web server.

Keep in mind that whether for using or creating content, Web proficiency represents a complex set of skills and considerable knowledge that you must master and continually update. You need to balance learning with practice.

Beyond learning by example, online sources of information can be found by exploring various sites on the Net in the form of Internet documentation of standards, protocols, and FAQs, as well as tutorials and applications (see netref 25).

There are lists on the Web that are maintained by individuals and companies who provide a Web search service. Performing the same service as form-based Web search engines, lists are grouped by topic under category hierarchies or in alphabetized indexes. The items in these lists are hypertext links to actual addresses on the Web where the information can be found. Some lists feature built-in search capabilities, but you can also use the Find command in your browser to find a particular item in the list. Yahoo is the most popular and extensive of the Web-based list services (see netref 26), though there are many smaller, but specialized lists.

The Web abounds with pages that contain lists that link sites on the Web for downloading software (see netref 27). Several lists review software and provide links for downloading. Also, software companies often use their Web sites as downloading platforms for beta and evaluation copies of their programs. They also provide e-mail links for support.

Information about the Web can also be found in a growing number of online newsletters and electronic magazines (often called e-zines or zines). For example, HotFlash is a weekly newsletter of the HotWired and WIRED magazine. It is delivered via e-mail. HotWired is the site for the Web version of WIRED magazine. It features articles, interviews, events, and links (see netref 28). WEBster is an online source of Web events, news, and information. WEBster is delivered every other week directly to your e-mail in box via an automated mailer and can also be accessed on the Web (see netref 29).

There are a growing number of integrated Web sites that employ a convergent media strategy in the way they leverage the Net to complement their television and radio broadcasts. Using a similar approach to simulcasts of concerts using television and radio, these shows support Web pages that let browsers access current and previous TV and radio shows through text transcripts and audio on-demand for Internet streaming playback. These Web sites also provide e-mail feedback and links to other shows and sites that cover related topics (see netref 30).

Internet E-mail

Internet e-mail is another popular service on the Internet. Through its use of open standards based on widely supported mail protocols such as SMTP and POP, it provides interoperability among diverse platforms. Anyone sending e-mail through the Internet can reach anyone else connected to the Internet wherever they are in the world and on whatever system they are using, as long as their systems comply with these proto-cols and standards. The Internet e-mail message format is described in the Internet Request for Comment, RFC822 (see netref 8).

Its store and forward mechanism is the basis for other Internet services and applications such as mailing lists and newsgroups (described below).

NOTE For information about e-mail see Chapter 8.

E-mail Remote Access of Internet Services

Besides sending and receiving messages with other people, e-mail can also be used to remotely access and use other Internet services (described below) such as ftp, archie, gopher, veronica, newsgroups, finger, and WAIS. One of the best sources for information on using e-mail remote access is a document entitled, "Accessing The Internet By E-Mail: Doctor Bob's Guide to Offline Internet Access" written by Bob Rankin (see netref 31). As he aptly states in that document, "As of late 1994, there were 150 countries with only e-mail connections to the Internet. This is double the number of countries with direct (IP) connections."

For people with "e-mail only" accounts, UNIX shell accounts, world-travelers, and people in countries who access the Internet through these local links, the e-mail remote access method may be the only means to use other Internet services. This method can also be used strategically as an economical batch method for using Internet services. It can save on time and connect charges.

Essentially, you create an e-mail message in the normal manner, except the destination is a special Internet server rather than a person. The body of the message is a series of commands associated with the Internet service you are using through e-mail remote access. For example, to use e-mail for file transfer, you send a message to an ftpmail server. This server performs the ftp actions, such as login to the remote host, get the specified files, and logout. Instead of issuing these commands directly with an ftp client, you type these commands in an e-mail message and send them to the ftpmail server, such as any one from the following list (the closer the better, but any will do):

ftpmail@sunsite.unc.edu (server located in southern U.S.)
bitftp@pucc.princeton.edu (server located in northern U.S.)
bitftp@vm.gmd.de (server located in Europe)
ftpmail@doc.ic.ac.uk (server located in the UK)
ftpmail@cs.uow.edu.au (server located in Australia)

First you need to find the ftp server and the file you want. Lists of these servers can also be found through e-mail (as described in Rankin's document). Once you have this information, you type the appropriate ftp commands in the body of your e-mail message. For example, to download Rankin's document, open a host named ubvm.cc.buffalo.edu and then change directories to NETTRAIN. Then get the document file named INTERNET.BY-EMAIL. Type each of the following ftp commands on separate lines in the body of your e-mail message:

```
open ubvm.cc.buffalo.edu
cd NETTRAIN
get INTERNET.BY-EMAIL
quit
```

Then type the address of one of the ftpmail servers in the To: header and send the message. Depending on how busy the server is, you can get the document via e-mail in minutes, hours, or days. Binary files such as programs can be downloaded this way by typing the ftp command named binary before the get command. When binary files are received via e-mail, you have to use the UUdecode utility program to convert it from encoded text back to binary file format.

You can also use e-mail remote access for other Internet services such as gopher, archie, veronica, finger, Whois, WAIS, World Wide Web, and USENET.

Finding an Internet User Address

Finding the e-mail address of someone who you believe has a current Internet e-mail address can be quite difficult. For starters, you'll only be able to find and reach a user at an address that is currently valid. The easiest method is to ask someone who has information that can lead to finding the address. Otherwise, you can guess where the user might be located and then access the appropriate address server to find out the address based on their name and/or affiliation.

> **NOTE** For more information about DNS and address servers, see Chapter 9.

Another way to find someone's e-mail address is to use the related Internet search services of Whois and White Pages.

Whois

The Whois service is composed of databases that contain information about administrators and individual sites on the Internet. Two of the largest sites contain most of this information: one for the military (nic.ddn.mil) and the other site for other hosts (whois.internic.net).

You can access Whois services at these sites using telnet to connect, then type whois and the name of a user. Other keywords such as domain, gateway, group, host, network, or organization can be used to find the corresponding types of information.

You can also use e-mail remote access for Whois searches by sending to whois@whois.internic.net (or service@nic.ddn.mil) with the word help in the message body. Automated reply mail sent to you will provide information on how use Whois via e-mail.

Likewise, WAIS, gopher, and even the World Wide Web offer access to Whois and other search services. With information provided by Whois, you can try to access address servers or contact administrators at these sites to obtain information that may lead to a user's e-mail address. Usually, you can address e-mail to the postmaster (as the user name) at these sites and request help in obtaining a user's address. As the postmaster is a real person and often a busy administrator, you should be patient and cordial in requesting this type of assistance.

White Pages

Although there is no online phone book for all Internet users, White Pages services (see netref 32), such as netfind and the Knowbot Information Service (KIS) can be used to find addresses.

If you know the name of the host, other utilities such as finger and Ph can query mail address servers at company, organization, school, and other sites for user addresses.

There are also several places on the Web where lists of White Pages sites can be found and used for form-based searching on a Web page. Many Web browsers, such as the Netscape Navigator, include built-in links to White Pages for Net searches.

Yellow Pages

The Web also has lists of Yellow Pages sites (see netref 33) to which you can link for a form-based search of information typically associated with traditional Yellow Page listings, such as businesses and other types of organizations. Some of these sites are free and others are specialized Yellow Pages listings that are part of a fee-based service. Some of the fee-based services allow a trial or limited number of free searches to let you try them out.

The term Yellow Pages, when used for this function, does not refer to the service provided by Sun's NIS (Network Information Services).

> **NOTE** For information about finding host names with DNS, see Chapter 9.

Mailing Lists

A mailing list provides a convenient way to share information with others on the Internet. It typically focuses on a particular topic, and allows people with similar interests to subscribe and post messages to the list, which are then redistributed to all subscribers of the list.

The basic types of mailing list are:

- An unmoderated mailing list does not have someone who acts as a moderator to govern membership or filter messages. Thus, this type lets anyone participate. All messages sent to the list are redistributed to its subscribers.

- A moderated mailing list has a moderator who reviews messages sent to the list. If the moderator feels they are appropriate, these messages are then redistributed through the list mailings to the subscribers.

- A digest mailing list has a moderator who compiles messages sent to the list into a single, large file which is then redistributed to the subscribers on a regular basis. A table of contents is usually included at the top of the file.

Mailing lists use the same procedure as e-mail but offer many-to-one and one-to-many capabilities around a given topic of interest. Listserv is the name used for mailing list servers and is often used as a general term for the source of the mailing list.

NOTE For information about listserv servers and subscribing to lists, see Chapter 10.

There are many mailing lists that offer up-to-date information about topics such as networking and the Internet. For example, one list provides descriptions, reviews, and downloading information for new Windows-based software (see netref 34).

The Web has sites and links that provides a convenient means of finding information about public mailing lists (see netref 35).

Newsgroups

Newsgroups are discussion groups that belong to USENET, an acronym for the user's network. USENET began in 1979 at Duke University and the University of North Carolina. Newsgroups are created by users around a unique discussion topic or purpose, which is not already address by another newsgroup.

Originally used by academics to share information on research topics, it has grown to support thousands of separate newsgroups. USENET is a network that is independent of the Internet, but it uses the store and forward mechanism to move its messages through the Internet.

Newsgroups contain uploaded messages called postings or articles that form multiple discussions. A user with client software called a newsreader can subscribe to one or more newsgroups to follow and contribute to these discussions. Users can view the messages in their newsreaders and post a response to a previous posting.

Often an original request or remark that is posted will start a discussion. Some postings that are made in response to it may generate a new discussion topic. This typically creates separate discussions called threads, which a good newsreader can automatically follow. It is not unlike the multiple conversations at a party in which you can variously follow and respond. Besides socially and professionally sharing ideas on topics of interest, many people use newsgroups to exploit the expertise of people on the Net for questions and answers, cooperative learning, and collaborative work.

> **NOTE** For information about establishing newsgroups and using newsgroup (NNTP) servers, see Chapter 10.

Newsgroup names are descriptive of their topics. Each name is composed of several short descriptive terms separated by periods. From left to right, each term in a newsgroup name becomes more specific to the discussion topic. Left-most terms are topic hierarchies that can be used to find more specific topics within. For example, comp is a high-level hierarchy that represents computer topics. The newsgroup named news.groups provides general discussion about newsgroups. The group named news.newusers.questions focuses on questions about netnews for new users.

Besides using a newsreader to select all newsgroups carried by your host, you can obtain a current listing of all newsgroups from the Internet (see netref 36). The Web also offers access to newsgroups through Web browsers. There are many sites where links to newsgroups or threads from discussions can be found. One handy site filters USENET groups to find one or more groups that are appropriate for you (see netref 37).

Agent is a newsreader for Windows and NT by Forte (see netref 38) that exhibits the key strategic feature of usable design (Figure 11-2).

This is evident upon installation, where an option to collect information about the user and newsgroup preferences can be automatically gathered from the preference files of other programs such as Netscape. This saves time and effort and lets users immediately login and begin reading the news from their preferred newsgroups. Other usable features include separate windows for groups, threads, and articles, support for e-mail, spelling checker, and automatic Web URL copying.

There are many sites on the Internet where you can download freeware, shareware, beta, or limited evals of commercial versions of newsreader and other client software (see netref 27). For example, a newsreader client called Free Agent can be downloaded from the Forte Web site.

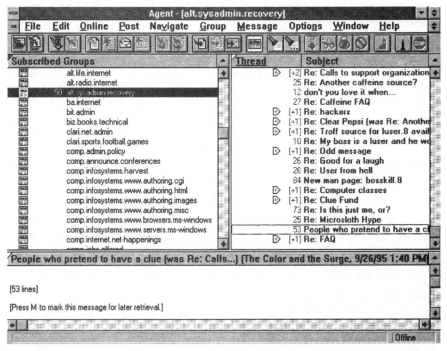

Figure 11-2. Agent E-mail and Newsgroup reader with multiple views of groups, headers, and articles (Forte).

File Transfer Protocol

As the oldest of the Internet protocols, the file transfer protocol, better known as ftp, is broadly supported by software vendors. Many types of ftp servers are available at most sites which you can access through the client software, Web browsers with integrated ftp, or via e-mail remote access. Of these three methods, the Web-based access of ftp servers is the most transparent because the browser automatically handles the login and logout. However, it is usually not as fast as an ftp client for downloading files.

Both client and server ftp software are available on the Net (see netref 27). Also, many network operating systems such as UNIX and Windows NT and TCP/IP utility packages such as Chameleon by NetManage include ftp server and/or client software.

When using the ftp service on the Internet to access directories on a remote host, you are often expected to perform an anonymous login. This refers to a login procedure that is common to many remote ftp servers. It requires that you type the word anonymous when you are presented with a prompt for username at login. After the next prompt for password appears, you should type in your full e-mail address in the format, username@host.domain.

NOTE For information about ftp servers, see Chapter 10.

File Compression

The size of files that are sent or received over the network has a direct effect on throughput. Whether through ftp, e-mail, or other methods, large files will increase the transmission time and in some instances the likelihood of transmission errors. If you are using dial-up connections, it will generally take much longer and also increase your line charges.

File compression programs can be used to decrease the size of a file. There are several types of compression algorithms that are used not only for transmission but for efficient use of storage space when archiving files. These are often identified by the filename extensions that are created when the archival files are created, such as .ZIP, .LZH, .ARJ, .ARC, .TAR, .GZ, .Z and others. Although formats such as ZIP have origins in the PC platform with support by programs such as PKZIP, many of these formats are supported in other platforms (such as ZIP format support by gzip under UNIX).

Although many archival programs can compress or decompress files in one of these formats, some programs can automatically identify and work with many formats. One example is WinZip by Nico Mak Computing (see netref 39). This archival program can be run under Windows or Windows 95 under its program icon or directly within the File Manager or Explorer (by clicking on a compressed file). Features include drag-and-drop operation, virus scanning, and automatic execution or application. An additional program called WinZip Self-extractor can create native Windows self-extracting ZIP files (i.e., that do not require a ZIP-compatible program to decompress files).

Archie

Archie is a companion search service for ftp. It was developed at McGill University in Canada. Archie helps users locate files and directories on anonymous ftp servers anywhere on the Internet. Administrators world-wide register anonymous ftp servers with the archie service. Once a month, the archie service runs a program that scans the directories and filenames contained on each of the registered ftp servers and generates a list of all the files and directories contained on all the registered servers. This list is referred to as the ARCHIE database and is maintained at locations around the world.

You can search for files with archie using several different methods. Archie client software included with utility packages such as Chameleon provides a graphical interface and flexible search criteria for finding files, specific Archie servers, or search keywords. Other archie clients use command-line prompts. If you don't have an archie client, you can use telnet to access an archie service on a host which supports it. For example, you can telnet to archie.mcgill.ca and login as archie. There are many sites on the Internet where you can download freeware or share-ware versions of this software (see netref 27).

Gopher

Gopher was originally developed in April, 1991, by the University of Minnesota to help students find answers to their computer questions. The gopher protocol specification can be found in RFC1436 (see netref 8). It offers distributed document search and retrieval by browsing through collections of information called gopherspace. Gopherspace is the information about sites and their directories and files as defined by the administrators of the many gopher servers around the world.

A user with a gopher client (such as the one bundled with Chameleon TCP/IP package by NetManage) connects to gopher server and is then presented with a menu that shows one or more gopher servers, their directories, and files. After navigating through the directory hierarchy and finding a document or file, the user can download the file or display the document through external text, image, video, or sound viewer applications.

The gopher+ protocol and client software, introduced in 1993, now allows information about items in addition to their content. Attributes include the +ADMIN that shows the source, +VIEW to view documents in alternate formats such as HTML, Microsoft Word, or PostScript, and +ASK to define a template for electronic forms. Upcoming enhancements may include security features and new user interfaces.

NOTE For information about gopher servers, see Chapter 10.

Veronica

Veronica is the companion search service for gopherspace (see netref 40). It actually stands for Very Easy Rodent-Oriented Net-wide Index to Computerized Archives. It performs a keyword search of most gopher-server menu titles in gopherspace. The result of the search produces a menu of gopher items. Each of these gopher items can link to a gopher site.

Veronica does not have to be started as another connection or another application; it is accessible from most top-level gopher menus.

TCP/IP Utilities

Besides providing the basic protocols for e-mail and file transfer, the TCP/IP suite of protocols supports a variety of widely supported network utilities or tools related to connectivity and communications.

- rlogin provides login to remote computers.
- Bind resolves host names to IP addresses.
- Ping echoes packets to test a network connection.
- LPR/LPD provides printing to a remote network printer.
- Ph provides network phone directory services for e-mail.
- finger lists users currently logged in at another host.

Many of these tools are included with Internet connectivity software such at NetManage Chameleon. Although these utilities are commonly used in system administration, network users often rely on them for connectivity and to determine their online status. For example, if continued clicking on a link in a Web document doesn't work, you can run Ping to test your connection. If you know someone's name and the name of the host, but not the e-mail address, you can use Ph to look for it.

> **NOTE** For information about servers for these special services, see Chapter 10.

ENHANCED SERVICES AND APPLICATIONS

Many other services and corresponding applications on the Internet are worth considering for personal and organizational uses. Some of the ones mentioned here have been around for some time, but are gaining new uses. Others are representative of more interactive and multimedia forms of communications.

Internet Relay Chat

Internet Relay Chat (IRC) is an Internet service that has been used for some time for real-time, text-based chat communications between two or more Internet users. Chatting takes place on IRC channels in a similar manner as on CB. IRC provides many self-descriptive text commands to control every aspect of the chat session, including listing all channels (LIST), selecting a channel (SELECT), joining a channel (JOIN), and getting help information (HELP). Private channels can be established and moderated using special mode (MODE) commands. The Internet is a source for many freeware, shareware, and commercial chat applications (see netref 27).

Besides standalone text-based chat programs, other applications use IRC as a component of their communications functions. Multi-user chat environments such as MUD (Multi-User Dungeon) applications (see netref 41), employ text windows in which the online visitors can communicate with the programmed script of the multi-user environment. They can also type messages with other online visitors. Although their names imply that these applications are typically designed as a multi-user adventure game, they can also be used for learning and conferencing applications. Several integrated Web sites employ MUD environments as a means of providing real-time interaction between online visitors.

Some commercial applications such as RUthere? (see netref 42) let users page other people online via their IP address to initiate chat. After registering online with an ID, you let the program run in the background. If someone wants to chat with you, a window will automatically appear. If you want to find an IP address or chat with somebody, you enter the e-mail address of the person with whom you wish to chat and then connect in chat mode. You type your message and then send it.

Other uses of IRC include applications that use channels to register online users of real-time audio or video communications such as IPhone and CU-SeeMe (described next).

Audio and Video

There are basically two ways that the high-bandwidth data of audio and/or video is transmitted over internetworks:

- Downloading a file and subsequently playing its audio or video data in viewers or helper apps.

- Using compression and streaming techniques to reduce the bandwidth demands and play audio and video in real time.

Downloading a file and playing it after the transmission delay is typically done with services like Internet Talk Radio (see netref 43) where large audio files can be selected and downloaded by Web links in a similar manner as using ftp, but where a viewer or helper application is launched when it is fully downloaded.

IPhone, also known as Internet Phone, by Vocaltec is audio software that provides real-time speech on the Internet (see Figure 11-3). It achieves this through audio compression and the use of IRC channels to register online users (see netref 44). Essentially, it gives Internet users a phone capability to call anywhere in the world someone else who is connected and using IPhone.

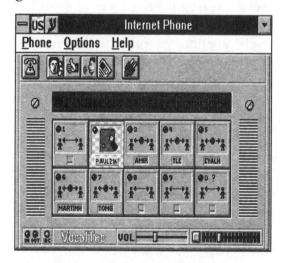

Figure 11-3. Internet Phone real-time voice and audio (VocalTec).

Using this Windows-based application with a PC equipped for sound, speakers, and microphone, you can conduct real-time audio communications over the Internet with a TCP/IP direct connection, or a dial-up connection using SLIP or PPP. Although it's used largely for talking to others who are also using this software on the Internet, it can handle any sounds that you transmit through your microphone, such as music or sound effects. The cost of an Internet Phone call anywhere in the world to someone who is connected to the Internet with this software is only the cost of your local connection to the Internet.

If you have full-duplex audio capability on each user's sound card, IPhone allows both users to speak and listen at the same time. With sound boards that support half-duplex, it only allows one person to transmit at a time. Once it automatically sets the proper recording level for your voice, it uses a voice-activation process to sense when you start and stop speaking. This eliminates the need to use the keyboard or mouse to indicate the beginning and end of a transmission. To handle the bandwidth at speech quality up to 11KHz, IPhone uses a proprietary compression technique to send voice packets and for decompression on the receiving end.

When users access the Internet via dial-up SLIP or PPP connections, they are dynamically assigned IP addresses. As the IP address changes with each login, IPhone can't use an IP address to identify users. Instead, it uses an Internet Relay Chat channel to register a user. Another user can identify the presence of a registered user in the IPhone Call dialog box. A user connects through one of many Internet Phone servers, which are special IRC servers designed to register users on the Internet Phone network.

Internet Streaming

Audio and video streaming applications employ the Internet Streaming Protocol to provide on-demand audiovisual data to clients.

Audio-on-demand and audio streaming represent emerging audio technologies that are bringing live and interactive audio to the Net without crippling its capacity by high bandwidth demands.

Audio applications that employ this protocol can deliver real-time audio content when a corresponding audio-on-demand Web link is selected. Using compression, the audio data is sent to the player application and begins playing within seconds on a multimedia-equipped computer. Real-time interactive control can include start, stop, pause, and re-positioning of the playback. Several audio-on-demand applications using this protocol are typically supported at Web sites.

Internet Wave by Vocaltec (see netref 45) provides audio-on-demand from Web servers through the use of the Internet Wave Player and the Internet Wave Encoder. The encoder converts standard audio files to Internet Wave files which are highly compressed, yet preserve the quality of the original file. It can create compressed files in several formats that support a range of Internet connection speeds and the sampling rate of the input audio file.

The player can be configured as a viewer with Netscape or other Web browsers. It offers intuitive controls on a player window that resembles an audio speaker. When an audio on-demand link for Internet Wave is recognized by the configured Web browser, the Internet Wave Player receives the audio stream and performs real-time playback through the computer's sound system.

TrueSpeech (see netref 46) is a family of speech compression and decompression algorithms and software developed by DSP Group, Inc. The TrueSpeech Player will play TrueSpeech as real-time, audio-streaming playback over the Internet, using low-bandwidth (8.5kbps) compression. The TrueSpeech encoder is bundled with Windows 95 and Windows NT for converting .wav and other file types to TrueSpeech format. TrueSpeech audio content can be added to Web documents and delivered by Web servers without the need for a special audio streaming server.

RealAudio by Progressive Networks, Inc. (see netref 47) is an audio-on-demand platform consisting of the RealAudio Player, RealAudio Encoder, and RealAudio Server. Transmission requires the use of the RealAudio Server.

> **NOTE** For information about audio and Internet streaming servers, see Chapter 10.

Internetwork applications that deliver video are more demanding of bandwidth than those that deliver audio. Compounding this is the typical inclusion of text and/or audio to accompany a video transmission. There are two basic strategies for delivering video on the internetworks: one is to reduce the bandwidth of the video signal to work with lower quality video signals and the other is to limit its use.

CU-SeeMe is software (see netref 48) that provides interactive video and voice communication via the Internet or any local TCP/IP-based network. It handles the challenge of delivering high-bandwidth signal by employing both compression for its audio-video data and IRC channels to manage online registration of CU-SeeMe services to users.

The CU-SeeMe client application provides person-to-person video conferencing (see Figure 11-4) with a compatible camera and video digitizer software, such as the ComputerEyes boards by Digital Vision (see netref 49) The client also allows users who are not transmitting video to "lurk" by only viewing the images transmitted by others. With a server called a Reflector, CU-SeeMe can provide group videoconferencing.

NOTE For more information about CU-SeeMe reflectors and other multimedia servers, see Chapter 10.

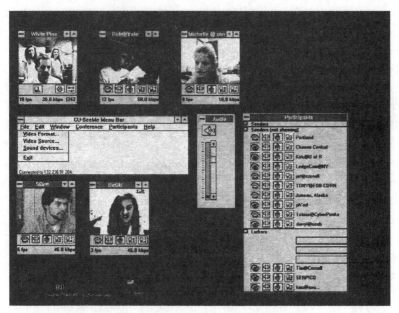

Figure 11-4. CU-SeeMe videoconferencing (White Pine).

What makes CU-SeeMe unique is that it uses no proprietary hardware and was specifically designed to perform over low-bandwidth network connections. Currently, video images over CU-SeeMe are transmitted in black and white at a slower frame rate than full motion video to reduce demand on the network. As the availability of ISDN lines and ATM switches becomes more commonplace, performance and quality will greatly improve.

CU-SeeMe software was developed at Cornell University with funding and cooperation from the National Science Foundation and other organizations. As the master licensee, White Pine will develop and enhance the software for Microsoft Windows, Macintosh and future desktop/set-top operating systems. Planned upgrades include color capability, improved audio fidelity, interactive whiteboard and application sharing, and a Windows NT-server version of the CU-SeeMe Reflector, and the eventual use of T.120 and H.320 standards for interoperability with other desktop video software and hardware.

StreamWorks by Xing Technology (see netref 50) is both an audio and video streaming client/server application. Using a highly-efficient compression technique, it can deliver high-quality audio and video over both LAN and Internet. It can support dial-up connections with modem speeds as low as 9,600 baud.

There are more advanced uses of real-time video over internetworks. These applications deliver higher video image quality and frame rates at the cost of more network bandwidth.

MBONE is an example of a high-end video Internet service. MBONE, an acronym for the Multicast Backbone, is a virtual network that operates over the Internet to provide high-bandwidth audio, whiteboard, video-conferencing and video broadcasts. It relies on routers equipped with the Internet Multicast IP protocol.

For a basic introduction to accessing the MBONE, read "Dan's Quick and Dirty Guide to Getting Connected to the Mbone." You can ftp to genome-ftp.stanford.edu then do an anonymous login and download it from the /pub/mbone/mbone-connect directory.

NOTE For more information about MBONE, see Chapter 10.

However, because of the increasing number of users and other applications that lay claim on the finite bandwidth of the internetworks, these high-bandwidth uses are currently limited in their application. Until new techniques and technologies can increase the capacity of the transmission media and decrease the load imposed by these high-end video applications, their use will be restricted in terms of how often transmissions occur and how many simultaneous users they can support.

Multimedia Chat and Conferencing

In addition to basic text and audio-video-conferencing services and applications, there are many multimedia-conferencing applications that are emerging on the Net. Typical of this group are graphical or animated environments. These can include text-based chat, the use of avatar-like graphics for visual representation, and audio, images, and animation.

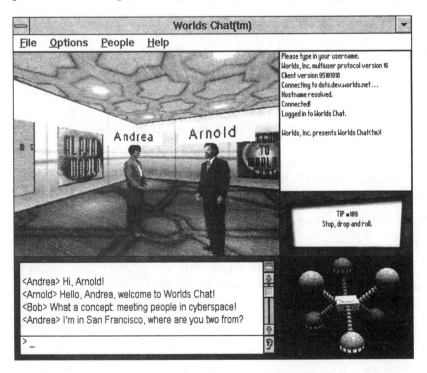

Figure 11-5. Worlds Chat™ VR chat and conferencing (Worlds Inc.).

WorldsChat is a robust audiovisual environment (see netref 51) that combines chat and virtual reality (VR) on the World Wide Web (see Figure 11-5). Worlds Inc., the maker of WorldsChat and other 3-D applications is a leading producer of social computing applications. These environments allow users to use their computers to communicate over regular phone lines and interact in a fully navigable graphical space (with sound) with other real people.

Users choose on-screen graphical images of people or other objects called avatars which then move through 3-D spaces (through cursor keys or mouse control) and interact with other users by typing of messages in text screens. Typed messages can be seen by anyone close to the user or may be privately directed (whispered) to a single user by typing that user's on-screen name and a colon before the message.

This software can be used for business conferences, interactive walk-though shopping malls, and many other conferencing and virtual reality applications. For example, Visa and Worlds Inc. will use this technology to establish virtual malls complete with virtual stores in which online visitors (using the client software) can enter and examine merchandise. If they want to make purchases, the transactions are made through a virtual bank using Secure Transaction Technology, an improved encryption technique. Other full-service banking will also be available. Real-time speech is planned to replace or supplement text-based interaction.

> **NOTE** For more information about network-based conferencing applications, see Chapter 8.

Interactive Multimedia

Although the Web offers interactivity by selectively activating links on Web pages, the original HTML specifications were limited in their direct support of interactive routines for animation, sound, and other programmed operations. One way that HTML was extended is through scripts that launch external programs through the Common Gateway Interface (CGI).

> **NOTE** For more information about CGI scripting, see Chapters 8 and 10.

Newer and more flexible enhancements are appearing in the form of languages and browser applications that can work with the Web. Netscape's Navigator Web browser provides enhanced support of interactive multimedia through its Live Objects support for content such as Java applets, frames, and Netscape inline plug-ins.

Hot Java (see netref 52) is an interactive multimedia browser application by Sun Microsystems (see Figure 11-6). The browser was originally released for Sun workstations and Windows NT. It uses a language called Java, developed by Sun Microsystems, that lets World Wide Web pages contain program code called an applet which can be executed on the browser. Java is based on a "virtual machine" which lets Java programs run on any system that has a version of Java. Also, Java can be used in applications on or off the Internet. Thus, interoperability is achieved through its presentation of interactive content across diverse hardware and software platforms. The Java language also provides some security by protecting applets from any unauthorized use.

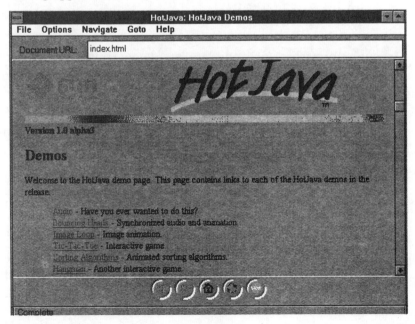

Figure 11-6. Hot Java browser (Sun Microsystems, Inc.)

The Java Development Kit (JDK) provides an integrated environment for Java script development. It can be used to develop interactive Java applets for the World Wide Web. Links to the applets can be added to an HTML page. Whenever a Hot Java browser encounters a web page containing a Java applet link, the applet can automatically execute, or the user can initiate the applet by clicking on a link that executes it.

Original applets are created and compiled directly with the Java language and using JDK, Java tutorials, and sample applets. For example, you can insert an HTML tag for an animation applet on a Web page by referring to an existing Java applet named "ImageLoopItem" as the source (SRC). After creating image files that make up an animation sequence (IMG) and storing them in a directory named "animate" at the same level as the HTML file, you would insert the following HTML coding on the Web page:

```
<APP CLASS= ImageLoopItem
   SRC= doc:/demo/
   IMG= animate >
```

Although animation and audio applets demonstrate the interactive multimedia potential of Java, applets can provide many other interactive functions. For example, an applet can be used to greet people by name. The applet can then present them with options that are customized to their personal preferences using the data that was previously entered in a Web form. This provides personalized interactivity for advertising, customer service, and similar applications on the Web.

Virtual Reality

Combining elements of hypermedia and virtual reality, a new breed of interactive audiovisual environments are making their way onto the Net.

Among the more animated environments on the Net are those that employ Virtual Reality Modeling Language (VRML) as an open standard for creating and visually exploring the virtual space of a three-dimensional (3-D) environment called a world. A VRML world is created using the text-based, descriptive statements of the VRML language, a subset of the OpenInventor format by Silicon Graphics. It is saved as an ASCII text file with .WRL as the filename extension. Thus, the source code for a world file can be created, viewed, and edited in any text editor or word processor that supports ASCII.

WebSpace by Silicon Graphics Inc. (see netref 53) and Template Graphics Software (see netref 54) is 3-D client software that lets you browse VRML worlds by moving through them under mouse or cursor control. Besides working as a standalone application, WebSpace can be used as an external viewer with Netscape and other Web browsers. It was originally available for UNIX, Windows 95 and Windows NT. The WebSpace package includes sample VRML worlds, as noted by the .WRL filename extension. Template Graphics also offers a cross-platform development platform called Open Inventor that uses the OpenGL rendering language for programming worlds and browsers. A toolkit called SceneCreator lets users create VRML worlds without programming.

WorldView by InterVista (see netref 55) is another VRML browser that can be run either in standalone mode or in conjunction with a World Wide Web browser such as Netscape. WorldView navigation is provided through mouse control of buttons in a control panel, including: Walk, Fly, and Inspect (which lets you move and tilt the 3-D model). Other controls include Move Forward/Move Backward, Move Left/Move Right, Look Left/Look Right, Look up/Look Down, Tilt Left/Tilt Right. A Crosshair button allows continuous and fluid Move and Rotate control through mouse movement (with Shift key for Pan, and with Control key for Pitch and Roll).

VRweb (see netref 56) is a VRML viewer/browser that is the result of a joint project between the Hyper-G development team at the Institute for Information Processing and Computer Supported New Media (IICM) in Graz, Austria, and the Mosaic team at NCSA. It has the advantage of being released originally for Windows users who are equipped with Win32s or Windows 95 or NT.

It operates both as a standalone viewer for VRML world files and as an external viewer with Mosaic, Netscape, or similar Web browsers. Its navigational tools include: Flip Objects, Walk, Fly, Fly To, and Heads Up. If offers multiple rendering options, including Wireframe, Hidden Line, Flat Shading, Smooth Shading, and Texturing.

WIRL, (formerly called WebView) by (see netref 57) is another VRML-based client. WIRL stands for Web Interactive Reality Layer. WIRL is a VR browser that is compatible with popular Web client/server products such as Enhanced Mosaic and Netscape. WIRL worlds can be created using VRCreator, VREAM's virtual-reality-creation software product. This will allow Web users to use a WIRL world on the Web. WIRL will support multimedia PC systems, as well as VR interface devices, including head-mounted displays, 3-D tracking systems, 3-D mice, gloves, and 3-D ball controllers to achieve immersive virtual reality on the Web.

The underlying VREAMScript language is high-level, and platform-independent, and extends VRML to allow complex virtual worlds to be quickly transmitted across the Internet. It allows WIRL worlds to possess attributes such as sound, motion, penetrability, throwability, weight, and elasticity. It also supports complex interactive cause-and-effect relationships, such as the ability to grab a cord to turn on a light. These attributes can be assigned to objects to create the interactive components of the 3-D world.

Remote Control

The Web and its ability to spawn external scripts and applications can be used to pass data to many devices that rely on computer data to operate under electronic control. This can be used for real-time remote control or for batch submission for subsequent operation (see netref 58).

There are many remote Web sites that use live video transmissions from cameras directly attached to computers (see Figure 11-7). Some of them display whatever the camera is showing. Other sites use CGI scripting to allow remote users to control the movements of the camera (see netref 59).

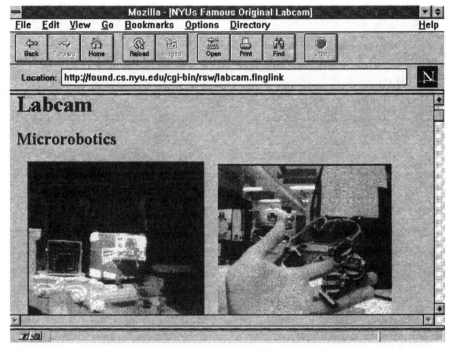

Figure 11-7. NYUs Famous Original Labcam (New York University).

Data entered into forms can be passed through CGI scripting as input to these devices. For example, Web users can submit requests in batch-mode to the Bradford Robotic Telescope (see netref 59) for specific observations and have the results available overnight.

Electronic Commerce

Since becoming the most popular of Internet services in the spring of 1995, the World Wide Web has also become the predominant platform for electronic commerce. At this point, the underlying technologies are emerging and their application is in the early stages of implementation. Two emerging technologies provide contrasting approaches to this problem: secure transaction and e-cash.

Secure Transactions

Secure transaction technologies are based on the exchange of credit data such as credit card numbers. For these types of transactions to be reliable, systems either encrypt the personal data that accompanies the transactional data or else an intermediary handles the exchange so that personal data does not need to accompany the transactional data.

For its popular Web products, Netscape employs Secure Socket Layer (SSL) and RSA encryption to protect vital personal and transactional data from being exploited when it passes between client and server. Also, Secure Courier provides a means of protecting the integrity and tracing the source of an encrypted transmission. Alternative methods include Secure Hypertext-Transport Protocol (S-HTTP), which adds to encryption the use of digital signatures to confirm the source.

Standards based on the use of these technologies will likely boost adoption and use (see netref 61). However, additional obstacles to the use of server-based security for electronic commerce exist. For example, an adequate number of online merchants must employ this type of server and there must be sufficient awareness of these merchants by consumers.

> **NOTE** For more information about security and other network protocols, see Chapter 7.

Virtual Accounts

Another method to secure online transactions is the use of a virtual account with an online intermediary such as a virtual bank. For example, First Virtual Holdings Incorporated (see netref 62) is a financial services company that makes use of an intermediary service to separate personal from transactional data. The service was created specifically to enable anyone with Internet access to conduct secure transactions worldwide using the Internet. The system is entirely secure, with no need for encryption, because sensitive financial information never travels over the Internet at all.

It operates a public-access information server called the InfoHaus, which enables anyone to become a merchant on the Internet quickly for almost no cost. To get an account and activate it for selling, all you need is e-mail and a checking account with First Virtual. To get an account and activate it for buying, all you need is e-mail access and a VISA or Mastercard to charge any purchases you make.

Electronic Cash

Electronic Cash, E-Cash, Digital Money, Digital Cash—no matter what the name, it all refers to the use of the electronic equivalent of hard currency. It's used as an alternative to secure transactions for buying products and services over the Net.

For example, NetCash is an e-cash service of the NetBank which is available on the Web (see netref 63). Using this service, you purchase a given amount of e-cash by sending funds in U.S. dollars to the NetBank in exchange for an equivalent amount of NetCash coupons. You can buy NetCash using the E-Mail Check Cashing service by sending an e-mail message to the NetBank. The coupon consists of the "NetCash US$" keyword, the dollar amount, and the serial number. A NetCash coupon included in the response message might look like this:

```
NetCash US$ 25.00 A123456B789012C
```

The cash value of your coupon is contingent on your bank honoring your check and remitting payment to the NetBank.

When you purchase a product or service, you send your NetCash coupon to a merchant via e-mail or from the merchant's Web pages. The merchant will tell you the recommended procedure to send him your coupon. The format of the e-mail message is:

```
From: user@home.net (User)
To: merchant@shopping.net (Merchant)
Dear Merchant,
Enclosed is payment for your product.
NetCash US$ 5.00 C345678D901234E
```

Doing Business on the Net

Although there is tremendous interest by both organizations as providers and online users as potential consumers, there are many hurdles that must be overcome before electronic commerce is fully implemented on global internetworks.

Foremost is that a sufficient number of users become familiar and feel confident with secure transactions and e-cash to support online buying and selling. Also, as the Internet is a global system, electronic commerce must account for international monetary exchange, trade, intellectual property, and other pertinent regulations and policies.

Despite the obstacles that must be overcome to move from adoption to use, some observations can be made even at this early stage of implementation on the Internet. Through media coverage and online observations, it is clear that businesses of all sizes are getting an early start by establishing a presence on the Web through which they can complement their offline business activities (netref 64).

Certain types of businesses can exploit the Web for electronic commerce because their product or service has a good organizational fit with the current technology and culture of the Net. Demographics on Web use obtained through online surveys (see netref 65) have established that the early adopters and users of the Net are young, well-educated, and technically savvy. Thus, for reasons of this fit, businesses in the electronics, computer, travel, finance, and related fields have identified this target audience and established an early presence. Other businesses will follow as the technological means to represent and sell their products is further developed and both the number and demographics of online users expands.

Many organizations are setting up shop on the Internet for reasons independent of current technology and use. They reason that electronic commerce is inevitable. They also recognize that the cost of admission is low, relative to the learning experience and promotional advantages of having an online presence at an early stage of implementation.

Certain business activities appear to be predominant, even if the return on investment is not yet clear or significant. The use of an online presence to complement traditional business activities is the most evident type of presence. To accommodate the needs of current and potential customers, many businesses are using an Internet presence to develop brand recognition and maintain product loyalty.

Although many companies support their online customers through e-mail, mailing lists, and other basic services, there is a growing trend towards providing these services through an integrated Web site. Web pages with graphics, sound, video, and real-time multimedia interaction can improve the quality of communications.

For businesses that established an early presence on the Net, a typical business objective was product recognition or brand recognition (see netref 66) or customer support (see netref 67), but many companies are now moving into direct marketing and online transactions (see netref 68).

Some of the most important concepts about promoting an online presence come from mistakes made by early adopters. Many companies raced to set up a Web site with no clear business goal or understanding of the technology and culture of the Web. What they learned was simply being first is not important. First impressions must be good to be lasting, but what is considered good in this new medium and what satisfies the expectations of its users?

Some small steps in understanding have come from lessons learned by these early adopters.

- Unlike waves of new technology that only represent incremental change, this is likely the beginning of a sea change on a global scale in the way business is done.

- Do your homework. Develop a first-hand understanding of the technology, culture, and demographics of the Internet.

- Develop a clear plan and test it before establishing an Internet presence. Try your ideas out locally before going globally. For example, use a local Web on your LAN until it is ready for the Net.

- The Web is not a broadcast medium. It supports many types of communications within a wide variety of services and applications.

- The Web is a "catch as catch can" medium, which means that you should adopt a convergent media strategy to draw visitors to your site. Include reference to your online presence (including the actual Web and e-mail addresses) in other media, such as print, television, and radio.

- The Web is not a passive medium. Learn what interactivity means, but don't look to standalone computer programs for a model because they never quite made the mark. Usable design is just coming into its own because producers are only now listening to their consumers. Instead, learn from other users and surf the Net with an eye for its underlying nature and benefits.

Many Web sites support CGI scripting that tallies the number of visits or "hits" during a given period, such as daily, weekly or total since inception. Quite often, these sites clearly display this in the form of a counter, usually near the bottom of the home page. What can these numbers tell you?

Popular Web sites not only get a lot of hits, they also benefit from word of mouth in a uniquely online manner. Not only do net surfers boast about interesting sites, but they also add links to those sites from their home pages.

You should explore some of these sites to see what they offer. Many of the more popular sites have learned to add value through content along with their promotional objectives. The content and the style of the site should be fun, interesting, useful, and interactive. It can also be made highly personal through CGI scripting, Java applets, and other interactive multimedia technologies. Integrated Web sites use several Internet services for a rich blend of personal and group interaction between you as the user, the producer, and other online users.

> **NOTE** For more information about establishing a presence on the Net, building an integrated Web site, and for an example of an integrated Web site, see Chapter 10.

If learning by example is any guide, then learning from the masters should apply, but you be the judge. Search for likely targets under keywords like Advertising or Web Production and link to the sites of those who do it for a living (see netref 69). For an unflinching look at the good, bad, and ugly of Web sites and applications, consult Web Review (see netref 70). This Web-based zine also provides pointers for tips and tools on Web production.

Although electronic commerce is in its infancy, it's growing fast and along with it, the norms and standards under which it takes place. Continuous learning is an essential strategy for getting online and riding the crest of change. Bon voyage!

REFERENCES

Net References

1. For the history of the Internet, use a Web or gopher client to access gopher://gopher.isoc.org/11/internet/history

For a Librarian's Guide to the Internet, www to http://www.faxon.com/Internet/LibGuide/LibTOC.HTML

2. www to http://www.internic.net/ then browse the InterNIC Directory and Database Services Home Page for information and statistics about the Internet. You can check on the latest Internet growth statistics by reading the corresponding Request for Comment documents (i.e., RFC1296 or more current RFC) that cover Internet growth statistics.

For graphs that depict Internet growth by number of hosts, ftp to ftp.isoc.org and search the directory named /isoc/charts

3. www to http://nii.nist.gov/ then browse the United States National Information Infrastructure Virtual Library for information about the NII or information superhighways. The Virtual Library provides explanations of the NII and how it works. It also provides systems developers with information on NII applications.

4. For information about the Global Information Infrastructure (GII) and the conferences and committees that help shape it, browse the following Web pages:

www to http://nii.nist.gov/whatgii.html for information on the subject, "What is the GII?."

www to http://www.ispo.cec.be/g7/g7main.html for information on the subject, "G-7 Information Society Conference."

www to http://info.ic.gc.ca/G7/poi-country.html for information on the subject, "GII Points of Interest Index by Country."

5. www to http://www.acm.org/sigcomm/sos.html then browse the SIGCOMM Web pages for information about the current status of the Internet, OSI, and related standards.

6. www to http://info.isoc.org/home.html then browse the information page of the Internet Society for links to information about its various sub-organizations and related sites, including standards, conference proceedings, usage charts, global connectivity maps, etc. Also, browse for proceedings in hypermedia form from its previous INET conferences.

7. For information about the Internet Architecture Board (IAB) and its meetings, www to http://www.iab.org/iab/ and browse the IAB home page where you can select an IAB Meeting Minutes link.

8. For access to RFC documents through the World Wide Web, www to http://www.cis.ohio-state.edu/htbin/rfc/rfc-index.html then search the RFC index list for the RFC by number. Click on the link to access the RFC source document. This index list contains the most recent RFCs.

If you prefer to use ftp to access RFC documents, then ftp to ds.internic.net then login as anonymous and search for an RFC in the /rfc directory. Or you can ftp to another repository such as nis.nsf.net in the directory named internet/documents/rfc.

9. For information about the IETF, www to http://www.ietf.cnri.reston.va.us/home.html then browse the IETF home page. You can also access IETF from a link on the IAB home page.

You can also ftp to ds.internic.net then login as anonymous and download documents from the IETF in the /ietf and /iesg directories.

10. For a list of Internet providers, access Yahoo via www to http://www.yahoo.com then select the following links (or add the following directory path to the end of the URL after yahoo.com): /Business/Corporations/Internet_Access_Providers/ then search the list by name, e-mail, or phone. For example, use the Find command in your browser to search for nearest provider by area code or 800 number.

For another Internet Service Provider Directory, www to http://www.commerce.net/directories/products/isp/isp.html

Other providers may be found by using their name (or search using the term, Internet provider) in a "Net Search" using any of the supported web search engines.

11. www to http://www.gti.net then view information on the Global Telecom, Inc. (GTI) home page for Internet access and service information, including points of presence, types of service, and establishing an account. GTI offers SLIP, PPP, and ISDN dial-up services and 24-hour services using frame relay and other technologies. Toll-free access supports nationwide connectivity.

12. www to http://www.netusa.net/ then view information on the Network-USA home page for Internet access and service information, including hardware and software resources and services.

13. For information about European Internet connectivity services and software, contact PIPEX in Cambridge, England via www to http://www.pipex.com/ or via e-mail to support@dial.pipex.com

14. www to http://www.w3.org/hypertext/WWW/WWW/ then browse for information and links related to the history of the Web and how to use it.

15. To access a Lynx client online, telnet to ukanaix.cc.ukans.edu then login as www and follow instructions on the screen.

16. For information about and downloading of Lynx, www to http://www.jackson.freenet.org/about_lynx/www_start.html

17. ftp to interport.net then access the FAQ file named sntfaq1.txt in /pub/pbrooks/slipknot and read about downloading sites, installation, and use. If you have access to the Web through Lynx or a graphical Web browser, you can access the SlipKnot home page via www to http://www.interport.net/slipknot/

18. For information about Mosaic, browse the Software Development Group pages at the NCSA Web site via www to http://www.ncsa.uiuc.edu/SDG/Software/Mosaic/

For more information about the NCSA, www to http://www.ncsa.uiuc.edu/General/NCSAHome.html

19. www to http://www.netscape.com/ then browse the Netscape home page for information about Netscape Navigator and other Web applications.

20. www to http://www.spry.com/ then browse the Spry home page for information about Internet Office.

21. www to http://www.mariner.ncd.com/ then browse the NCD Mariner home page for information about Mariner.

22. www to http://fox.nstn.ca/~harawitz/index.html then browse for information about the URL Grabber software by Brooklyn North Software Works.

23. For information about WAIS client/server search engines, www to http://www.wais.com/ then browse the WAIS home page. You can also e-mail to info@wais.com for information about WAIS.

24. Web search engines are plentiful and varied to meet the needs of Web crawlers and surfers in search of new haunts and troves of information.

For a meta-list of Web search engines for all types of information broken down by the following categories: information servers, software, people, publications, news/FAQs, documentation, and other categories, www to http://cuiwww.unige.ch/meta-index.html

The CUI W3 Catalog at the University of Geneva is a search interface to several Internet catalogs, www to http://cuiwww.unige.ch/w3catalog/

INFOSEEK which is available from Netscape can also be accessed via www to http://www2.infoseek.com/

The Harvest Information Discovery and Access System offers automated brokers that assist in conducting high-powered searches, www to http://harvest.cs.colorado.edu/

Lycos is an easy-to-use, yet helpful Web-based search engine that searches the entire Net, www to http://www.lycos.com/

The Open Text Index offers a variety of keyword search types, www to http://opentext.uunet.ca:8080/

For a form-based, Web search engine on a Web page, http://www.webcrawler.com/ then browse the Web Crawler page and fill in the fields of the form to conduct a search.

For another form-based, Web search engine on a Web page, www to http://www.cs.colorado.edu/home/mcbryan/WWWW.html then browse the World Wide Web Worm (WWWW) page and fill in the fields of the form to conduct a search.

25. The entire Web is an excellent resource for continuous learning. Here is a small sampling of the many sites that offer Web information resources:

For a list of frequently asked questions (FAQ) about the Web, access the Sunsite online library via www to http://sunsite.unc.edu/boutell/faq/

CERN is the original home of the Web. Start at the top and work your way down through the links to finds all things of a Web nature, www to http://info.cern.ch/

For information about the Internet and Web, access online documents in the Web Developer's Virtual Library via www to http://WWW.Stars.com/Vlib/

Netscape's page has links for creating a Web site: www to http://home.netscape.com/home/how-to-create-web-services.html

26. For an example of a Web "lists of lists" access Yahoo via www to http://www.yahoo.com/

27. There are many sites on the Web that describe and provide links for downloading freeware, shareware, and beta or evals of commercial software. Here are just a few:

The Virtual Shareware Library (VSL) offers descriptions, searching and downloading links for many platforms, including UNIX, Windows, and Macintosh, as well as DOS, OS/2, and other platforms, www to http://vsl.cnet.com/

Jumbo offers shareware downloading for multiple platforms, www to http://www.jumbo.com/

For the speed of downloading shareware with ftp, try these sites with an ftp client or with a Web browser. For PC and Windows shareware, ftp to ftp.cica.indianc.edu/pub/pc/ For Macintosh shareware, ftp to mac.archive.umich.edu/pub/mac

For review and downloading information about Windows based software, browse the Consummate Winsock Apps List (CWSApps List), www to http://www.hookup.net/cwsapps/ then view the information about reviews and downloading.

www to http://www.tucows.com/ then browse The Ultimate Collection of Winsock Software which contains reviews and links for downloading Windows-based programs.

28. www http://www.hotwired.com/ then browse the HotWired home page where you can subscribe, read articles, and participate in online interviews and forums. To sub-scribe to the HotFlash mailing list, send email to info-rama@hotwired.com with the message, subscribe hotflash, in the body of the message.

29. www to http://www.tgc.com/webster.html then browse the home page for information about a trial subscription. As this service also is offered through a mailing list you can request a trial subscription via e-mail to 4free@webster.tgc.com

30. Here are some examples of media convergence on the Web:

For an example of television and Web convergence, www to http://uttm.com/ then browse the UTTMlink home page. This is the Web version of the CBS News Up To The Minute television show offering overnight news with coverage of Internet and CD-ROM developments. Their Web pages include text, images, and audio on-demand playback of current and previous shows (using RealAudio, IWave, and TrueSpeech), e-mail feedback and opinion polls, and links to related sites.

www to http://www.tvnet.com/TVnet.html for links to TV stations, chat, and discussion areas.

For an example of radio and Web convergence, www to http://newsradio88.com/boot/archive/welcome.html then browse the home page of a popular WCBS radio program called Boot Camp (hosted by technology reporter, Fred Fishkin (www to http://www.pulver.com/ffishkin.html then browse his home page or contact him via IPhone). You can view or listen (with RealAudio or Vocaltec's IWave) to transcripts of shows on a variety of computer and networking topics. It also provides e-mail feedback and links to archives of previous shows and related sites.

Another example of radio netcasting is the Online computer information show from the Canadian west coast. You can hear them on CFAX 1070 or on the Web via www to http://www.islandnet.com/~online/online.html then browse its page, which offers current netcasts of shows featuring interviews and information about computer and networking. They support e-mail requests and questions for on-going shows. They also have show archives which are indexed with the URLs of guests who've appeared. If you heard someone interesting on a show, you can review the show and contact them on the Net. They support RealAudio and IWave audio-on-demand playback.

For radio information and links on the Internet, www to http://www.radiospace.com/welcome.html

For a radio newsgroup, subscribe to rec.radio.broadcasting

For an example of print and Web media convergence, www to http://www.bookwire.com/ then browse the pages and links for publisher and reader information, reviews, and book information indexes.

31. To get the document entitled, "Accessing The Internet By E-Mail: Doctor Bob's Guide to Offline Internet Access," email to: mail-server@rtfm.mit.edu with the Subject line blank and type only the following line in the body of the note:

```
send usenet/news.answers/internet-services/access-via-email
```

You can also retrieve this document via ftp to ubvm.cc.buffalo.edu then login as anonymous and get the file named NETTRAIN/INTERNET.BY-EMAIL

32. There are many ways to access White Pages which are needed because there are many separate lists of addresses:

For a FAQ about using White Pages services to find addresses, www to http://www.qucis.queensu.ca:1999/~dalamb/info.html

If you prefer telnet to login to a remote host to obtain a White Pages listing, telnet to wp.psi.net then login as Fred to search the White Pages listing by typing in the name of a user.

Netfind is a White Pages service which can use telnet to search address databases: telnet to ds.internic.net then login as netfind. No password is required.

The Knowbot Information Service is another White Pages search service which can search addresses: telnet to info.cnri.reston.va.us 185

33. For a master list with links to free and commercial Yellow Pages and search sites, www to http://www.yellow.com/

34. For a mailing list with descriptions, reviews, and downloading information for new Windows-based software, subscribe to the Critical Applications Distribution List (CADL) mailing list. Send a message with SUBSCRIBE CADL to Neuroses@mail.utexas.edu and include your e-mail address and your first and last name.

35. For a Web page index of public mailing lists by subject, www to http://www.NeoSoft.com:80/internet/paml/bysubj.html

www to http://scwww.ucs.indiana.edu/mlarchive/ then search through the mailing list archive.

For an ftp site that lists current mailing lists, ftp to ftp.nisc.sri.com then login as anonymous and access the file named interest-groups in the netinfo directory.

36. ftp to ftp.uu.net then login as anonymous and download the file in /archive/uunet-info/newsgroups

For a FAQ about newsgroups, use a Web browser or ftp client to ftp://rtfm.mit.edu/pub/usenet/news.answers/

For a Web page index of USENET newsgroups by subject, www to http://www.NeoSoft.com:80/internet/paml/bysubj-usenet.html

For a Web-based guide to newsgroups, www to http://www.faxon.com/Internet/LibGuide/Usenet.html

37. www to http://sift.stanford.edu/ then follow instructions for using SIFT to filter USENET newsgroups for topics in which you are interested.

38. www to http://www.forteinc.com/forte/agent/ then browse the Forte Agent news-reader page for information and downloading instructions about this product.

39. www to http://www.winzip.com/winzip/ then look at information about the WinZip compression program and how to download the shareware evaluation version or order the commercial version.

40. Veronica can be accessed from the Other Gophers menu on the University of Minnesota gopher server. From the Web, you can access it via www to gopher://futique.scs.unr.edu/11/veronica

41. For information and listings of multi-user chat applications and sites, try the following:

For Web access to MUD sites, MUD newsgroups, and MUD FAQs, www to http://www.absi.com/mud/

For a newsgroup which contains FAQs and announcements of new MUDs, subscribe to rec.games.mud.announce

42. www to http://www.personalnet.com/ then browse for information about RUthere?, how to download the freeware player program, and register with the commercial paging service.

43. www to http://www.ncsa.uiuc.edu/radio/radio.html then browse for information about Internet Talk Radio.

44. www to http://www.vocaltec.com/ then browse the Vocaltec home page for information about Internet Phone downloading an evaluation version (limited to a single 60 second transmission per session) and ordering the full version via the Web form or e-mail.

45. For information about Internet Wave, www to http://www.vocaltec.com/ then browse the Vocaltec home page for information about this application and downloading.

46. www to http://www.dsp.com/ then browse the DSP home page for information about the TrueSpeech player and other applications.

47. www to http://www.RealAudio.com/ then browse the Progressive Networks, Inc. RealAudio home page for information about the RealAudio Player, Encoder, and several types of servers.

48. For information about evals and the licensed, commercial verison of CU-SeeMe, www to http://www.wpine.com/ then browse the White Pine home page for CU-SeeMe product information.

For information about CU-SeeMe software, a mailing list, and links to other CU-SeeMe sites where it is used, www to http://www.jungle.com/msattler/sci-tech/comp/CU-SeeMe/

49. www to http://www.digvis.com/digvis then browse the Digital Vision home page for information about the complete line of ComputerEyes video digitizer hardware, software, and other products.

50. www to http://www.xing.com/ then browse the Xing Technology home page for information and to download the StreamWorks player.

51. www to http://www.worlds.net/ then browse the Worlds Inc. home page for information about downloading WorldsChat software, accessing WorldsChat and other VR world environments.

52. www to http://java.sun.com/ then browse the Sun Microsystems Java page for information about Hot Java, the Java language, and links to other sites that have applets made with Java.

53. www to http://www.sgi.com/ then browse the Silicon Graphics home page for basic information about WebSpace and for links to VRML worlds.

54. For information about availability of WebSpace and other software for various platforms from Template Graphics, www to http://www.sd.tgs.com/~template/WebSpace/monday.html

55. www to http://intervista.com/ then browse the InterVista home page for information about the WorldView VRML browser.

56. To download the VRweb client from the master site in Graz, Austria, which contains the newest versions, www to ftp://ftp.iicm.tu-graz.ac.at/pub/Hyper-G/VRweb/

You can also access VRweb at the NCSA mirror site via ftp to ftp.ncsa.uiuc.edu/Hyper-G/VRweb/

57. For information about WIRL (formerly called WebView), www to http://www.vream.com/ then browse the VREAM, Inc. home page for WIRL, VRCreator and other virtual reality programs.

58. For a Web page with links to remote control sites, www to http://www.jungle.com/msattler/sci-tech/comp/misc/remote-control.html

59. www to http://www.ts.umu.se/~spaceman/camera.html for a Web page with links to many live-camera sites on the Web.

60. For remote control of a telescope and receive observational data, access the robotic telescope at the Bradford Observatory www to http://www.telescope.org/rti/

61. For information about secure transaction standards for electronic commerce on the Internet, refer to the IETF site (see netref 9) and the following Web sites:

www to http://www.w3.org/ then browse the World Wide Web Consortium site.

www to http://www.terisa.com/ then browse the Terisa Systems site.

www to http://www.eit.com/ then browse the Enterprise Integration Technologies (EIT) site for information about S-HTTP standards.

www to http://www.netscape.com/ then browse the Netscape Communications Corporation site for information about SSL standards.

62. For an example of virtual accounts on the Web, www to http://www.fv.com/ then browse the First Virtual Holdings Incorporated site.

63. For an example of electronic cash on the Web, www to http://www.netbank.com/~netcash/ then browse for information about NetCash.

64. www to http://www.directory.net/ then browse the Open Market Commercial Sites Index for a comprehensive list of business sites on the Web.

65. For information and results of online Web surveys, browse the pages of the following sites:

For information about a Web user survey and its results, www to http://www.gatech.edu/pitkow/survey/survey-1-1994/

For another Web user survey and its results, www to http://www.cc.gatech.edu/gvu/user_surveys/survey-04-1995/

For the Internet Domain Survey, www to http://www.nw.com/ then browse the Internet Domain Survey page.

66. For businesses that put a unique online spin on product and brand recognition, browse the following Web site:

www to http://www.eat.com/tour/index.html for a tour of Little Italy in New York provided by Ragu.

67. For a business that puts a unique online spin on customer support, www to http://www.fedex.com/ then browse the Federal Express home page for information about using its online Airbill Tracking System.

68. For examples of direct marketing and online transactions:

www to http://www.rpi.edu/~okeefe/business.html for an updated list of 50 business sites, archives from previous sites, and a link to Web marketing information.

www to http://www.pizzahut.com/ to order a pizza.

69. Try some of these sites for a look at the ideas and work of advertisers and Web designers:

www to http://www.adage.com/ then browse the Advertising Age Web site, and for a critical look at online marketing and Web sites, visit the Interactive Media & Marketing section via www to http://www.adage.com/IMM/critique.html

www to http://www.thinkpix.com/ then browse the Thinking Pictures Web Site, creators of the Rolling Stones Web site.

Then visit The Rolling Stones Web Site, www to http://www.stones.com/

www to http://www.freerange.com/ then browse the Free Range Media home page.

For a guide to Internet advertising, www to http://www.missouri.edu/internet-advertising-guide.html

For a paper by the Coalition for Networked Information, www to http:/www.cni.org/projects/advertising/www/adpaper.html

70. For an unflinching look at the good, bad, and ugly of Web sites and applications, consult the Web Review e-zine via www to http://www.wr.com/

12

Disaster Recovery and Contingency

ABOUT THIS CHAPTER

Network planning and implementation is not complete without a documented plan for preventing and responding to disasters. It must be tested to confirm its reliability and constantly updated to account for changes.

This chapter provides an overview of different types of disasters and the steps that organizations can take in response to the risks they pose. It describes the means by which a disaster plan can be created and an overview of its structure and contents. Although disaster planning should be comprehensive for the entire organization and its operations, this chapter focuses on the component that covers disaster prevention, protection, recovery, and contingency for network systems.

OVERVIEW

Like most systems procedures, data recovery and contingency had its genesis during the era of centralized mainframe computing. Manned by specialized technicians concerned with controlling access and maintaining the smooth operation of a large system, backup and other procedures had to be strictly observed. Any failure or damage to the mainframe would bring down the entire operation. However, because the vital components of this system were concentrated in a secure data center, the prevention and recovery from the effects of disasters could be more easily assessed and repaired.

With the era of distributed systems, local and wide area networks, and client/server technology, the threat of damage to a center of operations is reduced by virtue of dispersed resources, but not eliminated. In other ways, distributed systems introduce new threats posed by the reduction of centralized control. It poses greater accountability for a larger number of users, who are more geographically dispersed and have much greater access to the system. Compounding this challenge are the many types of disasters that pose threats to the vital information resources of an organization.

As the events of the World Trade Center and Oklahoma bombings can attest, disaster can strike quickly and without warning and the effects on people and business are incalculable.

As cited in an *Information Week* article (DePompa, 1995) about disaster recovery, 150 of the 350 businesses in the World Trade Center were out of business a year after the bombing. Most of these businesses relied on mini-computer or PC networks with links to off-site data centers. Nonetheless, many of these businesses attributed their subsequent failure to the inability to re-enter the building for several days following the bombing. This illustrates the importance of a comprehensive disaster recovery plan.

Even for businesses with a well-rehearsed plan, it takes on average twice as long to recover as the downtime caused by the disaster (Wintrob, 1995). Disaster recovery must be immediate, thorough, and reliable for businesses to survive its effects. Even when a contingency site is contracted with a recovery service, there can still be secondary effects due to an inadequately rehearsed or specified plan, such as improperly configured routers (Welch, 1995).

In the move away from centralized systems toward client/server environments, many companies have not adequately planned for recovery and contingency. Although moving data centers and servers out of harm's way is a tactic being used by many, there is still an inadequate characterization and backup of mission-critical servers and data wherever they may be found within the enterprise.

With the increasing use of client/server systems and the reliance on LANs for mission-critical applications, the distribution of resources poses challenges that many companies are not willing to tackle. The complexity of the task is one reason, but price is another. Simply put, the distribution of information resources throughout an enterprise has multiplied the cost and effort of prevention, protection, and recovery in the event of disaster. The cost and complexity of this undertaking tends to drive disaster planning low on the agenda, in many cases so low that it is never fully implemented. Many business-recovery firms acknowledge that disaster planning is like a fad that fades in and out with each new disaster.

Gaining consensus and guidance for companies who have not fully implemented disaster plans is an important first step. With increasing media attention on the real effects of disasters upon businesses, several sources of statistics and advice are becoming more available in publications, training, and associations (see netref 1 and the section of this chapter entitled "Other Recovery Tools").

For example, beginning in 1993 and continuing thereafter on an annual basis, a survey of business vulnerability has been conducted by Comdisco and Palindrome. Its results are made freely available (see netref 2). Comdisco Disaster Recovery Services is a division of Comdisco, Inc., which provides services that help organizations reduce technology cost and risk. These services include equipment leasing and remarketing, business continuity and consulting. Palindrome Corporation provides scalable data protection and management software for enterprise LANs.

This study measures the vulnerability to disasters that limit access to the systems and data needed to operate them. The survey was conducted through interviews of 300 of the largest computer users in the United States (average revenue $2.5 billion).

The 1995 Vulnerability Index produced the following results with respect to LANs and disaster recovery and contingency:

- Thirty-seven percent did not have any computer disaster recovery plans in place.

- Of these, 70 percent had disruptions to computer operations compared to 64 percent of those with plans in place.

- Despite the growing reliance on LANs, only one-third have contingency plans or test recovery plans for their LANs (compared to two-thirds of data centers that have plans in place).

Disaster Planning

From the perspective of an organization, disasters are not what happens, but rather the effects they have on its operation and even survival. Although the effects of hurricane damage and similar types of disasters are often unavoidable, organizations must take actions to prevent, protect, and recover from their effects.

A useful disaster plan is one that takes the entire operation of the organization into account, including its people, its customers, its equipment, and many other assets. Although this chapter focuses on the part of a plan that concerns itself with the network and related computer systems, it is only part of a complete and comprehensive plan.

The disaster plan must be documented, tested, maintained, and upgraded to account for any changes that affect the plan. An organization must first analyze its liabilities to all types of disasters. Based on this assessment, the organization must provide for a comprehensive system of planning and action that includes two basic strategies: prevention and protection.

Prevention and Protection

Put simply, prevention is concerned with avoiding disasters, whereas protection is concerned with minimizing the effects if disasters should occur. Prevention and protection should be a part of system administration and network management, including backup and security procedures.

With the costs and complexity of disaster planning for client/server networks, much of the current responsibility is being placed on central information systems management. Multiple-tiers of planning are being considered by organizations, aimed at enterprise, departmental, and even workgroup levels.

Network managers at their level of control need to use advanced tools and procedures to avoid disasters that originate in the network itself. Greater emphasis should be placed on preventing disasters such as network outages through regular monitoring and analysis of network performance. Advanced network test equipment such as sniffers and software-based tools should be used to support these activities. Network management software and LAN re-configuration, through advanced components such as switching hubs, can prevent and limit the effects of disasters that originate with the network.

> **NOTE** For information about network components, see Chapter 3.

Specific disaster recovery and contingency training should be provided for systems personnel and users. Specifically, key personnel are assigned to maintain documentation and training for backup procedures, including the type of data backup and tape rotation. However, due to the sheer scope of it, much of the backup of client applications and data has to be assumed by users. Loss of critical data can occur through unintentional misuse of restore or formatting procedures by users. Regular user training and support in backing up and restoring data must be provided by systems personnel or outsourced trainers assigned that responsibility.

Mirroring and electronic vaulting are advanced backup procedures that are particularly appropriate for time-sensitive data. Mirroring is a backup procedure that is performed often enough to establish a mirror image of the system, applications, and/or data at another site. This mirror image can be used for a quick and reliable recovery in the event of disaster. Electronic vaulting is the regular storage of that information in secure storage media and storage locations.

Whether provided through a service or implemented as an enterprise solution, incremental mirroring of files can be achieved through services such as ISDN to selected storage sites where data is protected by compressed copy to rewritable optical disks. Advanced telecommunications and network services can be used to support the incremental backup to a mirrored server in distant and more secure location. Many companies in earthquake-prone locations and other disaster-prone areas, such as California, are setting up mirror sites in distant states.

In some cases, organizations are moving their entire data centers to remote locations and facilities that are considered at lower risk of disaster. For example, the Federal Emergency Management Agency (FEMA), which provides disaster assistance, has moved its network management from Washington D.C., to secure buildings on a mountain top 75 miles away in Virginia (see netref 3).

The new data center will handle telephone claims processing, Internet administration, and e-mail. They are using off-the shelf software and simultaneous processing to protect systems in the field. A Recovery Assistance Programs Information and Delivery Systems (RAPIDS) will handle calls from multiple disaster sites (Cohodas, 1995).

The disaster contingency problem is particularly acute with small LAN installations. Typically, networks are installed and managed by outsourced vendors and consultants who do not inform their clients of the details of contingency planning. Insufficient training and unreliable backup restoration procedures leave companies at a loss in the case of disaster.

> **NOTE** For information about system administration and security, see Chapters 6, 9, and 10.

Disaster recovery geared around the network infrastructure, including the transmission media, has been identified as key to limiting the effects and speeding recovery. Key components to include in training and the recovery plan include: cable system design, testing, and verification, separate or redundant cabling to key sites, and spare capacity built into the network to reroute away from failed cable segments. Administrative procedures, which include daily record-keeping and documentation of network operation and the use of network diagnostic tools, can help in both planning and recovery (Baxter and Shariff, 1995).

NOTE For information about transmission media, see Chapter 1.

Recovery strategies are beginning to take into account advanced telecommunications and network services (Kirvan, 1995). In locations where digital services such as ISDN are becoming available, they are being considered as a backup for private line services such as T1 and fractional T1. Similarly, if SONET rings are available and affordable, they should be considered as a backup for local network access. Wireless services such as satellite, microwave, infrared, and cellular should also be considered for backup and recovery. Diverse carrier arrangements, cable entrance, and the use of open standards for interoperability across multi-carrier systems become critical allies during the typically short window that is required for recovery.

NOTE For more information on network services, see Chapter 5.

Recovery and Contingency

This part of disaster planning covers the steps that must be taken in the event of a disaster. These steps should include damage assessment, control and repair, the use of emergency and contingency systems and facilities, and the measures taken to resume mission-critical and then complete operations.

This chapter focuses on the recovery and contingency component of a comprehensive plan and how it relates to the operation of the network and related computer systems. It characterizes several types of disasters and their effects, describes recovery and contingency, and describes the creation, testing, and maintenance aspects of a disaster plan that relates to these systems.

DISASTERS

There are many types of disasters that pose a threat to network operations. What impacts they have on the network inevitably has a significant effect on the organization. With increasing reliance on networks to provide both computing and communications, there is little distinction between the operation of a network and many of the operations associated with an organization.

In light of this, the means to prevent, plan, and execute recovery and contingency for each type of threat becomes critical. There are no reasonable alternatives. Most businesses suffer a 25 percent drop in revenues within the first week of disrupted network operation. When appropriate plans and actions have not been taken, effects of disasters can quickly degrade beyond the ability of the business to recover operations in a manner that ensures its survival.

And, like many natural disasters that take a toll on people and physical property, disrupted network operations can become a source of additional damage to the members of the organization and the surrounding community. This is especially critical when it occurs to telecommunications providers, hospitals, and other organizations which are needed for relief, security, and communications.

Disasters that affect network operations can be categorized in terms of their threat, types of damage, and the means by which you can plan prevention, recovery, and contingency measures.

Natural Disasters

Typically, the notion of disasters evoke thoughts of earthquakes, hurricanes, tornadoes, floods, and other natural events that might occur. These include more common occurrences such as damage from lightning, wind, rain, snow, and extremes of temperature (see netref 3).

Prevention and recovery procedures for natural disasters should focus on those that are typically associated with the region or area served by the network. Their effects should be anticipated in the design and maintenance of environment protection. Air-conditioning, power protection and backup, smoke and fire alarms, and related procedures must be matched by network systems monitoring. Any damage to equipment must be anticipated along with its repair or replacement. For mission-critical operations, fault-tolerant systems and contingency sites must be maintained in the event of catastrophic damage.

However, when viewed in terms of disruption of network operations, disasters extend beyond the types for which nature is the cause. Other types of disasters, from utility outages and power surges to arson, bombings, and other terrorist activities are no less devastating to the network and thus to the enterprise that depends on its constant and reliable operation. Even rodents chewing through a network backbone can wreak greater damage to operations than many of nature's more newsworthy events.

Human Disasters

Disaster can also occur through human intent or neglect, often with more precision and with more incalculable extent. Disgruntled former and current employees, hackers, and a host of other characters can be sources of disaster for which appropriate measures must be taken.

These threats largely fall under risk management and security aspects of network management. Understanding the nature of these problems is the beginning of calculating their risk and examining the appropriate security measures (see netref 4).

Security

Threats and breaches of network security are disasters caused by people within and outside the organization who seek to infiltrate, disrupt, steal, and/or cause damage via network communications. This can occur directly, as with people who break the password-protection on servers and login to the system surreptitiously to gain access to information resources. The term hacker is usually applied to someone who enjoys playing with system software vulnerabilities. Likewise, the words cracker or cracking is used to denote penetration of a system's integrity.

Although many can't see the distinction, there are good hackers and bad hackers. This distinction relates to their effect and not necessarily to their prowess. A bad hacker is someone who uses this knowledge to cause damage to other systems, whereas a good hacker does not intentionally do so. Although bad hackers are cause for legitimate and serious attention, so is the head-in-the-sand attitude by many whose responsibility is the security of their systems. Many observers comment on the Darwinian nature of this dichotomy, and in real-world terms, it is the survival of the fittest (system).

This Darwinian view can be taken further by claiming that system security would not be improved if not for attempts to penetrate it. This doesn't excuse the damage, but it does account for the development of anti-hacking and anti-cracking measures. For example, in the aftermath of the Internet Worm, a 1988 event that slowed Internet traffic, the Computer Emergency Response Team (CERT) was established (see netref 5).

The proliferation of internetworks and bulletin board systems (BBS) has opened up communications for all users. Unfortunately, this has also resulted in the dissemination of information and programs by bad hackers for anyone to attempt to replicate their work. Some of this software falls under the category of bad hacker toolkits, which require little expertise to penetrate systems through internetwork links (Neumann, 1995).

Until recently there have been few preventive and protective security methods outside of tight control of passwords and access, the use of proxy servers, or, in the extreme, the complete isolation of systems. Software such as COPS, Tripware, and Crack have been available for

UNIX systems, and were largely useful as a complement to traditional means of analyzing security breaks or vulnerabilities (see netref 6).

Fortunately, software known as good-hacker or anti-cracking toolkits are becoming available. Used as offensive tools to penetrate their own systems, wily network managers and system administrators can assess and correct weaknesses in the integrity of their own systems. For example, the SATAN program that was introduced in 1995, and similar programs initially construed as hacker tools, can be used by administrators to analyze weaknesses in their own systems (see netref 7).

SATAN operates on a rule-based system that uses known system vulnerabilities as a checklist for scanning host systems. It is easily extensible by modifying or adding rules in the text files that are read by the program. It was originally released to run under UNIX and can be used with a Mosaic or Netscape Web browser through direct or SLIP/PPP dial-up connections.

Virus

Sometimes disaster planned by bad hackers occurs by proxy through software, generically called a virus. Viruses are usually associated with a range of actions from disruptive messages indicating their presence to spreading damage among files. Although viruses can be sent through data communications channels to be attached to system, program, and data files in remote systems, their effect is increased by users who unwittingly spread a virus through copying and exchanging infected files. It spreads when they load these infected files onto a network from floppy disks or by modem.

Virus-protection software can usually detect and eliminate viruses (see netref 8) and even repair some files. However, it is a cat and mouse game in which new viruses are created that in turn require the development and use of new protection schemes. Auto-scanning workstations on bootup and establishing safe and legal procedures for user transfer of files offer some protection. Maintaining the latest versions of virus protection and continually testing communications and recovery procedures are also needed.

> **NOTE** For information about virus-protection software, see Chapter 9.

Other Threats

Other threats to the integrity of the network and business operations come from misuse or neglect of electronic and other systems used in support of networks. Last but not least, are the many disruptions and losses that occur through mismanagement of the network resources themselves, whether by administrators or users. The integrity of both data and applications can be protected through the use of backup and redundancy measures such as mirroring, duplexing, and RAID.

> **NOTE** For information about network security and administration, see Chapter 9. For information about RAID and other network components, see Chapter 3.

Assessing the Risks

There is no way to anticipate the occurrence of all disasters or calculate the risks they pose. Nonetheless, several steps can and should be taken to plan for the likelihood of disasters that have been known to happen in the areas served by your network.

The tremendous growth of networks and our increasing reliance on them make disaster planning a vital, yet difficult task to master for an organization. With centralized legacy systems, operators of a mainframe computer would usually concern themselves with a single physical plant in a secured area that also housed storage and communications devices. Terminals and peripherals such as printers that were located outside this protected area did not represent as great a concern in case of disaster.

With distributed computing environments, you must account for vital data and physical resources spread over LAN, WAN, and the Internet. Through remote connectivity, this also includes people and resources dispersed over a wide geographical area. You must also account for wireless access, virtual LANs, and other emerging technologies. It's a daunting task, but it's necessary to anticipate the actual risks to your organization.

At the earliest stage in your disaster planning, you should learn what people within your own organization know about the history of previous events of this kind and their outcomes. You can also check with other organizations that share geographical or operational similarities to get tips on the types of disasters that can occur, their effects, and ways to avoid and reduce their impact. Consider local and state agencies, including the police, weather service, and hospitals, all of which not only respond to disasters, but must also keep their systems intact during emergency operations.

RECOVERY

The goal of recovery is the resumption of normal business operations in the shortest possible time after a disaster occurs. The way to achieve this is to create and test a recovery plan in advance of disasters and deploy the plan in the event of a disaster.

Although many companies expect their information systems departments to provide disaster recovery plans, many plans ultimately reflect a balance of internal planning and outsourced services. In many cases, recovery services also provide consulting for the development and testing of the plan.

Because distributed systems have decentralized resources, there are more potential points of failure than with centralized systems or data centers. Planning for client/server systems is a complex and time-consuming task that is often left to specialists. However, there are significant costs involved. Economies can be found in strategic outsourcing of the planning, contingency, and recovery services as a complement to tapping in-house expertise.

The following sections contain examples of business recovery services, including their consulting, equipment, facilities, and software components.

Recovery Services

Business Recovery Services

IBM Business Recovery Services (BRS) are subscription-based services provided by Integrated Systems Solutions Corporation (ISSC), an IBM subsidiary (voice: 800-599-9950, also see netref 9). They help companies with mid-range to large systems prepare for catastrophic events. It supports business recovery services in 17 facilities across the United States. IBM BRS offers recovery support for the IBM Enterprise Systems product line and selected non-IBM mainframes as well at three locations across the country: Sterling Forest, NY, Tampa, FL, and Gaithersburg, MD.

Testing of recovery plans is performed by clients at an IBM BRS Center to compare actual performance to pretest objectives. Some test time is included in the large systems subscription and optional test time is available in eight-hour blocks. Remote testing capability is also available from a customer's location or at an IBM BRS Remote Customer Suite.

IBM BRS Client Services is provided for users with distributed environments. They offer comprehensive recovery solutions, from consulting and plan development, through testing and implementation. This service provides secure office buildings with work spaces wired to support Ethernet and Token Ring LANs, terminal emulation for large and mid-range systems connectivity, and voice solutions. Office equipment includes fax machines and copiers. A customer may elect to use this space, phones, and cabling infrastructure with equipment they supply, or to subscribe to an equipment configuration that meets their needs.

Preventative and protective services are also available. The Electronic Bulk Data Transfer service copies critical data off-site after it is created. This replaces or augments physical transfer of data to a remote, hardened vault. The Operating System Store and Edit service provides the customer with facilities to store an image of the production operating environment on direct access storage devices such as a high-speed magnetic disk subsystem. Customers can remotely access the data to keep the image current. Upon recovery, the image can initialize the hot site system without the usual delays in re-configuring the operating system and physically transporting data. The Electronic Journal Transport service provides real-time transfer of journal or log information of databases. Applied to a duplicate, daily image of data bases, these logs and journals can provide quick recovery of data.

SunGard Recovery Services Inc. of Wayne, PA (voice: 610-341-8700, also see netref 10) provides a wide range of recovery services, including consulting, planning, and contingency facilities, hot-site recovery, mobile data centers, and computer systems replacement. Two types of cold-sites are available: facilities with equipment and mobile cold-sites which are used at customer sites in the event of disaster.

Comdisco Disaster Recovery Services (voice: 708-698-3000, also see netref 2) is a division of Comdisco, Inc. It provides a world-wide network of fully-equipped Computer Recovery facilities (CRF) and Business Recovery Facilities (BRF), which are available to subscribers in the event of disasters that affect a customer's business environment or data center.

Comdisco Remote Testing is a methodology that lets asynchronous terminals, PCs, and remote terminal controllers appear to the host computer as locally-attached devices. This allows the subscriber to reduce travel costs and efforts by allowing key people to remain in their local areas during the disaster recovery testing process.

Comdisco Disaster Recovery Services Backbone Network is a dedicated and on-demand, high-speed, high-capacity network. It interconnects Comdisco Disaster Recovery Services facilities. A customer at one Business Recovery Facility can access any of the other Computer Recovery facilities. This can provide flexibility and redundancy of resources in managing the recovery. These facilities have a high degree of network resilience by using high-capacity network services gateways or SONET Fiber Rings to access multiple local and long distance carriers.

Comdisco Mobile Recovery Operations Center (COMROC) is a modular, transportable cold-site that can be assembled at a customer's location within 7 to 23 days. The units come complete with raised flooring, security systems, environmental equipment, and other critical data center equipment, and can replace an unavailable data center or provide a useable space for a variety of corporate functions. COMROC ranges in size from 1,200 to 9,600 square feet, and was designed for customers in need of long-term recovery environments.

Additional recovery support is also available from Comdisco, including professional services, customer training, toll-free help desk and bulletin board service, quarterly newsletter and the annual Solutions Conference.

Hewlett-Packard Business Recovery Services of Bellevue, WA (voice: 800-637-7740, also see netref 11) provides a range of business recovery services. These include consulting, planning, training, orchestrated rehearsals, use of off-site computing facilities, technical support, and restoration of computing systems and environments. The HP BRS can also deliver fully operational loaner systems to a customer's location of choice within 24 hours.

HP hot-site facilities are located in Valley Forge, Penn. and Federal Way, Wash. These fully configured recovery centers let a customer run critical computer operations while its disaster site is being restored. The centers include extensive telecommunications capabilities, HP 3000s, HP 9000s, network servers, and workstations.

Other providers of business recovery services, include AT&T Business Recovery Group (voice: 800-823-6305 and see netref 12), Digital Business Protection Services of Marlboro, MA (phone: 508-467-5111), Wang Laboratories Disaster Recovery Services of Lowell, MA (phone: 800-225-0654), and Weyerhaeuser Information Systems of Tacoma, WA (phone: 206-924-5302).

Business Recovery Consultation Services

Comdisco Professional Services (CPS) is a division of Comdisco, Inc., that provides consulting assistance to help organizations design and implement corporate recovery strategies that ensure business continuity.

CPS provides clients with recovery methodology comprised of an analysis phase, a planning phase and an assurance phase. Business exposures are qualified and quantified, a recovery organization and its action steps are identified and documented in a recovery plan. A quality assurance program is developed that ensures the ongoing maintenance of the business continuity program.

IBM Business Recovery Consultation Services provides clients with the capability to design, implement, and manage effective enterprise-wide recovery programs. Specific tasks include identifying a client's vital business processes, potential risks, critical technology and resources during disasters, and software applications to determine financial impacts of disasters. Other task areas include determining vulnerability and asset relationships, and plans for managing communications with the external media and employees during a disaster.

Consulting includes recovery plans that are designed for many levels of an organization, including corporate, campus, department, and data center. The consulting services can also provide as-needed support to clients who are developing a plan in-house, reviewing an existing plan, or evaluating the loss of a business process. Consulting can be applied to any part of a comprehensive disaster plan: managing risk, avoiding disasters, business recovery planning, anti-virus services, customer environment analysis, business impact analysis, and client/server customer and business impact analyses. Additional services include: testing, maintenance, a business recovery audit, and on-going training in support of a plan.

Recovery Software

Recovery software is available from software companies who specialize in recovery planning and from several business recovery services. It typically uses document templates and application macros to help users step through the creation and modification of a business recovery plan. Database applications and sample files typically assist the user in the specification of employee, equipment, facility, and other organizational aspects that must be specified in the plan. Here are two examples of recovery planning software, one from a software company and the other from a recovery service.

Phoenix by Binomial International (see netref 13) is a low-cost, yet comprehensive disaster recovery planning system. Binomial International of Ogdensburg, NY provides a recovery consulting service (voice: 800-361-8398 and fax: 613-692-2425). Out of this experience it has developed complementary tools in the form of seminars and software.

The Phoenix Recovery Planning System is composed of two basic components. The planning system includes a document template and macro. The plan template includes sections for protection, prevention, impact, teams, procedures, maintenance, testing, and training. This menu-driven package helps you build custom disaster recovery plans within the familiar environment of a word processor. It can be used for as many unique plans as you need. It is compatible with popular word processors such as WordPerfect (DOS and Windows), Word for Windows, and Ami Pro (Windows).

The custom database application lets you specify your business recovery inventory. It includes provisions for specifying hardware, software, systems, applications, other assets, suppliers, teams, people, and skills.

ComPAS (Comdisco's Plan Automation Software) is automated business continuity software that employs the recovery methodology of Comdisco. It guides you through a step-by-step process of developing, testing, and implementing a comprehensive, integrated continuity plan encompassing every aspect of your enterprise.

The plans provide complete, action-oriented task lists organized by function, department, and location. The software is compatible with popular spreadsheets, word processors, and other applications. It is available with a variety of sample plans for business function and work area recovery, and for mainframe and midrange data center recovery. Other sample plans are available.

Recovery software tools for assessing network liabilities, developing a plan, and other aspects of disaster planning are available from SunGard and other disaster-recovery services.

Other Recovery Tools

There are other recovery tools and services in the form of print and online publications and directories.

The Disaster Recovery Journal (see netref 1) provides coverage of disaster recovery topics in its print publication. It also provides other services including Contingency Planning Group Contacts and a Disaster Recovery Symposium & Exhibition.

Survive! is a magazine about business recovery published by Survive Inc., Morristown, NJ, a disaster recovery coordinators association.

The Disaster Recovery Yellow Pages is published by The Systems Audit Group Inc., Newton, MA. It provides a list of consulting services, recovery software, contingency sites, mobile vans, and emergency equipment.

CONTINGENCY

There are many alternatives for providing a contingency site for network operations in case of a disaster. These options range from having no contingency plans or sites to planning and maintaining full contingency.

Types of Contingency Sites

Typically, most contingency plans refer to any of three basic types of sites, appropriately called, hot, warm, and cold sites. These sites can be established and maintained within your organization or through outside providers.

Hot-Site

A hot-site is the most comprehensive and costly choice for contingency, yet it is the most capable and available choice when disaster disrupts normal operations. It generally offers the highest degree of support by providing all of the technology and security procedures of a normal installation. This includes an operating network with servers, workstations, printers, and other necessary network devices. It also includes backup software for mission-critical applications and data. The hot-site environment is protected with uninterruptable power systems, smoke alarms, air-conditioning, etc.

For example, IBM Business Recovery Services provide hot-site contingency facilities consisting of a computer center facility where the customer's subscription configuration is available for use in the event a disaster is declared. Hot-sites are available and fully operational within 24 hours after a disaster has been declared and for up to six weeks following a disaster. The facilities include data processing equipment, communications controllers, network connectivity, and operational/technical support for both IBM and non-IBM equipment.

In addition to the large systems configuration, the IBM BRS Center contains raised floor space, office space, office equipment, conference rooms and storage facilities as well as end-user space. The service also includes IBM personnel who are trained to assist with problem determination and other recovery issues during testing or recovery.

Cold-Site

A cold-site is the least costly choice for contingency, yet the most costly in terms of recovery time. It is essentially a reserved site where all aspects of the network and environment protection must be put into place before contingency network operations can take place.

For example, IBM Business Recovery Services provide a cold-site service called an Extended Support Facility. Their cold-site is available should facilities be needed beyond the six-week availability of the hot site. The Extended Support Facility contains all facilities necessary to support the installation of a customer's equipment, such as raised floor space and air conditioning. This cold-site is available for up to six months at no additional charge, as part of the IBM BRS subscription.

Warm-Site

A warm-site is a third type of service that fits the needs organizations that don't need or can't afford the full contingency of a hot-site. A warm-site typically offers the protection and availability of a hot-site, but without the presence of a network installation. When a disaster occurs, the client must install network hardware and software. Although this method offers a cost savings over maintaining a backup system, it introduces delay in contingency system startup.

CREATING A PLAN

The means by which you can create a disaster recovery plan can vary. You can develop it entirely in-house, use outside consultants and services, or use a mixture of both. No matter what method you choose, you should bear the primary responsibility for providing the content of the plan. This is especially true for characterizing the nature of your organization and its needs in case of disaster.

There are a few basic steps in developing a disaster recovery plan: designing, documentation, testing, and maintenance. Although each of these steps are critical to the success of a plan, the way that you carry out these steps should fit the needs and capabilities of your organization.

Creating an In-House Plan

A big part of getting a plan properly funded and supported is the justification of the considerable costs that are associated with a comprehensive recovery and contingency plan for client/server systems. First, you must identify mission-critical information wherever it may be found within the organization. Next, you must analyze its value and predict the financial and business impacts of a loss of that information over time. Statistics from disaster studies and company surveys can provide a source of data and analyses (see netrefs1 and 2).

The other part is true of any innovation that affects the enterprise. You must establish a leader and a team assigned with creating and executing this plan and they must get clear support from the highest levels of management.

Contracting the Plan with Outside Services

If the uncertainty and delays associated with developing in-house plans lead you to consider outside support, there are many options available. However, you can't afford to relegate the organizational decisions that should govern the plan.

Thus, no matter who you choose for help in preparing your plan, you must retain control of each step, including the all-important maintenance that keeps your plan current. This being said, help with your plan can come in many forms from one or more outside sources: from the providers of contingency sites, an auditor, and/or consultant. Their support can range from providing advice in selecting services to the actual documentation of the plan.

Recovery Services

Recovery services that provide contingency sites and services can also provide assistance with the development of your plan. Although there are savings and assurance by working with the same provider, keep in mind that their recommendations may be linked to selling their own related recovery services.

Auditors

The auditing services of an accounting firm represent another source of professional advice in formulating your plans, assuming that the firm has a proven track record for providing this type of service. Auditors are likely to work well with management and understand your business needs, but make sure they can adequately assess network technology as well.

Consultants

Independent consultants can offer advice and assistance in the formulation, testing, and documentation of your plans. As this type of service has increased in demand in recent years, it is not uncommon to find consultants who specialize in this work.

If you select wisely based on a proven track record, a consultant can provide a more independent point-of-view than larger firms that want to sell their related services. On the other hand, you have to take greater responsibility in the development of your plans to ensure that your needs are being served and protected.

Developing a Plan

The means you choose to create a disaster recovery plan can be varied. You can develop it entirely in-house, use outside consultants and services, or combine these methods. No matter what method you choose, you should bear the primary responsibility for providing the content of the plan. This is especially true for characterizing the nature of your organization and its needs in case of disaster.

Designing the Plan

The design of a plan can conform to existing plans or use standard components as published in books and articles, but the manner in which it is tailored to your organization is a vital part of this step.

The first step in design is planning. This is typically done by forming groups whose shared tasks are to analyze the organization and its vulnerability to various types of disasters.

One task is to analyze and document the various types of threats and their potential effect on the operations of the organization. Unfortunately, many organizations have prime locations for business that are also primed for disaster: California earthquakes, Florida hurricanes, and the fires and bombings endemic to many large cities (see netref 3).

So if your business is located in a major industrial center that has been associated with previous bomb threats and/or actual destruction of property, this type of threat should be analyzed in terms of the likelihood of it occurring and its possible effects.

The other task is called a loss analysis. It consists of examining and documenting the losses that would be associated with various types of disasters. It should be expressed as a monetary value per day due to loss of operations.

Generally these analyses are conducted through meetings with key members and departments within the organization (such as security, computer operations, and department heads, etc.). Like all activities of this sort, the participation and leadership of one or more top-level executives gives this work importance, priority, and urgency.

The network itself can be used to communicate and document these analyses through e-mail, conferencing, and other applications.

Documenting the Plan

The first steps in documenting the plan is to decide on the structure and basic content of the plan and who will do the writing and editing of its various sections.

Once this work is defined and delegated, an outline should be prepared for each section and the entire outline should be distributed to all members of the documentation team. Here is a model of a typical plan and how it is structured.

Overview

The overview of the plan should be prepared by a high-level executive of the organization. Its should describe the various components of the plan in an organizational rather than strictly technological perspective.

Organizational Profile

The organizational profile broadly characterizes the nature, history, goals, and objectives of the organization. It should be briefly stated in no more than a few pages. Much of the basic information can be transferred from annual reports, data sheets, business plans, and other mission statements.

Justification for Plan

The justification for the plan should begin with a section that describes the overall nature of the disaster recovery plan and how it addresses the needs of the organization. First and foremost, there should be a statement that characterizes the need and nature for protecting the people in the organization and the people it serves from the threat and effects of disasters. Another statement should address how this particular disaster recovery plan will protect the assets of the organization and how it can maintain the operations and minimize risks to these areas.

In particular, these statements should describe briefly how and why the disaster recovery plan will ensure against interruptions in operations and services and the threat of lawsuits (e.g., negligence), as well as how any pertinent regulatory issues will be addressed (e.g., environmental, etc.). This section should also contain an estimate of the monetary loss per day with and without the plan if certain mission-critical operations should be disrupted.

Disaster Prevention

Disaster prevention procedures should begin with a listing of the various inventories of the organization and how they are monitored and maintained. These inventories should include the physical inventory of equipment and materials, especially those which are used to maintain daily and critical operations. The network and its components are primary examples of this inventory. Inventories should also include facilities such as buildings, offices, storage sites, and transportation. Inventories of personnel must also be taken with respect to their roles and relation to operations in case of disaster.

Prevention strategies should include tactics for employing key personnel, facilities, and equipment to monitor operations. This should detail what type of drills, training, and documentation procedures will be use to keep these plans current.

Disaster Recovery

Disaster recovery procedures should be as inclusive and detailed as possible. This section should include a description of mission-critical systems and how they should be recovered in the case of various types of disaster. The list of mission-critical systems should take into account all systems that support operation of the network, including electric power and telecommunications.

Order of recovery and associated time frames for recovering each major function of the network should be established and documented. These should include voice and data links, processors, servers, network devices such as gateways, hubs, routers, bridges, operating systems, and each point-of-presence for services.

The critical systems should be ordered from the most critical to the least critical. For example, the first statement in a plan for a hospital might be worded in the following manner:

- The electric power must be restored immediately through a backup generator system.

- Voice communications to the disaster control center should be brought back online through cellular or satellite systems within ten minutes, and so on.

Specific procedures for each critical system should be listed along with trouble-shooting strategies. Similar procedures should be documented for loss of facilities, services, and related equipment such as lighting, air-conditioning, etc.

A separate section should list the members of in-house and contracted recovery teams and their responsibilities at each stage, including identifying problems; issuing alerts; notifying management, authorities, media, vendors, and customers; damage assessment and reporting; etc.

Using the results of analyses of disasters by type, an ordered procedure (with troubleshooting) should be made for each type of disaster, such as bombing, explosion, flood, fire, earthquake, tornado, security breaches, sabotage, vandalism, etc. It should also include loss of services such as communications point-of-presence, T1 lines, servers, etc. This procedure should be clearly stated and non-technical so that anyone can understand it.

For example, the emergency procedures for a loss of a critical LAN server or gateway might be listed as follows:

1. Report condition to LAN management.

2. Diagnose conditions and attempt correction following the troubleshooting checklist, including virus scan and clean.

3. Reboot, restore, or use backup server based on results of previous step.

4. Record initial actions in log.

A separate section should be devoted to the description of network operations recovery, including activating recovery and contingency procedures. This should include restoring services, rerouting voice communications, redirecting network backbones and router links, duplication and delivery of media, and the operations of network control and help centers.

The recovery section of the plan should also detail the steps that should be taken to restore normal operations, migrate operations back from the recovery site, and report on the disaster and the response.

Testing and Maintenance

The final section of the documentation should detail procedures for testing the recovery plans, maintaining the documentation, and training personnel to teach or refresh the knowledge and skills associated with disaster prevention and recovery. This section (or appendix) should also include lists and contact information arranged in order and categorized for quick access. This information should include primary and backup call lists for management and recovery teams, authorities, vendors, etc. It should also include hardware and software inventories, floor plans, network diagrams, contracts, operation guides, etc.

Testing the Plan

Testing the disaster recovery plan is critical to its success. This is not a pencil and paper test, but rather a dress-rehearsal for the real thing. People must walk-through the exact procedures and test the systems, facilities, and ultimately the plan itself. As a result of simulations and other tests, an analysis and additional testing will determine what adjustments are needed to the procedures and plan. Only then do the pencil and paper and word processors come into play with the modification of the plan to account for these adjustments.

Initial testing of the plan is the only way that you will establish a baseline for its effectiveness. As the plan must be updated to account for significant changes, the plan must test whenever known changes impact upon the plan. It should also be tested on a continuous basis according to a defined schedule to ferret out any unforeseen changes that require adjustment.

There can be many objectives in testing the plan. It should determine if all necessary steps are included in the plan, feasibility and compatibility of backup facilities and procedures, need for changes, training and rehearsal for recovery teams, demonstrate recoverability, and impetus for plan maintenance.

After a test plan has been completed, an initial test of the plan should be performed by conducting a structured walk-through test. The test will provide additional information regarding any further steps that may need to be included, such as changes in procedures that are not effective and other appropriate adjustments. The plan should be updated to correct any problems identified during the test. Initially testing of the plan should be done in sections and after normal business hours to minimize disruptions to the overall operations of the organization.

The types of tests should include checklist tests, simulation tests, parallel tests, and full interruption tests.

Maintaining the Plan

Besides regularly-scheduled testing, maintenance of the disaster recovery plan primarily requires training that covers the purpose and tasks of team leaders, team members, and to a lesser degree others in the organization who will provide a supporting role. Training must be conducted regularly and include rehearsals of actual tasks in simulation of different types of disasters.

Maintenance also includes regular review and modification of the plan based on the result of testing and in response to changes that occur in the assumptions and specifications upon which the plan was generated. These can include changes in the degree of risk or vulnerability assessment, or changes in personnel, the network, facilities, or other factors that would affect the intended results of the plan.

Some of the recommendations provided in the Phoenix planning software (see netref 13) are worth considering for the maintenance schedule and activities:

- At least every three months, the employee phone call list and equipment inventories must be recreated from their master source.

- At least every six months, review any changes that could affect protection, prevention, and resumption plans. Updates must be scheduled to accommodate any of these types of change. Team leaders must be provided with any changes to their plans and the readiness of their teams.

- At least every six months, an employee awareness program must be reviewed for new activities slogans and posters.

- At least every six months, the local fire department personnel should be invited to tour the premises to identify and potential hazards. They should also familiarize themselves with the building, its facilities, the emergency response plan, and those responsible for it.

- At least every six months, everyone identified as floor wardens must meet to review their assignments and to be briefed (if possible) by the fire department personnel on the proper use of the fire-fighting equipment in their areas.

Although maintaining a plan adds to the effort and cost, this process helps ensure that the greater investments of creating and testing the plan are not wasted. Some disasters can be prevented through this process. However, even when disasters cannot be averted, their devastating effects can be reduced through a plan that has been properly maintained. The confirmation can be found by looking at companies that quickly resumed operation after disasters such as the World Trade Center bombing and the California earthquakes.

REFERENCES

Bibliography

Baxter, L. and M. Shariff. March 1995. "Steps toward successful disaster recovery."*Telecommunications*, v29 n3 p61(2).

Cohodas, M. 1995. "Rescue Plan." *PC Week.* May 29, 1995, (12) 21:E1.

Kirvan, Paul. 1995. "Using Advanced Network Services for Disaster Recovery." *Communications News.* March, 1995, (32) 3:50.

Welch, D. 1995. "Details Can Make Disaster Recovery Plans a Success." *Network World*, April 24, 1995, v12 n17 p33(2).

Wintrob, S. 1995. "Most Users Ill-Prepared if Disaster Strikes." *Computing Canada.* April 26, 1995, v21 n9 p15(1).

Net References

1. www to http://www.drj.com/ then browse the Web site of the Disaster Recovery Journal. You can submit article ideas and comments via e-mail to the editor. Other information and links are available about Contingency Planning Group Contacts and the Disaster Recovery Symposium & Exhibition.

For information about Management and Professional Development courses that include Disaster Recovery topics such as Introduction to Disaster Recovery Planning (TTDR01), Communications Technologies (TTDR02), and Managing and Developing a Disaster Recovery Plan (TTDR03), www to http://www.cait.wustl.edu/cait/catalog/management/

2. www to http://www.comdisco.com/ then browse the Comdisco site for information about the Comdisco Recovery Service and the following items:

A report entitled, "The Vulnerability Index: Hidden Risks in Computer-Aided Productivity," is a scrollable Web page with links for more information. It describes the purpose and results of an annual survey of 300 of the largest computer users in the U.S., including businesses, government agencies, and non-profit organizations. For a copy of the survey results, as well as a free site-vulnerability assessment, call Comdisco at 800-272-9792.

A disaster recovery glossary with links to additional descriptions of glossary items.

3. www to http://www.disaster.org then look for links to many organizations and sources of information about different types of natural disasters, including current and historical lists.

For information about the APA Disaster Response Network www to http://www.apa.org/drn.html

For information about the Federal Emergency Management Agency (FEMA), www to http://www.fema.gov/

4. The Risk Forum addresses the risk considerations of computer and network system use. You can join it through its newsgroup or mailing list. It is moderated by Peter Neumann, a noted author, ACM committee chair and columnist.

To subscribe to the newsgroup, subscribe to comp.risks.

To subscribe to the mailing list, subscribe by sending e-mail to risks-request@CSL.SRI.COM

5. To subscribe to the CERT advisory mailing list, e-mail to cert-advisory@cert.org

6. For information about security issues and software:

www to http://www.process.com/news/whitesec.htp then browse the "Guide to Internet Security."

For Network/Computer Security Technology, www to http://www.tezcat.com/web/security/security_vendors.html then browse the Commercial Vendors page with links to vendor sites.

For information about hacker culture and issues:

www to http://swcp.com/pcaskey/hacker-faq.html then browse the Hacker FAQ.

www to http://www.2600.com/ then browse the 2600 Magazine home page.

www to http://www.fc.net/phrack.html then browse the Phrack Magazine home page.

7. For information about SATAN, www to http://www.tchk.com/satan_doc/html/docs/satan_doc.html

For a guide to getting started using SATAN, www to
http://mcrlabs.com/satan_doc/html/docs/getting_started.html

8. For information about virus-protection software and computer viruses, www to
http://www.datafellows.fi/cv.htm then browse the Data Fellows Virus Information
Centre.

9. www to http://www.brs.ibm.com/brsprdsv.html then browse the Web site of IBM
Business Recovery Service Products and Services.

10. www to http://www.sungard.com/srsg.htm then browse the Web site of SunGard
Recovery Services, Inc.

11. Hewlett-Packard Business Recovery Services did not have a unique Web site at the
time of writing. General information about HP can be browsed via www to
http://www.hp.com/

12. For information about the AT&T Business Recovery Group, browse the following
Web page. Read how its Disaster Recovery Team conducted a practice exercise demon-
strating the company's ability to replace an entire AT&T central office damaged or
destroyed by a natural or man-made disaster. www to
http://www.att.com/press/0895/950814.cha.html

13. www to http://www.binomial.com/ then browse the Binomial International Web
site for information about Phoenix, the Business Disaster Recovery Planning software.
You can request more information via e-mail to phoenix@binomial.com

For links to other disaster recovery sites on the Web, www to
http://www.binomial.com/links.html

Suggested Reading

Bates, R. 1994. *Disaster Recovery for LANs: A Planning and Action Guide.* New York:
Mc-Graw-Hill, Inc.

Chorakis, D. and H. Steinmann. 1990. *Intelligent Networks.* Boca Raton, FL:
Multiscience Press.

Neumann, P. 1995. *Computer-Related Risks.* Reading, MA: Addison-Wesley.

Wrobel, L. 1993. *Writing Disaster Recovery Plans for Telecommunications Networks and LAN.* Boston, MA: Artech House.

For articles on security and disaster-recovery planning from DowVision, a Web-based business and technology news service by Dow Jones, www to http://dowvision.wais.net/ then browse the pages, search for articles, or read the following articles:

"Expert offers companies five disaster planning tips," www to http://dowvision.wais.net/dvscripts/dvwaisr?79889454311651+1

"How vulnerable are your computer systems?" www to http://dowvision.wais.net/dvscripts/dvwaisr?79889454311651+10

For several articles on network security from Open Computing, select a title and plug the URL in your browser to access it.

"The Growing Professional Menace" (a cover story about security threats) http://www.wcmh.com/oc/features/previous/9507hkrs.html

Sidebars to cover story include: "Is SATAN Worth It?" "Keeping the Barbarians Out: Network Security, Firewalls, and External Security Products, Computer Crime & Information Warfare Timeline." http://www.wcmh.com/oc/features/previous/9507otsb.html#timeline

For an article entitled, "Palmtops In Disaster Recovery" by Michael Miora, www to http://www.penworld.com/is16/disatr.htm

13

Organizational and
Social Issues

ABOUT THIS CHAPTER

This chapter deals with human issues that underlie the planning and implementation of networks. It examines the individual response to networking as an innovation within the perspectives of organization and society. As innovations bring change, it is useful to consider frameworks by which people can work with change. Some of these frameworks are examined here as strategies for individuals and organizations to use networking.

There are also emergent social issues that individuals must face, such as censorship, privacy, intellectual property, and universal service. These are not limited to traditional domains. They also emerge in cyberspace and challenge us to resolve them anew.

ORGANIZATIONS AND SOCIETY

Compared to other social entities, such as the individual or society, organizations have only recently become a focus of research. Previous discussion in this book has been centered around networking strategies from the perspective of an organization. In this chapter, that notion will be explored, along with issues that relate to society. Let's briefly define these terms before examining some of these larger issues that networking invokes.

ORGANIZATIONS

Peter Drucker (1993, also see netref 1) a noted scholar on issues of management, technology, and society defines an organization by comparing it to other, more familiar social institutions: "society, community, family are, organizations do." He also describes an organization as possessing the following salient traits:

- It is a human group, composed of specialists working together on a common task.

- It is always specialized and defined by its task.

- To be effective, it concentrates on one central task.

- Its function is to make knowledge productive.

- Its product is the result of contributing specialists.

- Its task and mission must be clear.

- It appraises performance against objective measures.

- It builds into its structure the management of change.

- It learns to exploit new applications for success.

- It learns how to innovate.

In his book entitled, *Modern Organizations*, Amitai Etzioni, a noted sociologist (1964 and see netref 2), quotes Talcott Parsons (1960), who defines an organization as "social units (or human groupings) deliberately constructed and reconstructed to seek specific goals."

Through the definitions of organization posed by these scholars, it becomes clear that a functional view of this social entity prevails. This framework can apply to many types of organizations: formal and informal, large and small, online and offline. Whether it is an agency, a corporation, an association, or the emerging varieties being spawned in cyberspace, we will examine how organizations and their members respond to the innovation of networking.

Societies

Societies are large social entities that, like smaller units such as families and communities, are generally thought of as simply being. Although we often talk about society as if it were a single entity, it only applies in the collective or generic sense. There are many societies and the uniqueness of their component groups make them pluralistic. Nonetheless, it is the common bonds of their unique geography, biology, history, language, culture, economy, and politics that define a society, both among its members and to outside observers.

Although individuals, families, and communities are the traditional components of societies, scholars such as Drucker note that societies are also defined by many constituent organizations, especially in developed countries in which most social tasks are performed in clearly-defined groups composed of many specialists.

From this perspective, the Internet and its constituent users can be seen more as a society that is composed of many organizations. Although it may retain its origin as an organization with a clearly-defined task and mission, its underlying nature is societal and scalable. As it links more networks, it also links more individuals and organizations through their common membership. The Internet changes through the explosive growth and global diversity of its membership, yet coheres as it accommodates their diverse goals.

FRAMEWORKS FOR CHANGE

To effectively employ strategies to plan and implement network technology, it is important to consider how change takes place within a social setting.

Although research in these areas is relatively new, theoretical frameworks have evolved that may explain the role of network technology. Foremost is the view of network implementation as an innovation and the place it holds in the process of planned change.

Planned Change

Like an organism, an organization grows and survives through continuous change in its structure and ways of doing things, while retaining its underlying nature. These changes can result from challenges in the external environment or through internal forces. With certain exceptions, such as a natural disaster, changes in an organization are generally planned. Anticipating unpredictable and unwelcome change should also be part of planning; see Chapter 12, "Disaster Recovery and Contingency."

Network technology is often a tool of change. For example, it can be used as a strategic tool to gain competitive edge, such as upgrading to real-time data feeds for a trading floor. Strategic design and use of network components and services can solve the technological challenge, but the business objective will not be solved until the organizational component is worked out, i.e., getting people to use it productively. Thus, changes in your use of technology must be planned because it is inevitably part of a larger innovative process. This process includes changes to the internal structure of your organization.

> **NOTE** For information about network components, see Chapter 3. For information about networking services, see Chapter 5.

The innovation that occurs is actually the change that network technology brings to members of an organization. This change is observed in what sociologists refer to as changes in patterns of interaction. If the introduction of new technology does not result in this type of change, its presence cannot be considered an innovation.

Changes brought on by innovations affect the formal and informal statuses and roles of individuals in the organization. In the larger context, the introduction of network technology and the automation associated with it may result in business expansion in some cases or downsizing in others. Even when these changes don't profoundly affect the gain or loss of membership in an organization, innovation affects how people interact with each other and with the technology that is introduced.

No matter how large or small the effect, innovation poses a change in behavior. It threatens and actually changes existing norms, and when properly implemented, it replaces them with new (presumably improved) patterns of interaction. People anticipate the affects of planned change and experience it firsthand when it is implemented. How they respond to the innovation is critical in its ultimate success or failure.

Diffusion and Adoption of Innovations

There is considerable literature on the diffusion or spread of an innovation. When examining adoption from the individual perspective, researchers identified two key concepts: the change agents and the early or late adopter.

Change agents are people who help and influence others to adapt to the changes brought on by innovations. Their role was considered indispensable to implementation. Sometimes these agents are leaders of organizations, but they may also be people whose informal status is an opinion leader. Identifying these people and soliciting their support is vital to strategic implementation of networking in an organization.

Early and late adopters are people who adopt the innovation at earlier or later times along the continuum of diffusion. As later research revealed, these distinctions are primarily descriptive of how people collectively respond to innovation. Despite popular notions about people who always want the latest technology or people who are generally considered laggards, there are more fundamental determinants of individual response.

One of the other popular notions related to studies of diffusion of innovations is that of ubiquity. Although having wide and convenient access to new technology is vital to successful implementation of new technology, this alone does not compel people to use it or not. The company that makes a major outlay for networked workstations with Internet access on everyone's desk has only brought the change to people. It does not determine how and if they will actually use it for its intended purpose.

Subsequent research looked at how people's personality traits affected their adoption of new technology. Other studies examined demographics such as gender, age, religious beliefs, etc. It became clear over the course of many studies, however, that focusing on these factors alone did not adequately explain why the same individual would be receptive to some innovations and reject others (Giacquinta, 1973).

The need to understand receptivity to innovation by an individual in a social setting became the focus of subsequent research. The settings in which change took place were examined as factors for adoption of innovation. Organizational characteristics such as size, complexity, and stratification were examined as determinants of individual response to change within the organizational setting. Examining factory automation, farming methods, and educational reform produced little evidence that the size of an organization or its internal structure was sufficient enough to explain how people as individual members would adopt new technology.

Searching for more explanations, recent studies began looking at how a person perceives risks associated with using innovations. Actual or perceived risk associated with change was seen from the perspective of a threat to the status quo which would generally be resisted (Miles, 1964). In their comprehensive review, Rogers and Shoemaker (1971) identified several studies in which status characteristics were examined in studies of receptivity to innovation.

Status-Risk Theory

When considering your own response to innovations like networking, think about the benefit or risk that it poses to your status in the organization. Decisions that you make about using groupware or video-conferencing are typically associated with your role in the workplace.

For example, if you are rewarded for your individual achievements and knowledge, you probably won't find much benefit in using these types of networking applications where team effort and shared knowledge are emphasized. The perceived risk to your status as a top performer may prevent you from using a technology that you might otherwise find attractive.

It is within this context that we think status-risk considerations can shed light on how or if people will use network technology. Giacquinta (1975) formulated a status-risk theory that claims that the statuses that you hold will determine how you respond to innovations that are introduced in your organization. His status-risk model is as follows:

- All innovations contain varying degrees of possible benefits, risks, and uncertainties for you as a member of an organization, depending on your statuses there.

- Your response to innovation depends upon the degree to which you perceive risks to the perquisites (perks) that come with your statuses in the organization.

Thus, it is not necessarily the *actual* benefits or threats to status that are key determinants, but rather the *perceptions* that individuals in an organization have about the benefits and risks posed by specific innovations.

Developing a Status-Risk Profile

One application of this theory would be to use it as a predictive tool for the process of organizational change. For example, to anticipate member receptivity to an innovation based on their collective statuses, a profile of groups or individuals could be developed (Giacquinta, 1975b).

For small organizations, individual status-risk profiles could be developed, but this would be costly and impractical for larger organizations.

Instead, a combination of group and individual profiles could be developed along the following lines.

- Identify groups on the basis of shared statuses.

For example, a status group could be examined based on all individuals who have previous experience developing projects in workgroups. For this group, the benefits and risks perceived in using groupware may be different than those who have no experience working in teams.

- Once groups have been identified, a status-risk profile could be developed further by examining their multiple statuses and corresponding perceptions of risk with regard to using the innovation.

For example, some people with the multiple statuses of prior experience with working in teams and prior networking experience may welcome the use of groupware because they clearly see the benefits and will be considered experts whose ideas will be valued. But what about someone who has a lot of computer experience, but who is highly rewarded for individual achievement and personal knowledge, such as a sales rep? Will she or he accept the innovation or fight it?

- Finally, each identified perquisite would be paired with a description of what possible gain or loss to that perquisite might be perceived by members of that status group with respect to using the innovation.

For example, sales reps who are rewarded for individual accomplishments and covet their expertise are likely to sense a real threat or risk when using groupware. They will fear a loss of recognition (and bonuses) if they will have to learn a new computer application and share the rewards of team sales with others on the team. These are perceived losses. However, will the peer recognition of sharing their knowledge with others be considered a benefit? In some cases, yes, but perhaps other incentives may be needed.

Similarly, profiles could be developed for key individuals in the organization, such as executives or opinion leaders. For larger organizations, profiles could be developed for a few individuals who represent different status groups.

With initial information from these profiles, management or other change agents could develop a series of planned change meetings and negotiations to assess the impact of the innovation, in advance of and during its implementation. For example, a multi-stage planned change strategy could be employed consisting of the following tactics:

1. Define the innovation in terms of its potential or actual affect on the organization, including the patterns of interaction between its members.

2. Develop status-risk profiles of groups and key personnel before and after the innovation.

3. Anticipate and define the effects of the innovation on key personnel.

4. Conduct planned change meetings with key personnel to determine the perceived impacts and to negotiate how these impacts could be optimized to improve their receptivity. Also consider modifications to the innovation as necessary.

5. Provide the needed resources and continue the above process through the planning and implementation of the innovation.

Implications for Strategic Networking

There are implications of this theory for most organizations facing the kinds of change posed by emerging network technology. Whether in schools, businesses, or other types of organizations, managers and agents of change need to carefully examine the impact of network innovations as affecting statuses of each individual and the formal and informal patterns of interaction between all individuals in that organization.

For example, some individuals in information systems management may act as agents of change by establishing an organization's commercial presence on the Internet as a technological edge against competitors. This technological innovation could reap great benefits. By establishing an early presence, millions of new potential customers could be introduced to a line of products and services geared for the profile of current Internet users.

However, this planned change may be viewed by network managers and system administrators as posing many more risks than benefits. Foremost will be the valid concern for adequate network security. However, this innovation may also be perceived as posing risks to their organizational statuses. For example, they may fear a loss of prestige or power if they fear the idea of users gaining more control of their own applications and resources on the Net.

This is also likely to raise concern and resistance because of a perceived increase in workload if they have to quickly provide everyone Internet connectivity and applications. Perquisites accruing to marital, family, and community statuses may also be threatened by the necessity for longer hours spent at work.

Here is where planned change agents and committees can pave the way for anticipating these responses. These groups can develop plans in concert with individuals for meeting these challenges and getting their input into how the technology should be implemented (or in some extreme cases, whether it should be implemented at all).

Leaders and Vision

The adoption and use of innovation also requires vision and leadership. This comes from individuals who stick their nose into things and stick their neck out when its time to let others know about it. They are often risk-takers, and sometimes whistle-blowers or diehard fanatics. There are more of these people than history books can accommodate. This is fortunate because they are absolutely indispensable. Change doesn't come easy, and leaders are those who rise to the occasion when it comes to taking a stand on something and articulating it for the rest of us.

These people are called leaders, and the ones with long-term ideals we call visionaries. When it comes to dealing with the changes that these ideas and innovations bring with them, they are the avant-garde, the agents of change.

This moniker applies whether it's someone in the organization who latches onto the advantages of groupware and rallies everyone around it to push through its implementation, or if it's someone who moves something along on a more global scale.

The role of change agents is vital. In the field of computer networking, their numbers are many. Many of them are principals in leading computer companies, some are ensconced in ivory towers and think-tanks, while others cruise the Net and travel the world as modern-day preachers of global connectivity and communication.

It's hard not to acknowledge the influence that people like Douglas Englebart, Ted Nelson, or Tim Berners-Lee exerted on the development of networked hypermedia (what we now call the Web), or the conception of the "network as computer" by Scott McNealy of Sun, the leadership of the "father of the Internet," Vinton Cerf, or the advocacy of personal rights extended to cyberspace by John Perry Barlow and Mitch Kapor, as founders of the Electronic Frontier Foundation. Like most other aspects of the open, published, and self-documenting Internet, their continued presence and ideas are there for you to consider (see netref 3).

Leaders and visionaries as agents of change don't always see their ideas to fruition, nor do they always possess the persistence to do so, but their influence is part of the innovation and the ways that we use it. The list of leaders in computer networking is too long for this book and, thankfully, growing along with our use and reliance on the Net. The point is that organizations and societies are composed of people and some of these individuals are vital to our collective response to change.

No matter how much we assimilate the use of computers and networks as tools, these agents are instrumental in leading us up to the point of change and letting us take it the rest of the way.

THE LEARNING ORGANIZATION

When organizations respond to environmental and internal pressures to change, there is recognition of learning that is taking place at many levels. From the top down and from the bottom up, individuals, groups, and the entire organization itself can seek to understand and plan change through learning. It represents a new and potentially fruitful field of study called organizational learning.

Although some researchers see this type of learning occurring through the development of adaptive routines at the organizational level (not unlike the behaviorist's view of individual learning), there is also recognition of diverse learning styles as well as levels. Recent research in organizational learning recognizes the importance of serendipitous learning through often unintended variations of routine (Miner, 1990, 1991). Taken together, these offer a view of organizational learning that is similar to biological evolution.

What also appears in studies of organizations that successfully use technology is the notion of establishing and maintaining a culture of learning. This culture is the result of a conscious plan for keeping an organization growing through support of learning. This support is expressed in financial support of continued studies, in the development of programs that reward useful solutions to organizational needs, or in the recognition of creative challenges to routines that spur positive change.

It can also be employed through a strategic use of internetworking and communications between all individuals in the organization, facilitating messaging, collaboration, and conferencing. The organizational learning strategy can be enhanced with the use of strategic networking. For example, an organization can establish gateways to information services, research centers, and even strategic alliances with other organizations that employ networking technology.

Strategic networking applied to this type of learning can take its cue from the corporate and academic researchers whose needs and goals were the impetus for the Net and later the Web. If you want to see how they implemented the innovation, look no further than their Web sites, mailing lists, and newsgroups (see netref 4).

The Internet was founded on the notion that internetworking universities, government, and military organizations could enhance research and collaboration and that this dissemination of knowledge would benefit society (see netref 5).

That model has not only ably proven itself in fueling research that brought about the unprecedented growth in technology in the past two decades, but it has also generated a communications revolution where learning and commerce are flourishing along electronic information superhighways.

THE VIRTUAL ORGANIZATION

The virtual space created by internetworking and organizations that access it has given rise to new concepts that not only redefine the nature of organizations, but that of work as well. Besides the familiar concept of telecommuting, there are several variants on the word virtual, including the virtual office, the virtual campus, and the virtual organization. Actually, all of these concepts describe a similar, flexible approach to the workplace as defined by one or more working members conducting work via network access from remote locations.

Whether those members of the organization are sales reps, engineers, students, faculty, or consultants, they all perform their responsibilities using the network. Thus, a sales rep can handle orders and inventory checks through wireless and wired network access. Students can register for classes and link to curriculum information through the Web pages of a virtual campus and participate in group discussions via e-mail, mailing lists, and newsgroups.

Collectively, these situations characterize a technological innovation that can enhance the flexibility of an organization and, in some cases, completely redefine the manner in which it accomplishes its mission. The potential benefits are great, including lower operating costs, greater collaboration among members, and new avenues for conducting the tasks associated with the organization. Using networking technology can also mean employing a flexible workforce composed of a mixture of core employees and outsourced consultants and services.

Whether it is a small organization like a community college or a large organization like the federal government, information processing and communication can be enhanced through a wide range of organizational tasks. In some cases, a small company could strategically leverage network technology and a flexible workforce to gain as much, or possibly greater, global presence and informational advantage than a larger, but more traditional, organization. Here are some examples of how virtual organizations could use the Internet in several operational areas.

Research and Development

Research and development can be achieved through automated database search and retrieval and communication via e-mail. Consultants and researchers can communicate along lines of expertise, mutual interest and concern, irrespective of their geographical proximity, organizational alliances, and schedule. The store and forward nature of e-mail could greatly reduce time and costs associated with face-to-face meetings, phone calls, or other traditional methods of collaboration (see netref 6).

Marketing

Marketing could be greatly enhanced by conducting or accessing existing data using online surveys conducted via e-mail or the Web. Additional market data could be gathered on an ongoing basis through government, academia, and other organizations that maintain archives related to the targeted product, service, and customer base (see netref 7, and also 4 and 5).

Advertising

Using the Internet for advertising can have varying results. Firstly, it is a new and different medium than the traditional venues of print, radio, and TV. It has its own culture spawned by its leaders and early adopters. It's also an inherently different technology that's interactive and much more varied than what is presented in other media.

Social mores on the Internet are known as netiquette. They are not always obvious to the novice, but they are present nonetheless. For example, the Internet community of users object to blunt broadcasting of commercial information (called "spamming"). They will likely let such an abuser feel the heat of a "flame" in the form of angry e-mail responses or even online campaigns to disrupt or prevent such activities. These responses can flood your e-mail inbox and may even overload your server. It's obvious that the traditional forms of hard sell and non-interactive broadcast advertising can not be easily translated to this new medium.

However, there is room for advertising with value-added content. This can be in the form of useful information, attractive online presentations, promotions, and real interaction between the producer and consumer. The computing and communications nature of this medium can be exploited in rich presentation and interaction that reaches far beyond the capabilities of more traditional forms of advertising.

Finally, recognizing that the Net is a catch-as-catch-can medium, you must also use other media to get their attention. Many of your potential customers are either not on the Net or don't know you have established a presence.

You can develop a strategic ad campaign that employs media convergence. For example, using online marketing demographics of Internet users, a series of related print, radio, and television ads can include information for accessing a Web page or e-mail for special online information.

Curious about the nature of new online sites, potential customers will be drawn to a network connection that offers direct personal interaction This contact can establish product recognition as well as customer feedback and loyalty.

Strategic Alliances

Strategic alliances could be developed in these and other operational areas between organizations. These alliances could serve mutual interests and needs, including financing, venture capital, cooperative marketing, sales, and distribution.

One or more organizations could form a wholly virtual organization with a charter and lifespan centered around a specific task, such as the promotion of a product or service or other collaborative activity.

> **NOTE** For more information about using the Internet for business, see Chapters 10 and 11.

SOCIAL ISSUES

There are social issues that emerge with innovations such as networking. They represent challenges to both individuals and society. Some of these issues include: censorship, privacy, intellectual property, and universal service.

We need to resolve them anew in legal, political, economic, and other ways. Their resolution is paramount for global internetworking to continue its expansion and implementation.

Censorship

Social issues are often narrowly defined. For example, censorship represents only one side of the coin. The other side is freedom of expression. You can't consider one without the other. The balancing act between these two poles is what keeps the ball in motion (see netref 8).

Let's consider freedom of expression first. Without a perceived excess in free expression, there would not be a perceived need to censor it. Freedom of speech, the press, and the exercise of one's religion is ably represented in the First Amendment to the U.S. Constitution (see netref 9).

Although the perceived need for censorship is not unique to the Net, there are problems associated with the free flow of information and, to some degree, the issue of anonymity (see below). This is most compelling in the case of people who break the law and cause harm in cyberspace in the same way they might in person. These problems include people who prey on the innocence of minors, stalk and harass people, or push pornography.

Most people consider these acts wholly undesirable. That is why there are laws to protect people from these abuses. One common theme is that these laws should apply in whatever social context or medium in which the abuses occur. Policing cyberspace for abuses of this nature is an awesome task, but these laws need to be enforced.

Assigning liability to the providers of information services has been considered as a way to share the load of monitoring the flow of information. The reasoning is that responsibility for communications that break the law should rest with its origin or repositories. Besides the considerable cost that would have to be borne by these services, should they be solely responsible? Many feel that attempting to lay the blame or responsibility solely on the information services and providers is like saying that the telephone system should be responsible for the crimes and abuses that take place during telephone calls.

Another issue related to these abuses is the concept of license. The social vagaries of a new medium of expression don't necessarily equate with license to harm others or break the laws. Thankfully, there are many associations and groups who are attempting to enact specific policies and measures by which individuals can be protected without denying free expression. While the government considers legislation, these groups are working on concepts of internal control. They are also encouraging parents to exercise their responsibilities. Others are working with industry to create software and hardware that will prevent individuals from being exposed to potentially harmful material or contact.

In 1960, the critic A. J. Liebling said, "Freedom of the press is guaranteed only to those who own one." On the Net, individuals and groups not only have the freedom to personally express their ideas through free press and speech, but now they have the means. They can reach anyone in the world and exchange ideas. They can keep their attention if what they say and how they say it deserves a reading or hearing.

> **NOTE** For information about personal Web servers and integrated Web sites, see Chapter 10. For information about using network and Internet applications, see Chapters 8 and 11.

Privacy

Privacy on computer networks is primarily a means to keep others from monitoring your communications and using this information in ways that are harmful to you. This is not always so easy to do. For example, e-mail has been called the electronic postcard. This denotes the fact that when you send an e-mail message, it is likely to travel through many systems where human operators could easily read or change its contents without your knowledge. Examining the header of a received message reads like a road tour of mail servers. The routing of messages is rarely direct.

This problem requires a solution that is equivalent to a digital envelope. One way to make personal communications more private is to scramble the contents of the message through a process called encryption. When an encrypted message is received, it can be decrypted by someone who should be the intended receiver.

The entire concept of electronic commerce and online transactions awaits a clear sign that privacy of personal and financial information can be preserved.

The issue of privacy (see netref 10) also involves shielding your identity or other personal information. Sometimes you are protecting yourself from unwanted monitoring, and in other cases you are seeking anonymity. For example, using anonymous e-mail accounts, Internet users can protect themselves from scrutiny or potential harm. It is quite common in the most personal or politically oriented newsgroups to see people expressing viewpoints under the protection of pseudonymous names or anonymous e-mail addresses.

Anonymity can actually be a positive tool if it allows people to express themselves in a non-harmful way. It can stimulate the free exchange of ideas in a non-threatening forum.

> **NOTE** For more information on e-mail, privacy, and security, see Chapters 8 through 12.

Intellectual Property Rights

Intellectual property rights are closely associated with the issue of free exchange and flow of information. Intellectual property is typically defined and protected legally through copyrights, trademarks, and patents (see netref 11). Conversely, the free flow and exchange of information is vital to a free and democratic society, whether online, in print, or thru any other medium.

Traditionally, the need for free flow of information is acknowledged in the fair use precedents that academics and scholars enjoy in their freedom to use excerpts for scholarship.

There are technological, legal, and other hurdles to overcome in this new media before these rights can be recognized and protected. For example, some claim that the concept of protecting personal ownership of messages posted to newsgroups or chat forums is unfeasible or unjustified, especially when no copyright notice is provided with the information. However, there is no inherent reason why at some basic level this can't be accomplished.

As in the other areas of social concerns, balancing these needs will preserve the rights of creators with the rights of users.

Universal Service

Universal service (see netref 12) involves the provision (often by law) of a basic level of a service for a given segment of the population. It can apply to many types of services such as electric power and interstate highways. In communications, it applies to public access of telephone, television, cable, or computer networks.

Universal service is closely linked to the rights of free expression and the concept of free enterprise. It is particularly vital to underserved populations such as school children or people living in rural and remote areas, or people who cannot afford premium services.

Defining what universal service should mean in a given context such as the Internet or information superhighways involves a concerted effort by many interest groups, government, and industry to achieve some common ground. Beyond acknowledging the need for it, several issues must be resolved to establish a basic level of service:

- What is the quality of service?

- Should it be the same for everyone or should it be divided into premium and basic services?

- Who should bear the cost of providing universal service?

- To what degree should costs be borne by government subsidy, taxes, or industry?

Plans for information superhighways such as the National Information Infrastructure (NII) and the Global Information Infrastructure (GII) include discussion of universal service. The growth of the Internet represents the transition to broad bandwidth, global internetworks. Current providers of video and phone services are likely to be a part of this transition. For example, until two-way wireless or fiber networks can reach every home, school, and business, existing systems will have to be used. The fiber network of cable companies can provide a downlink, and the digital services, such as ISDN of the phone companies, can provide an uplink to broad-bandwidth network backbones. Although these systems already provide a high degree of universal service with respect to access, determining the degree and quality of content and its cost must still be resolved.

Some think industry should bear the full cost. In the extreme, this may discourage private investment and development. However, as networking increasingly is associated with leasing or selling rights to use the public airwaves or public land, taxpayers may feel that universal service is part of the bargain.

> **NOTE** For information about transmission media, see Chapter 1. For information about network services, see Chapter 5. For information about information superhighways, the NII, GII, and the Internet, see Chapter 11.

REFERENCES

Bibliography

Betz, F. 1987. *Managing Technology*. Englewood Cliffs, NJ: Prentice-Hall, Inc.

Bhalla, S. K. 1987. *The Effective Management of Technology. Columbus*, OH: Battelle Press.

Boddy, D. and D. Buchanan. 1986. *Mastering New Technology*. Oxford, UK: Basil Blackwell Ltd.

Drucker, P. F. 1993. *Post-Capitalist Society*. NY: HarperCollins Publishers, Inc.

Gattiker, U. E. 1990. *Technology Management in Organizations*. Newbury Park, CA: Sage Publications.

Giacquinta, J. B. 1975. Status, Risk, and Receptivity to Innovations in Complex Organizations: A Study of the Responses of Four Groups of Educators to the Proposed Introduction of Sex Education in Elementary School. *Sociology of Education*. 48:38-58.

Giacquinta, J. B. 1975(b) Status Risk Taking: A Central Issue in the Initiation and Implementation of Public School Innovations. *Journal of Research and Development in Education* 9(1):102.

Gross, N., J. B. Giacquinta, and M. Bernstein. 1971. *Implementing Organizational Innovations*. NY: Basic Books Inc., Publishers.

Miner, A. S. 1990. "Structural Evolution through Idiosyncratic Jobs: The Potential for Unplanned Learning." *Organizational Science*. 1:195-210.

Miner, A. S. 1991. "Organizational Evolution and the Social Ecology of Jobs." *American Sociological Review*. 56: 772-785.

Monger, R. F. 1988. *Mastering Technology*. NY: The Free Press.

Weiss, Joseph W. 1989. *The Management of Change*. NY: Praeger Publishers.

Net References

1. For information about Peter Drucker, www to
http://www.cgs.edu/0/drucker/homepage.html then browse The Drucker Graduate
Management Center.

2. For information about Amitai Etzioni, www to
http://town.hall.org:80/Archives/radio/IMS/Club/062893_club_HALL.html then
browse the town hall interview page and listen to the audio playback of Dr. Amitai
Etzioni, Communitarian, at the National Press Club.

3. Visit the sites of some agents of change. Their presence and communications
represent a work-in-progress, and you are part of it.

For information about Douglas Englebart and his work, www to
http://irss.njit.edu:5080/cgi-bin/bin/option.csh/pqr?sidebars/engelbart.html then read
"Toward Augmenting the Human Intellect and Boosting our Collective IQ."

Also, read:

www to http://www.collaborate.com/rules.html

www to http://flatwater.unl.edu/PhysicsHTML/Millikan.html

For information about Theodor Holm Nelson and his work, www to
http://irss.njit.edu:5080/cgi-bin/bin/view.csh?view=y then read, The Heart of
Connection: Hypermedia Unified by Transclusion

Also, www to http://xanadu.net/the.project then read about Xanadu.

For information about Tim Burners-Lee and his work, www to http://www.w3.org/ then
browse for information about hypertext and the World Wide Web.

For information about Scott McNealy of Sun and his work, www to
http://www.sun.com/

For information about Vinton Cerf and his work: For his document on the history of the
Internet, use Web or gopher client to gopher://gopher.isoc.org/11/internet/history
For information about the Internet Society and its work, www to
http://info.isoc.org/home.html

For information about John Perry Barlow, www to
http://www.cs.uidaho.edu/lal/cyberspace/eff/barlow/barlow.html

For information about Mitch Kapor, www to
http://www.kei.com:80/homepages/mkapor/

For information about the Electronic Frontier Foundation, www to
http://www.cs.uidaho.edu/lal/cyberspace/eff/eff.html

4. Visit the sites where the work of scholars and researchers can be seen as models of
net-based learning and communication: For University Libraries and Scholarly
Communication, www to http://www.lib.virginia.edu/mellon/mellon.html then browse
and read the Mellon study report.

www to http://www.acns.nwu.edu/ezines/academic.html then browse the list of
electronic journals and magazines from Academic publishers.

For a list with links to scholarly journals distributed via the World Wide Web, www to
http://info.lib.uh.edu/webjour.html

For a list of American universities, www to
http://www.clas.ufl.edu/CLAS/american-universities.html

For a list of College and University Home Pages, www to
http://www.mit.edu:8001/people/cdemello/univ.html

www to http://borg.lib.vt.edu/ then browse the information and listings of the Scholarly
Communications Project of VPI & SU.

5. For a look of the government's way of getting things done on the Net, visit these
sites:

You might want to make the FedWorld Information Network your only bookmark as it
links to many government sites via Web, gopher, telnet, and ftp. www to
http://www.fedworld.gov/

Similarly, browse the Federal Information Exchange List of WWW servers via www to
http://www.fie.com/www/us_gov.htm

www to http://www.whitehouse.gov then browse The White House.

www to http://www.house.gov then browse the House of Representatives.

http://thomas.loc.gov then browse Thomas Legislative Information on the Internet.

www to http://lcWeb.loc.gov/homepage/lchp.html then browse the Library of Congress.

www to http://www.census.gov then browse the Bureau of the Census.

6. For information about research in online communications, www to
http://web.bu.edu/SMGMIS/people/sproull.html

7. Survey research sites on the Web:

http://www.princeton.edu/~abelson/section1.html

http://www.cc.gatech.edu/gvu/user_surveys/

8. For sites that relate to the social issues of censorship and freedom of expression, consider these starting points:

For the EFF "Censorship & Free Expression" Archive, www to
http://kragar.eff.org/pub/Censorship/

For a list of links on Censorship, www to
http://www8.yahoo.com/Government/Politics/Censorship/

For a list of links on Censorship and the Net, www to
http://www8.yahoo.com/Government/Politics/Censorship/Censorship_and_the_Net/

9. For a Web page view of the U.S. Constitution, www to
http://www.law.cornell.edu/constitution/constitution.overview.html

10. For sites that relate to the social issues of privacy and anonymity, consider these starting points:

For a list of links on privacy, www to http://www8.yahoo.com/Law/Privacy/

For a privacy page with FAQs and links to resources, www to
http://snyside.sunnyside.com/cpsr/privacy/ssn/html/privacy.html

For the EPIC "Online Guide to Privacy Resources," www to
http://snyside.sunnyside.com/dox/program/privacy/epic.privlinks.html

For a privacy law link on Tort Resources, www to
http://chicagokent.kentlaw.edu/lawlinks/tort.html

11. For sites that relate to the social issues of intellectual property rights and the need for the free flow of information, consider these starting points:

For a list of links on intellectual property, www to http://www8.yahoo.com/Government/Law/Intellectual_Property/

For a page on intellectual property and law, www to http://chicagokent.kentlaw.edu/ipls/

For a page on intellectual property and society, www to http://host1.jmls.edu/orgs/ips.html

For a page on intellectual property and digital media, www to http://belladonna.media.mit.edu/people/mt/int-prop.html

For the U.S. Information Agency home page, www to http://www.usia.gov/hottopic/ip/1.html

12. For sites that relate to the social issues of universal service and free enterprise, consider these starting points:

For telecomunications regulations: universal service, www to http://charlotte.wiltel.com/telecomr/archive/0634.html

For an archive of postings to TAP-INFO: Cox Amendment to Limit Universal Service to Voice Grade Telephone, www to http://essential.org/listproc/tap-info/0162.html

For "Benton's Publications Catalog" home page, www to http://cdinet.com/cgi-bin/lite/Benton/Catalog/catalog.html

For the APT Web page, www to http://apt.org/apt/

For the Communications Policy Project page, www to http://cdinet.com/Benton/

For The Benton Foundation's Communications Policy Project, www to http://cdinet.com/Benton/home-large.html

For the home page of the FCC, www to http://www.fcc.gov/

For FCC releases and notices on universal service, www to http://cdinet.com/Benton/Goingon/fcc-notices.html

14

Resources

ABOUT THIS CHAPTER

This chapter provides contact information and brief network product and service descriptions. These listings are categorized under headings for vendors, publications, associations, and conferences and expositions.

USING RESOURCE INFORMATION

Due to the changing nature of contact information, we cannot be held responsible nor provide any assurance that these references will be accurate. This is especially true in the case of online addresses.

Recognizing this, we have tried wherever possible to refer to higher-level locations that are closer to the domain of the source, such as department or company names, numbers, and addresses. Additional address and content information about a source is provided to help you find it in the case of a changed address.

VENDORS

The following list of vendors represents a small sampling of networking products and services. For additional vendor information, check the Net References section at the end of chapters throughout this book, including business recovery services in Chapter 12. The products mentioned here and throughout this book are recognized as the trademarks and tradenames of their respective owners and are used for editorial purposes only.

3Com Corp., 5400 Bayfront Plaza, PO Box 58145, Santa Clara, CA 95052-8145, voice: 800-638-3266; 408-764-5000, fax: 408-764-5001, makers of LAN/WAN products, including network interface cards, hubs, and routers.

Adobe Systems Incorporated, 1098 Alta Ave., Mountain View, CA, 94043, voice: 415-961-4400 or 1-800-833-6687; Web: http://www.adobe.com/, develops, markets, and supports computer software products and technologies that enable users to create, display, print, and communicate electronic documents, such as Adobe Illustrator, Adobe Photoshop, the Adobe Acrobat series of PDF software, and Adobe PostScript fonts.

Adobe also provides the FrameMaker publishing line of products, 33 West San Carlos Street, San Jose, CA 95110, voice: 1-800-U4FRAME, fax: 408-975-6799, e-mail: salesinfo@frame, Web: http://www.frame.com/, makers of FrameMaker multi-platform desktop publishing software and the FrameMaker+SGML Structured Authoring Tool.

Artisoft, Inc., 2202 N. Forbes Blvd., Tucson, AZ 85745, voice: 800-233-5564; 520-670-7100, direct sales: 800-846-9726, fax: 520-670-7101, makers of the popular LANtastic network operating system and other LAN/WAN products.

askSam Systems, 119 S Washington Street (or) PO Box 1428 (Mail), Perry, FL 32347, voice: 1-800-800-1997 or 904-584-6590, fax: 904-584-7481, BBS: 904-584-8287, e-mail: sales@asksam.com, Web: http://www.asksam.com/, makers of askSam, a free-form database for DOS and Windows.

Avalan Technology, Inc., 116 Hopping Brook Park, PO Box 6888, Holliston, MA 01746, voice: 800-441-2281; 508-429-6482, fax: 508-429-3179, tech support BBS: 508-429-3671, makers of Remotely Possible/Sockets remote control software.

Banyan Systems Inc., 120 Flanders Rd., Westborough, MA 01581-5013, voice: 800-222-6926; 508-898-1000, fax: 508-898-1755, makers of VINES network operating system and other LAN/WAN products.

Berkeley Software Design, Inc., 5575 Tech Center Dr., Suite 110, Colorado Springs, CO 80918, voice: 800-800-4273; 719-593-9445, fax: 719-598-4238, makers of BSDI/OS network operating system and other communications and networking software.

Binomial International, 812 Proctor Avenue, Ogdensburg, NY 13669, voice: 613-692-4000 or 800-361-8398, fax: 613-692-2425, e-mail to phoenix@binomial.com, Web: http://www.binomial.com/, makers of Phoenix Recovery Planning System.

Borland International, Inc., 100 Borland Way, Scotts Valley, CA 95066-3249, voice: 800-233-2444 or 408-431-1000; Web: http://www.borland.com/, makers of Paradox and other integrated database applications, compilers, and languages.

Brooklyn North Software Works, Bedford, Nova Scotia, voice: 902-493-6080, fax: 902-835-2600, sales@brooknorth.bedford.ns.ca, Web: http://fox.nstn.ca/~harawitz/index.html, makers of URL Grabber software and distributor of HTML Assistant Pro software for the World Wide Web.

Capsoft Development Corp., 732 East Utah Valley Drive, Suite 400, American Fork, UT 84003, voice: 801-763-3900, fax: 801-763-3999, Web: http://www.itsnet.com/home/capsoft/public_html/, makers of HotDocs document template software.

CompuServe Internet Division, 316 Occidental Ave South, Suite 200, voice: 1-800-777-9638, 206-447-0300, fax: 206-447-9008, e-mail: info@spry.com, Web: http://www.compuserve.com/, makers of the Internet Office, Internet In A Box, Mosaic In A Box, and Internet In A Box For Kids.

Corel Corp., 1600 Carling Ave., The Corel Bldg., Ottawa, ON, CD K1Z 8R7, voice: 800-772-6735 or 613-728-8200, fax: 613-728-9790; Web: http://www.corelnet.com/, makers of Corel Draw, Ventura Publisher, and other graphics software.

Corning Optical Fiber Information Center, P.O. Box 7429, Union Station, Endicott, NY 13760, voice: 800-525-2524, ext. 908, fax: 800-834-3504, e-mail: fiber@corning.com, The Corning Optical Fiber Information Center is a free service of Corning Incorporated, Telecommunications Products Division.

DataBeam Corp., 3191 Nicholasville Rd., Lexington, KY 40503, voice: 800-877-2325, 606-245-3500, fax: 606-245-3528, e-mail: fs_win@databeam.com, provides standards-based collaborative software, such as Collaborative Computing Toolkit Series and FarSite document-conferencing software.

Delrina Corp., 895 Don Mills Rd., 500-2 Park Centre, Toronto, ON, CD M3C1W3, voice: 800-268-6082 or 416-441-3676, fax: 416-441-0333; Web: http://www.delrina.com/, makers of stand-alone and networked fax software.

Digi (division of Digi International, Inc.), 6400 Flying Cloud Dr., EdenPrairie, MN 55344, voice: 800-344-4273 or 612-943-9020, fax: 612-943-5398, Web: http://www.digibd.com/, develops and manufactures communications software and communications control systems for multiple platforms.

Digital Vision, Inc., 270 Bridge Street, Dedham MA 02026, voice: 617-329-5400, fax: 617-329-6286, e-mail: support@digvis.com, sales@digvis.com, BBS: 617-329-8387 (8,N,1), Web: http://www.digvis.com/digvis, makers of ComputerEyes Video Digitzers and TelevEyes Scan Converters for Mac and IBM PC Computers.

Distinct Corp., 12901 Saratoga Ave., Suite 4, Saratoga, CA 95070, voice: 408-366-8933, fax: 408-366-0153, developers of X-servers, TCP/IP application packages, and network resource sharing applications for Microsoft Windows.

DTI, Inc., P.O. Box 1276, Olympia WA 98507, voice: 360-493-0060, fax: 360-493-0567, e-mail: dti@wln.com, database specialist and consultant in transforming Data To Information.

Esker, Inc., 350 Sansome St., Ste. 210, San Francisco, CA 94104, voice: 800-88-ESKER or 415-675-7777, fax: 415-675-7775, develops TUN*UNIX software to provide MS-DOS to UNIX resource sharing. TUN*PLUS provides tools to transparently access UNIX hosts, run multiuser applications, share peripherals, and exchange messages from Windows/DOS desktops.

Exabyte Corp., 1685 38th St., Boulder, CO 80301, voice: 800-EXABYTE or 303-442-4333, fax: 303-447-7501, manufactures cartridge drives, DAT (Digital Audio Tape) drives, and mini-cartridge drives.

Firefox, Inc. (subsidiary of Firefox Communications, Ltd.), 2099 Gateway Plaza, 7th Fl., San Jose, CA 95110, voice: 800-230-6090, 408-467-1100, fax: 408-467-1105, Web: http://www.firefox.com/, develops NOV*IX Elite for Internet, an NLM-based product that provides users with a suite of Windows-based applications for accessing hosts and services on the Internet.

Forte, 2141 Palomar Airport Road, Suite 100, Carlsbad, CA 92009, voice: (main) 619-431-6400, (orders): 619-431-6496, fax: 619-431-6465, e-mail: agent-sales-human@forteinc.com, Web: http://www.forteinc.com/forte/, makers of Agent newsreader, 3D PC screen savers, and a line of collaborative Internet software navigation products.

Frontier Technologies Corp., 10201 N. Port Washington Rd., Mequon, WI 53092, voice: 800-929-3054 or 414-241-4555; fax: 414-241-7084; Web: http://www.frontiertech.com/, makers of Super TCP, a TCP/IP connectivity package for Windows.

Global Telecom, Inc. (GTI), 31 Market Street, Morristown, NJ 07960, voice: 201-285-9099, dial-up for Morristown, NJ: 201-285-0700, fax: 201-285-0728, e-mail: sales@gti.net, Web: http://www.gti.net, Global Telecom, Inc. (GTI), is an Internet Service Provider (ISP) offering a wide range of personal and business services, including dial-up access (ISDN, PPP, SLIP, and Shell) from various points throughout New Jersey and the Metro area, and direct Internet connections (56K, Frame Relay, T1) to anywhere in the continental United States. Enhancements include 24-hour support and toll-free access.

IBM (International Business Machines), Old Orchard Rd., Armonk, NY 10504, voice: 800-426-3333; 914-765-1900, direct sales: 800-426-7255 (IBM PC Direct), makers of a wide variety of network hardware and software including OS/2 Warp.

Insignia Solutions, Inc. (subsidiary of Insignia Solutions, Ltd.), 1300 Charleston Rd., Mountain View, CA 94043, voice: 800-848-7677, 415-335-7100, fax: 415-335-7105, Web: http://www.insignia.com/, makers of SoftWindows, for UNIX workstation users to run Microsoft Windows applications.

Internet Shopper Ltd., P.O. Box 6064, London, SW12 9XG, UK, voice: 44-181-673-7422, fax: 44-181-673-2149, email: sales@net-shopper.co.uk, makers of NTMail and other software for Windows NT, including servers for NNTP, FTP, SMTP, POP3, DNS, and WWW.

Ipswitch, Inc., 81 Hartwell Avenue, Lexington, MA 02173, voice: 617-676-5700, fax: 617-676-5710, email: info@ipswitch.com, Web: http://www.ipswitch.com/, makers of e-mail client/server software.

LANovation, 1313 Fifth St. SE, Minneapolis, MN 55414, voice: 800-747-4487 or 612-379-3805, fax: 612-378-3818, makers of LAN Escort, a comprehensive solution for managing Windows on NetWare LANs and WANs.

LaserMaster Corp. (subsidiary of LaserMaster Technologies, Inc.), 6900 Shady Oak Rd., Eden Prairie, MN 55344-9965, voice: 800-950-6868 or 612-944-9330, fax: 612-944-0522, develops printer enhancement products that increase printing resolution and accelerates printing of Windows applications.

Megahertz Holding, Inc. (subsidiary of U.S. Robotics Corp.), 605 North 5600 West, PO Box 16020, Salt Lake City, UT 84116-0020, voice: 800-LAPTOPS or 801-320-7000, fax: 801-320-6010; Web: http://www.xmission.com/~mhz/, makers of LAN/WAN modems and other communications products.

Microsoft Corp., One Microsoft Way, Redmond, WA 98052-6399, voice: 800-426-9400; 206-882-8080, fax: 206-93-MSFAX, makers of PC accessories/ peripherals, software, and applications including MS-DOS, Windows NT, and Windows 95.

MicroTest, Inc., 4747 North 22nd St., Phoenix, AZ 85016-4700, voice: 800-526-9675; 602-952-6400, fax: 602-952-6434, makers of data communications and test equipment, including the Pentascanner.

Mobile Satellite Products, 55 Commerce Drive, Hauppauge, NY, voice: 516-273-4455, fax: 516-273-4583, e-mail: info@mobilesat.com, manufacturers of satellite earth stations for voice, fax, and data, including the LYNXX Transportable Immarsat-B Earth Station.

NCD Software Inc., 350 N. Bernardo Avenue, Mountain View, CA, 94043-5207, voice: 800-416-1956, 415-694-0650, fax: 415-961-7711, e-mail: mariner_sales@ncd.com, Web: http://www.mariner.ncd.com/, makers of software products which include PC Xware, Z-Mail, and Mariner.

Network World, Inc., 161 Worcester Rd., Framingham, MA 01701-9524, voice: 800-643-4668 or 508-875-6400, fax: 508-820-1283, develops graphics and GUI software including Net Draw, a network drawing and layout package.

NETCOM, 3031 Tisch Way, San Jose, CA 95128, voice: 408-983-5950, fax: 408-983-1537, a national Internet provider with local access points in many major cities. NETCOM provides dial-up and direct connections (56KB and T1). NetCruiser software provides connectivity and popular Internet applications in an integrated package.

NetManage, Inc., 10725 North De Anza Blvd., Cupertino, CA 95014 USA, voice: 408-973-7171, fax: 408-257-6405, e-mail: info@netmanage.com, Web: http://www.netmanage.com/, makers of Chameleon software for Windows-based connectivity and TCP/IP applications.

Netscape Communication Corporation, 501 East Middlefield Road, Mountain View, California, 94043, Web: http://www.netscape.com/, makers of Web srvers and clients. Netscape, Netscape Navigator and the Netscape Communications logo are trademarks of Netscape Communications Corporation.

Network General Corp., 4200 Bohannon Dr., Menlo Park, CA 94025, voice: 800-764-3329; 415-473-2000, fax: 415-321-0855, makers of data communications and test equipment, including the Expert Sniffer Network Analyzer.

Network-USA Internet Services, P.O. Box 819, Commack, NY 11725, voice: 516-543-0234, Web: http://www.netusa.net/, e-mail: all-info@netusa.net, Internet provider for Long Island, NY area.

Nico Mak Computing, Inc., P.O. Box 919, Bristol, CT 06011, voice: 800-242-4775, fax: 713-524-6398, e-mail: info@winzip.com, Web: http://www.winzip.com/winzip/, makers of WinZip compression software for Windows.

Novell, Inc., 122 East 1700 South, Provo, UT 84606-6194, voice: 800-453-1267; 801-429-7000, fax: 801-429-5155, makers of the NetWare line of network operating systems, and other software systems and applications.

PinPoint Software Corp., 6531 Crown Blvd., Ste. 3A, San Jose, CA 95120, voice: 800-599-3200 or 408-997-6900, fax: 800-308-3777, develops networking and communications software including Click Net, the network diagramming tool.

PIPEX, 216 Cambridge Science Park, Cambridge, England CB44WA, voice: 44 (0)1223-250120, fax: 44 (0)1223-250121, e-mail: support@dial.pipex.com, provides European Internet connectivity services and software.

QUALCOMM Incorporated, 6455 Lusk Blvd., San Diego, CA 92121-2779, voice: 800-238-3672 or 619-587-1121, fax: 619-597-5058; Web: http://www.qualcomm.com/, makers of e-mail and communications software including Eudora Pro (Windows and Macintosh).

Quyen Systems, Inc., 1300 Piccard Dr., Suite 108, Rockville, MD 20850, voice: 800-827-1856 or 301-258-5087, fax: 301-258-5088, makers of netViz, the Windows network diagramming and documenting tool for documenting networks, systems and processes.

Shapeware Corp., 520 Pike St., Ste. 1800, Seattle, WA 98101-4001, voice: 800-446-3335 or 206-521-4500, fax: 206-521-4501, makers of Visio, a drawing program designed for business and technical users who need to create business and technical diagrams. Note: The network diagrams in this book were created using Visio and its network diagram templates.

SoftQuad Inc., 56 Aberfoyle Crescent, 5th floor, Toronto, ON, M8X 2W4, Canada, voice: 416-239-4801, fax: 416-239-7105, email: mail@sq.com, Web: http://www.sq.com, vendor of HTML and SGML software and services, including HotMetal PRO, Panorama PRO, Author/Editor, and other multi-platform, standards-based solutions for information management and electronic publishing.

StarNine Technologies, Inc., 2550 Ninth St., Suite 112, voice: 800-525-2580, 510-649-4949, fax: 510-548-0393, e-mail: sales@starnine.com, Web: http://www.starnine.com/, makers of Internet servers for the Macintosh, including the WebSTAR commercial Web server, the ListSTAR listserver and e-mail-on-demand server, and StarNine Mail server/client mail program.

SunSoft, Inc., (subsidiary of Sun Microsystems, Inc.), 2550 Garcia Ave., Mountain View, CA 94043-1100, voice: 800-SUN-SOFT; 415-960-3200, fax: 415-336-2473, makers of network operating systems and other software applications, including Solaris and Solstice SunNet Manager.

Symantec Corp., 10201 Torre Ave., Cupertino, CA 95014-2132, voice: 800-441-7234 or 408-253-9600, fax: 408-252-4694, Web: http://www.symantec.com/, develops remote connectivity products such as pcANYWHERE, and network management tools such as Norton Administrator for Networks.

Texas Imperial Software, 11028 Jollyville Rd #260, Austin TX 78759-4836, voice: 512-346-2729, fax: 512-346-2803, e-mail: alun@texis.com, makers of WFTPD, the Winsock FTP Daemon server software.

Trans-Ameritech Systems, Inc., 2342A Walsh Ave., Santa Clara, CA 95051, voice: 408-77-3883, fax: 408-727-3882, e-mail: order@trans-am.com, makers of LinuxWare CD-ROM version of Linux.

Traveling Software, 18702 North Creek Parkway, Bothell, WA 98011, voice: 206-483-8088, fax: 206-487-1284, Web: http://www.travsoft.com/, makers of wireless and wired connectivity products, including LapLink Wireless (software) with AirShare (hardware) and other versions of LapLink for cable-based connectivity.

Tribe Computer Works, 960 Atlantic Ave., Suite 101 Alameda, CA 94501-9941, voice: 800-77-TRIBE; 510-814-3900, fax: 510-814-3980, makers of LAN/WAN bridges, routers, gateways, and network software applications.

UniPress Software, Inc., 2025 Lincoln Highway, Edison, NJ 08817, voice: 908-287-2100, fax: 908-287-4929, e-mail: info@unipress.com, providers of Web services, distributors of connectivity, remote node, and remote control software.

U.S. Robotics Access Corp. (subsidiary of U.S. Robotics Corp.), 8100 N. McCormick Blvd., Skokie, IL 60076-2999, voice: 800-USR-CORP or 708-982-5010, fax: 708-933-5800; Web: http://www.usr.com/, makers of modems and other communications hardware and software.

VocalTec Inc., 157 Veterans Drive, Northvale, NJ 07647, voice: 1-800-843-2289, 201-768-9400, fax: 201-768-8893, e-mail: info@vocaltec.com, Web: http://www.vocaltec.com/, makers of Internet Phone and Internet Wave software.

VREAM, Inc., 2568 Clark Street, #250, Chicago, IL 60614, voice: 312-477-0425, fax: 312-477-9702, e-mail: info@vream.com, Web: http://www.vream.com/, makers of WIRL, VRCreator, and other virtual reality software for Windows 3.x, Windows NT, and Windows 95.

Wall Data, Inc., 11332 Northeast 122nd Way, Kirkland, WA 98034-6931, voice: 800-48-RUMBA; 206-814-9255, tech. support: voice: 206-814-3400, fax: 206-814-4300, tech. support BBS: 206-558-0392, makers of Rumba mainframe connectivity software.

White Pine Software, Inc., 40 Simon Street, Nashua, NH 03060, voice: 1-800-241-PINE, 603-886-9050, fax: 603-886-9051, e-mail: info@wpine.com, Web: http://www.wpine.com/, makers of connectivity software for the PC and Macintosh, including the eXodus X-server and CU-SeeMe desktop video-conferencing software.

Wildbear Consulting, Inc. 8-589 Beechwood Drive, Waterloo, Ontario, Canada, voice: 519-886-3683, fax: 519-886-3033 email: wildbear@wildside.kwnet.on.ca, Web: http://wildside.kwnet.on.ca/ makers of WinSmtp and other Windows-based Internet servers. For purchasing, contact Seattle Lab, voice: 206-402-6003, support@seattlelab.com, Web: http://www.seattlelab.com/.

Xircom, Inc., 2300 Corporate Center Drive; Thousand Oaks, California 91320; voice: 800-438-4526, fax: 805-376-9311, e-mail: sales@xircom.com, Web: http//www.xircom.com/, makers of CreditCard Ethernet+Modem II PC Card and other data communications equipment including modems, muxes, and network interface cards.

PUBLICATIONS

Consummate Winsock Apps List (CWSApps List) and The Critical Applications Distribution List (CADL) provide review and downloading information on the latest Net applications. For the CWSApps List, www to http://www.hookup.net/cwsapps/ To subscribe to the CADL mailing list, send a message with SUBSCRIBE CADL to Neuroses@mail.utexas.edu. Include your e-mail address and your first and last name.

Digital Media, Editorial Offices, 444 De Haro Street, Suite 126, San Francisco, CA 94107, voice: 415-575-3775, fax: 415-575-3780, e-mail: info@digmedia.com, and Web: http://www.digmedia.com/, publishes a print newsletter (Digital Media) and Digital Media Perspective, an electronic newsletter delivered via e-mail. For a free subscription, email to perspective-request@digmedia.com and type in the subject line: subscribe perspective. Also, type your full name, title, and organization in the message body.

HotWired Ventures LLC, email: hotwired-info@hotwired.com, Web: http://www.hotwired.com/, publisher of HotWired, online Web zine with articles about the Net and a wide range of related topics, online interviews and forums. To subscribe to the HotFlash mailing list, send email to info-rama@hotwired.com with the message, subscribe hotflash, in the body of the message.

libHiTech.a, P.O. Box 136, Lake Hiawatha, NJ 07034, voice: 201-334-8750, fax: 201-334-8750, e-mail: info@libhitech.com, support@libhitech.com, order@libhitech.com, Web: http://www.libhitech.com/libhitech/, an online source for computer and networking books (especially UNIX) at discount.

Tabor Griffin Communications, 8445 Camino Santa Fe, Suite 204, San Diego, CA 92121, voice: 619-625-0070, 800-795-4472, fax: 619-625-0088, e-mail: sos@webster.tgc.com (general information and assistance), human@webster.tgc.com (help from a real, live human being), publisher of WEBster, an online source of information about the World Wide Web and related Net topics and events.

ASSOCIATIONS

As there are many associations that support networking, we provide a brief online contact address and refer to the appropriate chapter(s) for more information.

American National Standards Institute (ANSI), www to http://www.ansi.org/ (for more information, see Chapters 1 and 4).

Association for Computing Machinery (ACM), www to http://www.acm.org/ (for more information, see Chapter 11).

ATM Forum, www to http://www.atmforum.com/ (for more information, see Chapter 5).

Building Industry Consulting Service International (BICSI), 10500 University Center Drive, Suite 100, Tampa, FL 33612-6415, voice: 800-242-7405 or 813-979-1991, fax: 813-971-4311.

Coalition for Networked Information (CNI), www to http:/www.cni.org/ (for more information, see Chapter 11).

CDPD Forum, www to http://www.cdpd.net/ (for more information, see Chapters 1 and 5).

Electronic Messaging Association (EMA), www to http://www.ema.org/ (for more information, see Chapters 8 and 11).

Fibre Channel Association (FCA), www to http://www.amdahl.com/ext/CARP/FCA/FCA.html (for more information, see Chapter 2).

IETF, www to http://www.ietf.org/ (for more information, see Chapters 9 and 11).

Institute of Electrical and Electronics Engineers, Inc. (IEEE), www to http://www.ieee.org/ (for more information, see Chapters 4 and 5).

International Standards Organization (ISO), www to http://www.iso.ch/ (for more information, see Chapters 1 and 9).

Internet Architecture Board (IAB), www to http://www.iab.org/iab/ (for more information, see Chapter 11).

Internet Society, www to http://info.isoc.org/home.html (for more information, see Chapter 11).

ITU Telecom Information Exchange Services (ITU TIES), www to http://www.itu.ch/ (for more information, see Chapter 5).

Open Software Foundation (OSF), www to http://www.osf.org/general/osf-info.html (for more information, see Chapter 4).

SMDS Interest Group, www to http://www.cerf.net/smds/smds-bgr.html (for more information, see Chapter 5).

SONET Interoperability Forum, www to http://www.adc.com/~don/sif/remote.html (for more information, see Chapter 5).

World Wide Web Consortium, www to http://www.w3.org/ then search web pages on the World Wide Web Consortium (for more information, see Chapters 7, 11, and 13).

X/Open, www to http://www.xopen.org/ (for more information, see Chapter 4).

CONFERENCES AND EXPOSITIONS

American Expositions, Inc., 110 Greene Street, #703, New York, NY 10012, voice: 212-226-4141, produces a variety of expositions and conferences on networking topics such as multimedia, electronic commerce, etc.

Digital Media, Editorial Offices, 444 De Haro Street, Suite 126, San Francisco, CA 94107, voice: 415-575-3775, fax: 415-575-3780, e-mail: info@digmedia.com, and Web: http://www.digmedia.com/, produces Digital World, Seybold conferences on electronic publishing, NetWorld+Interop, Windows Solutions, and others.

IDG, Web: http://www.idgwec.com/, publishes computer and networking books, magazines, and produces the Network World Unplugged conference.

Mecklermedia Conference Management, 20 Ketchum Street, Westport CT 06880, voice: 800-632-5537 or 203-226-6967, fax: 203-226-6976, e-mail: iwconf@mecklermedia.com, Web: http://www.mecklerweb.com/shows/, producer of Internet World and other trade shows.

NetWorld+Interop conference and **N+I On-line!** For information, visit the N+I On-line! Web: http://www.sbexpos.com/

World Wide Web Consortium (W3C) (http://www.w3.org/) sponsors an annual International World Wide Web Conference along with the Open Software Foundation (OSF) (http://www.osf.org/). The 4th annual conference was also sponsored by MIT (http://www.mit.edu/).

Index